Risk in Intellectual and Psychosocial Development

DEVELOPMENTAL PSYCHOLOGY SERIES

SERIES EDITOR
Harry Beilin

Developmental Psychology Program
City University of New York Graduate School
New York, New York

A complete list of titles in this series is available from the publisher.

Risk in Intellectual and Psychosocial Development

Edited by

DALE C. FARRAN

Center for the Development of Early Education
Kamehameha Schools/Bishop Estate
Honolulu, Hawaii

JAMES D. McKINNEY

Frank Porter Graham Child Development Center
The University of North Carolina
Chapel Hill, North Carolina

1986

ACADEMIC PRESS, INC.

Harcourt Brace Jovanovich, Publishers

Orlando   San Diego   New York   Austin
London   Montreal   Sydney   Tokyo   Toronto

COPYRIGHT © 1986 BY ACADEMIC PRESS, INC.
ALL RIGHTS RESERVED.
NO PART OF THIS PUBLICATION MAY BE REPRODUCED OR
TRANSMITTED IN ANY FORM OR BY ANY MEANS, ELECTRONIC
OR MECHANICAL, INCLUDING PHOTOCOPY, RECORDING, OR
ANY INFORMATION STORAGE AND RETRIEVAL SYSTEM, WITHOUT
PERMISSION IN WRITING FROM THE PUBLISHER.

ACADEMIC PRESS, INC.
Orlando, Florida 32887

United Kingdom Edition published by
ACADEMIC PRESS INC. (LONDON) LTD.
24–28 Oval Road, London NW1 7DX

LIBRARY OF CONGRESS CATALOGING-IN-PUBLICATION DATA

Main entry under title:

Risk in intellectual and psychosocial development.

Includes index.
1. Mental retardation—Diagnosis.   2. Mental illness
—Diagnosis.   3. Child development deviations—Diagnosis.
4. Child development—Testing.   I. Farran, Dale
Clark.   II. McKinney James D.   (James Donald), Date
RJ506.M4R57   1986   362.2   85-18492
ISBN 0-12-249630-2 (alk. paper)
ISBN 0-12-249631-0 (paperback)

PRINTED IN THE UNITED STATES OF AMERICA

86 87 88 89   9 8 7 6 5 4 3 2 1

Contents

v

PART II   Risk in Psychosocial Development

6 Psychopathology and Preventive Intervention in Infancy: A Clinical Developmental Research Approach

STANLEY I. GREENSPAN

7 Age-Specific Manifestations in Changing Psychosocial Risk

RICHARD Q. BELL

8 Psychosocial Risk: Which Early Experiences Are Important for Whom?

DALE C. FARRAN AND DAVID H. COOPER

9 Changes in Conduct Disorder over Time

LEE N. ROBINS

10 Problems and Perspectives for the Concept of Risk in Psychosocial Development: A Summary

DALE C. FARRAN

PART III   Risk Assessment and Public Policy

11 A Four-Dimensional Model of Risk Assessment and Intervention

KENNETH KAYE

12 Prevention Services for Risk Children: Evidence for Policy and Practice

BARBARA K. KEOGH, ANNE G. WILCOXEN, AND LUCINDA BERNHEIMER

Contributors

Numbers in parentheses indicate the pages on which the authors' contributions begin.

Richard Q. Bell (169), Department of Psychology, University of Virginia, Charlottesville, Virginia 22904

Lucinda Bernheimer (287), Division of Child Development, Department of Pediatrics, Los Angeles, California 90024

David H. Cooper (187), Department of Special Education, College of Education, University of Maryland, College Park, Maryland 20742

Dale C. Farran (187, 261), Center for the Development of Early Education, Kamehameha Schools/Bishop Estate, Honolulu, Hawaii 96817

Stanley I. Greenspan (129), Clinical Infant–Child Development Research Center, Division of Maternal & Child Health, HRSA & NIMH, Rockville, Maryland 20852

Ron Haskins (29), Frank Porter Graham Child Development Center, University of North Carolina at Chapel Hill, Chapel Hill, North Carolina 27514

Kenneth Kaye (273), Center for Family Studies, Northwestern University Medical School, Evanston, Illinois 60201

Barbara K. Keogh (287), Graduate School of Education, University of California, Los Angeles, California 90024

James D. McKinney (121), Frank Porter Graham Center Child Development Center, University of North Carolina at Chapel Hill, Chapel Hill, North Carolina 27514

David MacPhee[1] (61), Frank Porter Graham Child Development Center, University of North Carolina at Chapel Hill, Chapel Hill, North Carolina 27514

[1]Present address: Department of Human Development, Gifford Building, Colorado State University, Fort Collins, Colorado 80523.

John U. Ogbu (83), Department of Anthropology, University of California at Berkeley, Berkeley, California 94720

Craig T. Ramey (61), Frank Porter Graham Child Development Center, University of North Carolina at Chapel Hill, Chapel Hill, North Carolina 27514

Lee N. Robins (227), Department of Psychiatry, Washington University School of Medicine, St. Louis, Missouri 63110

Emmy E. Werner (3), Department of Applied Behavioral Sciences, University of California, Davis, California 95616

Anne G. Wilcoxen (287), School of Education, University of California, Los Angeles, California 90024

Preface

The idea that there are identifiable risk factors that can influence children's development is becoming more entrenched daily as a greater proportion of federal funds is devoted to preventive programs, as new training programs in this field are initiated, and as more publication space in journals is occupied with this topic. Yet none of the recent publications has analyzed the developmental significance of these risk factors. We appear to have leaped to the level of service delivery for prevention without having adequate information about two prior considerations: (1) Can we be reasonably certain about risk indicators? and (2) If we are certain, do we have data to support any particular intervention to forestall the consequences of the risk?

This volume deals with scholarly contributions to the first of these two questions, that is: What is the data base from which we draw our conclusions about risk? Clarke and Clarke's book, *The Myth of Early Experience*, was a major contributor to this area. It needs to be updated for several reasons: (1) there exist more recent data from longitudinal studies than they could summarize at that time; (2) though Clarke and Clarke's conclusions were radical at the time, more people may be able to view risk analytically today—because of Clarke and Clarke's work; and (3) they reviewed and synthesized information themselves, leaving themselves open to the charge that this was merely their point of view about risk.

This book consists of three major parts. The first two parts are organized along parallel lines: All chapters in each concern data from longitudinal projects with which the author(s) have been involved. Each presents a model of risk factors that could be generalized to other kinds of risk. In other words, the authors have used their particular data base as the source for examples about risk in general. Within each of the first two parts, the chapters proceed from a child focus to an environmental focus.

The third and final part consists of two chapters outlining what the data suggest for policy. Is prevention possible? For what kinds of outcomes? For what should we screen? Is our knowledge good enough to justify preventive efforts at all?

This book is a necessary and timely addition to the field. New policies are being considered, if not already enacted, at the national level concerning both research and service programs for families. There is a groundswell of interest in the topic: two new infant mental health journals in the past several years; the formation of the National Center for Clinical Infant Programs in 1977; training workshops for practitioners and professionals in infant assessment and intervention; the routine use of the Neonatal Assessment Behavior Scales (the Brazelton); and on and on. Each of these efforts involves assessment and intervention for infants already classified as at-risk. Few existing references critically evaluate the evidence for risk itself, and only a few present longitudinal data on the topic. This book is directed to a wide audience of professionals in research and service delivery as well as to policy analysis and policy making.

PART I

Risk in Intellectual Development

1

A Longitudinal Study
of Perinatal Risk

EMMY E. WERNER

Introduction

Most longitudinal studies that have followed children into adulthood have dealt with select and rather privileged samples of the human race: bright, middle-class Caucasians who lived in metropolitan areas of the Western world. Prospective studies of high-risk children provide a corrective. They include children who grew up in poor and/or unstable homes, and children from other races as well. They allow us to assess the long-term impact of genetic, individual, and family risk factors on children's development within a broader sociocultural context (Murphy & Moriarty, 1976; Rutter, 1979).

The Kauai Longitudinal Study provides us with an opportunity to examine the joint influences of reproductive risk and quality of caretaking environment on the development of a multiracial cohort of children in Hawaii, from the prenatal period to young adulthood. It allows us to examine children's vulnerability to a host of biological and psychosocial risk factors and to study their resiliency—that is, their capacity to cope effectively with internal and external stresses.

My objectives in this chapter are

1. to provide a longitudinal perspective on children's capacity to cope with perinatal stress, poverty, and family instability;
2. to discuss sex differences in vulnerability and resiliency in the first and second decade of life;

3. to examine the predictive power of a combination of biological and psychosocial risk factors;
4. to identify protective factors within the individual and the caregiving environment that differentiate between groups of high-risk children and youth who were resilient and peers who developed serious learning and/or behavior problems; and
5. to present a model of the relationships among risk factors at birth, stressful life events, and protective factors that seems to account for the range of adaptive and maladaptive outcomes observed in our study.

I conclude with a brief discussion of some of the implications of our findings for future research in child development and social action in behalf of children.

Methodology

The island of Kauai lies at the northwest end of the main chain of the Hawaiian islands, some 100 miles and half-an-hour's flight from Honolulu. Settled between the eighth and thirteenth century A.D. by voyagers from the Society Islands and Tahiti, the island was first visited by Europeans in 1778 when Captain Cook landed on its shores. In the nineteenth and twentieth centuries, Kauai encountered successive waves of immigrants from Southeast Asia and Europe, many of whom intermarried with the local Hawaiians.

The children in this study were a kaleidoscope of different ethnic groups: Japanese (33%), part and full Hawaiians (23%), Filipino (18%), ethnic mixtures other than Hawaiian (14%), Portuguese (6%), Anglo-Caucasians (3%), Chinese (1%), Koreans (1%), and Puerto Ricans (1%). Most of the fathers worked as semiskilled or unskilled laborers on the island's sugar plantations; most of the mothers did not graduate from high school and half had only 8 years or less of formal education.

A detailed account of the methodology of our study and our data base can be found in three books: *The Children of Kauai* (Werner, Bierman, & French, 1971); *Kauai's Children Come of Age* (Werner & Smith, 1977); and *Vulnerable, but Invincible* (Werner & Smith, 1982).

The study began in 1954, with an assessment of the reproductive histories and the physical and emotional status of the pregnant women in the community in each trimester, from the fourth week of gestation to delivery. A total of 3,735 pregnancies was reported, of which 2,203 consisted of all women with pregnancies beginning in 1954, 1955, and

1956. These resulted in 240 fetal deaths and 1,963 liveborn from the cohort of 1955 births and the cohort of 1956–1957 births.

The study continued with an evaluation of the cumulative effects of perinatal stress and the quality of caretaking environment on the physical, cognitive, and social development of 698 children from the 1955 birth cohort in the postpartum period and at 1 year, 20 months, and 10 and 18 years. The assessments included evaluations by pediatricians of the severity of prenatal and perinatal complications, home interviews and observations in the prenatal and postpartum periods and at 1 year by public health nurses, psychological and pediatric examinations of the children and interviews with their principal caretakers at 20 months, primary mental abilities and perceptual-motor tests in grade five, teachers' evaluations of classroom behavior at age 10, home visits and family interviews by social workers at age 10; and scholastic aptitude, achievement, and personality tests and in-depth interviews conducted by clinical psychologists with high-risk youth at age 18. In addition, there were diagnostic tests by specialists for children who were considered to be at risk on the basis of the examinations given at birth, and at ages 2, 10, and 18 years.

Records on file in community agencies for members of the 1955 birth cohort and their families were monitored for more than two decades. These included social service records, records of family physicians and hospitals, the public and mental health departments, the police and the family court, the department of special education, and vocational rehabilitation agencies. The Mental Health Register for the State of Hawaii provided us with referrals for inpatient and outpatient treatment for the youth and their families.

Attrition rates remained relatively low: Of the 1955 birth cohort, 96% participated in the 2-year follow-up, 90% in the 10-year follow-up, and 88% in the 18-year follow-up. For two high-risk groups from the 1955 birth cohort (the offspring of psychotic parents and the teenage mothers) we now have data that extend to their 25th year of life (Gonsalves, 1982; Johnston, 1981). A follow-up of the high-risk youth at age 30 is planned for 1985.

While the focus of this report is on young people who were vulnerable, we could not help being deeply impressed by the resiliency of most children and youth and their capacity for positive change and personal growth. This is especially remarkable because our study took place during a period of unprecedented social change that included statehood for the former territory of Hawaii, the arrival of many newcomers from the U.S. mainland, and the aftereffects of two prolonged wars in Southeast Asia (Korea and Vietnam).

Results

Our study was conducted on a small island with medical, public health, educational, and mental health services that compare favorably with most communities of similar size on the U.S. mainland. In spite of this, the magnitude of the casualties during pregnancy and the first two decades of life was impressive.

The Casualties

Deleterious biological effects resulting in reproductive casualties exerted their peak influence in the very early weeks of pregnancy, when 90% of the fetal losses in our study occurred. Of pregnancies reaching 4 weeks gestation, an estimated 237 per 1000 ended in loss of the conceptus. The rate of loss formed a decreasing curve from a high of 108 per 1000 women in the 4–7-week period to a low of 3 at 32–35 weeks of gestation. In contrast, neonatal and infant mortality rates were very low on Kauai: There were only 13.8 deaths under 28 days per 1000 liveborn and *all* were attributed to pre- and perinatal causes (as were 4 of the 10 remaining deaths between 28 days and 2 years). The liveborn were classified as to presence and severity of handicapping conditions and estimates made of the type of services required for them.

Approximately one out of every three children in this birth cohort had some learning or behavior problems during the first decade of life. By age 10, more than twice as many children needed remedial services for such problems than were in need of medical care for physical handicaps.

Approximately one out of every five youths had records of serious delinquencies or mental health problems in the second decade of life. The majority of such troubled youth had mutliple problems—that is, a combination of delinquency and mental health problems among the boys, or mental health problems and teenage pregnancies among the girls. Some of the children and youth had been exposed to major perinatal insults that prevented normal development; many more lived in chronic poverty or in a persistently disorganized family environment. Frequently, biological and psychosocial risk factors interacted and exposed them to cumulative stresses too difficult to cope with unaided. The interplay between perinatal and psychosocial risk factors was already discernible in prenatal interviews with their mothers.

Emotional Stress in Pregnancy and Perinatal Risk

Our analysis of the prenatal interviews indicated that emotional factors predictive of reproductive risk for women with little economic or emotional support differed from the factors predictive for women from middle-class families. Among middle-class women, negative feelings about the pregnancy, psychological trauma experienced during the pregnancy, and the woman's anxiety and inability to express herself freely in the prenatal interviews were significant predictors of such perinatal risk factors as difficult delivery (prolonged first stage of labor), birthweight below 2500 gm, poor condition of the newborn (respiratory distress, jaundice, convulsions, gastrointestinal problems), congenital defects, and central nervous system (CNS) dysfunctions noted in the neonatal period. First-trimester interviews yielded more items predictive of perinatal risk than later prenatal interviews for middle-class women.

Fewer prenatal interview items were significant predictors of perinatal risk among poor women or women living in unstable, disorganized homes. In all three trimesters, the father's unhappiness about the coming baby, as perceived by the woman, and in the second and third trimester, the mother's lack of preparedness for the baby were significant predictors of such perinatal risk factors as difficult labor, low birthweight, and poor condition of the newborn.

The anxiety expressed by lower-SES mothers in the prenatal interviews tended to focus on long-term life stresses over which they had little control. The anxiety expressed by the middle-class mothers tended to focus more specifically on the pregnancy experience.

Incidence of Pre/Perinatal Complications

A clinical rating based on the presence of conditions thought to have had a deleterious effect on the fetus or newborn was made for each child at the beginning of the study. A pediatrician scored the severity of some 60 complications occurring during the prenatal, labor, delivery, and neonatal periods as follows: 0, not present; 1, mild; 2, moderate; and 3, severe. (A summary of the scoring system is presented in Table 1). After all conditions were scored, the pediatrician assigned to each infant an overall score from 0 to 3. This was based on clinical judgment, taking into account the number, type, and severity of unfavorable conditions present. Cases with overall scores of 2 and 3 were reviewed independently by a second pediatrician.

For 56% of the newborn, the prenatal and perinatal periods were free from complications. Thirty-one percent suffered from complications of only a mild nature. For 10%, complications of moderate severity were present, and for 3%, complications were considered severe. Of the infants who died before the 2-year follow-up, more than 75% were from

Table 1

Summary of Scoring System for Prenatal–Perinatal Complications:
Kauai Longitudinal Study

Mild (Score 1)	Moderate (Score 2)	Severe (Score 3)
Mild: preeclampsia, essential hypertension, renal insufficiency or anemia; controlled diabetes or hypothyroidism; positive Wasserman and no treatment; acute genitourinary infection 3rd trimester; untreated pelvic tumor producing dystocia; treated asthma	Marked: preeclampsia, essential hypertension, renal insufficiency or anemia; diabetes under poor control; decompensated cardiovascular disease requiring treatment; untreated thyroid dysfunction; confirmed rubella first trimester; nonobstetrical surgery: general anesthesia, abdominal incision or hypotension	Eclampsia: renal or diabetic coma; treated pelvic tumor
Second or third trimester vaginal bleeding; placental infarct; marginal placenta previa; premature rupture of membranes; amnionitis; abnormal fetal heart rate; meconium stained amniotic fluid (excl. breech); confirmed polyhydramnios	Vaginal bleeding with cramping; central placenta previa; partial placental abruptio; placental or cord anomalies	Complete placenta abruptio; congenital syphilis of the newborn
Rapid, forceful or prolonged unproductive labor; frank breech or persistent occiput posterior; twins; elective cesarean section; low forceps with complications; cord prolapsed or twisted and oxygen administered to newborn	Chin, face, brow, or footling presentation; emergency cesarean section; manual or forceps rotation, mid forceps or high forceps or breech and oxygen administered under 5 minutes	Transverse lie; emergency cesarean section; manual rotation, mid forceps or high forceps or breech extraction and oxygen administered 5 minutes or more
Breathing delayed 1–2 minutes; intermittent central cyanosis and oxygen administered under 1 minute; cry weak or abnormal; bradycardia	Breathing delayed 3–5 minutes; gasping intermittent central cyanosis and oxygen administered over 1 minute; cry delayed 5–15 minutes	Breathing delayed over 5 minutes; no respiratory effort; persistent cyanosis and oxygen administered continuously; cry delayed over 15 minutes

Table 1 (*Continued*)

Mild (Score 1)	Moderate (Score 2)	Severe (Score 3)
Birth injury excl. central nervous system; jaundice; hemmorrhagic disease mild; pneumonia, rate of respiration under 40 and oxygen administered intermittently; birth weight 1800–2500 gm and oxygen administered intermittently or incubator or other special care; oral antibiotic to newborn; abnormal tone or Moro reflex; irritability	Major birth injury and temporary central nervous system involvement; spasms; pneumonia, rate of respiration over 40 and oxygen administered intermittently; apnea and oxygen administered intermittently or resuscitation under 5 minutes; birth weight 1800–2500 gm, fair suck and oxygen administered or incubator; antibiotics administered intravenously; cry absent	Major birth injury and persistent central nervous system involvement; exchange transfusion; seizure; hyaline membrane disease; pneumonia, rate of respiration over 60 and oxygen administered continuously, resuscitation over 5 minutes; birth weight under 1800 gm and oxygen administered or special feeding; meningitis; absent Moro reflex

the small group with severe perinatal complications. Among the surviving children, only 2% had suffered severe perinatal stress.

Distributions of perinatal scores in our study were not significantly different by ethnic group or socioeconomic status (SES) of the mother. The fact that the women of Kauai had easy access to medical care provided by the sugar plantations and used it freely during their pregnancies may be responsible for the lack of subcultural differences in the overall incidence of perinatal complications observed in our study.

However, the proportion of babies with birthweight of 2500 gm or less, born after less than 37 weeks gestation ("premature") and after 37 weeks or more ("dysmature"), was highest for mothers in the lowest SES group.

Pre/Perinatal Risk: Short-versus Long-Term Impact

During the developmental examinations at 20 months we found a direct relationship between severity of perinatal stress and the proportion of children considered to be below normal in physical and intellectual development. This trend was especially pronounced among the children who had experienced moderate and severe perinatal stress. In the latter group, pediatricians diagnosed most of the congenital defects requiring long-term ($<$ 6 months) specialized medical care.

Table 2

2-, 10- and 18-Year Outcomes by Severity of Perinatal Stress: 1955 Birth Cohort, Kauai Longitudinal Study

Criteria	Total cohort ($n = 698$) (%)	Moderate perinatal stress ($n = 69$) (%)	Severe perinatal stress ($n = 14$) (%)
At age 2 years			
Pediatricians' rating of physical health status below normal	14.2	23.1	35.7
Psychologist's rating of intellectual development below normal	13.5	21.5	28.6
Cattell IQ > one SD below mean	9.6	15.4	21.4
At age 10 years			
Physical handicap	6.0	7.0	22.2
PMA IQ > one SD below mean	10.7	9.9	30.6
In MR class or institution	2.3	3.5	16.7
At age 18 years			
Physical handicap	6.0	6.0	14.5
Mental retardation	3.0	6.0	29.0
Serious mental health problem	3.0	9.0	14.5
Delinquency record	15.0	17.0	21.5
Teenage pregnancy	6.0 (F)	14.0 (F)	—
Proportion of children and youth with some problem at 2, 10, or 18 years	33.0	36.0	79.0

On the basis of both test performance and observations of the child's behavior, the psychologists independently rated 29% of the children with severe perinatal complications as below normal in intellectual status and another 29% as "questionable." Of those with moderate perinatal complications, 22% were considered to be below normal and 12% questionable.

By 10 years, differences found between children exposed to various degrees of perinatal stress and those born without perinatal complications were less pronounced than they were at age 2 and differences centered on a small group of survivors of moderate and severe perinatal stress (see Table 2). The highest proportion of children who had suffered moderate or severe perinatal complications was found among the youngsters with physical handicaps related to CNS impairment, among children requiring placement in special institutions or special education classes for the mentally retarded (MR) and learning disabled (LD), and among children considered in need of long-term mental health (LMH) services of more than 6 months duration. Four out of five children in this group were "acting-out"; the other had been diagnosed as childhood neuroses or as schizoid or sociopathic personalities.

By 18 years, four of five survivors of the small group who had suffered severe perinatal stress had persistent and serious physical, learning, or mental health problems, which had been documented in a variety of agency records. Among them were youth who were MR, or who displayed schizoid, paranoid and obsessive–compulsive behavior, and youth with growth retardation, orthopedic problems, and speech and hearing problems. The rate of mental retardation in this group was 10 times that found in the total cohort; the rate of serious mental health problems (requiring in- or out-patient treatment) was 5 times; and the rate of significant physical handicaps was more than 2 times that amount.

Among the survivors of *moderate* perinatal stress, the rate of serious mental health problems was three times that for the 1955 cohort as a whole, and the rate of mental retardation and of teenage pregnancies was twice the normal amount. The teenage pregnancies in this group comprised half of all abortions for the total cohort.

Perinatal Risk and Behavior Differences among Twins

Among the cohort of births, there were 14 liveborn twin pairs. The secondborn members of two twin pairs (one monozygotic [MZ], one dizygotic [DZ]), both males, died in infancy, one at 29 days (cause of death: malnutrition, pneumonia, and poor constitution), the other at 2 months, 14 days (cause of death: anemia, pneumonia, strangulated hernia). The 12 intact twin pairs who survived to age 18 consisted of five monozygotic (MZ), four dizygotic (DZ), and three twin pairs of undetermined zygosity.

There were nine sets of twins (five MZ, four DZ) among the 12 intact surviving pairs who were discordant on one or more behavior variables in infancy (i.e., maternal ratings of infant temperament at 1 year, psychological test results at 20 months). Among these discordant twins (as among the twins who had died), the secondborn had experienced more adverse perinatal events than the firstborn: four secondborns had a perinatal score of 2 and one a perinatal score of 3. All four breech births among the discordant twins were secondborn. Among the one set of discordant twins who were delivered by Ceasarean section, the secondborn was cyanotic. Cyanosis, delayed breathing, and/or jaundice were noted in seven instances among the discordant twin pairs, always in the secondborn.

Among the discordant twins, birth sequence was found to be more often related to within-pair differences in temperament, cognitive skills, and personality factors than birthweight, favoring the firstborn on maternal ratings of activity at year 1, Cattell IQ at 20 months, PMA reasoning skills, CNS integrity (fewer errors on the Bender-Gestalt test), and school achievement at 10 years, and in reading skills, intellectual efficiency, self-acceptance, and flexibility in late adolescence. This trend was even more significant for the small group of MZ twins alone.

It appears that *perinatal* as well as *genetic* factors contributed to relatively stable differences in temperament and cognitive skills among twins, and these differences may have significantly affected the child–caretaker relationship (see also Werner, 1973).

Joint Influences of Reproductive Risk and Quality of Caretaking Environment

In the 1955 birth cohort, we found significant interaction effects between characteristics of the caretaking environment and degrees of perinatal stress that produced the largest deficits for the most-disadvantaged children and those living in the most-disorganized homes. This was evident at each follow-up stage (see Tables 3 and 4).

As early as 20 months, these effects were seen in several ways:

1. Children growing up in middle-class homes who had experienced the most severe perinatal complications had mean scores on the Cattell Infant Scale almost comparable to children with no perinatal stress who were living in poor homes.
2. The most developmentally retarded children (in physical as well as intellectual status) were those who had both experienced the most severe perinatal complications and were also living in the poorest homes.
3. SES differences provided for a greater difference in mean Cattell scores (34 points) for children who had experienced severe perinatal stress than did perinatal complications for children living in a favorable environment (4 points).

A similar trend was noted when we examined the interaction effects between perinatal risk and family stability ratings. The latter were based on pre-and postnatal interviews and home visits at age 1 year, which gave evidence of family cohesiveness or upheaval (i.e., presence/absence of marital discord, parental psychopathology, long-term separation of child from primary caretaker).

The correlation between SES (based on father's occupation, standard of living, condition of housing) and family stability ratings was low (.21).

Table 3

Physical Health Status, Cattell IQ and PMA IQ by SES and Perinatal Stress

| | Severity of perinatal complications | | | |
| | None (N = 388) | Mild (N = 222) | Moderate (N = 69) | Severe (N = 14) |
Variable				
Physical health status at age 2 yrs (below normal): percentage				
(Very) high SES	7.5	16.7	16.7	50.0
Middle SES	10.9	15.9	22.0	22.2
(Very) low SES	12.2	13.8	21.4	66.7
Cattell IQ at age 2 yrs: mean score (and standard deviation)				
(Very) high SES	102 (12)	100 (11)	104 (20)	95 (13)
Middle SES	100 (12)	100 (11)	98 (14)	91 (8)
(Very) low SES	98 (11)	96 (12)	93 (12)	61 (37)
PMA IQ at age 10 yrs: mean score (and standard deviation)				
(Very) high SES	112 (11)	113 (12)	114 (11)	110 (11)
Middle SES	108 (12)	106 (13)	105 (12)	101 (13)
(Very) low SES	98 (11)	100 (11)	99 (12)	94 (14)

Table 4

Physical Health Status and Cattell IQ by Family Stability and Perinatal Stress

| | Severity of perinatal complications | | | |
| | None (N = 388) | Mild (N = 222) | Moderate (N = 69) | Severe (N = 14) |
Variable				
Physical health status at age 2 yrs (below normal): percentage Family stability				
(Very) high	11.1	16.1	24.4	25.0
Adequate	6.8	16.7	7.7	33.3
(Very) low	26.7	0	33.3	66.7
Cattell IQ at age 2 yrs: mean score (and standard deviation) Family stability				
(Very) high	100 (11)	100 (12)	99 (16)	94 (8)
Adequate	99 (11)	98 (10)	96 (8)	73 (16)
(Very) low	96 (12)	90 (10)	83 (6)	77 (8)

However, the difference in mean Cattell IQs between infants who had experienced severe perinatal stress but were growing up in a stable family environment (94) and those with serious perinatal stress who grew up in an unstable caretaking environment (77) was nearly as dramatic as that found for differences between the infants from middle-class and poor homes. Unstable caretaking environments also produced a significant increase in the proportion of children in poor health at 20 months, especially among those who had undergone severe perinatal stress, and in spite of the availability of prepaid and easily accessible health care services provided by the plantations.

By 10 years, the effects of the quality of the caretaking environment appeared even more powerful:

1. Children both with and without severe perinatal stress who had grown up in middle-class homes achieved mean PMA IQ scores well above average.
2. PMA IQ scores were seriously depressed in children from low-SES homes, particularly if they had experienced severe perinatal stress.
3. The family's SES showed significant associations with rate of serious learning and behavior problems. By age 18, ten times as many youth with serious coping problems were living in poverty as had survived serious perinatal stress.

In sum, perinatal complications were consistently related to later impaired physical and psychological development *only* when combined with persistently poor environmental circumstances (i.e., chronic poverty and/or family instability). Children who were raised in more affluent homes, with an intact family and a mother with good education, showed few, if any, negative effects from reproductive stress, unless there was severe CNS impairment.

Sex Differences in Vulnerability and Resistance to Stress

Sex differences in susceptibility to both biological and psychosocial stress were noted; boys appeared to be more vulnerable in childhood and girls more vulnerable in adolescence. At birth, more boys than girls in our study had been exposed to moderate or severe perinatal stress (M:3.6%; F:2.7%). More than half of the boy babies, but less than one-fifth of the girl babies with the most serious perinatal complications died in infancy—most in the neonatal period. Four-fifths of *all* the deaths among the boys in this cohort up to age 2 years, and two-thirds of all the deaths among the girls were due to severe pre/perinatal complications.

Among the survivors, the incidence of perinatal complications, by degree of severity, was approximately the same for boys and girls (2%), but more of the most seriously stressed girls stayed alive. A slightly higher proportion of boys had recognizable congenital defects at birth (M:10.2%; F:7.9%), but a higher proportion of girls weighed less than 2500 gm when they were born (M:6.5%; F:9.5%). Throughout the first decade of life, more boys than girls were exposed to serious illnesses requiring medical care, and more boys than girls had serious learning and behavior problems necessitating remedial services or special-class placements for the MR and LD.

Boys who were at high risk because of biological factors (moderate to severe perinatal stress; congenital defects) were also more vulnerable amidst a disordered caretaking environment than girls with the same predisposing conditions. There were significant sex differences in the effects of poverty, and family instability, which led to a higher rate of childhood problems—that is, need for long-term remedial education, need for LMH services and repeated serious deliquencies—for such high-risk boys than for high-risk girls. Factors contributing to the boys' vulnerability appeared to be their physical immaturity in childhood, more stringent expectations for male sex-role behavior, and problems in aggression control.

Trends were reversed in the second decade of life: The total number of boys with serious learning problems dropped, while the number of girls with serious behavior problems rose. Dependency and problems associated with teenage pregnancies and marriages appeared to be major contributing factors to the increase in mental health problems among the girls in late adolescence.

Related to these trends was the cumulative number of stressful life events experienced by each sex that led to disruptions in their family unit: Boys with serious coping problems had experienced more adversities than girls in childhood (such as departure of older sibs, sporadic maternal employment, marital discord, maternal mental health problems, father absence, divorce, and remarriage of mother). Girls with serious coping problems reported more stressful life events in adolescence (such as problems in their relationships with their parents, parental divorce or chronic conflict that led to temporary separation of one parent from the family, and maternal mental health problems). Among girls with serious mental health problems by age 18 years, a high proportion became pregnant, married during their teens, and reported marital stress of their own. Among both sexes, significantly more such stressful life events were reported in childhood and adolescence for lower-class than for middle- and upper-class children.

In sum, sex differences in susceptibility to biological and psychosocial stress changed with time and with the different cognitive and social demands of childhood and adolescence. Overall, however, more females than males in this birth cohort appeared to be able to cope successfully, in spite of reproductive risks, chronic poverty, or family distress during the first two decades of life.

The Predictive Power of Biological and Psychosocial Risk Factors

About a dozen variables were among key predictors of serious coping problems (mental retardation, learning disabilities, serious mental health problems, and delinquency) in our study.

Among the biological variables were moderate to severe perinatal stress, a congenital defect at birth, and a moderate to marked physical handicap at age 10. Among the variables that characterized the caregiving environment were a low level of maternal education; a low standard of living, especially at birth, but also at ages 2 and 10 years; and a low rating of family stability between birth and age 2 years. Among the behavioral variables were maternal ratings of very low or very high infant activity level at year 1, a Cattell IQ score below 80 at age 2 years, and a PMA IQ score below 90 at age 10.

Singly or in combination, these variables appeared in our multiple regression equations as key predictors of serious learning and behavior problems, with the predictive power increasing steadily from birth to age 2 years, from ages 2 to 10, and from ages 10 to 18. Correlations across time were generally slightly higher for girls than for boys. Predictions for children from poor homes could be made with greater certainty than for children from middle-class homes, reflecting a greater likelihood of some continuous malfunction of the child–caretaker/child–environment interaction across time for the children of poverty than for the children of affluence.

The presence of *four or more* of these predictors in the records of the children by age 2 years appeared to be a realistic dividing line between most children in this cohort who developed serious learning and/or behavior problems by age 10 or 18 and most of the boys and girls who were able to cope successfully with the developmental tasks of childhood and adolescence (see Table 5). We chose this cutoff point to select the resilient children.

Resilient Children in Chronic Poverty

The resilient children (42 females, 30 males) had *each* encountered four or more such cumulative risk factors before age 2 years, but they had

Table 5

Cumulating Early Predictors of Learning and Behavior Disorders (1955 Birth Cohort, Kauai)

Number of predictors present	Criteria (%)					
	MR by 10 years	LD by 10 years	LMH by 10 years	Delinquent by 18 years	Mental health problems by 18 years	No problem at 10 or 18 years
1 or more	100.0	100.0	100.0	100.0	100.0	97.6
2 or more	100.0	100.0	100.0	100.0	100.0	70.6
3 or more	100.0	100.0	92.0	90.0	88.0	49.2
4 or more	100.0	81.0	75.0	72.0	70.0	26.9
5 or more	88.0	54.0	54.0	54.0	50.0	9.1
6 or more	60.0	27.0	37.0	30.0	27.0	2.2
7 or more	44.0	18.0	16.5	16.0	18.0	.6
8 or more	20.0	4.5	4.0	9.0	7.5	0
9 or more	16.0	4.5	4.0	3.0	3.0	0
10 or more	12.0	0	4.0	3.0	3.0	0

managed to cope successfully with chronic poverty, with constitutional vulnerabilities, and with family instability. All of them "worked well, played well, loved well and expected well" (Garmezy, 1976) when we last interviewed them at age 18. None had developed any serious learning or behavior disorders or sought or received any mental health services during the first two decades of their lives.

A number of constitutional, ecological, and interpersonal variables discriminated, over time, between these high-risk resilient children and high-risk peers of the same age, sex, and low SES who developed serious coping problems in childhood and/or adolescence: A significantly higher proportion among the resilient ones were firstborn children. Although rates of perinatal stress, low birthweight, congenital defects, and physical handicaps were above the norm in this group, the resilient children had fewer serious illnesses and recuperated more quickly than their high-risk peers who developed serious coping problems.

Their mothers perceived them to be "very active," "cuddly," "affectionate," "good-natured," and "easy to deal with" when they were infants, and independent observers noted their pronounced autonomy and positive social orientation when they were toddlers. Developmental exams in the second year of life showed advanced self-help skills and age-appropriate sensorimotor and language development for most. In middle childhood, these children possessed adequate problem-solving and communication skills and their perceptual–motor development was age appropriate. Parents' and self-reports indicated a balance between instrumental and expressive activities and interests that were not sex-typed.

Characteristics that differentiated between high-risk resilient youth and youth with serious coping problems in adolescence were (1) better verbal skills (including reading), (2) an internal locus of control, (3) a positive self-concept, and (4) higher scores on the California Psychological Inventory (CPI) scales—responsibility, socialization, achievement, and femininity for *both* sexes, reflecting a more androgynous, nurturant, and responsible attitude toward life. Resilient girls differed from high-risk girls with problems in adolescence on a number of additional personality dimensions, such as dominance, sociability, achievement via independence, intellectual efficiency, and a sense of well-being.

Key factors in the caregiving environment that appeared to contribute to the stress resistance of resilient children in the midst of chronic poverty were (1) the age of the opposite-sex parent (younger mothers for resilient males, older fathers for resilient females); (2) the number of children in the family (four or fewer); (3) the spacing between the index child and nextborn sibling (more than 2 years); (4) alternate caretakers available to the mother within the household (father, grandparents, older siblings); (5) the workload of the mother (including steady employment outside of the household); (6) the amount of attention given to the child by the primary caretaker(s) in infancy; (7) the availability of a sibling as caretaker or confidant in childhood; (8) the structure and rules in the household in adolescence; and (9) the presence of an informal multigenerational network of kin and friends, including neighbors, teachers and ministers, who were supportive and available for counsel in times of crisis.

For the resilient girls, early mother–daughter relationships had been consistently positive, and there were other females present as support for them in the household during childhood and adolescence. Permanent absence of the father and long-term employment by the mother outside of the household seemed to push them into the direction of greater autonomy and competence, which included care for younger sibs.

Resilient boys were more often firstborn sons, and grew up in households that were less crowded. There were fewer children, but some adult male models were present in their families, who provided rules and structure in their lives.

Structure and strong social bonds were absent among the high-risk children who had difficulties coping under duress. The lack of emotional support was most devastating to children with a constitutional tendency toward withdrawal and passivity, with low-activity levels, and irregular sleeping and feeding habits. These youngsters were more often later-born children in large families whose mothers were more often pregnant again and gave birth to younger sibs before the index child was 20 months old. They appeared to be less active and less socially responsive to their mothers when they were infants and appeared less autonomous to independent observers during the 20-month developmental examinations.

During childhood, they were sick more often and they moved and changed schools more often as well. They also lost siblings or close friends through departure or death and were exposed to more family discord and permanent father absence than the resilient children. There were fewer alternate caretakers in the household for these children, even though many of their mothers worked (but more sporadically), and more parental marriages in this group ended in divorce or separation of one parent from the family.

By age 18, most of these youth had an external locus-of-control orientation and a very low estimate of themselves. They felt that events happened to them as a result of luck, fate, or other factors beyond their control. They considered professional assistance sought and obtained by community agencies to be of little help to them.

Resilient Offspring of Psychotic Parents

Similar characteristics were found to differentiate the resilient offspring of psychotic parents from offspring who developed serious problems of their own. This sample in our study is small; hence the results are only suggestive, but they complement our findings from the high-risk children who grew up in chronic poverty. (The two groups did not overlap.)

Twenty-nine children, or some 4% of the birth cohort (27 singletons, 1 set of twins), were the offspring of parents who had received treatment for serious psychiatric problems (Johnston, 1981). Eleven children, including a set of male twins, had mothers whose primary diagnosis was depression, eight children had mothers who were diagnosed as schizophrenic, five had schizophrenic fathers, and five had depressed fathers. In this small group, the proportion of children who had experienced moderate–marked perinatal stress was twice as high as that of the cohort as a whole (24% vs. 12%). Offspring of schizophrenic mothers had the highest proportion of moderate to marked perinatal complications (40%); offspring of depressed mothers had a rate equal to that of the cohort as a whole.

By the time they reached age 10 years, twelve of the 29 offspring (some 40%) had developed serious learning and/or behavior problems; by the time they reached age 18, 16 of the 29 youth (55%) showed evidence of serious coping problems, such as antisocial behavior or serious mental health problems—a rate more than twice that for the cohort as a whole. There were twice as many boys as girls in this group of troubled youngsters. The majority had mothers with serious mental health problems, most with a diagnosis of schizophrenia.

Among the 13 resilient offspring of psychotic parents who had not developed any serious coping problems during the first two decades of life, the majority were offspring of depressed mothers. They had fewer congenital defects at birth than those who developed serious coping problems in childhood and adolescence.

The resilient youngsters in this group had not been separated from their primary caretaker for extended periods of time during infancy, and home observers noted that their mothers' way of coping with the children at age 1 year was predominantly positive. The mothers considered these infants to be "good natured" and "even tempered" babies.

Independent observers commented on their social orientation, their autonomy, and their advanced self-help skills during the 20-months developmental exam. Teachers' classroom observations and group test results at 10 years indicated that they possessed superior problem-solving and verbal skills, that they could focus their attention, and that they could control their impulses in the classroom.

Self-reports in late adolescence reflected a strong conviction among the resilient offspring of psychotic parents that they were in control of their lives. Like the resilient youngsters who lived in chronic poverty, they drew upon the emotional support of alternate caretakers in the household (for example, a grandmother or older sibling) or peer friends to buffer the stresses associated with parental psychopathology. They also reported a smaller number of cumulative life stresses in childhood than the offspring of emotionally disturbed parents who had developed serious coping problems. *Internalization of parent by child? "say Freud. Why not, in these cases?*

Resilient Teenage Mothers

Twenty-eight women in the 1955 birth cohort on Kauai became pregnant before age 18. Most came from poor homes. As infants, this group had been exposed to higher rates of moderate perinatal stress than the cohort as a whole, and they, in turn, had delivered a higher rate of babies with perinatal complications.

By age 25, when 20 of the women (71% of the original group) were interviewed, they had given birth to a total of 45 children, of whom 18 (40%) had either weighed less than 2500 gm, and/or were born prematurely, and/or had experienced some problems in the perinatal period (e.g., surgery or birth defects requiring hospitalization). As in other populations of teenage mothers, perinatal risk had increased with recidivism rate among the teenage mothers on Kauai. But at the time of the 25-year interview, all women reported that their children were healthy and doing well in school (Gonsalves, 1982).

The educational, vocational, and marital attainment of the women in this sample was above the national average for adolescent mothers. Since the 18-year follow-up, 90% of the pregnant teenagers had completed their high school education, and 25% had gone on to college. Ninety-five percent had worked full- or part-time since adolescence, and only one woman had to rely on welfare support. A third of the original teenage marriages had ended in divorce (a proportion lower than that of the national average of 50% for married teenagers), but second marriages or steady relationships were, with few exceptions, rated stable and satisfactory. Only 2 (10%) of the women were still struggling financially and emotionally at the time of the 25-year follow-up.

At age 25, the Nowicki Locus of Control scores of the teenage mothers were significantly more internal than their scores in late adolescence, indicating that they had greater faith in the control of their own fate than at age 18. The women with the most-internal scores in this group had attained the highest level of education and reported the greatest marital stability and satisfaction at age 25. They reported a balance of high social support and a moderate amount of stressful life experiences in the transition period between late adolescence and young adulthood. They had relied predominantly on relatives and friends to help with finances and child care during hard times, while they went to school and work and acquired new competencies and skills and a sense of responsibility that placed them above the national norms for adult women on the CPI.

The general improvement in the status of this high-risk group presents a positive contrast to the negative consequences generally reported in studies of teenage mothers that are drawn from more select samples, such as juvenile homes and psychiatric clinics, during periods of acute crises.

Discussion

The results of our longitudinal study, based on a whole cohort of children in an entire community, over an extended period of time, provides us with a more hopeful perspective than can be obtained from short-term studies of problem children. Most young people in this cohort were competent in coping with their problems, chose their parents as their role models, found their family and friends to be supportive and understanding, and expressed a strong sense of continuity with their families in values attached to education, occupational preferences, and social expectations.

The Likelihood of Persistence of Childhood Disorders

Looking across a spectrum of more than two decades of development, it appears that the majority of learning and behavior problems identified in childhood improved spontaneously by the time the cohort reached young adulthood. In the absence of early biological stress and early family instability, the majority of such problems appeared to be temporary, though at the time painful, responses to stressful life events.

The cumulative number of such stressful life events experienced in adolescence differentiated significantly high-risk children whose status improved from those whose status deteriorated. Improved youth also had better relationships with their parents during their teens and shared parental attention with fewer children in the household.

Children with learning and/or behavior problems that persisted had higher rates of moderate to severe perinatal stress, low birthweight, and CNS dysfunctions noted by pediatricians in infancy, and they tended to live more often in chronic poverty or amidst parental psychopathology than children whose problems were transient. They also tended to elicit more negative responses from their caretakers.

SES and Vulnerability

Although most of the children and youth with serious and persistent learning and behavior problems in this community were poor, it needs to be kept in perspective that poverty alone was not a sufficient condition for the development of serious coping problems. A low standard of living, especially at birth, increased the likelihood of exposure of the infant and young child to *both* biological and psychosocial risk factors. But it was the *joint* impact of perinatal risk stress and early family instability that led to serious and persistent learning and behavior problems in both middle-class and lower-class children.

Regardless of SES infants with so-called "difficult" temperaments who interacted with distressed caretakers in disorganized, unstable families had a greater chance of developing serious and persistent coping problems than did infants perceived as rewarding by their caretakers and who grew up in stable supportive homes.

Support Systems

We were impressed by the pervasive effect of the quality of mother–child interaction in infancy and early childhood that could be documented as early as year 1 by public nurses who observed in the home and that were verified independently by pediatricians and psychologists in observations before, during, and after developmental screening examinations at age 2 years. The role of the father appeared more crucial in middle childhood and adolescence, especially for the children with learning disabilities (most of whom were boys) and for the pregnant teenagers. His understanding and support or lack of it, his consistent enforcement of rules or lack of it, appeared to play a crucial role in the positive or negative resolution of the developmental problems of his children. Parental attitudes differentiated between high-risk youth with learning and behavior problems who improved in adolescence and those who did not; exposure to different types of intervention by community agencies had a lesser impact.

We had *not* anticipated the considerable influence of alternate caretakers, such as grandparents, older siblings, aunts and uncles, parents of boyfriends or girlfriends, and peers on the children and youth in this cohort. The emotional support of such elders or peer friends was a major ameliorative factor in the midst of poverty, parental psychopathology, and serious disruptions of the family unit.

Among the people of Kauai, an informal network of kin and neighbors, and the counsel and advice of ministers and teachers were more often sought and more highly valued than the services of the mental health professionals, whether they were counselors, psychologists, psychiatrists, or social workers.

Competence and Locus of Control

Equally pervasive appeared to be the effects of competence in reading and writing standard English among the children of Kauai. Competence in these skills was a major ameliorative factor among the resilient youth who coped well in spite of poverty or serious disruptions of their family unit. Lack of these skills led to cumulative problems in coping with cognitive as well as with affective demands in middle childhood and adolescence.

Finally, the degree to which the youth had faith in the effectiveness of their own actions was related not only to the way in which they used their self-help skills and intellectual resources but also to positive changes in behavior. An internal locus of control was a significant correlate of improvement. An external locus of control—that is, a pronounced lack of faith in the effectiveness of one's own actions—was especially notable among the serious and persistent learning and behavior disorders. Crucial for these children was not failure per se, but loss of control over reinforcement, a lack of synchrony between their actions and feedback from their environment. On the contrary, the experience of the resilient children in coping with and mastering stressful life events by their actions appeared to build immunity against such learned helplessness, and fostered an attitude of hopefulness instead.

A Transactional Model of Human Development

The results of the Kauai Longitudinal Study appear to lend some empirical support to a transactional model of human development, which takes into account the bidirectionality of child–caregiver effects (Sameroff & Chandler, 1975). It is the balance between risk factors, stressful life events, and protective factors in the child and the child's caregiving environment that appears to account for the range of adaptive or maladaptive outcomes encountered in this birth cohort.

For the children in our study, biological (temperament, health) factors appeared to show their greatest influence in infancy and early childhood; ecological factors (household structure and composition) and cognitive skills gained in importance in childhood; and inter- and intrapersonal factors, such as self-esteem and locus of control, gain influence in adolescence, judging from the weight assigned to these variables in our discriminant function analyses.

The relative impact of risk factors, stressful life events, and protective factors within the child and his/his caregiving environment differed not only with the stage of the life cycle, but also with the sex of the child and the sociocultural context in which she/he grew up. In this cohort, boys were often more at risk at birth and experienced more life events perceived as stressful in the first decade of life, while the picture was reversed for the girls in the second decade.

As disadvantage and the cumulative number of stressful life events increased, more protective factors in the individual and his/her caregiving environment were needed to counterbalance the negative aspects in their lives and to ensure a positive developmental outcome.

To the extent that the children and youth were able to *elicit* predominantly positive responses from their environment, at each stage of their life cycle, they were found to be stress-resistant, even if they had experienced perinatal stress, and lived in chronic poverty or in a home with a psychotic parent. To the extent that they elicited negative responses from their environment, they were found to be vulnerable, even in the absence of biological stress or serious financial constraints (Werner, 1984, 1985).

Optimal adaptive development thus appears to be characterized by a balance between the power of the person and the power of the (social and physical) environment (Wertheim, 1978). Intervention in behalf of children and youth may be conceived as an attempt to create or restore this balance, either by decreasing their exposure to biological factors and cumulative life stresses, or by increasing the number of protective factors (competencies, sources of support) that they can rely on within themselves or their caregiving environment.

Implications

At present we need to know more about a wide array of what Antonovsky (1979) has called "generalized resistance resources," which seem to be as important as sources of strength for the survivors of concentration camps (which he studied in Israel) as for the making of resiliency and stress resistance in high-risk children and adolescents. Among them are (1) adaptability on the biological, psychological, and sociocultural levels; (2) profound ties to concrete, immediate others; and (3) (formal and informal) ties between the individual and his/her community. We need to identify more systematically the positive effect of these variables in contributing to "resiliency" and "invulnerability," and provide some additional support where they are lacking.

Future research in the study of vulnerability and stress resistance needs to consider the consequences of changing demographic trends (such as later age of marriage and childbirth, smaller families and single parenthood) as well as changing sex-role expectations that may alter substantially the nature of the caregiving environment and the stress resistance of contemporary children and youth in our society.

We need to know more about the role of alternate caregivers, whether they are siblings, grandmothers, kith, or kin, as sources of support in times of stress. Outside of the family unit, there is need to explore other informal sources of support. Among the most frequently encountered in our study were peer friends, teachers, ministers, and neighbors.

The central component of effective coping with the multiplicity of inevitable life stresses appears to be a sense of *coherence* (Antonovsky, 1979), a feeling of confidence that one's internal and external environment is predictable, that life has meaning, and that things will work out as well as can be reasonably expected. But what gives one these feelings of coherence?

A young child maintains a relatively small number of relationships that give feedback and shape a sense of coherence. We have seen that even under adverse circumstances, change is possible when an older child or adolescent develops new competencies and meets people who give her/him positive reinforcement and a reason for commitment and caring.

References

Antonovsky, A. (1979). *Health, stress and coping: New perspectives on mental and physical well-being.* San Francisco: Jossey-Bass Publishers. Holocaust RA418 .A66

Garmezy, N. (1976). *Vulnerable and invulnerable children: Theory, research and intervention* (No. 1337). Master lecture on developmental psychology. Washington, DC: American Psychological Association. WID-LC RJ499 .G37 X

Gonsalves, A. M. (1982). *Follow-up of teenage mothers at age 25: A longitudinal study on the island of Kauai.* Unpublished master's thesis in Child Development, University of California at Davis.

Garmezy: Stress, Coping & Development in children : BF 723.S75 S77 1983 (Gutman + Psych research)

Johnston, K. (1981). *Children of parents treated for mental health problems: A longitudinal assessment.* Unpublished master's thesis in Child Development, University of California at Davis.

Murphy, L., & Moriarty, A. (1976). *Vulnerability, coping and growth from infancy to adolescence.* New Haven: Yale University Press. w·O-ιC BF 921. M863 1976

Rutter, M. (1979). Maternal deprivation, 1972–1978: New findings, new concepts, new approaches. *Child Development, 50,* 283–305.

Sameroff, A., & Chandler, M. J. (1975). Reproductive risk and the continuum of caretaking casualty. In F. D. Horowitz (Ed.), *Review of Child Development Research* (Vol. 4). Chicago: University of Chicago Press.

Werner, E. E. (1973). From birth to latency: Behavioral differences in a multi-racial group of twins. *Child Development, 44,* 438–444.

Werner, E. E. (1984). Resilient Children. *Young Children, 40* (1), 68–72.

Werner, E. E. (1985). Stress and Protective Factors in Children's Lives. In A. R. Nicol (Ed.) *Longitudinal Studies in Child Psychology and Psychiatry.* Chichester, England: Wiley.

Werner, E. E., Bierman, J. M., & French, F. E. (1971). *The children of Kauai: A longitudinal study from the prenatal period to age ten.* Honolulu: University of Hawaii Press.

Werner, E. E., & Smith, R. S. (1977). *Kauai's children come of age.* Honolulu: University Press of Hawaii.

Werner, E. E., & Smith, R. S. (1982). *Vulnerable, but invincible: A longitudinal study of resilient children and youth.* New York: McGraw-Hill. Gutman f Soc. Relations : HQ 792.US 04

Wertheim, E. S. (1978). Developmental genesis of human vulnerability: Conceptual re-evaluation. In E. J. Anthony, C. Koupernik, & C. Chiland (Eds.), *The child in his family: Vulnerable children* (Vol. 4). New York: Wiley. Gutman: RJ 499 .A1 C42 1979 v. 4

2

Social and Cultural Factors in Risk Assessment and Mild Mental Retardation

RON HASKINS

Introduction

Because the particular factors that cause mild retardation are un-known, there has emerged a great deal of interest in risk assessment. The logic underlying the concept of risk goes something like this: (1) there are many children who display no known biological or physiologi-cal damage or syndromes, and yet who fail in school, perform poorly on tests, and in general demonstrate inadequate intellectual functioning; (2) because these children demonstrate no evidence of gross abnormality, the causes of the condition are probably environmental; (3) because the condition occurs almost exclusively in low-income families, the environ-mental causes must be correlated with family income and, in all proba-bility, with children's rearing environments; and (4) thus, any child born into these environments could be considered at risk for subnormal intel-lectual growth.

Although this chain of assumptions is rarely spelled out in this way, it does seem that something similar to this pervades popular thinking about the concept of risk as it applies to inadequate mental develop-ment. The last two links in the risk chain serve as the focus for this chapter. In particular, I examine the social and cultural factors that de-velopmental psychologists and educators have posited as candidates for the environmental conditions that lead to deficient intellectual develop-ment. It is necessary to begin with a few remarks on the definition and epidemiology of mental retardation in order to clarify the group of individuals addressed in subsequent parts of the chapter.

Problems of Definition

Focusing on social and cultural factors in retardation prompts one to consider the definition of mental retardation. Groups, such as the American Association on Mental Deficiency (AAMD), who have offered definitions of retardation could well be accused of semantic gamesmanship. Whereas many previous definitions had focused on intellectual impairment alone (see Shonkoff, 1982), the 1959 AAMD definition was a step forward, in that both intellectual impairment (as indexed by IQ) and impairment of adaptive behavior were required as criteria of mental retardation (Heber, 1959). However, the definition also posited a class of retardates—known as the borderline retarded—who were between 1 and 2 standard deviations below the mean on an IQ test. This definition created a previously unknown group of retarded individuals with IQs between 85 and 70, though the definition did stipulate that deficits in adaptive behavior were also required. Assuming a normal distribution of IQ, and a population of children below 18 of about 80 million in 1959, the AAMD definition created up to 11 million newly retarded individuals. By 1973, the AAMD had decided that these 11 million children were no longer retarded by returning to the more traditional cutoff score of 70 or 2 standard deviations below average.

Behind this semantic and statistical confusion lurks a real issue. The issue is joined by both Ogbu (1978) and Mercer (1970) from their respective views as cultural anthropologist and sociologist. Both critics assert that mental retardation should not be defined for bureaucratic and professional convenience on a statistical basis. A valid diagnosis of mental retardation requires evidence that individuals demonstrate significant functional deficits in their own social or cultural environments. As Mercer (1970) argues most convincingly, the school is the primary social system that defines its members as retarded on grounds of both intellectual and adaptive deficits. But the school diagnosis is not benign, as it often results in segregation from normal students and in whatever effects accrue from the stigma associated with the label, "mentally retarded." Such effects, of course, must be balanced against the putative benefits of special services offered by the schools.

Nonetheless, that the school's diagnosis does not necessarily accord with the diagnosis of other sectors of the culture such as the family, neighborhood, and workplace is suggested by extensive data showing that the prevalence of retardation is greatest during the school years (see

Goodman & Tizard, 1962; Gruenberg, 1964; Lapouse & Weitzner, 1970). The problem of accepting the school definition of retardation is further suggested by very substantial data showing that school achievement correlates rather poorly with success in the work place (Featherman, 1980; Jencks, 1972, 1979; Kennedy, 1948). The implication of both types of data is that there is not a necessary fit between adaptive skills in the schools and adaptive skills in the wider society.

These definitional issues highlight two important points. First, the idea that a valid definition of retardation will ever be achieved is dubious at best. The changes in the AAMD's definition only symbolize the underlying problem that effective adaptation based on cognitive skills varies across historical time, developmental period, and sociocultural context. Second, the definitional issue carries political undertones, and may rouse serious and emotional opposition from various cultural groups (Mercer, 1977).

In the remainder of this chapter, I ignore these definitional issues and focus instead on the social and cultural factors that may place biologically normal children at risk for displaying retarded intellectual development in the 50 to 70 IQ range. I begin with a brief overview of the epidemiology of mental retardation.

Epidemiology of Mental Retardation

The epidemiology of mental retardation is a complex and sometimes baffling discipline. If IQ were normally distributed, we would expect about 2.28% of a random sample to be retarded (below IQ 70) and about 0.18% to be severely retarded (below IQ 50). In fact, there is substantial evidence to indicate that the prevalence of retardation is less than expected for mild retardation (IQ 50–70) and greater than expected for severe retardation (Grossman, 1973; Shonkoff, 1982). On this latter point, Kushlick and Blunden (1974) have reviewed several published studies on prevalence rates in school-age populations. The range of prevalence in these studies extends from 3.3 to 5.8 per 1000 (about 0.33 to 0.58%)—a range above the normal curve estimate of 1.8 per 1000.

By contrast, the prevalence of mild retardation (IQ 50–70) is probably much less than the expected rate of somewhat above 2%. Tarjan, Wright, Eyman, and Keeran (1973) have argued that the actual rate is likely to be about 1%. In addition to elevated death rates among retardates, Tarjan and his colleagues hold that when adaptive behavior is added to the definitional criteria, many individuals with IQ scores in the retarded range are found not to be retarded. In short, though they have low IQ scores, many individuals are able to adapt effectively to the demands of their environment. Mercer (1970), as suggested, would support the lower prevalence rate of about 1%. Although Mercer found a prevalence rate of 21.4 per 1000 (2.1%) below IQ 70 in Riverside, California, this rate was cut by more than 50%—to 9.7 per 1000 (about 1%)—when a test of adaptive behavior was added to the definitional criteria.

The appropriate conclusion seems to be that about 1% of a given population will be mildly retarded if we require IQ scores and assessments of adaptive behavior as the dual criteria for the diagnosis of mental retardation.

Regardless of what prevalence rate we select, it is widely agreed that nonbiological factors are the primary cause of retardation in the 50–70 IQ range, and that at least 70% of retarded individuals are in this group. This conclusion is strongly suggested by the finding from epidemiological studies that, whereas severe and profound retardation (IQ below 50) does not occur disproportionately in the lower classes, mild retardation does. Rutter's (Rutter, Tizard, & Whitmore, 1970) studies of the Isle of Wight in England, for example, showed that the vast majority of cases of mild retardation occurred in low-income families. Further, Birch and his colleagues (1970) concluded from their epidemiological study of Aberdeen, Scotland that prevalence rates in upper classes were nearly zero, and that the prevalence rate among those from the lowest SES group was nine times the prevalence rate in the upper class. Finally, data from the Collaborative Perinatal Project in the United States revealed that IQs between 50 and 69 at age 7 were 11 times as frequent among lower SES as compared with upper SES white families, and about 7 times as high among lower SES as compared with upper SES black families (see Shonkoff, 1982).

These epidemiological considerations form the primary justification for the intent of this chapter (see also Stein & Susser, 1962). If prevalence rates for moderate retardation are so much higher among low-SES families, and if children in this group of retardates have no clear biological problems, we might assume that social and cultural factors play an important role in placing a child at risk for mild retardation. In the remainder of this chapter, then, I review evidence about what these social and cultural risk factors might be—and whether they might be subject to modification.

Social and Cultural Factors in Mental Retardation

Interaction of Social and Biological Factors

Regardless of one's view of the evidence for genetic effects in causing mild retardation (see Jensen, 1969; Kamin, 1974), other biological conditions seem to be quite pertinent as risk factors in at least some cases. Although these are not our major concern here, such biological conditions must be mentioned because they seem to interact with sociocultural factors to produce retarded development. These conditions occur during the prenatal (e.g., cytomegalovirus), perinatal (e.g., low birthweight, hypoxia), and postnatal (e.g., malnutrition) periods, and often have a greater prevalence among low-income populations. An example proves instructive.

Cytomegalovirus (CMV) is an intrauterine infection that can be transmitted to the fetus. Its frequency in the United States is about 1% of live births, and the rates are higher in neonates born to low-income and younger women (Hanshaw, 1981). Neonates with CMV are often asymptomatic, thereby making the condition especially pernicious because its presence may not, indeed usually is not, detected until later childhood—if ever. The long-term sequelae of the condition include reduced hearing acuity and deficient mental development—outcomes which in all likelihood are related.

A study by Hanshaw and his colleagues (1976) examined the IQs of 44 children who as neonates had asymptomatic CMV (as determined by cord serum specimens). These children were given a pediatric exam, a hearing exam, and several psychological tests between 3.5 and 7 years of age, as were a group of 44 children matched on age, sex, race, and several other factors, and a random sample of children born in the same hospital as the CMV group. The mean IQ of children in the CMV group, though normal, was significantly less than that of children in the other two groups. Further, a disproportionate number of all children below IQ 90 were from the CMV group; all seven children with an IQ below 79 were in the CMV group, and nearly 30% of children in the CMV group, as compared with less than 7% in the other two groups, were found to have hearing loss. Of greatest interest, however, were the findings that: (1) whereas only 38% of all children were in low-income families, 68% of the CMV group were from low-income families; and (2) among low-income families the IQ difference between children in the CMV group and the other two groups was significant; by contrast, there were no IQ differences between CMV and non-CMV middle-class children.

Two important generalizations are implied by these results, both of which are seen frequently in the studies I review. First, low-income infants and children have a greater risk of exposure to a potentially harmful condition—in this case intrauterine infection with CMV. Second, low-income children are more likely to show long-term sequelae of a given condition than middle-income children with the same condition (see Sameroff & Chandler, 1975). Although this second generalization will be dealt with in greater detail, note that middle-class infants who were positive for CMV did not show lower IQs in subsequent years, whereas low-income children positive for CMV did demonstrate lower IQs. The obvious conclusion to be drawn from these two facts is that both biological and sociocultural variables must be taken into account in understanding mental development in general and mental retardation in particular. The importance of social and cultural risk factors becomes even more apparent when studies of family effects on development are examined.

Family Effects

Several approaches have been taken to show that families exert a major influence on the intellectual development of their children (Clarke-Stewart & Apfel, 1978; Hess, 1970). With few exceptions, these studies confound genetic and environmental effects because the family provides all of the genetic background and much of the environmental background— particularly during the preschool years—enjoyed by their children. Although only a few of the studies I review permit the disentangling of genetic and environmental factors, we can nonetheless have at least some confidence in the importance of environmental factors examined by most of the studies. For example, experimental intervention studies are relatively impervious to criticism on genetic grounds when the studies (1) randomly assign children to treatments, (2) present one group with an enriching experience, and then (3) compare the average intellectual development or school achievement of children in the two groups. Whatever the genetic effects might be, the logic of random assignment dictates that they are equally represented in both groups. Even the typical observational or interview study of specific family practices and their effects on development can be granted some immunity from the genetic criticism. Only in the case where genetic differences covary with specific parenting practices does the relation between parent practice and child outcome confound genetic and environmental effects. It seems somewhat unlikely that parents who give their children better genes would also have genes for intelligence that cause them to perform particular parenting behaviors at higher rates or, as seems more important, under particular circumstances. Many of the studies reviewed here control to some extent even for this possible confounding by examining parent practices within particular ethnic and socioeconomic groups.

Recall from the section on epidemiology that a disproportionate number of mildly retarded children come from low-income families. Indeed, some investigators claim that virtually no mildly retarded children are reared in middle-class families (Birch, Richardson, Baird, Borobin, & Illsley, 1970). It is not surprising, then, to learn that there is a well-established link between family social or socioeconomic status (SES) and children's intellectual development. What is meant by SES? Although income, education, or occupation—or some combination of the three—have almost always served as indexes of SES, it would appear that occupation is the primary variable that average people use to classify each other according to prestige. In fact, the great hierarchy of occupations, though not written in stone, is surprisingly similar across Western societies (and even emerging nations), stable across time, and clearly apprehended by children as young as age 9 (see Kohn, 1979). There are doubtless serious issues involved in how we operationalize SES (see Mueller & Parcel, 1981), but these are ignored here.

My interest in this chapter, however, is not simply in the relation between measures of SES and intellectual development. Rather, the intent is to discover whether variations in environments provided by families of differing SES contribute to variations in intellectual development. If so, it is then necessary to outline the specific social experiences or cultural factors that are most closely associated with intellectual growth.

I begin by citing three excellent studies that demonstrate the very substantial power of the family environment to shape intellectual development. Two of these are adoption studies and are therefore particularly well suited to the purposes of this review. Whereas natural or biological families confound the developmental contribution of genes and childrearing environment, adoptive families break this confounding because they supply only environment and not genes to their children.

In the first of these studies, Sandra Scarr and her associate David Weinberg (1976) studied 130 black (or interracial black and white) children adopted by middle-class white families in Minnesota. Because the mean IQ of blacks in the midwestern part of the United States is 90 (compared with a national average of 85 for blacks and 100 for whites), if the mean IQ of adopted blacks were greater than 90, one could conclude that family environment contributes to intellectual growth. Nor should we overlook the fact that conducting this study with black children was an especially important achievement because of the widespread belief, popularized by Arthur Jensen (1969) and William Shockley (1971), that black–white IQ differences were genetically determined.

Results showed that the mean IQ of the 130 black and interracial adopted children was 106.3; the mean IQ of the 99 black children adopted before 1 year of age was 110.4. It seems clear, then, that whatever the proportion of variance in IQ scores accounted for by genetic factors, there is ample environmental variance to permit substantial IQ changes by placement in favorable family environments. Indeed, from the Scarr and Weinberg study, we might conclude that the range of reaction for IQ scores is at least 20 points—that is, the difference between the average IQ of 90 for blacks reared in the midwest and the average IQ of 110 for early-adopted blacks in the Scarr and Weinberg study. More to the point, the social and cultural influences of families can be seen to exert a powerful influence on development.

A second and equally remarkable adoption study was conducted by Skeels and his associates (Skeels, 1966; Skeels, Updegraff, Wellman, & Williams, 1938). In this study, which was initiated during the 1930s, infants were transferred from a barren orphanage environment to a home for retarded girls. In effect, the infants were adopted by the retarded females—who ranged in age from 18 to 50 years, with mental ages from 5 to 12 years. According to Skeels, the infants were given constant attention by both the retarded girls and the ward attendants; were played with, talked to, and trained almost constantly; and were taken on frequent excursions outside the ward. On average, infants were 19 months of age when transferred to the home for retarded girls, and spent an average of 19 months in the home.

The first row in Table 1 summarizes the effects of this treatment on the infants' intellectual development. The second row summarizes the intellectual development of a comparison group of 12 infants who remained in the orphanage during approximately the same period of life as the 13 experimental infants. Examining the first column of IQ data shows that shortly before transfer to the home for retarded girls, the mean IQ of the experimental infants was 64.3; at a comparable age of about 17 months, the mean IQ of comparison infants was 86.7. Within a few months after transfer, however, the mean IQ of experimental infants had increased dramatically to 90.5—a gain of about 25 points. By contrast, over roughly the same period of development, comparison infants declined about 15 IQ points to 71.1. At the end of the experimental period, when both groups of infants were approximately 3 years of age, the IQ of adopted infants had increased to 91.8, while the IQ of comparison infants continued to fall dramatically.

Summarizing these results produces two major conclusions. First, placing biologically normal infants who are developmentally delayed in a stimulating environment produced substantial IQ gains. Second, leaving infants in an extremely deprived environment, in which they received only minimal care and stimulation, produced equally dramatic declines in intellectual development. Unfortunately, we have no information about the specific types of stimulation received by experimental infants that produced the impressive IQ gains, nor the experiences of

Table 1

IQ Scores for Two Groups Before, During, and Near the End of Placement

| | Test occasion | | | | | |
| | 1^a | | 2 | | 3 | |
Group	IQ^b	Age^c	IQ	Age	IQ	Age
Experimental	64.30	18.30	90.46	33.78	91.76	45.31
Comparison	88.68	24.19	71.08	27.66	60.50	53.15

[a]The first test occasion for the experimental group was just before placement in the home for mentally retarded girls; the second test was given a few months after placement; the third test was given near the end of placement.
[b]Most tests were Kuhlmann-Binet's; a few were Stanford-Binet's.
[c]In months.

which comparison infants were deprived that produced the dramatic IQ declines. What we do know is that a complete change in rearing environment resulted in a reversal of delayed IQ development. As in the case of maternal stimulation studies, as well as in the Scarr and Weinberg (1976) adoption study, children reared in environments in which they received substantial amounts of social stimulation and individual attention demonstrate normal intellectual development. Again, the power of family social influences on intellectual development is apparent.

The story of this remarkable study does not end, however, with the results summarized thus far. In an extraordinary display of tenacity, Skeels (1966) located all 25 experimental and comparison children some 20 years later. The information obtained from this follow-up study constitutes some of the most dramatic results in the history of developmental research. First, all 13 experimental subjects were self-supporting and none were wards of an institution; all but two had formed stable marriages. On the other hand, 4 of the 11 living members of the comparison group (one had died at age 15 in an institution for the retarded) were in state institutions. Another lived in an institution for the retarded, but was paid as an employee. Of the remaining 6, 3 were dishwashers, 1 was usually unemployed, 1 was a part-time cafeteria worker, and 1 was a typesetter. Thus, only 1 of the 11 living members of the comparison group was employed in other than a menial occupation. Further, only 2 of the 11 had ever married, and 1 of these was divorced.

Equally impressive was the fact that the experimental group had an average of 11.7 years of education, all save 2 had completed at least 10 years of school, and 8 of the 13 had graduated from high school. Comparison group members, by contrast, had completed an average of less than 4 years of schooling, and only 1 had completed junior or senior high school. Finally, the average income of the experimental group was slightly above the average for the state in which the adults lived, and greater by a factor of nearly four than the income of comparison group members.

In many respects, the Skeels study represents the ideal outcome for which subsequent intervention programs with mildly retarded children have aimed. Not only does it demonstrate the power of social influences on intellectual development, but it also demonstrates that environmentally induced retardation can be prevented, with consequent benefits for both the retarded individuals and society.

In the third study, Firkowska and her colleagues (1978; see also Czarkowski et al., 1977) studied the children of families headed by mothers and fathers with jobs of varying status in Warsaw, Poland. The characteristic that makes this study so interesting—besides the fact that it included an entire age cohort of 13,625 children—is that Warsaw is a city with few of the amenities enjoyed by wealthy families in capitalist nations. Because the city was leveled during World War II and rebuilt along socialist lines:

> people of all levels of education and all types of occupations live in apartments that closely resemble each other, shop in identical stores that contain the same goods, and share similar catering and cultural centers. Schools and health facilities are equipped in the same way and are uniformly accessible. (p. 138)

The authors conclude, then, that Warsaw presents an opportunity to minimize the differences in physical environments and privileges outside the family that usually accompany status prestige in capitalist societies, and permits a more refined test of the impact of family childrearing practices, as distinct from material factors, on intellectual development. In effect, Firkowska and his colleagues were able to study the equivalence of middle-class and working-class families in capitalist societies, while controlling for the vast differences in resources that distinguish upper and lower classes in capitalist nations.

Based on tests administered when children were about 11 years old, the study revealed that family variables were more closely associated with Raven IQ scores than variables describing the district in which children lived or variables describing the school they attended. Further, there was a direct and striking relation between an index of parent education and job status and their children's Raven scores.

These three studies, then, provide strong evidence that family environments can have substantial effects on intellectual development.

They do not, however, provide us with information about the particular practices or processes in which families engage that influence intellectual development. Fortunately, a number of studies do provide evidence on these points.

While reviewing these studies, it should be kept in mind that the most direct approach to uncovering the family practices associated with mild retardation would include a comparison of families with mildly retarded children and matched families with normal children. Because so few studies of this type have been conducted, we focus on studies that have compared the practices of lower-class and middle-class families. The justification for this approach is that, as argued in the preceding section on epidemiology, disproportionate numbers of mildly retarded individuals are reared by lower-class families, while middle-class families produce very few mildly retarded children.

The approach taken to reviewing these studies is straightforward. First, we examine evidence concerning differences in childrearing practices between lower-class and middle-class families. Second, we examine evidence concerning the family practices that are related to intellectual development. Third, we compare the family practices that differentiate lower-class and middle-class families with those that seem related to intellectual development. A correspondence between the two sets of practices suggests that family childrearing patterns may play an important role in the etiology of mild retardation.

SES Differences in Childrearing Practices

Studies of differences in the behavior of low-income and middle-class mothers in the first year of life have produced somewhat conflicting results. Whereas Lewis and Wilson (1972) found low-income mothers to exhibit more touching, holding, smiling at, and playing with their 3-month-olds at home, Ramey, Farran, and Campbell (1979) failed to find differences between middle-income and low-income mother–child dyads at 6 months in a laboratory setting. Data reported by Tulkin and Kagan (1972) complicate matters further as these investigators found striking differences favoring middle-class mothers. The middle-class mothers of 10-month-olds, as contrasted with low-income mothers, were more interactive, engaged in more face-to-face encounters with their babies, issued more verbalizations to the babies, and entertained them more, especially by giving objects. In addition, middle-class mothers responded to a higher percentage of infant vocalizations and with shorter latency.

At least two studies employing Caldwell's HOME scale, which uses a combination of observations and ratings, have also shown substantial differences in the environments of lower- and middle-class homes during the first year of life (Caldwell, 1967; Ramey, Mills, Campbell, & O'Brien, 1975). In fact, the Ramey et al. study found significant differences on all six HOME subscales; a group of predominantly middle-class mothers provided emotional and verbal responsivity, avoided restriction and punishment, organized the physical and temporal environment, provided appropriate play materials, involved themselves in the child's activities, and provided for variety in daily stimulation at higher levels than a group of very low-income mothers.

By contrast with studies of SES differences in the first year of life, studies of mothers and infants over 2 or 3 years of age have consistently found differences in maternal behavior. Zegiob and Forehand (1975) found that low-income mothers of 4- to 6-year-olds more often criticized and less often questioned their children in a laboratory session. Kamii and Radin (1967) found low-income mothers to be less responsive to their child's expressed needs and to initiate less contact with their children. Like Zegiob and Forehand, Kamii and Radin also observed middle-class mothers to be less commanding and more consulting with their 4-year-olds. Borduin and Henggeler (1981) essentially replicated these results, as did Hanson (1975), Wachs, Uzgiris, and Hunt (1971), Walters Connor, and Zunich (1964), and Zunich (1961).

Similarly, studies in which mothers were observed teaching their children have consistently shown SES differences favoring middle-class mothers. Hess and Shipman (1965, 1967), for example, found that middle-class mothers of 4-year-olds used more cognitive control and less punitive control than low-income mothers. Further, middle-class mothers were more effective at motivating their children, provided their children with better orientation to task requirements, and used more positive and less negative reinforcement. Similarly, Bee and her colleagues (1969) found that middle-class mothers were less controlling and disapproving of their children, gave them more information, asked more questions, spent more time on task, and more often told children what they were doing right than lower-class mothers.

Thus, inconsistencies in published studies of infants give way to clear SES differences in maternal behavior beginning at least by age 2 or 3. Of the preceding studies, as well as others (see reviews by Clarke-Stewart & Apfel, 1978; Deutsch, 1973; Freeberg & Payne, 1967) not discussed here, it might be said that four findings are more or less consistent. First, there are rather consistent differences in use of influence and control techniques by middle- and lower-class mothers. Middle-class mothers use fewer direct commands, less disapproval, and more positive reinforcement. Second, nearly all the studies find higher levels of involvement by middle-class mothers; they spend more time in actual play or teaching, provide more structure to their children in both free-play and problem-solving situations, and observe their children attentively when not directly involved with them. Third, several studies find middle-class mothers to be more responsive to their children in the sense of anticipating and meeting their needs and responding to a higher proportion of their signals or requests for assistance. Fourth, middle-class mothers tend to be better teachers than lower-class mothers. In addition to their aforementioned more positive approach to control, they also involve their children in a greater variety of experiences, orient them to tasks more thoroughly, and supply them with more information.

Relations between Childrearing Practices and Intellectual Development

Of what consequences are these SES differences in maternal behavior? Such differences are meaningless unless it can be shown that they are related to differences in child outcome. The task before us, after all, is to examine the contribution of social and cultural factors to intellectual development.

Several maternal behaviors have been shown to be related with developmental outcomes during the first year of life. With rare exceptions (e.g., Lewis & Goldberg, 1969), simple caretaking-behaviors such as touching, holding, breastfeeding, and so on, do not seem of great moment (Caldwell, 1964). On the other hand, responsiveness to infant signals such as crying and vocalizing does seem to be important. Lewis and Goldberg (1969) found that the proportion of infant cries and vocalizations to which mothers responded at 12 weeks was correlated with a habituation-like measure of learning. Donovan and Leavitt (1978) found that mothers of infants who received high scores on the Uzgiris–Hunt scales, as compared with mothers of low-scoring infants, tended to respond to or to stimulate their infants when the infants were attentive to the mothers. Further, Lewis and Coates (1980) found that although total amount of stimulation was either negatively correlated or unrelated with performance on the Bayley Mental Development Index (MDI), maternal responsivity and interaction were both positively correlated with MDI performance. All these studies (see also Yarrow, Rubenstein, & Pedersen, 1975), then, suggest that the mother's sensitivity and responsiveness to her infant during the first year of life are positively related to cognitive outcomes.

A second important set of relations between maternal and child development variables in infancy might be called the provision of appropriate stimulation and variety of experience. Beckwith (1971) found the number of places mothers took their infants to be correlated with Cattell scores; several studies have found the variety in stimulation and provision of appropriate play material subscales on Caldwell's HOME to be associated both with level of development and with increases in test performance across time (see review by Elardo & Bradley, 1981); and Ruddy and Bornstein (1982) found encouraging infants to attend to objects and other types of stimulation at 4 months to be associated with vocabulary size at 12 months.

Third, Beckwith (1971), found that a combination of low verbal stimulation and high restrictiveness was negatively associated with Cattell scores.

Turning to mothers with older preschool children, one also finds several significant relations between childrearing practices and developmental outcome. First, various measures of maternal speech are associated with intellectual development. Communication accuracy between mother and child in a referential communication task was correlated with IQ at age 6 and with school readiness at ages 5 and 6 in a study by Dickson, Hess, Miyake, and Azuma (1979). This finding is particularly impressive because it remained statistically significant even when the child's IQ and family SES were partialled out, and because the same relationship was found in both a sample of American and a sample of Japanese children. Borduin and Henggeler (1981) found mothers' use of questions with 4-year-olds to be correlated with IQ and performance on the Peabody Picture Vocabulary Test. Similarly, Clarke-Stewart and her associates (1979) found maternal descriptive speech to be correlated with IQ in a longitudinal study of children between 24 and 30 months.

Several investigators (Blank, 1975; Nelson, 1973; Schachter, 1979; Snow et al., 1976; Tough, 1977) have argued that it is not so much the form or the frequency of mothers' speech that seems related with child outcome as it is the responsivity of maternal speech to children's talk and behavior. On the basis of an elaborate study of black low- and middle-income and white middle-income mother–child pairs, for example, Schachter (1979) concluded that advantaged mothers more frequently adapted and adjusted their speech to support the child's behavior. In general, it would appear that maternal speech, and particularly its use in responding to the child's activities and in promoting reasoning and thinking, both differentiate middle-class and low-income mothers and are positively related to intellectual development (see review by Farran, 1982).

Closely related to the dimension of maternal speech is a set of behaviors that might be called "provision of intellectual experiences." I have already noted that several studies found Caldwell's HOME to be related with development. Bradley and Caldwell (1976), for example, found the HOME subscale on provision of appropriate play materials (as well as other subscales) to be associated with increased IQ scores between 6 and 36 months.

In a similar finding, based on somewhat more sophisticated observations of maternal behavior in the home, Carew (1977) has shown a variety of what she called "intellectually valuable experiences" (p. 191) to be associated with IQ. More specifically, using home observation measures based on White's (White & Watts, 1973) work, Carew recorded the occurrence of four types of experiences thought to promote intellectual development: verbal/symbolic, spatial/fine motor, concrete reasoning/problem solving, and expressive/artistic. In the first category, for example, she recorded instances in which the child learned to recognize objects, understand and use labels, say or write letters or numbers, or talk about pictures. Two results from this study bear emphasis. First, the frequency of these intellectual experiences in the home between 12 and 33 months was highly correlated ($r = .76$) with Binet IQ at age 3 years. Further, in a multiple regression analysis, a measure of SES added virtually nothing to the variance in IQ scores accounted for by these measures of intellectual experience. It would appear, then, that "intellectually valuable experiences" are associated with SES, and that they are specific and process-related measures that may underlie the frequently reported SES–IQ correlation. Second, Carew found that the source of these intellectual experiences is not the child but people, and usually the mother, in the child's home setting.

In a similar home observation study of poor children between 12 and 36 months of age, McGlaughlin and her colleagues (1980) also found intellectual interactions with the mother to be associated with language development; direct teaching by the mother in unplanned situations was also strongly related with language development. Thus, the role of the mother in creating situations that promote intellectual growth is again seen to be quite important.

A third factor that seems related to intellectual development during the preschool years is a dimension of attachment, warmth, and positive interactions. For example, Matas, Arend, and Sroufe (1978) found that secure attachment at 18 months was associated with persistence and competence at 24 months. Hatano, Miyaki, and Tajima (1980) observed that warm concern in an observational setting was associated with IQ in

4-year-olds. Similarly, in a longitudinal study, Clarke-Stewart and her associates (1979) found that positive interactions between mothers and children in the home were correlated with IQ in 2-year-olds.

Finally, as was the case during the infancy period, several studies with older children have shown that maternal directions and commands are negatively associated with intellectual development (Borduin & Henggeler, 1981; Clarke-Stewart, 1973; Hatano, Miyaki, & Tajima, 1980).

Interestingly, these same maternal behaviors have been found to be associated with intellectual development in school-age children. Although the measures of maternal speech are not as refined in these studies as in the studies with preschool children, maternal speech has nonetheless often been found to be associated with the child's verbal or intellectual ability (Bing, 1963; Milner, 1951). Wolf (1964) found situations for learning in the home and parent assistance in learning to be correlated with IQ in 10-year-olds, and Bing (1963) found mothers' voluntary assistance and pressure for improvement to be associated with verbal ability. Regarding warmth and attachment, Milner (1951) found that good readers at age 6 had positive interactions with their mothers in the home. Finally, the factor of maternal negative behavior continues to be inversely related with intellectual outcome in children through at least 12 years of age (Kent & Davis, 1957; McCall, Appelbaum, & Hogarty, 1973; Milner, 1951; Walberg & Marjoribanks, 1973).

Three studies deserve special emphasis in this section on relations between the child's home social environment and intellectual development. These studies are especially important because all have focused on children who either met the criteria for mild retardation or showed evidence of serious educational problems.

The first study, conducted by Cunningham, Reuler, Blackwell, and Deck (1981), examined differences in the mother–child relations of normal and mildly retarded children between 18 and 54 months of age. Observing mothers and children in both a free play and a task situation, these investigators found that retarded children were less interactive and less responsive than normals. For their part, the mothers of retarded children initiated fewer social acts, were more controlling, and reinforced their children less for compliance with maternal direction. In addition, mothers of retarded children used less-complex language. Although a correlational study of this type does not allow one to disentangle behavioral differences attributable to children from those attributable to mothers, the findings do suggest that several of the aforementioned relations between maternal behavior and child intellect apply to retarded children and their mothers.

An excellent study by Wilton and Barbour (1978) provides even more direct evidence of differences in the social stimulation received by children at risk for retardation and that received by normal children. Moreover, the study confirms a number of the aforementioned relations between maternal behavior and development. An especially compelling feature of this study is the selection of subjects. More specifically, the children judged to be at risk for mild retardation were selected because they had older siblings in a public school class for special students; the contrast group was selected from younger siblings of students in regular classes. The logic of this design is that if special-class students were retarded because of inadequate stimulation they received at home as youngsters, then their younger siblings should also be experiencing the same type of deficient stimulation. Another attractive feature of this form of subject selection was that children in both groups were from homes of low SES, thereby controlling, at least in part, for SES factors while implicitly recognizing that not all low-income homes are deficient and therefore at risk for producing retarded children.

Interestingly, the stimulation received by a younger group of high-risk preschoolers, who averaged about 2 years of age, was no different than that received by comparison children. By contrast, an older group of high-risk children, who averaged about 3 years of age, experienced a number of deficiencies. More particularly, high-risk children interacted less with their mothers, spent less time in the type of highly intellectual activities found by both White and Watts (1973) and Carew (1977) to be associated with accelerated intellectual development, had mothers who taught them less often and encouraged them less, and had mothers who had more difficulty controlling them. This study, although based on a rather small sample, provides evidence that mild retardation is associated with preschool home environments that do not provide sufficient instruction and intellectual stimulation.

A final study again provides evidence of the relation between social experience in the home and intellectual development. Like Cunningham et al. (1981), Norman-Jackson (1982) conducted home observations involving the younger siblings of older children. In this case, however, the older siblings were not retarded; rather, they were poor readers with normal IQs (about 90), as contrasted with good readers with similar IQs.

Home observations revealed that, although the preschool siblings of successful readers did not enjoy higher rates of verbal exchange with their parents, they did have higher rates of verbal exchange with parents and school-age siblings combined. Further, parents of successful readers were four times as likely to encourage as they were to discourage verbal interaction with their preschool siblings. Parents of unsuccessful readers were equally likely to discourage as to encourage verbal interaction.

When the younger preschool siblings had themselves entered the public schools, it was found that 71% of them were in the same reading classification as their older sibling. These children were then divided into successful and unsuccessful readers on the basis of their reading performance. Comparing the preschool data for these newly constituted groups provided a nearly complete replication of the earlier findings; namely, that successful readers had more verbal interaction with parents and siblings combined (though not with parents alone) than unsuccessful readers, and that parents of successful readers were seven times as likely to encourage as to discourage verbal interaction. By contrast, parents of unsuccessful readers were about twice as likely to discourage as to encourage verbal interaction.

By way of summary, then, the preceding studies seem to provide evidence that some childrearing practices that differentiate lower-class and middle-class families are also practices that influence intellectual development. More specifically, although the issue is less clear in the first year of life than later, four sets of social influences seem of particular importance: (1) language, and especially language responsive to the child's activities; (2) control and influence techniques, especially moderate use of punitive controls and direct commands and greater dependence on reasoning and positive reinforcement; (3) warmth and positive relations between family members and the child; and (4) arranging the environment so as to encourage opportunities for learning new facts, reasoning, and thinking. A calculated guess would indicate that this last factor is especially important for intellectual development or, more important for our purposes, that its absence is especially detrimental to normal intellectual growth.

Some Caveats

Although the preceding studies seem to demonstrate that social and cultural factors in the home differentiate SES groups, and that these very social factors seem related to intellectual outcomes, the studies must be interpreted within the framework of several caveats.

First, nearly all the studies collected data on several variables but found significant correlations or differences on only a few. Ramey et al. (1979) found significant correlations for only 1 of 6 variables at 6 months and only 2 of 6 at 20 months; Tulkin and Kagan (1972) found significant relations on 12 of 23 variables; Walters, Connor, and Zunich (1964) on 5 of 17 variables; and Kamii and Radin (1967) on 3 of 22 variables. These ratios suggest some capitalization on chance in both the significant differences between SES groups and the associations between maternal behavior and child outcome reported in the literature.

Even more ominous for the findings, in one of the few studies with systematic attempts at replication, Clarke-Stewart et al. (1979) obtained identical observational and child test data on a primary and on four replication samples. These data permitted 120 correlations between maternal and child variables. Only about half of these 120 were replicated in at least one of the four samples, and only 5 of the 120 were replicated in all four samples. Consider further that the criterion for replication selected by Clarke-Stewart was simply whether the correlations were significant or nonsignificant in two samples, and one begins to realize that we are not dealing with precision in this business of seeking relations between maternal behavior and child outcomes.

Second, I have said too little in this review about dyadic effects. As Bell has repeatedly argued (1968, 1971), influence in parent–child interaction goes both ways. Thus, it is possible that some of the behavioral differences between upper- and lower-income mothers are attributable in some degree to differences between upper- and lower-income children. Like the preceding studies, for example, Farran and Haskins (1980) found that low-income mothers were more directly controlling than middle-class mothers. However, closer inspection of the data revealed that both groups of mothers tended to tell their children what to do when the children were not actively engaged in any activity. But because low-income children were in this state twice as often as middle-class children, low-income mothers more often suggested activities for them. It is difficult to know to what extent dyadic effects of this type account for the aforementioned SES differences in maternal behavior, but it is definite that very few studies have looked for these types of dyadic effects.

A third caveat concerning the findings reviewed here is that nearly all the studies focused on single maternal behaviors. By contrast, using factor scores derived from home observational data, Clarke-Stewart (1973; Clarke-Stewart et al., 1979) found a constellation of maternal behaviors that was highly related with child outcomes. More specifically, a factor of optimal maternal care that included positive emotion, stimulation, and responsiveness was highly correlated with a factor of child competence that included cognitive, language, and social development. As Clarke-Stewart argues, this finding suggests that it is not so much the frequency of specific maternal behaviors that influences development as it is a pattern of maternal variables that incorporates several of the single variables other studies have shown to be related to development. I can see no empirical basis in the literature for resolving this issue, but its importance for future research and intervention is clear.

Another important caveat is that the studies are quite restrictive in their definition of social environment. There is now enough evidence in the literature to indicate that the nearly exclusive focus on mothers as the only factor in the social environment of infants and children is not justified. Recall that Norman-Jackson (1982) found that parents of successful readers did not provide more verbal stimulation than did parents of unsuccessful readers. However, when verbal stimulation from older siblings was combined with that of parents, successful readers did receive more verbal stimulation in the home. The obvious conclusion is that siblings represent an important part of the home social environment that stimulates intellectual growth.

And if siblings are important, what about fathers, friends, neighbors, uncles, aunts, and grandparents? The evidence is now beginning to accumulate on the importance of fathers (see, e.g., Radin, 1973), but we can only guess at the importance of these other actors. Nonetheless, one study provides extremely provocative evidence in this regard. Landau (1976) observed male infants of 2, 4, 7, and 11 months of age from lower- and middle-class environments both in a kibbutz and among Bedouin tribesmen. Although there were no differences in the overall rates of social stimulation received by infants in these environments, Landau found that infants had frequent social exchanges with up to eight familiar adults. Further, older infants received a progressively smaller proportion of their total stimulation from mothers. And of even greater importance, the mothers' contribution to total social stimulation received by infants varied radically across various types of stimulation. Thus, for example, mothers represented an average of 80% of the words and sentences to which infants were exposed, but only 45% of the play activity.

Until similar studies have been done in various SES groups in the United States, Landau's findings should be interpreted with caution. Nonetheless, if Norman-Jackson's results are representative, the literature on SES differences in mother–child interaction could be quite misleading. This possibility would be especially true if lower-class, as compared with middle-class, infants and children receive relatively more of their stimulation from people other than their mother—as ethnographic observations by Stack (1974) have suggested is the case.

Finally, although nearly every published study produced at least one significant correlation between maternal behavior and child outcome, and despite the fact that some of these correlations are replicated across several studies, it must be observed that the correlations tend to be quite moderate. Most seem to be in the range of .3–.4, which would translate to well less than 20% of the variance in child outcome that is accounted for by maternal behavior. And even this amount of variance could be shared with other unmeasured variables that are correlated with the maternal variables. In any case, people who would interpret these studies must bear in mind that the typical correlations between maternal and child variables are not very strong.

Ecological Studies and Considerations

Studies of family environments are notable for their rigor and, at least in several cases, for the convergence in findings. But, as Bronfenbrenner (1977) and others (Ogbu, 1978) have noted, these studies are also limited in several respects. At a most obvious level, they cannot answer questions about why parents raise children the way they do. Even if we knew exactly what parenting behaviors caused particular types of intellectual development at particular ages, we would still want to know what factors impinge on families to determine their selection and use of childrearing practices. Further, as children begin to move beyond the family to spend an increasing proportion of their time in schools, churches, peer groups, and street activities (see Medrich, 1977), influences outside the family must have a substantial developmental impact.

Nonetheless, educators and developmental psychologists have continued to emphasize both the importance of the family environment and the early years of life in accounting for development. White (1979) has stated the position most succinctly: "much that shapes the final human product takes place during the first years of life" (pp. 182–183). Further, White and many others leave little doubt that the mother's skills are the central factor in the shaping process. Thus, for example, Connolly and Bruner (1974) have emphasized the "hidden curriculum of the home" in accounting for the development of competence during the preschool years.

The ecological approach to mental development stands in stark contrast to the family-centered approach. For our purposes, the position taken by Ogbu (1978, 1981, 1982, this volume) can be cited to indicate the essential outline of an ecological approach to retardation. Simplifying considerably, let us take subsistence as an example of an ecological factor that influences development. Every group within a given society must earn a living. Due to historical and other broad factors (each of which are themselves aspects of ecology), different groups in American society have different means of achieving subsistence. As adults in all cultures at all times have attempted to do, adults in American SES groups defined by different modes of subsistence will attempt to pass on to their children the specific knowledge and general skills requisite to achieving subsistence. Notice that this model of development stands the family-centered approaches—such as those reviewed here earlier—on their head. It is not so much that childrearing practices followed by SES groups determine subsistence skills acquired by children as it is that subsistence skills determine childrearing practices.

Three examples will indicate the value of this approach. As previously noted, Kohn (1979) has argued that the differences in childrearing practices, and especially discipline, between working-class and middle-class families are explained by the workplace requirements faced by parents. Thus, Kohn argues that working-class families stress conformity to external authority and rules in their childrearing because these are salient characteristics of the subsistence environments occupied by factory workers. By contrast, middle-class parents, whose professional and business sector jobs require self-direction and manipulation of symbols, encourage their children to develop these competencies, especially by appeals to reasoning, guilt, and psychological punishments in their choice of disciplinary techniques. In both cases, instrumental competencies required by the work world drive childrearing practices and not vice versa.

The cross-cultural work of Barry, Child, and Bacon (1959) provides a second example of the value of the ecological approach (see also LeVine, 1970; Whiting, 1963). The authors first define two contrasting types of societies on the basis of subsistence types—namely, the low-food accumulation cultures typified by hunter–gatherers, and the high-food accumulation societies typified by farmers. Barry et al. further posit a two-step process to get from subsistence requirements to childrearing practices. First, it is in the nature of things that the personality types required by these two types of subsistence differ greatly. Hunter–gatherer societies value individuality, assertiveness, and risk taking because these are the skills requisite to successful subsistence activities. By contrast, agricultural societies value responsible, conservative, cooperative adults. In addition to reviewing empirical evidence that adults in several hunter–gatherer and agricultural societies in fact value and display these respective sets of characteristics, Barry and his colleagues rated the childrearing practices of 104 societies and found them generally congruent with the personality type needed for the societies' subsistence activities.

The point of these studies is that subsistence tasks "generate adaptive, functional personal activities or instrumental social–emotional competencies. These qualities are perceived as useful by parents and other child-rearing agents and are taught by appropriate techniques" (Ogbu, 1981, p. 419).

Following this same line of reasoning, Ogbu (1978, 1982) argues that school failure among American blacks can only be understood with reference to the types of subsistence activities open to them as adults.

Black children grow up with the understanding, based on direct observation, that discrimination, unemployment, and menial jobs are the lot of many blacks, especially among adolescents and young adults. Indeed, black children must be prepared to occupy an economic environment characterized by "marginal conventional economic resources and a substantial amount of nonconventional resources or 'street economy' " (Ogbu, 1981, p. 423).

Ogbu goes on to argue not only that childrearing practices of black parents are informed by the parents' understanding of ghetto economy, but also that parenting practices are shaped by the very forces to which black parents must teach their children to accommodate. Thus, marginal participation in conventional economic activity makes it difficult for black males to participate in childrearing; parents are often forced to rely on friends and relatives for goods and services (see Stack, 1974); and parents must often themselves participate in street culture to fulfill social and economic needs.

Such parents do not value the same personal attributes as white, middle class parents. Although the goals of both groups—economic security, power, social prestige—seem to be similar, the competencies needed to achieve the goals differ substantially. As a result, according to Ogbu, black parents are likely to use very different childrearing practices than middle-class parents:

> Among such techniques are the contrasting treatment of the infant with abundant nurturance, warmth, and affection and their scarcity in postinfancy; establishment of a child–adult contest relationship in the postinfancy period; inconsistent demands for obedience in sanctions and in other ways of relating to the child; and the use of verbal rebuffs and physical punishment. These techniques probably promote functional competencies like self-reliance, resourcefulness, ability to manipulate people and situations, mistrust of people in authority, ability to 'fight back' or to ward off attacks, etc. (1981, p. 424).

An important implication of Ogbu's theory concerning the ecology of competent development among black children is that direct intervention to change childrearing practices is doomed to failure. Even if the parents' childrearing techniques could be changed, the child would still need to develop competencies to become prepared for subsistence activities. This reasoning underlines the importance of ecological approaches by emphasizing the social, cultural, economic, and historical context, which is in substantial part beyond the family's control, that impinges on children and shapes their development. Needless to say, Ogbu's (1978) approach is incompatible with the use of terms such as "mild retardation" and especially the practice of assigning responsibility for inadequate intellectual development to family childrearing prac-

Table 2

Select Social Indicators of Kerala State and India
as a Whole

Indicator	Kerala	All India
Literacy (%)	60.4	29.5
Number of patients treated per 1,000 population	2.0	85.3
Crude infant mortality rate	55.0	122.0
Crude birth rate	26.9	35.9
Female literacy (%)	54.0	19.0
Women never married (%)	22.0	7.0

tices—that is, to "deficiencies" in black and low-income families (1981, p. 420).

A further implication of Ogbu's approach to understanding competent development is that broad societal forces play a major role in creating the circumstances that foster school failure and the use of terms such as "mild retardation" to label children whose competencies are not congruent with those of the dominant culture. Such broad societal forces are a major theoretical target of ecological approaches. To a substantial degree, ecological approaches to child development intend to force researchers out of their laboratories and single-variable studies to a consideration of equally important, though more difficult to study, factors that lie outside the child's immediate environments of home, neighborhood, and school (Bronfenbrenner, 1977).

Though examples of how such broad factors can influence development are difficult to find, at least one study provides interesting results that are consistent with the ecologists' emphasis on broad cultural factors in accounting for development.

Ratcliffe (1978) has summarized extensive evidence to demonstrate that social reforms in Kerala, India have resulted in several important changes in living conditions and in the status of individual citizens. Kerala is an extremely poor state with a per capita income of about $80— about two-thirds the all-India average. Yet Kerala has achieved a set of social indicators that is beyond expectations for such a poor state. A few of these indicators are summarized in Table 2.

The data in Table 2 indicate that, despite an extremely low-level of economic development, Kerala has embarked on a path of social development that has already brought its social indicators to a level just below many modern and highly industrialized nations. As compared with all-India averages, the literacy rate in Kerala is greater by a factor of two, many more of its citizens receive medical care, its infant mortality rate is about half, its birth rate is about 75%, its female literacy rate is more than double, and more than three times as many women never marry.

How are these outcomes to be explained? The answer appears to lie in the political development of Kerala's citizens. Beginning in the 1950s, the Communist party became very active in Kerala and subsequently secured a series of election victories. At one point, in fact, Communists controlled the legislature of Kerala and forced a number of important land reforms. In subsequent elections, although the Communists did not control the legislature, they did retain a substantial political influence and played an important role in further social reforms.

Three examples can be cited to demonstrate the type of reforms that differentiate Kerala from other Indian states, and that affected what might be called the political and social ecology of the state. First, unlike other states in India, Kerala implemented a limited but effective series of land reform measures in the late 1950s and early 1960s. A number of studies have concluded that these land reforms have served to reduce wealth and income inequalities, and to provide low-income farmers with a stake in Kerala's economy (e.g., Ratcliffe, 1978).

Second, wage rates in Kerala are the second highest among Indian states, and 1974 legislation provided employment security to laborers, improved the conditions of work, and provided retirement benefits to employees. These measures, of course, have served to promote the equitable distribution of wealth among all Kerala's citizens.

Third, government expenditures have tended to focus on low-income rather than privileged citizens. Thus, for example, whereas other Indian states tend to concentrate their educational expenditures on universities that cater primarily to the upper classes, Kerala spends 86% of its educational resources on primary and secondary schools that serve the low-income and working classes.

The information summarized by Ratcliffe, then, demonstrates how social and economic changes can influence the immediate environment in which people live. Changes in infant mortality, literacy rates, and the conditions of employment can be expected to establish a radically different environment in which children and families live. If ecological theory is correct, these changes will have a direct influence on childrearing practices and thereby on intellectual development.

It seems appropriate to emphasize the fact that family-centered and ecological approaches to development are not incompatibile. Ecological forces establish a set of influences that impinge on children's development by influencing conditions in the home, school, and community. But complete understanding of development will still require knowledge about the immediate social environment that directly affects the child.

Conclusions

Seven conclusions seem appropriate. First, despite definitional and epidemiological issues, a substantial portion of people judged to be retarded fall in the 50–70 IQ range. Because of the lack of biological or physiological problems evident in this population, social and cultural factors are often assumed to underlie the low-IQ scores of this group and their problems with adaptation to school environments. Second, most—some would say nearly all—of these individuals live in lower-SES families.

Third, there are several differences in the childrearing practices of lower- and middle-SES families, and many of these differences have been found to be associated with intellectual growth. More specifically, four dimensions of parental behavior seem especially important, and may play a role in the etiology of mild retardation: (1) language responsive to the child's talk and activities; (2) minimum use of punitive discipline, control, and direct commands, with a concomitant emphasis on reasoning and positive reinforcement; (3) warmth and positive social interactions; and (4) arranging the natural environment to promote learning and reasoning. Fourth, a number of individuals—in addition to the mother—are sources for these types of stimulation.

Fifth, consideration of ecological factors impinging on the family and on the child in environments outside the home throws the correlational relations listed above into sharp relief. The ecological perspective implies that children from economically disadvantaged families may undergo socialization to cope with a substantially different environment than privileged families.

Sixth, entirely different intervention strategies would be supported from the perspective of the family socialization model and the ecological model of development. Whereas the former views family differences as deficits to be corrected through parent education and training, the latter views the causes and therefore the remedies of mild retardation to lie in broad societal forces such as discrimination and the distribution of income and resources.

Finally, the information on social and cultural factors reviewed here seems consistent with two generalizations concerning risk. The first conclusion is that risk is a viable concept in that research has identified several conditions within the family environment that differentiate low-income and middle-class families, that are correlated with developmental outcomes, and that are responsive to intervention. Indeed, data from several studies (Andrews et al., 1982; Gordon, 1973; Madden, Levenstein, & Levenstein, 1976; see also Clarke-Stewart & Apfel, 1978) demonstrate that, at least under some circumstances, the behavior of low-income mothers can be changed and these changes can lead to positive changes in intellectual outcomes.

On the other hand, a second conclusion supported by the preceding ecological studies, as well as several additional considerations, suggests that the enterprise of identifying children at risk and intervening on an individual or family basis may not solve the problems of educational or income inequality that plague our society. A full consideration of these points goes beyond my purpose in this chapter, but I would like to close by outlining the basic argument.

In the first place, as Finkelstein and Ramey (1980) have shown, current techniques of identifying infants at risk for developmental deficits are not very precise. Identifying all infants and children from low-income environments as at risk for subnormal intellectual development makes little sense, both because far more of these children demonstrate normal than deficit intellectual development (Broman, Nichols, & Kennedy, 1975) and because the cost of intervening with all these children would be immense.

Moreover, some might argue that available techniques of intervention with individuals and families have not produced very impressive results. Although some projects have produced excellent short-term results, on the whole it seems appropriate to conclude that social science has yet to demonstrate intervention techniques that can produce substantial and cost-efficient intellectual benefits on a broad scale (Clarke-Stewart & Apfel, 1978). Thus, even if infants and children at risk for mild retardation could be efficiently identified, it is not entirely clear that current intervention techniques could reliably deter the predicted deleterious outcomes.

Finally, our society has not yet given sufficient attention to structural changes in the economy and techniques of income redistribution that may be more effective in producing equality of education and income (see Jencks, 1972, 1979).

In a word, even the substantial advances in knowledge about social and cultural factors that influence intellectual development should not at present be interpreted to mean that the enterprise of identifying infants and children at risk and supplying them with individual and family intervention will produce the hoped-for results.

References

Andrews, S. R., Blumenthal, J. B., Johnson, D. L., Kahn, A. J., Ferguson, C. J., Lasater, T. M., Malone, P. E., & Wallace, D. B. (1982). The skills of mothering: A study of Parent

Child Development Centers. *Monographs of the Society for Research in Child Development,* 47 (6, Serial No. 198).

Barry, H., Child, I. L., & Bacon, M. K. (1959). Relation of childtraining to subsistence economy. *American Anthropologist, 61,* 51–63.

Beckwith, L. (1971). Relationships between attributes of mothers and their infants' IQ scores. *Child Development, 42,* 1083–1097.

Bee, H. L., Van Egeren, L. F., Streissguth, P., Nyman, B. A., & Leckie, M. (1969). Social class differences in maternal teaching strategies and speech patterns. *Developmental Psychology, 1,* 726–734.

Bell, R. Q. (1968). A reinterpretation of the direction of effects in studies of socialization. *Psychological Review, 75,* 81–95.

Bell, R. Q. (1971). Stimulus control of parent or caretaker behavior by offspring. *Developmental Psychology, 4,* 63–72.

Bing, E. (1963). Effect of childrearing practices on development of differential cognitive abilities. *Child Development, 34,* 631–648.

Birch, H., Richardson, S., Baird, D., Borobin, G., & Illsley, R. (1970). *Mental subnormality in the community: A clinical and epidemiologic study.* Baltimore: Williams & Wilkins.

Blank, M. (1975). Mastering the intangible through language. In D. Aaronson & R. W. Ricker (Eds.), *Developmental psycholinguistics and communication disorders.* New York: New York Academy of Science.

Borduin, C., & Henggeler, S. (1981). Social class, experimental setting, and task characteristics as determinants of mother–child interaction. *Developmental Psychology, 17,* 209–214.

Bradley, R., & Caldwell, B. M. (1976). The relationship of infants' home environments to mental test performance at fifty-four months: A follow-up study. *Child Development, 47,* 1172–1174.

Broman, S. H., Nichols, P. L., & Kennedy, W. A. (1975). *Preschool IQ: Prenatal and early developmental correlates.* Hillsdale, NJ: Erlbaum.

Bronfenbrenner, U. (1977). Ecological factors in human development in retrospect and prospect. In H. McGurk (Ed.), *Ecological factors in human development.* Amsterdam: North-Holland Publishing Co.

Caldwell, B. M. (1964). The effects of infant care. In M. L. Hoffman & L. W. Hoffman (Eds.), *Review of child development research* (Vol. 1). New York: Russell Sage.

Caldwell, B. M. (1967). Descriptive evaluations of child development and of developmental settings. *Pediatrics, 40,* 46–54.

Carew, J. (1977). Social class, experience and intelligence in young children. In H. McGurk (Ed.), *Ecological factors in human development.* Amsterdam: North-Holland Publishing Co.

Clarke-Stewart, K. A. (1973). Interactions between mothers and their young children: Characteristics and consequences. *Monographs of the Society for Research in Child Development, 38,* (6–7, Serial No. 153).

Clarke-Stewart, K., & Apfel, N. (1978). Evaluating parental effects on child development. In L. Shulman (Ed.), *Review of research in education.* Itasca, IL: F. E. Peacock Publishers.

Clarke-Stewart, K. A., Vanderstoep, L., & Killian, G. (1979). Analysis and replication of mother–child relations at two years of age. *Child Development, 50,* 777–793.

Connolly, K. J., & Bruner, J. J. (Eds.). (1974). *The growth of competence.* London: Academic Press.

Cunningham, C., Reuler, E., Blackwell, J., & Deck, J. (1981). Behavioral and linguistic developments in the interactions of normal and retarded children with their mothers. *Child Development, 52,* 62–70.

Czarkowski, M., Firkowska-Markiewicz, A., Ostrowska, A., Sokotowska, M., Stein, Z., Susser, M., & Wald, I. (1977). Some ecological, school, and family factors in the intellectual performance of children: The Warsaw study—preliminary results. In P. Mittler (Ed.), *Research to practice in mental retardation* (Vol. 1). Baltimore; University Park Press.

Deutsch, C. P. (1973). Social class and child development. In B. M. Caldwell & H. N. Ricciuti (Eds.), *Review of research child development* (Vol. 3). Chicago: University of Chicago Press.

Dickson, W. P., Hess, R. D., Miyake, N., & Azuma, H. (1979). Referential communication accuracy between mother and child as a predictor of cognitive development in the United States and Japan. *Child Development, 50,* 53–59.

Donovan, W. L., & Leavitt, L. A. (1978). Early cognitive development and its relation to maternal physiologic behavioral responsiveness. *Child Development, 49,* 1251–1254.

Elardo, R., & Bradley, R. H. (1981). The Home Observation for Measurement of the Environment (HOME) Scale: A review of research. *Developmental Review, 1,* 113–145.

Farran, D. (1982). Mother–child interaction, language development and the school performance of poverty children. In L. Feagan & D. C Farran (Eds.), *The language of children reared in poverty: Implications for education and intervention.* New York: Academic Press.

Farran, D., & Haskins, R. (1980). Reciprocal influence in the social interactions of mothers and three-year-old children from different socioeconomic backgrounds. *Child Development, 51,* 780–791.

Featherman, D. L. (1980). Schooling and occupational careers: Constancy and change in worldly success. In O. G. Brim & J. Kagan (Eds.), *Constancy and change in human development.* Cambridge, MA: Harvard University Press.

Finkelstein, N. W., & Ramey, C. T. (1980). Information from birth certificates as a risk index for educational handicap. *American Journal of Mental Deficiency, 84,* 546–552.

Firkowska, A., Ostrowska, A., Skolowska, M., Stein, Z., Susser, M., & Wald, I. (1978). Cognitive development and social policy. *Science, 200,* 1357–1362.

Freeberg, N., & Payne, D. T. (1967). Parental influence on cognitive development in early childhood: A review. *Child Development, 38,* 65–87.

Goodman, M., & Tizard, J. (1962). Prevalence of imbecility and idiocy among children. *British Medical Journal, 1,* 216–219.

Gordon, I. J. (1973). *An early intervention project: A longitudinal look.* Gainsville: University of Florida, Institute for Development of Human Resources.

Grossman, H. (1973). *Manual on terminology and classification in mental retardation: 1973 version* (Special Publication Series No. 2). Washington, DC: American Association on Mental Deficiency.

Gruenberg, E. (1964). Epidemiology. In H. Stevens & R. Heber (Eds.), *Mental retardation: A review of research.* Chicago: University of Chicago Press.

Hanshaw, J. (1981). Cytomegalovirus infection. *Pediatrics in Review, 2,* 245–251.

Hanshaw, J., Scheiner, A., Moxley, A., Gaeu, L., Abel, V., & Scheiner, B. (1976). School failure and deafness after "silent" cogenital Cytomegalovirus infection. *The New England Journal of Medicine, 295,* 468–470.

Hanson, R. (1975). Consistency and stability of home environmental measures related to IQ. *Child Development, 46,* 470–480.

Hatano, G., Miyaki, K., & Tajima, N. (1980). Mother behavior in an unstructured situation and child's acquisition of number conservation. *Child Development, 51,* 379–385.

Heber, R. (1959). A manual on terminology and classification in mental retardation. *American Journal of Mental Deficiency, Monograph Supplement, 64(2).*

Hess, R. D. (1970). Social class and ethnic influences on socialization. In P. H. Mussen (Ed.), *Carmichael's manual of child psychology* (3rd ed., Vol. 1). New York: Wiley.

Hess, R. D., & Shipman, V. C. (1965). Early experience and the socialization of cognitive modes in children. *Child Development, 36,* 869–886.

Hess, R. D., & Shipman, V. C. (1967). Cognitive elements in maternal behavior. In J. P. Hill (Ed.), *Minnesota symposia on child psychology* (Vol. 1). Minneapolis: University of Minnesota Press.

Jencks, C. (1972). *Inequality.* New York: Basic Books.

Jencks, C. (1979). *Who gets ahead?* New York: Basic Books.

Jensen, A. R. (1969). How much can we boost IQ and scholastic achievement? *Harvard Educational Review, 39,* 1–123.

Kamii, C. K., & Radin, N. L. (1967). Class differences in the socialization practices of Negro mothers. *Journal of Marriage and the Family, 29,* 302–310.

Kamin, L. J. (1974). *The science and politics of IQ.* Potomac, MD: Erlbaum.

Kennedy, R. J. R. (1948). *The social adjustments of morons in a Connecticut city.* Hartford, CT: Mansfield-Southbury Training Schools.

Kent, N., & Davis, D. R. (1957). Discipline in the home and intellectual development. *British Journal of Medical Psychology, 30,* 27–33.

Kohn, M. L. (1979). The effects of social class on parental values and practices. In D. Reiss & H. Hoffman (Eds.), *The American family: Dying or developing?* New York: Plenum.

Kushlick, A., & Blunden, R. (1974). The epidemiology of mental subnormality. In A. M. Clarke & A. D. B. Clarke (Eds.), *Mental deficiency: The changing outlook.* New York: Free Press.

Landau, R. (1976). Extent that the mother represents the social stimulation to which the infant is exposed: Findings from a cross-cultural study. *Developmental Psychology, 12,* 399–405.

Lapouse, R., & Weitzner, M. (1970). Epidemiology. In J. Wortis (Ed.), *Mental retardation: An annual review* (Vol. 1). New York: Grune & Stratton.

LeVine, R. A. (1970). Cross-cultural study in child psychology. In P. H. Mussen (Ed.), *Carmichael's manual of child psychology* (3rd ed., Vol. 2). New York: Wiley.

Lewis, M., & Coates, D. (1980). Mother–infant interaction and cognitive development in twelve-week-old infants. *Infant Behavior and Development, 3,* 95–105.

Lewis, M., & Goldberg, S. (1969). Perceptual-cognitive development in infancy: A generalized expectancy model as a function of the mother–infant interaction. *Merrill Palmer Quarterly, 15,* 81–100.

Lewis, M., & Wilson C. D. (1972). Infant development in lower-class American families. *Human Development, 15,* 112–127.

Madden, J., Levenstein, P., & Levenstein, S. (1976). Longitudinal IQ outcomes of the mother–child home program. *Child Development, 47,* 1015–1025.

Matas, L., Arend, R., & Sroufe, A. (1978). Continuity of adaptation in the second year: The relationship between quality of attachment and later competence. *Child Development, 49,* 547–556.

McCall, R. B., Appelbaum, M. I., & Hogarty, P. S. (1973). Developmental changes in mental performance. *Monographs of the Society for Research in Child Development, 38* (3, Serial No. 150).

McGlaughlin, A., Empson, J., Morrissey, M., & Sever, J. (1980). Early child development and the home environment: Consistencies at and between four preschool stages. *International Journal of Behavioral Development, 3,* 299–309.

Medrich, E. A. (1977). *The serious business of growing up: A study of children's lives outside of school (Children's Time Study)*. Unpublished manuscript, University of California, Berkeley.

Mercer, J. (1970). Sociological perspectives on mental retardation. In C. Haywood, (Ed.), *Socio-cultural aspects of mental retardation*. New York: Meredith Corporation.

Mercer, J. (1977). Cultural diversity, mental retardation, and assessing the case for non-labeling. *Care and Intervention, 1,* 353–362.

Milner, E. (1951). A study of the relationship between reading readiness in grade school children and patterns of parent–child interaction. *Child Development, 22,* 95–112.

Mueller, C. W., & Parcel, T. L. (1981). Measures of socioeconomic status: Alternatives and recommendations. *Child Development, 52,* 13–30.

Nelson, K. (1973). Structure and strategy in learning to talk. *Monographs of the Society for Research in Child Development, 38,* (1–2, Serial No. 149).

Norman-Jackson, J. (1982). Family interactions, language development, and primary reading achievement of black children in families of low income. *Child Development, 53,* 349–358.

Ogbu, J. U. (1978). *Minority education and caste: The American system in cross-cultural perspective.* New York: Academic Press.

Ogbu, J. (1981). Origins of human competence: A cultural–ecological perspective. *Child Development, 52,* 413–429.

Ogbu, J. (1982). Societal forces as a context of ghetto children's school failure. In L. Feagans & D. C. Farran (Eds.), *The language of children reared in poverty: Implications for evaluation and intervention.* New York: Academic Press.

Radin, N. (1973). Observed paternal behaviors as antecedents of intellectual functioning in young boys. *Developmental Psychology, 8,* 369–376.

Ramey, C., Farran, D., & Campbell, F. (1979). Predicting IQ from mother–infant interactions. *Child Development, 50,* 804–814.

Ramey, C. T., Mills, P., Campbell, F. A., & O'Brien, C. (1975). Infants' home environments: A comparison of high-risk families and families from the general population. *American Journal of Mental Deficiency, 80,* 40–42.

Ratcliffe, J. (1978). Social justice and the demographic transition: Lessons from India's Kerala state. *International Journal of Health Services, 8,* 123–144.

Ruddy, M. G., & Bornstein, M. H. (1982). Cognitive correlates of infant attention and maternal stimulation over the first year of life. *Child Development, 53,* 183–188.

Rutter, M., Tizard, J., & Whitmore, K. (1970). *Education, health and behavior.* London: Longman.

Sameroff, A. J., & Chandler, M. J. (1975). Reproductive risk and the continuum of caretaking casualty. In F. D. Horowitz (Ed.), *Review of child development research* (Vol. 4). Chicago: University of Chicago Press.

Scarr, S., & Weinberg, R. (1976). I.Q. test performance of black children adopted by white families. *American Psychologist, 31,* 726–739.

Schachter, F. (1979). *Everyday mother talk to toddlers: Early intervention.* New York: Academic Press.

Shockley, W. (1971). Morale, mathematics, and the moral obligation to diagnose the origin of Negro IQ deficits. *Review of Educational Research, 41,* 369–377.

Shonkoff, J. (1982). Biological and social factors contributing to mild mental retardation. In K. Heller, W. Holtzman, & S. Messick (Eds.), *Placing children in special education: A strategy for equity.* Washington, DC: National Academy Press.

Skeels, H. M. (1966). Adult status of children with contrasting early life experiences. *Monographs of the Society for Research in Child Development, 31* (3, Serial No. 105).

Skeels, H., Updegraff, R., Wellman., B. L., & Williams, H. M. (1938). A study of environmental stimulation: An orphanage preschool project. *University of Iowa Studies in Child Welfare, 15*, No. 4.

Snow, C. E., Arlman-Rupp, A., Hassing, T., Jobse, J., Joosten, J., & Vorster, J. (1976). Mother's speech in three social classes. *Journal of Psycholinguistics Research, 5*, 1–20.

Stack, C. B. (1974). *All our kin: Strategies for survival in a Black community.* New York: Harper.

Stein, Z., & Susser, M. (1962). The social distribution of mental retardation. *American Journal of Mental Deficiency, 67*, 811–821.

Tarjan, G., Wright, W., Eyman, R., & Keeran, C. (1973). Natural history of mental retardation: Some aspects of epidemiology. *American Journal of Mental Deficiency, 77*, 369–379.

Tough, J. (1977). *The development of meaning: A study of children's use of language.* New York: Wiley.

Tulkin, S. R., & Kagan, J. (1972). Mother–child interaction in the first year of life. *Child Development, 43*, 31–41.

Wachs, T., Uzgiris, I., & Hunt, J. (1971). Cognitive development in infants of different levels and from different environmental backgrounds: An explanatory investigation. *Merrill-Palmer Quarterly, 17*, 283–317.

Walberg, H. J., & Marjoribanks, K. (1973). Differential mental abilities and home environment: A canonical analysis. *Developmental Psychology, 9*, 363–368.

Walters, J., Connor, R., & Zunich, M. (1964). Interaction of mothers and children from lower-class families. *Child Development, 35*, 433–440.

White, B. L. (1979). *The origins of human competence: The final report of the Harvard preschool project.* Lexington, MA: Health.

White, B. L., & Watts, J. C. (1973). *Experience and environment.* Englewood Cliffs, NJ: Prentice-Hall.

Whiting, B. B. (1963). *Six cultures: Studies of child-rearing.* New York: Wiley.

Wilton, K., & Barbour, A. (1978). Mother–child interaction in high-risk and contrast preschoolers of low socioeconomic status. *Child Development, 49*, 1136–1145.

Wolf, R. M. (1964). *The identification and measurement of environmental process variables related to intelligence.* Unpublished doctoral dissertation, University of Chicago.

Yarrow, L. J., Rubenstein, J., & Pedersen, F. A. (1975). *Infant and environment.* Washington, DC: Hemisphere.

Zegiob, L. E., & Forehand, R. (1975). Maternal interactive behavior as a function of race, socioeconomic status, and sex of the child. *Child Development, 46*, 564–568.

Zunich, M. (1961). A study of relationships between child rearing attitudes and maternal behavior. *Journal of Experimental Education, 30*, 231–241.

3

Developmental Retardation: A Systems Theory Perspective on Risk and Preventive Intervention

CRAIG T. RAMEY AND DAVID MACPHEE

Introduction

Understanding risk mechanisms is a prerequisite to cost-effective prevention programs. Without detailed knowledge of the etiology of a particular psychopathology, mental health professionals cannot determine where best to concentrate limited resources. Without a clear understanding of the mechanisms causing the disorder, we can have only vague hunches to guide the creation and implementation of prevention programs. To focus preventive efforts on a group that as a whole does not really need additional services results in public dismay at the costs for the relatively few beneficiaries. To choose a program that focuses inadvertently on mechanisms unrelated to pathology can lead either to despair about society's ability to solve a high-priority problem or (worse) to harm of the intended beneficiaries through stigma or outright damage. However, we rarely possess either the epidemiological data or adequate information about treatment effectiveness to design efficient prevention programs. Such has been the case with developmental retardation.

In this chapter, we discuss some contemporary perspectives on risk and the prevention of retarded development. The central theme of our presentation is the complex, transactional nature of development. We argue that traditional models of risk fail to account for the range of developmental outcomes observed in individuals exposed to the same risk factors, and that more sophisticated models are needed to explain changes in risk status. Our general systems model not only illuminates the interplay of forces causing developmental retardation but also pinpoints loci where prevention programs may have the greatest effect. Fundamentally, then, development is a dynamic, multiply determined process, and so efforts to predict it and prevent it from going awry will need to be broader in scope, yet tailored more specifically to types of families or children's stages of development.

Risk for Developmental Retardation

The power and elegance of any risk equation is inherently limited by how well the predictor and outcome variables are defined. We consider poverty-as-risk in later sections; our definition of the outcome variable deserves explication first. In contrast to the traditional absolutist position of adopting a predetermined IQ score as evidence of mental retardation (see Grossman, 1973; Heber, 1959), we have taken an intraindividual relativistic position. Here, the primary focus is on deviations from optimal intellectual or social functioning within individuals or groups. Developmental retardation, then, is a relative decrement in cognitive and/or social skills compared to the phenotypic value that would be obtained in an optimal environment. This definition shifts the focus of prevention and remediation from an arbitrary, often politically motivated classification score to the individual's learning potential. The Achilles' heel of our definition is that the reference point is *potential,* or the individual's capabilities that would have developed under optimal circumstances.

Cost-effective prevention of developmental retardation depends on the ability to identify those persons who are most likely to experience such outcomes—that is, those persons who are at high risk for dysfunctional development. *Risk* can be defined as any condition or variable that increases the likelihood of an abnormal developmental outcome. *Prevention efforts,* in turn, attempt to modify the strength of relationships between particular conditions and their outcomes. In the case of developmental retardation, poverty predicts later mild mental retardation and associated school failure.

Traditional conceptions of risk, however, have not provided an adequate understanding of the genesis of retarded and atypical development among the poor. One of the biggest limitations has been the emphasis on univariate risk factors. While variables such as poverty are correlated with atypical development in group data, they are not sensitive enough to identify, without many false positives, those specific individuals who appear to need some form of intervention. For example, although 75% of mild mental retardation occurs among the poor, only 2% to 10% of the poor are likely to become mentally retarded by traditional criteria (Begab, 1981; Richardson, 1981).

The inability of traditional models of risk to account for individual variations in outcome suggests that a change in perspective is in order. Our first goal, then, is to describe current conceptions of risk and their inadequacies. The thrust of our argument is that characteristics of persons and their environments may make individuals more or less vulnerable to the effects of general and univariate risk factors such as poverty. Our presentation is organized around a general formula that Albee (1982) proposed for general psychopathology:

$$\text{Incidence} = \frac{\text{Organic factors} + \text{stress}}{\text{Coping skills} + \text{self-esteem} + \text{social–material resources}}.$$

Components of a Risk Model

Perspectives

The traditional concept of risk embraces several assumptions about development that warrant detailed examination. First, risk is couched in terms of predicted abnormal outcomes, and thus is a deficit model of development. The implications of this orientation are manyfold. The notion of deviations from expected developmental pathways assumes that we know a fair amount about population norms or control groups not exposed to the risk factor. Unfortunately, such baselines for comparison often are absent or deficient. Adherence to a deficit model also implicitly places programmatic emphasis on remediation of the pathological process rather than *enhancement* of normal development. Identifying an individual as at risk for developmental retardation also raises the issues of unjustified labelling and potential self-fulfilling prophecies.

Second, risk has been understood largely within an actuarial framework. Showing that a statistical relationship exists between risk condition X and outcome Y, however, does not necessarily illuminate the contributing developmental processes. Fundamentally, *risk* as traditionally used in psychology is a prediction in want of an explanation. The statistical association between poverty and developmental retardation, for instance, tells us little about the functional relationships between the risk factors and the outcome. Unfortunately, an inadequate understanding of the mechanisms involved in any particular adverse developmental outcome leaves one hard pressed to generate precisely targeted and hence cost-effective programs.

Traditional risk research has been hampered by three other limitations, each of which can be attributed to an oversimplified concept of development. First, reliance on predictions from one point in time to a later outcome assumes that development is linear for individuals and that the magnitude of risk remains constant over intervening time periods. Second, risk frequently has been restricted in research practice to a small number of variables, typically fewer than three and often only one or two. Even though developmental theory is donning the mantle of a multivariate, transactional paradigm, risk remains too frequently couched in univariate terms such as maternal IQ or social class. Third, risk conditions have typically been viewed as properties of either the organism or the environment rather than their transactions.

New perspectives on risk are, however, beginning to emerge as the intrinsic limitations of the traditional definition have become apparent. The position that holds the greatest promise for understanding the effects of poverty—and efforts to ameliorate those effects—can be labelled as the *functional perspective*. Recognizing the flaws in the traditional concepts of risk, this emerging orientation emphasizes the multivariate, transactional nature of development. Thoman (1982, pp. 166–169), for example, advocates assessment of risk status based on (1) multivariate indices—to include biological and social factors that might be related to developmental processes; (2) repeated measures—to increase reliability and to assay ongoing coping or adaptation; and (3) measures of performance—to tap variations in functioning within risk status. The potential power of the functional perspective is its explicit recognition of development as a dynamic, multiply determined process.

Organic Factors and Stress

Most risk research on mild mental retardation has not paid sufficient attention to the interrelationships among biological predispositions and environmental stresses, even though we know these insults to be more common among the poor (see Ramey & Finkelstein, 1981, for a discussion of this issue).

Conditions that affect the biological integrity of the organism will increase the risk for developmental retardation for several reasons. If the insult is severe enough to affect morphology, the organism's ability to conduct transactions with the environment may be reduced, with concomitant impairment in the cognitive, social, and motivational spheres. Another product of organic insults might be direct impairment of cognitive processing; risk factors such as anoxia, fetal malnutrition, and obstetrical medications are presumed to operate in this manner. At a subtler level of influence, risk conditions may deflect the expected course of development by interfering with the child's self-righting tendencies (Sameroff, 1979) or the ability to adapt to changes in the environment. These selected examples reinforce the argument that changes in the individual's functional status or developmental plasticity need to be assessed.

A cluster of mechanisms related to stress also are germane to the association between poverty and developmental retardation. *Stress* is a definitional quagmire and so requires comment first. We follow Pearlin and Schooler (1978) and Rutter (1981) in defining *stress* as an unpleasant mental and emotional state resulting from strain. *Strain,* as defined by Rutter (1981), is a force requiring adaptation, while Pearlin and Schooler (1978) define it in terms of "enduring problems that have the potential for arousing threat" (p.3) or frustrations, usually in major social roles. Viewing risk in terms of stress moves the focus from relatively stable biological limitations to a consideration of how the organism *responds to changes* or to chronic problems in the environment.

One explanation for the relationship between strain and stress is that organisms are reluctant to make fundamental changes. Pearlin, Lieberman, Menaghan, and Mullan (1981) postulate that change causes disequilibrium and a struggle to reestablish homeostasis; if continued long enough, this struggle results in stress. As Pearlin et al. (1981) and Rutter (1981) note, though, this process depends on the magnitude (or duration) of change and the amount of control over it. Small amounts of change and disequilibrium may, in fact, be beneficial if the challenges are mastered and effectance motivation is thereby increased.

Changes or problems that the organism cannot control may result not only in stress, but also in a lack of instrumentality, which lowers the individual's sense of mastery and self-concept, a by-product that exacerbates the inability to respond to strains in the future. The incapacity to cope with strains—and its consequences for self-esteem and subsequent effort—is most apparent in situations where there is little control over events, such as in transactions with impersonal institutions. It is worth noting, for example, that severely disadvantaged mothers in our research report both an extreme external locus of control shortly after their child's birth (Ramey & Campbell, 1976) and low self-esteem, which in turn are related to quality of the home and ultimately to their children's intellectual development (Ramey & Newman, 1979).

Thus, one aspect of poverty as a risk factor may be that disadvantaged children may not experience sufficient numbers of events that would lead to a sense of mastery (Ramey, MacPhee, & Yeates, 1982); as adults, the problems and institutions they confront often resist solutions based on individual initiative. *Risk*, in sum, is defined here as disequilibrium resulting from environmental changes and the inability to control those changes. Intervention efforts, from this view, would focus on the individual's ability to cope with or to change the conditions that create strain.

A second mechanism related to stress focuses on the behavioral repertoire of the organism rather than on the environment. Pearlin et al. (1981) postulated that strains may cause stress if the organism has learned inappropriate or nonoptimal modes of functioning, such that behavior cannot be appropriately modified to meet changing circumstances. In this vein, we have argued elsewhere (Ramey, MacPhee, & Yeates, 1982) that children from the lower socioeconomic strata may learn behaviors that are not valued or that are specifically disapproved by the dominant culture. Thus, poverty may be a risk factor to the extent that it affects the strategies individuals use in confronting personal crises and/or in their transactions with middle-class institutions. Intervention efforts for socially disadvantaged children based on this mechanism, therefore, might best be primarily oriented toward adaptational skills, or teaching the individual how to change to meet the changing demands of the environment, rather than on teaching specific content or specific skills.

Coping and Adaptation

In the past, not much research has been focused on factors that can compensate for the detrimental effects of risk variables such as poverty. Lately, however, we have come to recognize that individuals' strengths must be taken into account. As Albee's (1982) equation suggests, these strengths can be attributes of the organism (coping skills and self-esteem) or the environment (social and material resources). These factors also make the organism more or less vulnerable to the effects of a given risk condition.

Coping has been defined by Lazarus and Launier (1978) as "efforts, both action-oriented and intrapsychic, to manage environmental and internal demands . . . which tax or exceed a person's resources" (p. 311). Pearlin and Schooler (1978) go on to specify that coping mechanisms can take the form of modifying the stressful situation, redefining the meaning of the problem (e.g., attaching less importance to it), or management of stress symptoms. Rutter's (1981) review and data from Pearlin and Schooler (1978) show that a variety of personal qualities are associated with effective coping, including sex, age, temperament, intelligence, and above all, mastery and self-esteem.

Pearlin and Schooler have suggested that instrumentality is a key concept: Successful coping depends on (1) recognizing a situation as the source of the problem, (2) knowing which strategies or resources to call on to modify the situation, and (3) having the confidence (or internal locus of control) to maintain a sense of self-worth while attempting to gain control. Coping mechanisms seem to have the largest effect in areas where control is possible (e.g., marriage and parenting), while they are relatively ineffective in dealing with impersonal or institutional problems such as racism. To reiterate, successful coping depends on situation-specific mechanisms, on flexible capabilities, and on the important relationship between the individual's sense of competence and how amenable the situation is to change.

Coping usually is defined in terms of psychological resources, but individuals also can obviously rely on material and, especially, social resources, which are frequently in short supply in poverty situations. Cobb (1976) argues that support is not the extent or frequency of contact with social networks; rather, it is *information* that the person is cared for (intimacy), is valued (esteem support), and belongs to a network (mutual obligation). Research on stress clearly demonstrates the critical role of social supports in mediating the effects of problematic events or risk factors. Finally, studies by Turner (1981) and by Bee et al. (1982) found that social supports were especially critical for lower-SES (socioeconomic status) individuals who were under stress. These data suggest, then, that the risk for later developmental retardation in children of disadvantaged families depends on the social support system of the family. Analyses by Ramey, Yeates, and MacPhee (1982) buttress this point by demonstrating that children of poor, teenage, unwed, and low-IQ mothers have children at greatest risk for developmental retardation, but that children from similar backgrounds who were provided with developmental supports via educational day care developed normal intelligence.

In sum, an even broader perspective on risk is required than the one offered in the previous section. In accordance with Albee's (1982) equation, risk status must be evaluated at the individual level of vulnerability. In particular, the risk for dysfunctional development depends on an evaluation of the organism's relative deficits (organic, stress) and strengths (coping mechanisms, resources). We argue, therefore, that the time has come to redefine risk as a property of the system within which the human organism develops.

A General Systems Model of Risk

Although practical limitations have hampered the development of preventive programs for developmental retardation, our limited models for general developmental processes have been an even greater hindrance. During the 1960s and early 1970s when early educational intervention was seen as a vehicle for reducing poverty, the prevalent attitude was that children of poverty lived in an inadequate environment and that the early environment was the critical factor in later intellectual growth. These assumptions about the nature of development translated into prevention strategies that emphasized direct instruction in cognitive skills, with the aim of "innoculating" the child against further privation. Ramey and Haskins (1981) have noted that a medical model such as this assumes a permanent and unitary relationship between environmental deprivation (the "pathogen") and school failure (the "disease"). Further, it was assumed that one "innoculation" would last forever.

As a number of reports have since shown (e.g., Zigler & Valentine, 1979), the intentions of earlier social policies were laudable but rested on tenuous assumptions about the processes of development. For example, hereditarian proponents (e.g., Jensen, 1969, 1981) have attributed differences between developmentally retarded, socially disadvantaged children, and middle-class children to the global wellspring of genetics without postulating either specific genetic mechanisms or adequately acknowledging genotype–environment interactions. Environmentalists have been equally vague in identifying causal models, frequently emphasizing only one developmental domain, such as language (e.g., McClearn & DeFries, 1973), mother–child interactions (e.g., Hess & Shipman, 1965), or anomie (e.g., Ogbu, 1978) as the major agent.

The skepticism about simple models of development culminated in several seminal review papers, including those by Clarke and Clarke (1976) and Sameroff (1975). Both monographs argued that (1) development involves the action of complex regulatory processes (environmental *and* constitutional); and (2) later outcomes have multiple causes such that there are few isomorphic continuities in development. Additional challenges to traditional assumptions also forced researchers to consider more-complex models of development. Some of the trends that have crept into current theorizing include bidirectionality of infant–caregiver effects (Bell, 1968), Bronfenbrenner's (1977) ecology of human development, and the idea of plasticity throughout the lifespan, as opposed to the notion of a critical period in early childhood (Clarke & Clarke, 1976).

In brief, researchers have come to appreciate more fully the complex nature of development.

The crowning blow to the main effects and interactional models of development popular through the 1950s and 1960s was Sameroff's (1975) transactional model. In this model, Sameroff argued that the child modifies the environment at the same time that the environment is acting on the child. Constitutional factors are partially responsible for individual differences in behavior (e.g., temperamental variables such as reactivity or sociability) and for the ability to compensate following insult (see Parmelee & Michaelis, 1971, and Sameroff, 1979, for a discussion of self-righting tendencies). Environmental variables affect, among other things, the biological integrity of the organism, morphological characteristics, and what is learned. When the two—the continuum of reproductive casualty and the continuum of caretaking casualty—are interwoven in development, intellectual deficits may be amplified or reduced.

In some respects, the transactional model is incomplete because the intervening variables are left unspecified. For instance, the continuum of caretaking casualty, translated into psychological variables, would go beyond SES and parental education to include patterns of dyadic interaction, modes of communication, and teaching strategies. In this way, the notion of a supportive environment (see Yarrow, Rubenstein, & Pedersen, 1973) is defined in terms of specific behaviors that can be examined for their contribution to later competencies or deficits. Ultimately, the task is to construct a model of development that (1) specifies the variables and processes constituting a supportive environment and (2) defines the desired product of our endeavors, be it adaptation to the environment (Parmelee, Kopp, & Sigman, 1976), social competence (Zigler & Trickett, 1978), or intellectual development (Ramey, Farran, & Campbell, 1979).

A variation on general systems theory (Bertalanffy, 1975; Miller, 1978) has proven to be quite useful in guiding our work on risk and the prevention of developmental retardation at the Frank Porter Graham Center. This model was developed by Ramey, MacPhee, and Yeates (1982) and is presented schematically in Figure 1. Several aspects of this model have a direct bearing on the design of prevention programs.

1. In systems theory, an outcome is the product of a multitude of forces that interact. Such interdependence of causal mechanisms— *the emergence principle*—means that prevention efforts focused on only one variable or level may have unanticipated effects in other areas.

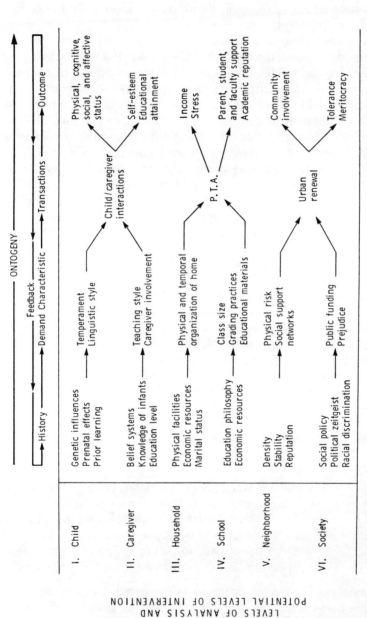

Figure 1. A general systems model illustrating developmental paths at different levels of analysis. The flow chart illustrates important variables and processes but is not exhaustive.

2. Living systems have different levels of complexity and functioning. Further, complex interactions can occur *within* each level as well as *across* levels such that, for example, societal processes such as racism can influence functioning at the level of the family.
3. Each variable within a system has a range of stability (Miller, 1978)—that is, it is maintained in equilibrium by transactions with the environment and by other variables within the system. Any variable that forces the system beyond its range of stability is called a *stressor*, producing strain in the system.
4. In the human, cybernetic processes operate to regulate behavior. In terms of development, this means that there is constant feedback and regulation such that the child continuously adapts to the environment. However, in cases where self-regulatory mechanisms are unable to cope with strain in the system, disorder or maladaptive behavior may result, as in developmental retardation, unless outside resources are used.
5. The child is seen as an active (rather than reactive) agent, eliciting responses from the environment at the same time he or she is adapting to its demands.

Several other terms in the general systems model (Figure 1) need further explication. By the *history* of the component, we mean the effects of previous transactions that are not manifested as observable behavior. This may be thought of as the probability of an action given the history of the individual (an actuarial concept). History at the different levels can be thought of in terms of genotypes, teratogenic effects, and prior learning (the child); general knowledge of child development, and attitudes and beliefs that have been inculcated by society and upbringing (the caregiver); the social status of the family; the reputation of a neighborhood or school; and the social policies and values advocated by a society. Historical variables are assumed to influence behavior but they cannot be observed directly. Thus, a central issue in studying behavioral development is to determine, for example, how history (e.g., a family's SES) is related to parental action (e.g., teaching strategies; language), and how these components affect and are affected by other components. In the domain of developmental retardation, the major problem has been to translate a global etiological factor such as poverty into characteristics of the environment that actually influence the child's mental development.

Transactions, as used in the general systems model, imply an interactional process among components that is, at least, bidirectional. A good example is behavioral interactions between infant and caregiver. The

behavior of each participant can be attributed to distal determinants—
for example, general expectancies about the partner's behavior based on
previous encounters and knowledge—and proximal influences such as
the infant's temperament, predominant state, and physical attrac-
tiveness; or the caregiver's demand characteristics such as general
warmth and current mood. At another level of analysis, transactions
between the neighborhood and society, through the mechanism of reve-
nue sharing, might result in urban renewal or benign neglect depending
on the political force of the neighborhood and current funding policies.
It is important to note that transactions can occur between *any* two or
more levels as well as among components within levels. Thus, a myriad
of relationships between components are possible, leaving the attribu-
tion of cause in rather murky waters.

Finally, the endpoint of this stream of reciprocal cause and effect
includes a number of *outcome* variables that also must be measured in an
ecologically valid manner at the appropriate level of analysis. In the case
of developmental retardation (an individual and societal construct), we
would want to know about the intellectual and social competence of the
child in a number of settings and about the ability of the child to adapt to
the environments of home, school, neighborhood, and society. These
global, ill-defined terms must be translated into valid assessment instruments in order to do justice to the complexity of development. In retrospect, it is apparent that developmental retardation can be caused by a
large number of factors, both within the organism (e.g., temperamental
variables; limited self-righting strategies), within the dyad, and at the
level of societal norms, as well as others. When these intra-, inter-, and
supracomponent processes are combined, the inadequacy of simplistic
models becomes all too evident.

Our conceptual model for developmental retardation contains two
other major process components not diagrammed in Figure 1 that illustrate the interplay of ontogenetic history and transactions with the environment. These components concern the functioning of subgroups
within the society (*sociocultural difference component*) and the child's contingency history (*reinforcement-motivational component*). In the past, each
has been perceived as a competing explanation for developmental retardation. Our general systems model, however, views them as comple-
mentary processes that act at somewhat different levels of analysis.

Sociocultural Difference Component

As noted before, a growing body of epidemiological literature suggests that individuals from the lower socioeconomic strata are most at
risk for retarded intellectual and adaptive behavior (Ramey & Finkel-

stein, 1981). Poor individuals with minority-group status are particularly likely to develop educational handicaps during the public school years (Mercer, 1977; Ramey, Stedman, Borders-Patterson, & Mengel, 1978; Richardson, 1975). We now think that the sociocultural difference component operates through three primary mechanisms.

First, disadvantaged sociocultural subgroups may learn complex modes of intellectual and social adaptation but learn ones *not valued* by the larger culture. Linguistic style is a good example. Baratz and Baratz (1970) argued for instance that lower-class black dialect was equally complex as standard English, and that while it was different from standard English it was not inherently deficient. Second, sociocultural subgroups may learn modes of functioning specifically disapproved by the larger society. For instance, aggressive or assertive interactions—particularly in the school system—may be construed as disrespectful and difficult behaviors even when there is no apparent damage.

Third, the larger society may form stereotypes of sociocultural subgroups and actively or unwittingly, but systematically, discriminate with respect to intellectual and adaptive opportunities to the point of creating a self-fulfilling prophecy. A study by Haskins, Walden, and Ramey (1983) concerning ability grouping in kindergarten and first grade illustrates this point. In assigning children to high- or low-ability groups within their classrooms, teachers reported using their own informal observations of the child's ability and teacher-made tests. None of the other factors assessed, including standardized tests, teacher recommendations, the child's interest in school work, or information about the child's home or background, were reported as influential in teachers' placement of children in ability groups. To the extent that personal bias may operate in assigning to low-ability groups, the structure and functioning of those groups seems likely to nurture their disadvantage through reduced exposure to new material and a social stigma that fosters a lower self-concept. This point led us into the second major process component of our model, which is important throughout the developmental period, but especially during infancy.

Reinforcement-Motivational Component

It is our contention that high-risk children are frequently reared in an environment with inadequate or inappropriate behavioral contingencies. In turn, this has been implicated as a cause of lowered effectance motivation and reduced success in mastery situations. Further, it is likely that the deficient contingency history is begun during infancy and can be observed during the second year of life, as assessed by declining intelligence scores in poverty-level children (Ramey, Farran, & Campbell, 1979; Ramey & Haskins, 1981). Support for this thesis accrues from two converging lines of our research.

First, Finkelstein and Ramey (1977) and Ramey and Finkelstein (1978) have reported a series of 4 experiments suggesting that increased amounts of response-contingent stimulation during the first year of infancy enhances subsequent learning performance when treated infants are compared to controls. Their findings are consistent with earlier reports by Watson and Ramey (1972), and with Lewis and Goldberg's (1969) idea of a generalized expectancy for effectiveness that derives from the responsiveness of the mother to her infant's behavior.

A second empirical theme has focused on social responsiveness to infants' operant behaviors (such as smiling and vocalizing) as a major determinant of the infant's subsequent cognitive and social development. Two major types of information are relevant to caregiver–infant interactions and developmental retardation. The first type of evidence concerns the interactional differences between low-risk dyads (typically middle class) and high-risk dyads (e.g., from poverty environments). Farran and Ramey (1980), Lewis and Wilson (1972), Tulkin and Kagan (1972), and others have reported social class differences in mother–child interaction during infancy (see a review by Ramey, Farran, Campbell, & Finkelstein, 1978). However, it has always been unclear from comparative social-class research whether the observed behavioral differences were causally related to cognitive growth or whether they were merely correlates of more-basic social-class differences. Therefore, a different line of research is becoming increasingly influential in implicating caregiver–child interactions as causally important. This second type of evidence concerns variations in parenting style within lower-class dyads. Bee and associates (1982), Clarke-Stewart, VanderStoep, and Killian (1979), and Ramey, Farran, and Campbell (1979) have reported positive correlations of substantial magnitude between stimulating, interactive, and responsive behaviors and children's cognitive development during the first 3 years of life within disadvantaged samples. Further, Bee et al. (1982) found that in general, the same factors predicted child intellectual outcome in high- and low-SES families. Thus, the dimension of social responsivity, from a reinforcement–motivational perspective, is a plausible explanation for differences in children's intellectual development.

Illustrations of Poverty-as-Risk

Much of our presentation to this point has been in abstract terms. In order to make the transition from theory to application, we review some of the variables that are associated with a poorer prognosis for later intellectual performance in both disadvantaged and middle-class families. The necessity for a functional perspective becomes apparent—a perspective that abandons static, global constructs such as social class to ask what experiences or dimensions of the environment influence development.

Within- and across-class research has illuminated some key variables associated with children's success in school and social relationships. These fall into three broad categories. The most pervasive influence on mental development, within both lower- and middle-class samples, appears to be encouragement of development. This construct often subsumes the parents' achievement motivation (McCall, Appelbaum, & Hogarty, 1973), engaging in intellectual activities, and providing a variety of stimulation for the child (see Gottfried & Gottfried, 1984). The implication for intervention programs is clear: Teach parents to be teachers and, to an extent that is possible and ethical, inculcate the valuation of intellectual achievement.

Another general category of proximal influences on cognitive development is the quality of social interactions and relationships. Three processes are important. First, Wachs (1984) has found that verbal interactions between siblings and contingent verbal responsiveness by adults are associated with positive development, across ages and social classes. He argues that intervention programs could foster development by emphasizing to the parent the necessity for verbal responsiveness, regardless of its content, and by working with the target child's older siblings. Second, maternal involvement also has been a key variable that reappears throughout the early-experience literature, perhaps because of its relationship to verbal interaction. Gottfried and Gottfried (1984) discovered that the family climate predicts cognitive development. Family cohesion—help, commitment, and support—was especially important. This cluster of variables related to the child's social system provides a sturdy podium for advocating family-centered intervention that includes siblings and the cohesiveness of the other members.

The third cluster of variables is related to the organization of the physical environment. Stimulation that increases distractability—a high amount of noise, a low rooms:people ratio, and a barrage of unstructured experience (e.g., TV)—has a detrimental effect on the child (see Gottfried, 1984). Similarly, an environment that severely restricts visual and physical exploration is associated with depressed cognitive development, across and within social class. One form of intervention, based on the notion of mediated experience, could help solve the first problem. Feuerstein (1979) argues that adults fulfill a critical role in the child's development when they regulate and interpret experiences for the child. Instructing parents in the value of a stimulus shelter, or a place in the house to call their own, or monitoring television viewing may be a step toward increasing the child's attentiveness and ability to derive the most benefit from what stimulation is experienced.

All of these recommendations are subject to a major caveat. Wachs (1979) argues that although some experiences have a global effect on development, most are both age and organism specific. That is, stimulation designed to enhance development must be matched to the developmental level of the child as well as to individual characteristics (e.g., sex, type of preexisting deficit, or temperament). This conclusion is based on new, yet persuasive, evidence that some experiences (e.g., disciplinary practices) are beneficial at some ages (after 24 months) and for some infants, but may be benign or even harmful at other stages of development. Intervention programs, then, will need to employ a combination of broad-band (e.g., verbal responsiveness, variety of stimulation) and narrow-band (e.g., age-specific) experiences for the at-risk child.

Conclusions

Two implications of the general systems model speak to the design of intervention programs. The first is a corollary of the level-of-analysis principle: In order to prevent later pathology, we must identify components of the system where intervention *can* occur before retardation is evident. For instance, proposed remedies for breaking the cycle of poverty have included educational programs delivered to children and/or parents (the level of the child and/or family), guaranteed annual income experiments (the level of the family), urban renewal and job programs (the family and neighborhood), and civil rights laws that foster the establishment of a true meritocracy (the family and society).

The crucial question, though—and the second implication of the model—is where intervention *should* be focused. Ideally, one would want a prevention strategy that produced powerful, permanent effects with a minimum of money and effort. Invoking a cost-effectiveness criterion, we may find that some loci in the system produce greater effects than others. Furthermore, we can infer from the emergent principle that intervention at several points may produce synergistic effects (i.e., more dramatic changes than prevention aimed at isolated components). For example, Bronfenbrenner (1975) reviewed the effects of early intervention programs and concluded, among other things, that (1) center-based programs with cognitive curricula produced greater gains than play-oriented programs; (2) parent intervention yielded benefits that extended to younger siblings, and to the attitudes and feelings of the parents; and (3) families who are under the most economic and psychological stress are the ones least likely to become involved in an intervention program.

What this suggests is that a combination of approaches may be the most effective. These might include quality day care, family education, and social services that move the family into a broader social-support network. The goal of preventing developmental retardation should be to ensure a supportive environment for the child, and a rearing atmosphere where caregivers attend to the needs of the child with a maximum of flexibility and resources. This sensitivity of the caregiver to the child is constrained by time, economics, education, and societal norms, so that prevention components geared to supporting the family may indirectly benefit the child, although no experimental evidence has been generated, to our knowledge, concerning this pathway of influence for severely disadvantaged children. Therefore, a major task for the future is to identify those components of a supportive environment that are most amenable to effective intervention.

At the core of systems theory is the idea of interactive influences—that is, all properties of complex systems have multiple causes rather than single causes. Thus, various interventions may initiate a series of *ripple effects* or unintended consequences, either positive or negative. As the Lazar consortium (1978) was to discover, early educational interventions have a number of ripple effects, including parent satisfaction and involvement, health-related benefits, a lower dropout rate in high school, and fewer cases of delinquency. On the other hand, intervention may have undesirable side effects. For example, the parents may abdicate responsibility for the child; aggressiveness in social interactions with peers may increase (Finkelstein, 1982; Schwartz, Strickland, & Krolick, 1974), and the parent's philosophy or style of childrearing may clash with that of the intervention program. In brief, the general systems model cautions us to be aware of the potential side effects of preventive interventions.

Another implication of the general systems model is that modifiability and learning tend to strike a balance over time (see Bateson, 1979). While children and adults may be justly viewed as dynamic individuals constantly adapting to changes in the environment, learning and hierarchical organization of behavior patterns are also taking place. This interplay of plasticity and learning has crucial significance for the timing of intervention and for the reversibility of its effects. Clarke & Clarke (1976), in discussing this issue, liken development to a wedge where there is "a greater potential responsiveness during early life . . . tailing off to little responsiveness in adulthood" (pp. 271–272). From a systems perspective, then, early intervention (during the period of greatest sensitivity) must be coupled with continuous enrollment or booster treatments to ensure both continuity and the learning of adaptive behavior patterns not demanded at earlier periods (for a more complete discussion of this issue, see Ramey & Baker-Ward, 1982). Early and prolonged enrichment is even more critical in those cases where the individual's self-righting tendencies (i.e., intrinsic plasticity) or ability to learn is impaired.

One final implication of the model concerns general strategies for conducting an intervention program. Recall that equal emphasis is placed on the contribution of the child to its own development and on the characteristics of the environment. As a consequence, the most effective prevention will capitalize on the unique capabilities of any given individual (the supportive-environment theme) while emphasizing transactions that are most effective in fostering later competence. Therefore, curriculum development (what is most effective for children in general) and research on learning styles (what is most suited to a particular individual) go hand in hand to exploit individual strengths and overcome weaknesses. While this implication may seem so obvious as to be a timeworn adage, its full realization depends on a comprehensive knowledge of child development, a flexible and individually tailored curriculum, an intimate acquaintance with each child's abilities, and an active program of research directed at discovering what works for given categories of child characteristics. With such a tack, we may be able to make progress in our efforts to prevent the insidious effects of development gone awry.

References

Albee, G. W. (1982). Preventing psychopathology and promoting human potential. *American Psychologist, 37,* 1043–1050.

Baratz, S. S., & Baratz, J. C. (1970). Early childhood intervention: The social science base of institutional racism. *Harvard Educational Review, 40,* 29–50.

Bateson, P. (1979). How do sensitive periods arise and what are they for? *Animal Behaviour, 27,* 470–486.

Bee, H. L., Barnard, K. E., Eyres, S. J., Gray, C. A., Hammond, M. A., Spietz, C. S., & Cook, B. (1982). Prediction of IQ and language skill from perinatal status, child performance, family characteristics, and mother–infant interaction. *Child Development, 53,* 1134–1156.

Begab, M. (Ed.). (1981). *Psychosocial influences and retarded performance: Vol. 2. Strategies for improving social competence.* Baltimore: University Park Press.

Bell, R. Q. (1968). A reinterpretation of the direction of effects in studies of socialization. *Psychological Review, 75,* 81–95.

Bertalanffy, L. V. (1975). *Perspectives on general system theory.* New York: George Braziller.

Bronfenbrenner, U. (1975). Is early intervention effective? In M. Guttentag & E. L. Struening (Eds.), *Handbook of evaluation research* (Vol. 2). Beverly Hills, CA: Sage Publications.

Bronfenbrenner, U. (1977). Toward an experimental ecology of human development. *American Psychologist, 32,* 513–531.

Clarke, A. M., & Clarke, A. D. B. (1976). *Early experience: Myth and evidence.* London: Open Books.

Clarke-Stewart, A. K., VanderStoep, L. P., & Killian, G. A. (1979). Analysis and replication of mother–child relations at two years of age. *Child Development, 50,* 777–793.

Cobb, S. (1976). Social support as a moderator of life stress. *Psychosomatic Medicine, 38,* 300–314.

Farran, D. C., & Ramey, C. T. (1980). Social class differences in dyadic involvement during infancy. *Child Development, 51,* 254–257.

Feuerstein, R. (1979). *The dynamic assessment of retarded performers.* Baltimore: University Park Press.

Finkelstein, N. W. (1982). Aggression: Is it stimulated by daycare? *Young Children,* September, 3–9.

Finkelstein, N. W., & Ramey, C. T. (1977). Learning to control the environment in infancy. *Child Development, 48,* 806–819.

Gottfried, A. W. (Ed.). (1984). *Home environment and early cognitive development.* New York: Academic Press.

Gottfried, A. W., & Gottfried, A. E. (1984). Home environment and cognitive development in young children in middle-class families. In A. W. Gottfried (Ed.), *Home environment and early cognitive development.* New York: Academic Press.

Grossman, H. J. (Ed.) (1973). *Manual on terminology and classification in mental retardation* (1973 Revision). American Association on Mental Deficiency. Special Publication Series, No. 2.

Haskins, R., Walden, T., & Ramey, C. T. (1983). The effects of ability grouping on teacher and student behavior. *Journal of Educational Psychology, 75,* 865–876.

Heber, R. (1959). A manual on terminology and classification in mental retardation. *American Journal of Mental Deficiency, 64* (Monograph supplement).

Hess, R. D., & Shipman, V. C. (1965). Early experience and the socialization of cognitive modes in children. *Child Development, 34,* 869–886.

Jensen, A. R. (1969). How much can we boost IQ and scholastic achievement? *Harvard Educational Review, 39,* 1–123.

Jensen, A. R. (1981). Raising the IQ: The Ramey and Haskins study. *Intelligence, 5,* 29–40.

Lazar, I., & Darlington, R. (Eds.). (1978). *Lasting effects after preschool.* Final report. HEW Grant 90C-1311 to the Education Commission of the States.

Lazarus, R. S., & Launier, R. (1978). Stress-related transactions between person and environment. In L. A. Pervin & M. Lewis (Eds.), *Perspectives in international psychology.* New York: Plenum.

Lewis, M., & Goldberg, S. (1969). Perceptual-cognitive development in infancy: A generalized expectancy model as a function of mother–infant interaction. *Merrill-Palmer Quarterly, 15,* 81–100.

Lewis, M., & Wilson, C. D. (1972). Infant development in lower-class American families. *Human Development, 15,* 112–127.

McCall, R. B., Appelbaum, M. I., & Hogarty, P. S. (1973). Developmental changes in mental performance. *Monographs of the Society for Research in Child Development, 38*(3, Serial No. 150).

McClearn, G., & DeFries, J. (1973). *Introduction to behavioral genetics.* San Francisco: W. H. Freeman.

Mercer, J. R. (1977). Cultural diversity, mental retardation and assessment: The case for nonlabeling. In P. Mittler (Ed.), *Research to practice in mental retardation: Vol. 1. Care and intervention* Baltimore: University Park Press.

Miller, J. G. (1978). *Living systems.* New York: McGraw-Hill.

Ogbu, J. V. (1978). *Minority education and caste: The American system in cross-cultural perspective.* New York: Academic Press.

Parmelee, A. H., Kopp, C. B., & Sigman, M. (1976). Selection of developmental assessment techniques for infants at risk. *Merrill-Palmer Quarterly, 22,* 177–199.

Parmelee, A. H., & Michaelis, R. (1971). Neurological examination of the newborn. In J. Hellmuth (Ed.), *Exceptional infant: Vol. 2. Studies in abnormalities* New York: Brunner / Mazel.

Pearlin, L. I., Lieberman, M. A., Menaghan, E. G., & Mullan, J. T. (1981). The stress process. *Journal of Health and Social Behavior, 22,* 337–356.

Pearlin, L. I., & Schooler, C. (1978). The structure of coping. *Journal of Health and Social Behavior, 19,* 2–21.

Ramey, C. T., & Baker-Ward, L. (1982). Psychosocial retardation and the early experience paradigm. In D. Bricker (Ed.), *Handicapped and at-risk infants* (pp. 269–289). Baltimore: University Park Press.

Ramey, C. T., & Campbell, F. A. (1976). Parental attitudes and poverty. *Journal of Genetic Psychology, 128,* 3–6.

Ramey, C. T., Farran, D. C., & Campbell, F. A. (1979). Predicting IQ from mother–infant interactions. *Child Development, 50,* 804–814.

Ramey, C. T., Farran, D. C., Campbell, F. A., & Finkelstein, N. W. (1978). Observations of mother–infant interactions: Implications for development. In F. D. Minifie & L. L. Lloyd (Eds.), *Community and cognitive abilities: Early behavioral assessment.* Baltimore: University Park Press.

Ramey, C. T., & Finkelstein, N. W. (1978). Contingent stimulation and infant competence. *Journal of Pediatric Psychology, 3,* 89–96.

Ramey, C. T., & Finkelstein, N. W. (1981). Psychosocial mental retardation: A biological and social coalescence. In M. Begab (Ed.), *Psychosocial influences and retarded performance: Vol. 1. Strategies for improving competence.* Baltimore: University Park Press.

Ramey, C. T., & Haskins, R. (1981). The causes and treatment of school failure: Insights from the Carolina Abecedarian Project. In M. Begab, H. C. Haywood, & H. Garber (Eds.), *Psychosocial influences and retarded performances: Vol. 2. Strategies for improving competence.* Baltimore: University Park Press.

Ramey, C. T., MacPhee, D., & Yeates, K. O. (1982). *Preventing developmental retardation: A general systems model.* In L. A. Bond, & J. M. Joffe (Eds.), *Facilitating infant and early childhood development.* Hanover, NH: University Press of New England.

Ramey, C. T., & Newman, L. S. (1979). *Maternal attitudes and child development in high risk families.* Unpublished manuscript, University of North Carolina, Chapel Hill, NC.

Ramey, C. T., Stedman, D. S., Borders-Patterson, A., & Mengel, W. (1978). Predicting school failure from information available at birth. *American Journal of Mental Deficiency, 82,* 524–534.

Ramey, C. T., Yeates, K. O., & MacPhee, D. (1982, August). *Risk variation in disadvantaged families: A systems approach to conceptualizing and preventing developmental retardation.* Invited symposium paper presented at the International Association for the Scientific Study of Mental Deficiency, Toronto, Canada.

Richardson, S. A. (1975). Reaction to mental subnormality. In M. J. Begab & S. A. Richardson (Eds.), *The mentally retarded and society: A social science perspective.* Baltimore: University Park Press.

Richardson, S. A. (1981). Family characteristics associated with mild mental retardation. In M. J. Begab, H. L. Haywood, & H. L. Garber (Eds.), *Psychosocial influences in retarded performance: Vol. 2. Strategies for improving competence*. Baltimore: University Park Press.

Rutter, M. (1981). Stress, coping, and development: Some issues and questions. *Journal of Child Psychology and Psychiatry, 22*, 256–323.

Sameroff, A. J. (1975). Early influences on development: Fact or fancy? *Merrill-Palmer Quarterly, 21*, 267–294.

Sameroff, A. J. (1979). The etiology of cognitive competence: A systems perspective. In R. B. Kearsley & I. E. Siegel (Eds.), *Infants at risk: Assessment of cognitive functioning*. Hillsdale, NJ: Erlbaum.

Schwartz, J. C., Strickland, R. G., & Krolick, G. (1974). Infant day care: Behavioral effects at preschool age. *Development Psychology, 10*, 502–506.

Thoman, E. B. (1982). A biological perspective and a behavioral model for assessment of premature infants. In L. A. Bond & J. M. Joffe (Eds.), *Facilitating infant and early childhood development*. Hanover, NH: University Press of New England.

Tulkin, S., & Kagan, J. (1972). Mother–child interaction in the first year of life. *Child Development, 43*, 31.

Turner, J. R. (1981). Social support as a contingency in psychological well-being. *Journal of Health and Social Behavior, 22*, 357–367.

Wachs, T. D. (1979). Proximal experience and early cognitive–intellectual development: The physical environment. *Merrill-Palmer Quarterly, 25*, 3–41.

Wachs, T. D. (1984). Proximal experience and early cognitive–intellectual development: The social environment. In A. W. Gottfried, (Ed.), *Home environment and early cognitive development*. New York: Academic Press.

Watson, J. S., & Ramey, C. T. (1972). Reactions to response contingent stimulation early in infancy. *Merrill-Palmer Quarterly, 18*, 219–227.

Yarrow, L., Rubenstein, I., & Pedersen, F. (1973). *Infant and environment: Early cognitive and motivational development*. New York: Halsted.

Zigler, E., & Trickett, P. K. (1978). IQ, social competence, and evaluation of early childhood intervention programs. *American Psychologist, 33*, 789–798.

Zigler, E., & Valentine, J. (Eds.). (1979). *Project Head Start: A legacy of the War on Poverty*. New York: Free Press.

4

Castelike Stratification as a Risk Factor for Mental Retardation in the United States

JOHN U. OGBU

The Problem

The concept of being at risk in intellectual development implies that some children under some conditions may not develop normal intelligence. That is, they may not develop the mental capacity to absorb complex information or to grasp and manipulate abstract concepts that would, for example, enable them to do normal academic work at school (Travers, 1982; Wigdor & Garner, 1932b). Children who do not develop this mental capacity are said to be mentally retarded, and their retardation may range from mild to severe. The mildly retarded are labeled educable and classified in the public school system as educable mentally retarded or EMR. They are the children placed in special education classes.

In the past, children were classified as EMR mainly on the basis of their IQ test scores. The assumption was (and still is among many psychologists and educators) that IQ or ability tests measure some global, enduring quality of cognitive functioning—the broad capacity to learn, reason, and grasp abstract concepts (Travers, 1982). Moreover, IQ test scores have been shown to correlate well with other measures of intellectual functioning, like school grades. Following the passage of PL 94-142 by Congress, schools are now required to include other criteria, such as judgment based on interviews with children and their parents, children's developmental histories, their medical histories, and so on, before a decision is made to classify them as EMR. However, it is reported that although many states require their schools to use other assessments, IQ "continues to play a predominant role in the classification of EMR children" (Bickel, 1982, p. 197).

Children from lower socioeconomic status (SES) and from certain racial and ethnic minorities (e.g., blacks, Native Americans, Mexican Americans, native Hawaiians, Puerto Ricans) generally have lower IQ-test scores than white children and are overrepresented in the EMR category. This overrepresentation increases dramatically when emphasis is placed on IQ test scores as a criterion for classification (Bickel, 1982). Thus many lower-SES and minority children are potentially at risk in intellectual development.

This chapter focuses on the lower test scores of black Americans and their overrepresentation in the EMR classes. I choose to focus on blacks for two reasons. One is that the gap between blacks and whites is the largest and is roughly about one standard deviation (Linn, 1982). This difference persists whether the test is verbal or nonverbal. It also persists when blacks and whites come from similar socioeconomic background (Baughman, 1971; Jensen, 1969). The large gap has adverse consequences for blacks in situations where IQ test scores are used to select people for education or jobs. For example, Linn (1982) points out that "A cutoff score on an ability test that would select half (50%) of the whites from the general population would select only about 16 percent of the blacks. One that would select 20 percent of the whites would select only about 3 or 4 percent of the blacks" (p. 366). At the other end, a cutoff score would tend to select a disporportionate number of blacks. This can be seen in Table 1, where the information is based on the analysis by a panel of the National Academy of Sciences of a nationwide data collected by the U.S. Office of Civil Rights. The table shows that blacks are three times as likely to be classified as mildly mentally retarded compared to whites—that is, 3.46% versus 1.07% of the black and white populations, respectively (Wigdor and Garner, 1982b).

The lower IQ-test scores of blacks have elicited a number of explanations. Some explanations stress biological factors, the nature of family and home environment; others point to the quality of instructions at school or to the bias in the assessment process as the main cause. In general, most explanations stress the individual child's attributes. There has been a noticeable failure on the part of social scientists to place the problem of low IQ-test scores or mental retardation of the minorities in their proper broader sociocultural context. It is true that some social

Table 1

Nationwide Special Education Placements, by Sex and by Race or Ethnicity[a]

Classification	Race or ethnicity				Sex			
	Percentage		Log-odds (Male–female)	Q	Percentage		Log-odds (Male–female)	Q
	Minority	White			Male	Female		
Educable mentally retarded (EMR)	2.54	1.06	0.89	.42	1.65	1.19	0.37	.18
Trainable mentally retarded (TMR)	0.33	0.19	0.55	.27	0.25	0.20	0.26	.13
Seriously emotionally disturbed (SED)	0.42	0.29	0.37	.18	0.48	0.16	1.14	.52
Specific learning disabilities (SLD)	2.29	2.30	0.01	.01	3.22	1.33	0.92	.43
Speech impaired (SI)	1.82	2.02	−0.09	−.04	2.40	1.53	0.48	.24
None of the above	92.60	94.12	—	—	92.00	95.59	—	—

[a]From Finn, Jeremy D. (1982). Patterns in special education placement as revealed by the OCR surveys. In *Placing children in special education: A strategy for equity* (p. 324). Washington, DC: National Academy of Sciences Press.

scientists have suggested that the lower test scores might be due to "cultural differences" or "cultural bias" (Eells, Davis, Havighurst, Herrick, & Tyler, 1952; Hilliard, 1981; Jackson, 1975; Jensen, 1980). However, this explanation focuses primarily on differences in sociocultural features of the home, neighborhood, and the minority population itself, which are assumed to influence school and test behaviors of individual students. What is neglected is the pervasive and enduring collective influence of the forces of the wider society on minority status, which causes the test scores of minorities to be lower than those of the dominant group.

This chapter is concerned with those broader societal forces as a source of the lower IQ-test scores or mental-retardation labels among black Americans. We argue that these societal forces work in two ways to produce the lower test scores. On the one hand, they deny blacks the opportunity to participate in those activities that require and stimulate the development of white middle-class types of cognitive skills or IQ; and on the other hand, they cause blacks to respond in some ways that actually promote low test scores. The broader societal forces to be considered are principally the pattern of racial or castelike stratification and the technoeconomic and sociopolitical barriers it generates, particularly job ceiling and inferior education. In order to show how forces outside the immediate environment of the family and neighborhood affect the IQ of a population, I define IQ contextually and from a non-Western-centric perspective. Once I define IQ from that point of view, I suggest an alternative explanation of group differences in IQ test scores, especially the difference between dominant and subordinate groups. The case of black Americans is then presented to illustrate how the wider societal forces adversely influence the test scores of subordinate groups. The final section of the chapter raises some policy questions.

An Alternative View of IQ and Its Origins

I need to make two important distinctions to avoid a Western-centric definition of intelligence and to explain more satisfactorily why blacks and similar minorities score lower than whites in current IQ tests. One distinction suggested by Scribner and Cole (1973) is between intelligence as cognitive skills and intelligence as cognitive capacities and processes. The other distinction is among the genetic potential for intellectual or cognitive development, the cognitive repertoire and patterns of a population, and IQ as a sample of the latter for special purposes (Vernon, 1969).

Universal Cognitive Capacities versus Culture-Specific Cognitive Skills

Scribner and Cole (1973) argue that cognitive capacities and processes are universal attributes. That is, members of every known human population remember, form concepts, generalize, operate with abstractions, think symbolically, and reason logically. Inner-city black Americans, suburban white Americans, Ukranians of Russia, Ibos of Nigeria, and Maori of New Zealand share these intellectual attributes. If these capacities are genetically based, then all human populations share the underlying genes.

Cognitive skills, on the other hand, vary from culture to culture. They are the different ways in which members of a given population use the universal cognitive processes to solve specific problems in their ecological niche. For example, the problems that face one population may require and facilitate a high degree of verbal ability; those of another may encourage numerical and mathematical skills (see Ginsburg, 1982); in a third, spatial-perceptual skills may be more adaptive and prominent (Seagrim & Lendon, 1980). In some cultures, the situation may require and encourage a combination of some or all of these skills. Furthermore, how one remembers, generalizes, reasons logically, and so on may vary from culture to culture. The repertoire and pattern of cognitive skills are thus theoretically culture-specific.

In general, I want to stress two points. One is that populations tend to differ in repertoire and pattern of cognitive skills when they live in different *macro environments*—that is, when they have different economic, technological, or sociopolitical realities that pose different cognitive problems. The other point follows—namely, that populations do not differ in repertoire and pattern of cognitive skills or intelligence mainly because they follow different methods of raising children. They may, in fact, follow different childrearing practices because the childrearing method of each population is more appropriate for inculcating the adaptive cognitive and other competencies required by its adults for competence (Ogbu, 1979, 1981a).

Cognitive skills, not cognitive processes or capacities, are what IQ tests attempt to measure. But IQ as represented in IQ-test scores does not represent the overall intelligence or cognitive repertoire and pattern of any individual or any population, not even that of the white middle-class who invented the tests. The limited scope of IQ is made clear in the next distinction.

Genetic Potential, Adaptive Cognitive Skills, and Sampled Cognitive Skills (Intelligence A, B, and C)

Vernon (1969) has suggested distinguishing among (1) intelligence A, or genetic potential for cognitive development; (2) intelligence B, or cognitive skills for a population—that is, the observed and culturally recognized intelligent and nonintelligent behaviors; and (3) intelligence C, or intelligent behaviors sampled for specific purposes, such as predicting academic performance. For an individual child, *intelligence A* is the innate capacity inherited from his or her parents for cognitive development. It represents his or her potential for cognitive development. For members of a given population or culture it is also their genetic potential for cognitive development.

Intelligence B refers to cognitive behavior of all kinds in the manner that members of a given population regard as intelligent or nonintelligent. It is the product of the interaction between the genetic potential (intelligent A) and nurture (both micro and macroenvironmental forces). It corresponds to Cole and Scribner's cognitive skills, which vary cross-culturally, and to changes in response to environmental changes. Because intelligence B is not fixed, it may rise or fall with technoeconomic and sociopolitical changes. Vernon has suggested, for example, that the intelligence B of Western peoples has probably changed remarkably and increased as a result of industrialization, urbanization, bureaucratization, and education. The cognitive problems posed by these changes require solutions that emphasize absorbing complex information, manipulating abstract concepts, grasping relations, and symbolic thought. These skills were probably initially utilized in dealing with specific problems in the industrial, bureaucratic, urban, and education settings, but in the course of time they came to permeate almost every activity of the daily life, work, and school of the middle class.

Under the impact of Western technology, economy, and emergent bureaucracy, as well as urbanization and Western-type education, I find this kind of cognitive development or cognitive acculturation taking place among various peoples in Africa and other parts of the world. There, I find people acquiring Western middle-class type of cognitive skills, or intelligence B, at school and at work, and moreover, I find that these skills appear to be permeating their activities outside school and work settings. As a result of their cognitive acculturation, those who participate in Western-type schooling, economy, and urban living become differentiated in cognitive repertoire and pattern or in intelligence B from their parents, siblings, and other members of their culture (Cole, Gay, Glick, & Sharp, 1971; Cole & Scribner, 1974; Greenfield, 1966; Scribner & Cole, 1973; Seagrim & Lendon, 1980; Sharp, Cole, & Lave, 1979; Stevenson, 1982). In other words, contrary to the critical-period hypothesis, significant cognitive development does take place *after* early childhood and even in adulthood. Equally important, the new segment of the indigenous population begins to use childrearing techniques that inculcate and reinforce the emerging cognitive attributes.

Intelligence C refers to those cognitive skills or behaviors that IQ tests are designed to elicit. These cognitive skills that make up IQ tests are deliberately and carefully selected for specific purposes, like predicting academic performance or job performance (Travers, 1982; Vernon, 1969, Wigdor & Garner, 1982a). Because the items are carefully selected and the tests are standardized, intelligence C or IQ is considered more scientific and objective than intelligence B. But IQ is more circumscribed because it excludes many cognitive skills and behaviors that white middle-class people would consider important for their survival.

What then is IQ? Whence does it come from? IQ is a special and circumscribed form of intelligence. Its origins lie in the cognitive requirements of the macroenvironment of Western middle-class people, particularly the cognitive requirements of middle-class jobs and education. Individuals acquire these preexisting, adaptive, or functional skills because they need them to become competent adults in the middle-class world. The process by which individuals acquire the preexisting functional cognitive skills includes family childrearing practices, play, and other age- and sex-appropriate cultural activities, as well as formal education where those activities exist.

An Alternative Explanation of Differences among Populations in IQ

IQ, as I have argued, is a special kind of intelligence sampled to reflect and predict cognitive requirements for middle-class jobs and education. Populations that participate in middle-class-type occupations and schooling will tend to resemble one another on IQ test scores. For example, I would suggest that the IQ of middle-class populations in the United States, Japan, Britain, Italy, Russia, and Hong Kong will tend to be similar because these populations are involved in similar technoeconomic and bureaucratic activities requiring and encouraging similar cognitive competencies. At the same time, these middle-class populations will differ in IQ from the lower-class populations of their respective countries to the extent that the latter are involved in different kinds of technoeconomic and bureaucratic activities with different cognitive requirements.

As also noted earlier, lower-SES people and members of other non-middle-class populations, such as ethnic and racial minorities in industrial nations, as well as peoples in developing nations, have their own cultural activities, which may require and encourage cognitive skills similar to those nurtured by middle-class activities. Emphasis may vary; but there are overlaps. Therefore, populations may still differ in IQ-test scores even though their members are involved in activities requiring and encouraging similar cognitive skills. This is particularly true among coexisting but stratified populations in industrialized societies.

Another factor, besides differences in technoeconomic activities, which accounts for differences in IQ between populations, is how members of a given population perceive and respond to the tests in relation to how they perceive and adjust to their technoeconomic and sociopolitical realities. These perceptions or this epistemology and the resulting behavioral adjustments or coping mechanisms are culturally shared. They are products of the population's historical experiences; they are not generally consciously articulated by members of the population. Nevertheless, they influence how individual members approach test-taking, how they perceive and respond to the tests.

That is, whether a person comes to the test with positive and instrumental attitude and whether or not he or she makes a concerted effort to maximize scores will be affected by the conscious and unconscious assumptions about IQ tests which he or she shares with other members of his or her culture. If he or she comes from a population that defines IQ test scores as a useful and essential instrument for getting ahead, he or she will make a concerted effort to maximize the scores. A population defining IQ test scores that way will often incorporate testing into its folk theory of getting ahead, and teach its children the instrumental perceptions and approach to the tests consciously and unconsciously, and the children will tend to internalize the appropriate beliefs and attitudes, as well as to learn and apply behaviors that enhance high IQ test scores.

In some other populations, IQ tests may not be seen as helping one to get ahead. Indeed, they may be seen as serving just the opposite function (Williams, 1972). Therefore these tests will have a different status in the people's theory of getting ahead. They will tend to be invested with negative attitudes, stripped of supportive beliefs and instrumental behavior, attitudes, and beliefs. Nor will instrumental behavior, attitudes and beliefs be emphasized in children's upbringing nor in children's own attitudes and behaviors. The members of such a population will probably score low on the IQ tests even if their activities require and encourage white middle-class type of cognitive skills.

The lower IQ-test scores of castelike minorities appear, however, to be due to the two phenomena: namely, (1) limited participation in middle-class occupations and schooling requiring and encouraging middle-class IQ; and (2) an epistemology with coping mechanisms in which IQ tests are not strongly regarded as an instrument for getting ahead. The case of black Americans to which we turn next illustrates both.

Castelike Stratification between Blacks and Whites

There are several problems with most theories of stratification. One is that most fail to recognize the coexistence of two forms of stratification in American society: one based on achieved criteria of education, job, and income—that is, class; the other based on birth-ascribed criteria due to skin color or racial caste membership.

Examination of the employment and educational histories of blacks will show, however, that most stratification theories are based on wrong suppositions. First, it is the job ceiling and related barriers, not inadequate IQ, which have historically resulted in the underrepresentation of blacks in middle-class jobs. And, more importantly for the theme of this chapter, the relationship between middle-class jobs and IQ works just as well in the opposite direction: Participation in middle-class occupations and schooling gives rise to the type of cognitive skills elicited in IQ tests, to perceptions of opportunities for participation in these presumably rewarding activities (e.g., high income, social prestige), to perceptions of the tests as enhancing one's opportunities for the same, and acts as a culturally sanctioned incentive motivation to maximize test scores.

Race appears to be a significant variable in test scores only when racial groups are locked in a rigid, more or less castelike, stratification. This is evident in studies of various racial populations in the United States and elsewhere. In the United States, for example, some nonwhite minorities do relatively well on IQ tests (Wigdor & Graner, 1982a). Chinese Americans and Japanese Americans, among others, do just as well as the whites on IQ tests. Moreover, two populations belonging to the same race and living in the same country may not necessarily do equally well on IQ tests. For example, in Japan, the Buraku outcastes score significantly lower than the Ippan dominant group (DeVos, 1973; DeVos & Wagatsuma, 1967). Yet in the United States, where the Buraku and the Ippan are not stratified in a subordinate/dominant relationship, the performance of the two groups is just about equal (Ito, 1967). Race is, therefore, a significant variable in IQ test scores and academic achievement only when the racial groups are stratified in a castelike subordination, such as between blacks and whites in the United States (Ogbu, 1977). This is in part because the subordinate racial caste is largely excluded from middle-class jobs and education that require and stimulate middle-class type cognitive skills, and in part because of the kinds of responses subordinate group members make to their situation. Both the kind of epistemology or interpretation of reality that subordinate groups make and the kind of coping mechanisms they develop often tend to reinforce low IQ-test scores.

History of Stratification

For centuries, the stratification between blacks and whites in the U.S. closely resembled a caste system, with blacks as the subordinate caste (Berreman, 1960; Davis, Gardner, & Gardner, 1965; Dollard, 1956; Warner, 1970). Although more flexible today, American racial stratification still retains some features of a caste system. For example, like other caste systems it has a rule, which is somewhat implicit, about affiliation of offsprings of intercaste matings: all known children of black/white mating are automatically defined as black and forced to affiliate with blacks (Berreman, 1967). It is the persistence of this and other features that leads us to call it a castelike stratification and to call blacks a castelike minority. We are also using *castelike* as an analytic tool to describe any racial, ethnic, or other kinds of stratification that are not based on achieved criteria, appear more rigid than class, and are more or less permanent (Ogbu, 1977, 1978, 1981b).

Under castelike stratification, generations of black Americans have occupied a different and inferior ecological niche from that occupied by whites, including place of residence (involuntary segregation and "ghettoization"), employment and other economic opportunities (job ceiling and business exclusion), political participation (exclusion and control), educational opportunities (segregated and inferior education). Space does not permit even a brief description of the historical patterns and trends in each of these matters. But interested readers may consult sources on the following: involuntary segregation and ghettoization (Forman, 1971; Kusmer, 1976; Weaver, 1948), job ceiling and economic exclusion (Drake & Cayton, 1970; Frazier, 1957; Greene & Woodson, 1930; Norgren & Hill, 1964; Ross & Hill, 1967; Thernstorm, 1973), political exclusion and control (Factor, 1970; Hamilton & Carmichael, 1967; Myrdal, 1944; Spear, 1967; Stone, 1948), segregated and inferior education (Bond, 1981; Bullock, 1970; Kluger, 1977; Ogbu, 1978; Weinberg,

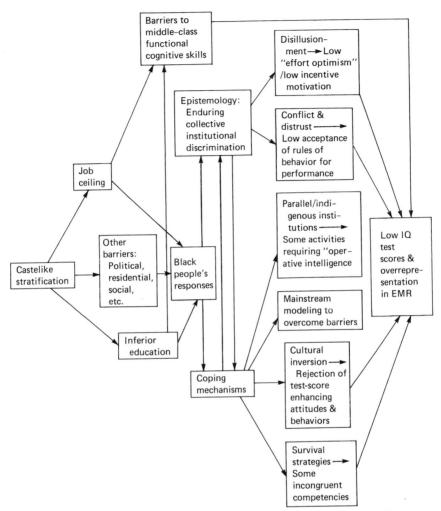

Figure 1. Societal forces influencing performance on IQ tests and representation in EMR.

1977). However, because jobs and education are directly related to the issue of IQ test scores and mental retardation of blacks, we attempt a brief summary of their experiences in these matters. We first show how, under castelike stratification, blacks have been largely excluded from those more-desirable middle-class occupations requiring and promoting middle-class IQ; then I show a similar exclusion from middle-class schooling. Thereupon, I describe black responses: perceptions and interpretations of their exclusions, the coping mechanisms they developed in consequence, and the implications of the perceptions and coping mechanisms for the IQ test scores. Figure 1 is a schematic representation

of these castelike barriers in jobs (job ceiling), education and other domains, as well as the black responses and their presumed lines of influence on black test scores and representation in EMR.

How Castelike Stratification Causes Lower IQ
and Disproportionate Representation of Blacks in EMR

JOB CEILING AND EXCLUSION
FROM MIDDLE-CLASS OCCUPATIONS

Myrdal (1944) has observed that American society "does not demand
equality of economic rewards independent of an individual's luck, ability and push. It merely demands equality of opportunity" (p. 671). That
is, there should be free and fair competition for desirable social and
economic positions. However, in the past, blacks and other nonwhites
were excluded from such free and fair competition when they had the
requisite educational credentials and ability. This was as true in the
South as it was in the North (Norgren & Hill, 1964).

A concept we have found useful in analyzing the employment of
experiences of blacks from the Emancipation to the 1970s is *job ceiling*.
We use it in the original sense employed by Drake and Cayton (1970)
and by Frazier (1957) to mean that (1) blacks are not permitted to com-
pete freely as individuals for any jobs they desire and for which they
have the educational qualification and ability; (2) blacks are not allowed
to obtain a proportionate share of the more-desirable middle-class jobs,
solely because of their race; and (3) as a result of these restrictions,
blacks are largely confined to the least-desirable, non-middle-class jobs.
Jobs in American society may be divided into two categories according
to the values Americans place on them. The more desirable jobs are
middle-class jobs, which are above the job ceiling; these would include
professional (e.g., architecture, engineering), technical, official, proprie-
tary, clerical, sales, and skilled-craft jobs. These jobs require more education or training and are valued more because they bring high income
and social prestige. The remaining jobs fall below the job ceiling and
include semiskilled operative work, personal and domestic service, common labor, and farm labor. These jobs do not require much education
and are not desired because they pay low wages and have little or no
prestige. Jobs above the job ceiling were traditionally regarded as jobs
for whites, while those below the job ceiling were jobs for blacks. Exceptions, as is shown in the following, occurred mainly when the jobs
above the job ceiling were within the black community or were in segregated institutions (e.g., teaching, clergy).

Table 2

Nonwhite as a Percentage of All Employed Persons in the South, 1940, 1950, 1960, and 1970, and Index of Nonwhite Participation[a]

Job ceiling	Percentage nonwhite				Index of nonwhite participation			
	1940	1950	1960	1970	1940	1950	1960	1970
Professional, technical and kindred workers	11.3	9.8	8.9	3.9	66.5	45.2	46.8	23.4
Farmers and farm managers	25.8	24.3	17.6	0.7	151.8	12.0	92.6	4.2
Managers and administrators, except farm	3.1	3.8	2.9	2.1	18.2	17.6	15.3	12.6
Clerical sales, and kindred workers	2.4	3.8	4.1	7.6	14.1	17.5	21.6	45.5
Craftsmen, foremen, and kindred workers	8.0	7.8	8.0	4.5	47.1	35.9	42.1	27.0
Operatives and kindred workers	15.5	18.5	17.6	20.8	91.2	65.3	92.6	129.6
Domestic service	60.5	84.6	79.7	30.0	355.9	389.9	419.5	179.6
Service, except domestic	—	40.0	37.3	11.6	—	184.3	196.3	69.5
Farm laborers and foremen	47.2	41.3	46.0	2.9	277.7	190.3	246.8	17.4
Laborers, except farm	50.2	49.7	47.4	11.3	295.3	229.0	249.5	67.7
Total, all persons employed	17.0	21.7	19.0	16.7	—	—	—	—

[a]From Ogbu, J. U. (1978). *Minority Education and Caste: The American System in Cross-Cultural Perspective* (p. 150). New York: Academic Press.

Table 3

Nonwhite as Percentage of All Employed Persons in the North, 1940, 1950, 1960, and 1970, and Index of Nonwhite Participation[a]

Job ceiling	Percentage nonwhite				Index of nonwhite participation			
	1940	1950	1960	1970	1940	1950	1960	1970
Professional, technical and kindred workers	1.4	1.6	2.3	3.9	41.2	35.6	41.1	59.1
Farmers and farm managers	0.3	0.3	0.2	0.7	8.8	6.7	3.6	10.6
Managers and administrators, except farm	0.9	1.2	1.3	2.1	26.5	26.7	23.2	31.8
Clerical sales, and kindred workers	0.8	1.8	2.9	5.6	23.5	40.0	51.8	84.9
Craftsmen, foremen, and kindred workers	1.4	2.2	3.0	4.5	41.2	48.9	53.6	68.2
Operatives and kindred workers	2.8	5.7	7.1	9.4	82.4	126.7	126.8	142.4
Domestic service	—	33.9	29.3	30.0	—	753.3	523.2	454.6
Service, except domestic	15.3	11.6	12.0	11.6	460.0	257.8	214.3	175.8
Farm laborers and foremen	1.4	1.6	2.2	2.9	41.2	35.6	39.3	43.9
Laborers, except farm	8.6	12.9	13.2	11.3	252.9	264.4	235.7	171.2
Total, all persons employed	3.4	4.5	5.6	6.6	—	—	—	—

[a]From Ogbu, J. U. (1978). *Minority Education and Caste: The American System in Cross-Cultural Perspective* (p. 152). New York: Academic Press.

Table 4

Nonwhite as Percentage of Total Civilian Labor Force, United States, 1940, 1950, 1960, and 1970, and Index of Nonwhite Participation[a]

Job ceiling	Percentage nonwhite				Index of nonwhite participation			
	1940	1950	1960	1970	1940	1950	1960	1970
Professional, technical and kindred workers	3.6	3.6	4.9	5.0	36.4	37.5	47.6	52.1
Farmers and farm managers	12.9	11.5	7.7	3.4	130.3	119.8	74.8	35.4
Managers and administrators, except farm	1.3	1.9	2.3	2.7	13.1	19.8	22.3	28.1
Clerical sales, and kindred workers	1.1	2.3	3.8	6.3	11.1	24.0	36.9	65.6
Craftsmen, foremen, and kindred workers	2.7	3.7	4.9	6.5	27.3	38.5	47.6	67.7
Operatives and kindred workers	5.7	9.1	10.7	13.2	57.5	94.8	103.9	137.5
Domestic service	47.1	57.6	53.9	52.5	475.8	600.0	523.9	546.9
Service, except domestic	15.6	19.0	20.1	17.0	157.6	197.9	195.2	177.1
Farm laborers and foremen	24.8	20.8	25.0	19.0	250.5	216.7	242.7	197.9
Laborers, except farm	20.4	26.0	25.8	20.5	206.1	260.4	250.5	213.5
Total, all persons employed	9.9	9.6	10.3	9.6	—	—	—	—

[a]From Ogbu, J. U. (1978). *Minority Education and Caste: The American System in Cross-Cultural Perspective* (p. 153). New York: Academic Press.

I use this concept of job ceiling to examine black experiences first in the South and then in the North. The representation of blacks above and below the job ceiling is presented in Table 2 for the South, Table 3 for the North, and Table 4 for the entire country. The nature of the U.S. Census data permits these tables to be prepared from 1940. Had classification of occupation for previous decades been the same, the extension of the table would have shown even more severe effects of the exclusion.

Employment history of blacks in the South from Emancipation may be divided into four broad periods. From 1861 to 1900, the distinction between "white jobs" and "black jobs" was firmly established by law and custom. Blacks were restricted to work in agriculture and in domestic and personal service and they could not advance even in some skilled trades where they dominated before Emancipation. Various mechanisms that displaced them from skilled occupations included re-enactment of the "black codes" (i.e., statutes that had governed the behavior of blacks before Emancipation), vagrancy laws, lawsuits for breach of contract, and the activities of the Ku Klux Klan. The emergence of craft unions between 1865 and 1885 reinforced black displacement from skilled crafts. But the final straw was the entry of white women into industrial workforce, partly because they became a new source of competition for "black jobs," especially those of black women. But more important was the fact that Southern code dictated that white women and blacks could not work together. Consequently, several Southern states passed laws drawing the color line in occupations even more sharply.

Only in segregated black communities and in public institutions like schools and hospitals serving blacks exclusively did blacks have the opportunity to achieve occupational status above the job ceiling (see Frazier, 1957; Greene & Woodson, 1930; Johnson, 1943; Marshall, 1968; Myrdal, 1944; Ross, 1967).

The job ceiling continued to influence the pattern of black employment during the second period, 1900–1940. Many blacks left agricultural labor for city jobs, but the latter were also traditional "black jobs" of semiskilled and unskilled labor. Here, however, any technological innovation making a particular "black job" easier or cleaner resulted in whites displacing blacks. Such a job was usually redefined as a "white job." A black business, professional, and white-collar class began to emerge during this period but it was almost totally dependent on the needs and support of the segregated black community and segregated institutions, though federal civil service in a few border cities like Washington, D.C., was also a source of white-collar work. However, note how the job ceiling and segregation acted to skew black occupational distribution: it allowed for the growth in number of black teachers and preachers (who made up ⅔ of the professional class), but it provided no place for black architects, accountants, civil engineers, managers of industry, natural scientists, lawyers and judges, technicians and other positions requiring and promoting white middle-class skills (Callis, 1935; Frazier, 1957; Greene & Woodson, 1930; Myrdal, 1944).

Between 1940 and 1960, available data permit a closer look at the way the job ceiling operated to restrict blacks to menial occupations. Table 2 shows the occupational distribution of blacks in this period. In spite of the labor shortage during World War II, blacks were not hired in the three top occupational categories within the general economy controlled by whites. Changes in black representation above the job ceiling occurred within black communities and in postal and other government jobs in the border cities. Black gains in the general economy during this period were in entering various jobs below the job ceiling. For example, many blacks displaced from skilled trades like bricklaying, plastering, and cement-finishing during the Great Depression were able to re-enter these occupations during the war. Blacks were also hired in significant numbers as semiskilled operative workers to take the place of white workers who moved into jobs above the job ceiling. Increases in the number of blacks among sales and clerical workers occurred in the black community and in the federal civil service in border cities. But black gains in wage labor during World War II did not change their pattern of employment, which continued to 1960.

Various studies show that the exclusion of blacks from desirable middle-class occupations prevailed through the early part of the 1960s. A good example is Vivian Henderson's (1967) study of black employment in private firms with federal government contracts, in Tennessee state government civil service, as well as in several Southern cities. His findings led him to conclude that "whether in the assembly line or elsewhere in the plant or business, blacks did not work side by side with whites, especially in jobs with advantages in income, responsibility, potential upgrading, and cleanliness" (p. 78). He further reports that black skills and abilities continued to be underutilized because skills and training were not the basis of black occupational status.

Since the passage of the Civil Rights Act of 1964, some blacks have gained entry into more skilled labor and other middle-class jobs above the job ceiling, both in the private and public sectors. Title VII of the Civil Rights Act bars racial discrimination in employment. Other forces that have also enabled blacks to gain entry into occupations above the job ceiling include the Equal Employment Opportunity Commission established in the 1960s, and blacks collective struggle, or protests and boycotts of white business (see Hill, 1968; Ladenburg & McFeely, 1969).

But subsequent studies have also shown that the job ceiling still remains an effective barrier to black employment in the private sector, as well as in cities like Memphis and Houston (Collins & Noblitt, 1970: Ross, 1973).

The national pattern from 1940 to 1970 is shown in Table 4. It is a product of the combination of forces/events affecting the separate regions. What needs to be emphasized is that the low black representation in middle-class jobs above the job ceiling in any region and nationally is not caused by lack of education, IQ, or genetic endowment. It is the legacy of the job ceiling under castelike stratification. Almost every study of black employment in the periods reviewed, whether in the South (e.g., Henderson's study in Memphis and Houston, 1967) or in the North (e.g., Thernstroms' study in Boston, 1973) or nationally (e.g., Norgren & Hill, 1964) has concluded that blacks were excluded from middle-class jobs through a job ceiling because they were a castelike minority, not because they lacked education and training. Thus, after studying black employment history, including extensive complaints filed with various state Fair Employment Practices Commissions, Norgren and Hill (1964) concluded that

> The main causal factor accounting for the greater magnitude of the occupational gap between [blacks and whites] is also fairly apparent. Owing to widespread racial discrimination in employment a large proportion of Negroes with college education and an even larger proportion of Negro high school graduates are unable to find jobs commensurate with their educational qualifications. This situation has been alleviated to some extent in a few Northern states with established and reasonable well-administered FEP laws. In the remainder of the North, however, there is still a widespread disparity between the level of educational attainment among Negroes and their representation in the upper half of the occupational spectrum. The disparity is even wider in the South where Negroes are still debarred from most clerical, sales, and professional jobs and virtually all managerial employment. (p. 84)

Kahn's study (1968) shows the adverse effects of the job ceiling for college-educated blacks. He found that before the mid-1960s, blacks with some college education were employed as service workers and laborers in numbers five times greater than whites with similar education. And 10% of black women with college degrees were doing domestic service. Kahn concluded from these and other statistics that "such a distribution cannot be explained in terms of lack of training" (p. 21). As a further illustration, before the mid-1960s, the greatest black–white unemployment gap occurred among those with 4 or more years of college education, with a ratio of 3.31 (as compared to 0.74 for people with 4 years of schooling or less). And those most adversely affected were young college-educated blacks. Some social scientists (e.g., Killingsworth, 1967) tried to explain the situation by saying that the unemployed college-educated blacks were young and their families did not teach them appropriate manners of speech, dress, and behavior. Yet, within a decade and with the raising of the job ceiling, these college-educated young blacks became the most employable of all blacks. And they have not only achieved parity of employment with young college-educated whites, but, significantly, young college-educated black females earn about $1000 a year more than their white peers (Wilson, 1978), apparently with no demonstrable changes in the way black families groom their children for the labor force.

In general, the wider societal forces of the 1960s have raised the job ceiling to the extent of increasing dramatically within a decade black representation above the old ceiling. For example, Brimmer (1974; see also Ross, 1973) reports that between 1960 and 1970, black employment in the two top-level job categories nearly doubled. Black professional and technical workers increased by 128%, even though the increase for the general population was only 49% during the same period. And blacks working as managers, officials and proprietors rose by 100%, while the rise for the general population was only 23%. Young college-educated blacks have benefitted most from the new employment opportunities, as they are the ones actively sought after by employers. Thus, Freeman (1976), cited in Wilson (1978), reports that the average number of recruitment visits by representatives of corporations to predominantly black colleges rose from 4 in 1960 to 50 in 1965 to 297 in 1970. I do not have the figures for black employment in more-recent years, but they are likely to show even further increases in black representation above the job ceiling.

Significant as these increases are in black employment above the job ceiling, it is important to stress two points about the change. One is that current changes illustrate again that the course of change in black occupational status is peculiar; it is different from the course of change among whites. Specifically, before 1960, blacks gained access to desirable jobs outside the black community and federal civil service mainly during periods of national crisis or labor shortages. These included periods of economic growth (1900–1908), restriction of immigration (1922–1929), national emergencies due to war (World War I, World War II, Korean War, and Vietnam War), and intense pressures from civil rights groups, such as occurred during World War II and in the 1960s. Even in such periods, employers did not readily or willingly accept black workers; rather, blacks advanced through political pressures, executive orders, and special legislation and court decisions. The dramatic gains since the mid-1960s merely confirm Myrdal's earlier observation that black employment advances are not normal, but the result of unique events (Myrdal, 1944). The gains since the mid-1960s are primarily due to forces referred to earlier, not because of the emergence of a generation of well-educated blacks or changes in the nature of employment requirements.

The second point to be emphasized is that these changes have not reached all segments of the black community. Non-college-educated blacks, lower-class blacks, and/or inner-city blacks remain largely unhelped by these developments. Of course, in the 1960s, the increase in the pool of jobs caused by the Vietnam War and social programs led to increase in employment of blacks in all sectors of the occupational ladder. In the early 1970s, a decrease in the pool of jobs not only slowed down the employment of non-college-educated blacks but also resulted in loss of jobs by those already employed, partly because they were the last hired and therefore the first to be fired. This loss of jobs among non-college-educated blacks has continued into the 1980s. And under the economic policy of the Reagan administration, black unemployment sometimes passed 18%, nearly twice the national average.

Note that the greater unemployment of non-college-educated blacks is not because they are less educated than non-college-educated whites. This can be seen from the fact that when the pool of jobs increased, as in the late 1960s, the employment gap decreased (12.5% black and 10.2% white underclass were unemployed in 1970). However, when the pool of jobs decreased, the exclusion of blacks increased; in consequence, black underclass unemployment in 1977 was 10% higher than white underclass unemployment: 25.6% black as compared to 15.6% white. This situation has led Newman to point out that "it is illogical to conclude that the black underclass is less employable than the white American underclass, unless white is included in the 'goods' and services and skills being offered in the marketplace" (Newman, 1979, pp. 96–97).

In summary, castelike stratification produces a job ceiling that excludes blacks from middle-class jobs, from those jobs that require and encourage middle-class education and cognitive skills or IQ. Also, the job ceiling generates a pattern of occupational advancement for blacks divergent from whites. Blacks do not advance by virtue of their educational advancement and ability like whites do. Rather, they are forced to rely on uncertain periodic national crises and on the goodwill of the government as the patron who can protect their rights to employment above the job ceiling. The effect of the latter on black educational attitudes and efforts is an unresearched problem. High unemployment and underemployment resulting from the job ceiling lead, of course, to poverty, with all that it implies for both adults and the developing child.

INFERIOR EDUCATION OR EXCLUSION
FROM MIDDLE-CLASS EDUCATION

Developments and public rhetoric of the 1980s tend to mask the fact that before 1960, there was no explicit public policy or concerted effort to provide blacks and whites with equal educational preparation for similar jobs above the job ceiling.

It is true that the education of lower-class whites has always been inferior to that of middle-class whites (Hollingshead, 1949; Sexton, 1961; Warner, Havighurst, & Loeb, 1944), but it is equally true that because of castelike stratification at every class level, the education of blacks has been even more inferior. I have described elsewhere a detailed historical pattern of black schooling (Ogbu, 1978); here, I only summarize the salient features. Three relevant points emphasized in this summary are (1) black education is different from white education; (2) it is inferior to white education; and (3) it is determined by white epistemology or white people's conception of the place of blacks in society at a given period.

Thus, while slavery lasted blacks received occasional education in the bible because their masters believed that it would make them more obedient and faithful. After the Civil War, blacks remained in the peon-like status of sharecropping or in the Negro jobs of domestic service and unskilled labor, and education followed suit. The ruling white elites believed that the tenant system would break down if black children, as future laborers, received the same kind of education as whites, because such education would encourage them to question the high rates of interest and the exploitative method of account keeping used by the planters in dealing with illiterate tenants. Consequently, academic training for blacks was de-emphasized and black education was starved of funds (Bond, 1981; Bullock, 1970; Ransom & Sutch, 1977; Vaughn, 1974; Weinberg, 1977).

As the South urbanized, most blacks were initially provided with some industrial education, chiefly for cooking and low-grade building skills. But when many desirable factory jobs began to require special training, ironically, the curriculum of black schools could emphasize classical or academic rather than industrial training, while white schools got the necessary funds and began to emphasize industrial education (Bond, 1981; Myrdal, 1944; Weinberg, 1977).

In general, inferior education in the South was institutionalized in legally segregated schools. And the processes by which that inferiority was maintained included shorter school terms, inferior curriculum and inadequate textbooks, less transportation, fewer library services, fewer supplies, less-qualified teachers, lower teacher salaries, and heavier teaching loads (Bond, 1981; Pierce et al., 1955). Legal segregation was officially ended by the United States Supreme Court in 1954, but actual desegregation did not begin until late 1960s, due to white opposition (Ogbu, 1978).

Black education in the North was not necessarily better. Although in the North, blacks had access to more schooling, the quality of that schooling was less than that of the Northern white; moreover, it further deteriorated when more blacks moved from the South. As black ghettoization in Northern cities increased, black education became even more segregated and inferior. An example of how Northern school systems kept black education inferior is seen in a study in Chicago for the U.S. Commission on Civil Rights. In the 1961–1962 year, Chicago school system spend almost 25% less money per pupil in black schools than in white schools, paid teachers in black schools 18% less than the salaries paid to teachers in white schools, and spent 50% less money on nonteaching operating expenses in black schools. Black schools had 46.8 pupils per classroom as compared to 30.9 pupils per classroom in white schools (Sexton, 1968). The education committee of the NAACP in San Francisco found similar differences in the treatment of black and white schools in the late 1960s, a finding that contributed to a later court order for San Francisco to integrate its schools. And as recently as 1972, the school district of Washington, D.C. spent, on the average, progressively less money per pupil as the number of black children increased in a given school.

Cognitive Implications of the Job Ceiling and Inferior Schooling

The implications of the exclusion of blacks from middle-class occupations and from free and fair competition for the same, as well as exclusion from middle-class education, are at least twofold. First, it affects the nature of the difference in IQ test scores, which has been stressed by Jensen (1969) and Bruner and Connolly (1974). Jensen says that blacks do less well in that portion of IQ tests that results in what he calls "level 2 intelligence." This is similar to what Bruner and Connolly call "operative intelligence," which they point out is lacking among inner-city blacks.

But a close examination suggests that operative intelligence and level 2 intelligence are very much the kind of intelligence that Baumrind (1977) and Vernon (1969) tell us middle-class people developed when they began to do what have become typically middle-class jobs: jobs involving scientific analysis of various kinds of problems; scientific control and exploitation of environment; planning and implementation of long-range and large-scale economic programs; and others in the ur-ban/industrial bureaucracy. We contend that the exclusion of blacks from such middle-class jobs and related activities might have affected the extent to which they developed and emphasized white middle-class operative intelligence. We also contend that exclusion from middle-class superior schooling functions like middle-class occupations to promote analytic skills, abstract thinking, and grasping of relations.

The other implication is that the job ceiling and the exclusion from fair and free competition for desirable positions, based on individual train-ing and ability, have probably discouraged blacks from incorporating positively IQ test-taking into their folk theory of success. This has not encouraged the emergence of a strong incentive motivation toward the tests as a culturally sanctioned phenomenon. This point is more fully discussed here subsequently, in the context of black epistemology and responses.

How Castelike Stratification Causes the Lower IQ Test Scores of Blacks

Even though blacks have been largely excluded from middle-class jobs and schooling, they have, like most other people, indigenous activities that require and encourage operative intelligence. For example, some blacks have long had middle-class jobs in segregated communities and institutions, and some blacks attend schools that approximate white middle-class schools. Other activities in the inner-city, like hustling, pimping, preaching, and the like, appear also to require and encourage operative intelligence.

Yet, hustlers, pimps, and preachers and other smart people in black communities may not have done well on IQ tests and were probably public school dropouts. Indeed they were probably the kind of people whom as children Jensen says that outside test situations behaved more intelligently than their test scores would suggest. In other words, black children who are as intelligent as white children may not necessarily score as high as their white peers on IQ tests and other standardized tests or do as well in school. Why do blacks not do as well? To explain this apparent discrepancy, I must go beyond psychometric observa-tions, test construction, experimentation and differences in cultural traits; I must turn to black epistemology or their perceptions and in-terpretations of reality as well as turn to their coping responses to their subordination.

BLACK EPISTEMOLOGY

Black Americans, like other castelike minorities, have developed an epistemology that is consistent with their experiences, an epistemology that reflects their encounter with the job ceiling and other barriers. That is, black perceptions and experiences of the job ceiling, inferior schooling, and similar barriers in other societal institutions have shaped how they perceive and interpret their place in American society and institutions or how they see and interpret their social realities.

This epistemology is characterized by a kind of collective institutional discrimination perspective. Many blacks believe that they cannot advance into the mainstream of society (i.e., become middle-class) through individual efforts in the manner that works for whites where whites or white representatives are judges. Even among the relatively successful, black professional and business people tend to believe that white people would not allow a black person to advance to the full extent of his or her ability and training, whereas a white person is believed to have a chance to advance all the way. These perceptions of their historical pattern of opportunity structure have given rise to several coping responses, many of which directly or indirectly adversely affect black IQ test scores and academic efforts.

COPING RESPONSES

I briefly describe four of the several coping responses of blacks which may adversely affect their IQ test scores. One response that may actually contribute to higher test scores is described first. I may call this *mainstream modeling* to overcome castelike barriers. However, it involves more than just patterning one's attitude and behavior after those of middle-class whites, for it often includes overdoing these. Mainstreamers recognize the existence of the job ceiling and other castelike barriers against blacks, but they are determined to succeed in spite of the barriers. They further believe that in order to succeed under the caste system a black person must work twice as hard as a white person or be twice as good as the white. And because they want to succeed, they are willing to pay the price of working harder to be better qualified than the white competitors. In our Stockton study, some informants appeared discouraged by the idea of working twice as hard as the white; but for some other informants, it was actually a motivating force to succeed in school. We interviewed some adults and some young people who attributed their successful graduation from high school or college to their determination to succeed in spite of castelike barriers (Ogbu, 1974, 1977).

Among the responses that may adversely affect IQ test scores and school performance is disillusionment, leading to failure to develop "effort optimism" or incentive motivation toward schoolwork and tests as a culturally sanctioned norm. I referred earlier to an aspect of this response, as absence of a culturally sanctioned incentive motivation. This is apparently a widespread response, and Shack (1970) has suggested how it might have evolved historically. He notes that the absence of a job ceiling among whites historically enabled them to receive adequate payoffs for their educational efforts—that is, to get jobs and wages commensurate with their training and ability.

This experience appears to have encouraged whites to develop effort optimism toward school and work, which is summed up in the white maxim: "If at first you don't succeed, try, try again." Effort optimism means being serious, determined, and persevering in academic work, test taking and the like. It appears, on the other hand, to be less a characteristic of blacks because of their different experience. For, according to Shack, faced with a job ceiling, blacks seem to have learned that social and economic rewards are not porportionate to educational efforts; consequently, they tended to develop a different maxim: "What's the use of trying?" The disillusionment and its consequences for effort are, thus, not of recent development. In her survey of black writers from 1900 to 1930, Sochen (1972) found that although many accepted the American Dream with its ethic of individual hard work, thrift, and discipline, there were some who simultaneously rejected it because, due to castelike barriers, it was meaningless and irrelevant to black Americans.

The adverse effects of disillusionment about schooling on older black students are demonstrated in an article sent to the *Newsweek* "My Turn," column by a 15-year old boy from Wilmington, Delaware (Hunter, 1980). The article describes two types of black teenagers in the inner-city: the "Rocks," who constitute the majority, have given up hope of making it in mainstream economy through white middle-class strategy of test scores and school credentials. They therefore stopped trying to do well in school or go to school at all. The "Ducks," or "Suckers," are the few, the "minority of the minority" who still hope to succeed through schooling. They are derided because they go to school everyday and even want to go to college; they do not use drugs or drink. The "Ducks" are regarded as "wasting their time waiting for a dream that won't come true" because even their parents cannot find jobs.

Cultural inversion is another response that can contribute to the lower IQ test scores and lower academic performance. *Cultural inversion* means acting, defining behaviors or events, and investing values and meanings to behaviors, events and situations opposite to those characteristic of members of another group, particularly members of a dominant group.

For example, members of X subordinate group may define things, events, and situations as being X's because they are not Y's, not the dominant group's; then they would define other behaviors, events or situations as not being X's because they are Y's. Holt (1972) says that among black Americans, inversion occurs in language and communication through the process of investing positive values to negative terms (e.g., "nigger") used by whites to describe blacks. This and other speech devices permit blacks to repudiate white stereotypes, to turn the tables against whites or to manipulate whites.

Cultural inversion involves what we referred to earlier as secondary cultural differences, which subordinate groups develop as a part of their coping mechanisms (Ogbu, 1982). This type of coping is in the form of opposition between the subordinate and the dominant group cultures, and it often results in two opposing models or two opposing cultural frames of reference. Individuals, especially from the subordinate group, attempting to cross the cultural boundaries, to behave like a member of the other group, both encounter opposition from members of their own group and arouse painful and discouraging inner conflict through a sense of betrayal to their group and uncertainty of acceptance by members of the other group (DeVos, 1980).

Cultural inversion in an education context appears in the tendency for some blacks to define both academic requirements and the instrumental attitudes and behaviors that enhance school success and high test scores as white and therefore not black. Boykin's (1980) description of a black cultural frame of behavior in opposition to a white cultural frame of behavior illustrates this situation. Boykin says that black children want to learn when they begin school but are "turned off" by an educational process that confronts them with "artificial, contrived, and arbitrary competence modalities" (i.e., with white ways of teaching and learning). However, note that children from some other nonwhite groups do learn more or less successfully and are not turned off as blacks are; the difference is that those other children do not define school requirements in opposition to their own cultural norm. It is not merely that children behave differently but that they behave in opposition to the required form.

A study by Petroni (1970) shows clearly that labelling academic and certain extracurricular activities as "white" and "not black," can have adverse effects on the schoolwork of black children. Petroni found that blacks in one high school regarded athletics as legitimate and appropriate activities for black participation and praised those blacks who excelled in them. On the other hand, they defined as white, and therefore not black, academic work and conventional school political organization, as well as certain extracurricular activities traditionally dominated by whites. Consequently, they condemned any black students who excelled in academic work or were actively involved in the "white activities." Such black students were labelled as "Uncle Toms" and socially unacceptable. This posed a serious dilemma for the students doing well in school or wanting to succeed. Our own observations in Stockton support Petroni's suggestion that fear of being called an Uncle Tom or accused of acting white may prevent some black students from making the necessary efforts to do well in school and in tests. Some Stockton students thought that doing well in school is "doing the whiteman thing" or acting white.

As a way of coping with the job ceiling and inferior education, blacks have also developed a number of *survival strategies* or alternative ways of meeting their subsistence and self-esteem needs. Some of these may not necessarily help students score high on IQ tests or do well in school. Among the survival strategies are collective struggle or civil rights activities, clientship or Uncle Tomming, and hustling and related activities. The attitudes, knowledge, skills, and rules of behavior for achievement fostered by these strategies are not always compatible with those required to do well on tests and in school. For example, collective struggle teaches children not to accept personal responsibility for failure but to blame the system. Clientship teaches them that societal success (including getting good jobs, wages, and promotions) does not necessarily depend on exerting personal efforts in the way advocated by the dominant group or in following rules of behavior for achievement that work for whites, such as obtaining school credentials or having high IQ test scores. Rather, access to good jobs, wages, and promotion depends on white patronage, which can be won by being dependent, compliant, and manipulative. Hustling teaches children to succeed or make it without working, or without accepting the conventional work practice of being employed by white people. Instead, a person should be smart, investing efforts and know-how in exploiting and manipulating others for desired goods and position. These survival strategies are a part of black culture learned by children more or less from preschool years. Children who enter school with some knowledge and competence in the survival strategies may perform poorly on IQ tests and in schoolwork, and as they get older and become more competent, their difficulties with the IQ tests and academic work increase.

A fourth response to the job ceiling and inferior education is hostility and distrust toward the public schools and IQ and other tests associated with it. This hostility has grown out of a long history of unpleasant experience with the schools and with white society in general. Throughout the history of public school education in America, blacks have come to perceive their frequent exclusion and discrimination as designed to prevent them from qualifying for the more desirable jobs open to whites. Consequently, a significant thrust of black collective struggle has been forcing whites and the schools to provide them with equal education; the thrust has thus not been toward working in cooperation with the schools to maximize academic accomplishments.

Initially, blacks were fighting against total exclusion from the public schools. For over a century, they have fought against inferior education in segregated and in integrated schools. Where blacks attend segregated schools, these schools are theoretically black schools, so that one might expect blacks to identify and work with such schools. However, the identification and cooperation have often been undermined by a simultaneous perception of the segregated schools as inferior. This perception results in diverting attention and efforts toward struggle for integration and equalization of education. These events, in turn, frequently generate a feeling that the public schools cannot be trusted to educate black children because of their gross and subtle mechanisms of discrimination. The conflicts also force schools to treat blacks defensively and to resort to various forms of control, paternalism, or contest. The schools' responses, too, divert efforts from educating black children. On the basis of these observations, which can be documented in almost every American city where blacks live, we would suggest that the black–school relationship, riddled with conflicts and suspicion would make it difficult for blacks to accept and internalize the schools' goals, standards, and teaching and learning approaches. Moreover, this situation would contribute to low test scores and low school performance among black children.

In summary, these responses—disillusionment, survival strategies, cultural inversion, and distrust—are logical within the context of the castelike stratification and the epistemology it generates. They work independently and cojointly to inhibit the development of a strong cultural orientation toward academic or intellectual pursuits, especially among inner-city blacks, and they serve to place black children at risk for being labeled retarded or school failures.

Why Blacks Score Lower Than Whites of Comparable Class and Than Other Minorities

The fact that, on the average, blacks score lower on IQ and other tests than whites of comparable socioeconomic background and than some other minorities of similar socioeconomic background has led to some puzzling questions and speculations. We first try to explain the class phenomenon; then we deal with that of minority status.

Castelike Stratification versus Class Stratification

The debate over the relative weight of influence of castelike stratification and class stratification involves three related questions: Is the class situation more influential than castelike status? Do blacks, on the average, score lower than whites because of black lower-class background? Why do blacks score lower than whites, on the average, of similar socioeconomic background?

The first two questions are embodied in criticisms of my own work, especially my thesis that where castelike stratification co-exists with class stratification, as in the United States, the former is basic to the social structure, and therefore the ultimate determinant of the lower IQ and poorer school performance of blacks and similar subordinate groups (Ogbu, 1978). My critics (Bond, 1981; Gordon & Yeakey, 1980; van den Berghe, 1980; Wilson, 1980; Yeakey & Johnson, 1979) say that I have not paid enough attention to class factors. Some go on to assert that the ultimate cause of inequality in American life is corporate capitalism or economic domination—that is, class (Gordon and Yeakey, 1980; Yeakey and Johnson, 1979). I reject their counter formulation for two reasons. One is racial or castelike stratification, hence castism or racism exists in precorporate capitalist and precapitalist societies, such as among the precolonial Ibos of Nigeria (Ogbu, 1981), the Nupe of Nigeria, the Beni Amer of East Africa, and the Tira of Sudan (Nadel, 1954), precolonial Rwanda (Maquet, 1968), the Senufo of West Africa (Richter, 1980; Todd, 1977), and the Konso of Ethiopia (Hallpike, 1972).

The other reason for rejecting the counterformulation is that if economic inequality were the more fundamental, I would expect the labor market or corporate capitalism to treat blacks and whites of similar social class background alike; but it does not (Harrison, 1972; Myrdal, 1944; Norgren and Hill, 1964; Thernstorm, 1973). The differential treatment of blacks and whites of similar class background by the labor market of corporate capitalism is illustrated by Thernstorm's study (1973) of blacks and of Irish, Italian, and Jewish immigrants in Boston from the late nineteenth century to 1970. The study shows that a large socioeconomic gap (e.g., predominance of blacks in menial labor) between blacks and the white groups, which persisted throughout the period, could not be attributed to differences in rural background, education, community environment, family pattern, or culture. Rather, the author concluded, racial barriers to employment—such as job ceiling—were the main cause of the relative lack of black progress (p. 217).

Critics err also in responding to the second question: whether or not blacks score lower on IQ tests and do less well in school, on the average, because of their lower-class background. Those interpreting the lower performance as a function of lower-class background tend to believe that American castelike stratification has been largely dismantled and replaced with class stratification. As a consequence, they think, black population is now polarized into two classes: middle-class blacks who are making it or succeeding like middle-class whites; and the black underclass, who are not making it (van den Berghe, 1979; Wilson, 1980). The difficulty with this view is that, on the average, blacks do less well than whites who come from similar socioeconomic background, including middle-class blacks. That is, middle-class blacks are *not* succeeding in school or scoring as high on IQ tests as middle-class whites (Haskins, 1980; Jencks, 1972; Jensen, 1969, 1980; *Oakland Tribune*, 1980; U.S. District Court for Northern California, 1979; Wigdor and Garner, 1982a).

The answer to the third question—why blacks do less well than whites of comparable socioeconomic background—lies in the influence of castelike stratification described previously. I have described elsewhere (Ogbu, 1977, 1978, 1981b) major differences between class and castelike stratification and suggested possible different educational implications. What needs to be stressed here is the differential implication of the absence of a job ceiling in American white class system and its presence in the castelike stratification. I would suggest that castelike stratification gives class membership in the subordinate group an added disadvantage: a white American who is lower class is only lower class with some impaired access to jobs and education, but he or she does not face a job ceiling. A black American who is lower class is also a member of a subordinate racial group who, in addition to impaired access due to lower-class status, faces a job ceiling. Thus one can speak of lower-class blacks as being involved in *a double stratification.*

Membership in a double stratification generates the distinct type of cognitive orientation or epistemology described earlier, which is not found among the white lower class. This is the tendency to blame the system rather than oneself for personal and group failures. Unsuccessful whites often blame themselves and their luck (Sunnett & Cobb, 1972). Unsuccessful blacks, however, tend to blame the system or society. They see racial barriers in employment and education as the primary causes of their poverty and other social ills. What distinguishes blacks from whites—particularly, what distingquishes lower-blacks from lower-class whites—is not that their material conditions (education, jobs, income, etc.) are different but rather that the way the blacks perceive, interpret, and respond to their situation is different. And these differential perceptions, interpretations, and responses have serious adverse implications for the test scores and school performance of blacks and similar minorities.

Minority Status

Minority status per se does not result in persisting low test scores or persisting disproportionate school failure. Therefore we must distinguish those minorities characterized by these problems—namely, castelike minorities, like blacks, Native Americans, and Native Hawaiians—from other types that are not, such as immigrant minorities like Chinese, Filippinos, Japanese, and Punjabi Indians. Castelike minorities are those who have been incorporated into their country or into American society more or less involuntarily and permanently and then relegated into menial positions through legal and extralegal devices. They have almost no escape but must carry on a continual struggle to lighten their subordination. Castelike minorities are characterized by the collective institutional discrimination perspective already described, with its consequences for test scores and school performance.

Immigrant minorities, on the other hand, came to America more or less voluntarily to improve their economic, political, or social status. They may hold menial jobs, lack political power, and have little or no prestige. However, these objective socioeconomic facts do not reflect their true status, because the immigrants may evaluate their position differently. They may, in fact, consider their menial position in America better than what it was in their original homeland, or they may see their menial position in America as only a temporary setback. Furthermore, their reference groups are their peers in their homeland, the people they compare themselves with and usually find much evidence of self-improvement and good prospects for their children because of better opportunities; they do not compare themselves with white middle-class Americans (Shibutani & Kwan, 1965). Also, immigrants have at least the symbolic option to leave America and return home or go elsewhere if things become too unbearable. Although they do not share the culture of the white middle-class Americans, the cultural distinctiveness is not a part of an oppositional process (Ogbu, 1978, 1983). Thus, immigrant minorities may interpret (like castelike minorities) their economic, political, and other problems in America in terms of collective institutional discrimination perspective, but unlike castelike minorities they do not see this situation as permanent; nor do they allow it to overwhelm them. For this reason, they are more able to maintain hope and instrumental attitudes and behaviors in their children, enabling the latter to do well in IQ tests and in school.

Conclusion

The main argument of this chapter has been that the lower IQ-test scores of black children, resulting in their overrepresentation among the educable mentally retarded, are the consequence of the position of blacks in a castelike system of stratification. This position subjects them to menial jobs, schooling, and related activities that do not require or promote white middle-class type cognitive skills or "operative intelligence" emphasized in some portions of the IQ tests. Furthermore, the status of blacks in the stratification system denies them adequate and equitable rewards for their tests and academic efforts, thereby discouraging them from developing a strong belief that it pays to maximize test scores or work hard in school. Some blacks are, of course, involved in indigenous and other activities requiring and promoting operative intelligence as well as rewarding efforts. But some of the ways in which blacks respond to the aforementioned inequities of the castelike stratification, particularly to the job ceiling and inferior education, actually reinforce the lower test scores and poor school performance. For these reasons, the test scores of black children do not reflect their true ability.

As societal forces permit more and more blacks to gain access to jobs above the job ceiling and to better schooling, the proportion of black children with higher test scores will increase. However, the elimination of the gap between black and white test scores will depend also on the extent to which the castelike inequities are eliminated and–or are perceived to be eliminated by blacks. Some black children, including those at risk, will always benefit from remedial programs and avoid classification as mentally retarded; some other black children, for other reasons, including differential experiences, perceptions and interpretations, will continue to do as well as or better than their white peers. But the overrepresentation in the EMR-labeled population is a collective problem not solved entirely by remedying assumed individual deficiencies.

References

Alland, A. (1973). *Human diversity*. Garden City, NY: Doubleday.

Barnes, J. A. (1947). The collection of genealogies. *Rhodes–Livingston Journal: Vol. 5. Human problems in British Central Africa*.

Baughman, E. (1971). *Black Americans*. New York: Academic Press.

Baumrind, D. (1977). *Subcultural variations in values defining social competence: An outsider's perspective on the black subculture*. Unpublished manuscript.

Berreman, G. D. (1970). Caste in India and the United States. *The American Journal of Sociology, 66*, 120–127.

Berreman, G. D. (1967). Caste in cross-cultural perspective: Organizational components. In G. DeVos & H. Wagatsuma, (Eds.), *Japan's invisible race: Caste in culture and personality*. Berkeley: University of California Press.

Bickel, W. E. (1982). Classifying mentally retarded students: A review of placement practices in special education. *Placing children in special education: A strategy for equity* (pp. 182–229). Washington, DC: National Academy of Sciences Press.

Birch, H. G. & Gussow, J. D. (1970). *Disadvantaged children.* New York: Harcourt Brace Jovanovich.

Bloom, B. S., Davis, A., & Hess, R. (1965). *Compensatory education for cultural deprivation.* New York: Holt.

Bond, G. C. (1981). Social economic status and educational achievement: A review article. *Anthropology and Education Quarterly, 12,* 227–257.

Boykin, A. W. (1980). *Reading achievement and the social cultural framework of reference of Afro American children.* Paper presented at NIE Roundtable Discussion on Issues in Urban Reading.

Brimmer, A. F. (1974). Economic development in the black community. In E. Ginzberg and R. M. Solow, (Eds.), *The great society: Lessons for the future.* New York: Basic Books.

Brookover, W. B., & Erickson, E. L. (1965). *Society, schools and learning.* Boston: Allyn and Bacon.

Bullock, H. A. (1970). *A history of Negro education in the south: From 1619 to the present.* New York: Praeger.

Callis, H. A. (1935). The training of Negro physicians. *Journal of Negro Education, 4,* 32–41.

Ciborowski, T. J. (1979). Cross-cultural aspects of cognitive functioning: Culture and knowledge. In A. J. Marsella, R. G. Tharp, & T. J. Ciborowski, (Eds.), *Perspectives on cross-cultural psychology.* New York: Academic Press.

Cole, M., Gay, J., Glick, & Sharp, D. W. (1971). *The cultural context of learning and thinking: An exploration in experimental anthropology.* New York: Basic Books.

Cole, M., & Scribner, S. (1974). *Culture and thought: A psychological introduction.* New York: Wiley.

Collins, T. W., & Noblitt, G. W. (1979). *Stratification and resegregation: The case of Crossover High School, Memphis, Tenn.* (Final Report, NIE Contract Grant No. 400-76-009). Washington, DC: The National Institute of Education.

Connolly, K. J., & Bruner, J. S. (1974). Introduction. In K. J. Connolly & J. S. Bruner, (Eds.), *The growth of competence.* London: Academic Press.

Davis, A., Gardner, B. B., & Gardner, M. R. (1965). *Deep South: A social anthropological study of caste and class* (abridged ed.). Chicago: University of Chicago Press.

DeVos, G. A. (1973). Japan's outcasts: The problem of the Burakumin. In B. Whitaker (Ed.), *The fourth world: Victims of group oppression* (pp. 307–327). New York: Schocken Books.

DeVos, G. A. (1980). Ethnic adaptation and minority status. *Journal of Cross-Cultural Psychology, 11,* 101–124.

DeVos, G. A., & Wagatsuma, H. (Eds.). (1967). *Japan's invisible race: Caste in culture and personality.* Berkeley: University of California Press.

Dollard, J. (1957). *Caste and class in a southern town* (3rd ed.). Garden City, NY: Doubleday.

Drake, St. C., & Cayton, H. R. (1970). *Black metropolis: A study of Negro life in a northern city* (Vols. 1 & 2). New York: Harcourt Brace Jovanovich.

Eells, K., Davis, A., Havighurst, R. J., Herrick, V. E., & Tyler, R. W. (1952). *Intelligence and cultural differences: A study of cultural learning and problem-solving.* Chicago: University of Chicago Press.

Eysenck, H. J. (1971). *The inequality of man.* San Diego, CA: EDITS.

Factor, R. L. (1970). *The black response to America: Men, ideals and organization from Frederick Douglass to the NAACP.* Reading, MA: Addison-Wesley.

Finn, J. D. (1982). Patterns in special education placement as revealed by the OCR surveys.

In *Placing children in special education: A strategy for equity* (pp. 322–381). Washington, DC: National Academy of Sciences Press.

Fishbein, H. D. (1976). *Evolution, development and children's learning.* Pacific Palisades, CA: Goodyear.

Forman, R. E. (1971). *Black ghettos, white ghettos, and slums.* Englewood Cliffs, NJ: Prentice-Hall.

Frazier, E. F. (1957). *The Negro in the United States.* New York: Macmillan.

Freeman, R. B. (1976). *The overeducated American.* New York: Academic Press.

Gartner, A., & Riessman, F. (1967). *The lingering infatuation with I.Q.: A review of Arthur R. Jensen's educability and group differences.* Unpublished manuscript.

Gay, J., & Cole, M. (1967). *The new mathematics and an old culture: A study of learning among the Kpelle of Liberia.* New York: Holt.

Ginsburg, H. P. (1982). *Rethinking the myth of the derpived child: New thoughts on poor children.* Unpublished manuscript.

Goody, J. & Watt, I. (1968). The consequences of literacy. In J. Goody (Ed.), *Literacy in traditional society* (pp. 27–68). Cambridge: Cambridge University Press.

Gordon, E. W., & Yeakey, C. C. (1980). Review of minority education and caste. *Teachers College Records, 526–529.*

Greenfield, P. M. (1966). On culture and conservation. In J. S. Bruner, R. R. Oliver, & P. M. Greenfield (Eds.), *Studies in cognitive growth.* New York: Wiley.

Hallpike, C. (1972). *The Konso of Ethiopia.* Oxford: Clarendon.

Hamilton, C., & Carmichael, S. (1967). *Black power: The politics of liberation in America.* New York: Random House.

Harrison, B. (1972). *Education, training and the urban ghetto.* Baltimore, MD: Johns Hopkins University Press.

Haskins, R. (1980). *Race, family income, and school achievement.* Unpublished manuscript.

Henderson, V. W. (1967). Region, race and jobs. In A. M. Ross & H. Hill, (Eds.), *Employment, race and poverty.* New York: Harcourt Brace Jovanovich.

Herzog, J. D. (1976). The socialization of juveniles in primate and foraging societies: Implications for contemporary education. In J. I. Roberts & S. Akinsanya (Eds.), *Education patterns and cultural configurations: The anthropology of education.* New York: David McKay Co.

Hill, H. (1968). Twenty years of state fair employment practices commissions: A critical analysis with recommendations. In L. A. Ferman, J. L. Kornbluh, & J. A. Miller, (Eds.), *Negroes and jobs.* Ann Arbor: University of Michigan Press.

Hilliard, III, A. G. (1981). *The IQ test on trial* (Part 3). Unpublished manuscript.

Hollingshead, A. (1949). *Elmtown's youth.* New York: Wiley.

Holt, G. S. (1972). Inversion in black communication. In T. Kochman (Ed.), *Rappin' and stylin' out: Communication in urban black America.* Chicago: University of Illinois Press.

Horton, R. (1967). African traditional thought and western science: Part 1. From tradition to science. *Africa, 27,* 50–71.

Horton, R. (1967). African traditional thought and western science: Part 2. The closed and open predicaments. *Africa, 37,* 155–187.

Hunt, J. McV. (1969). *The challenge of incompetence and poverty: Papers on the role of early education.* Urbana: University of Illinois Press.

Hunter, D. (1980, August). My turn: Ducks vs. hard rocks. *Newsweek,* 2.

Ito, H. (1967). Japan's outcastes in the United States. In G. A. DeVos & H. Wagatsuma (Eds.), *Japan's invisible race: Caste in culture and personality.* Berkeley: University of California Press.

Jackson, G. D. (1975). On the report of the ad hoc committee on educational uses of tests with disadvantaged students: Another psychology view from the Association of Black Psychologists. *American Psychologist, 33–93.*

Jencks, C. (1972). *Inequality.* New York: Basic Books.

Jensen, A. R. (1969). How much can we boost IQ and scholastic achievement? *Harvard Educational Review, 39,* 1–123.

Jensen, A. R. (1972). *Statement of Dr. Arthur R. Jensen, Senate Select Committee on Education, February 24, 1972.* Unpublished manuscript.

Jensen, A. R. (1980). *Bias in mental testing.* New York: The Free Press.

Johnson, C. S. (1943). *Backgrounds to patterns of Negro segregation.* New York: Crowell.

Kagan, J. (1973). What is intelligence? *Social Policy,* July/August, 88–93.

Kahn. T. (1968). The economics of inequality. In L. A. Ferman, J. L. Kornbluh, & J. A. Miller, (Eds.), *Negroes and jobs.* Ann Arbor: University of Michigan Press.

Katzman, D. M. (1973). *Before the ghetto: Black Detroit in the nineteenth century.* Urbana: University of Illinois Press.

Kerber, A., & Bommarito, B. (1965). Preschool education for the developing cortex. In A. Kerber & B. Mommarito (Eds.), *The schools and the urban crisis.* New York: Holt.

Killingsworth, C. C. (1967). Negroes in a changing labor market. In A. M. Ross & H. Hill (Eds.), *Employment, race, and poverty: A critical study of the disadvantaged status of Negro workers from 1865 to 1965.* New York: Harcourt Brace Jovanovich.

Kluger, R. (1977). *Simple justice.* New York: Vintage Book.

Kusmer, K. L. (1976). *A ghetto takes shape: Black Cleveland, 1870–1930.* Urbana: University of Illinois Press.

Ladenburg, T. J., & McFeely, W. S. (1969). *The black man in the land of equality.* New York: Hayden Book Co.

Linn, R. (1982). Ability testing: Individual differences, predicting and differential prediction. *Ability Testing: Part II. Uses, consequences and controversies.* Washington, DC: National Academy of Sciences Press.

Maquet, J. J. (1968). *The premise of inequality in Ruanda.* London: Oxford University Press.

Marshall, R. F. (1968). lndustrialization and race relations in the southern United States. In L. A. Ferman, J. L. Kornbluh, & J. A. Miller (Eds.), *Negroes and jobs.* Ann Arbor: University of Michigan Press.

Marshall, R. F., & Briggs, Jr, V. M. (1966). *The Negro and apprenticeship.* Baltimore: The Johns Hopkins University Press.

Means, J. E. (1968). Fair employment practices legislation and enforcement in the United States. In L. A. Ferman, J. L. Kornbluh, & J. A. Miller, (Eds.), *Negroes and jobs* (pp. 458–496). Ann Arbor: The University of Michigan Press.

Musgrove, F. (1953). Education and the culture concept. *Africa, 23,* 110–126.

Myrdal, G. (1944). *An American dilemma: The Negro problem and modern demomocracy.* New York: Harper.

Nadel, S. F. (1954). Caste and government in primitive society. *Journal of Anthropological Society of Bombay, 8,* 9–22.

Newman, D. K. (1979). Underclass: An appraisal. In C. V. Willie (Ed.), *Caste and class controversy.* New York: General Hall.

Norgren, P. H., & Hill, S. E. (1964). *Toward fair employment.* New York: Columbia University Press.

Oakland Tribune (1980, August 7). U.C. study on minorities in college (p. 1).

Ogbu, J. U. (1974). *The next generation: An ethnography of education in an urban neighborhood.* New York: Academic Press.

Ogbu, J. U. (1977). Racial stratification and education: The case of Stockton, California. *ICRD Bulletin, 12.*

Ogbu, J. U. (1978). *Minority education and caste: The American system in cross-cultural perspective*. New York: Academic Press.

Ogbu, J. U. (1979). Social stratification and socialization of competence. *Anthropology and Education Quarterly, 10,* 3–20.

Ogbu, J. U. (1981a). Origins of human competence: A cultural-ecological perspective. *Child Development, 52,* 413–429.

Ogbu, J. U. (1981b). Education, clientage, and social mobility: Caste and social change in the United States and Nigeria. In G. D. Berreman (Eds.), *Social inequality: Comparative and developmental approaches*. New York: Academic Press.

Ogbu, J. U. (1981c). Review of caste and class controversy. *Harvard Educational Review, 51,* 205–209.

Ogbu, J. U. (1982). Cultural discontinuities and schooling. *Anthropology and Education Quarterly, 13*(3), 290–307.

Ogbu, J. U. (1983). Minority status and schooling. *Comparative Education Review, 27*(2), 168–190.

Petroni, F. A. (1970). Uncle Toms: White stereotypes in the black movement. *Human Organization, 29,* 260–266.

Pierce, T. M., et al. (1955). *White and Negro schools in the south: An analysis of biracial education*. Englewood Cliffs, NJ: Prentice-Hall.

Ransom, R. L., & Sutch, R. (1977). *One kind of freedom: The economic consequences of emancipation*. New York: Cambridge University Press.

Reese, H. E. (1968). *Deprivation and compensatory education: A consideration*. Boston: Houghton Mifflin.

Richter, D. (1980). Further consideration of caste in West Africa: The Senufo. *Africa, 50,* 37–54.

Ross, A. M. (1967). The Negro in the American economy. In A. M. Ross & H. Hill, (Eds.), *Employment, race and poverty*. New York: Harcourt Brace Jovanovich.

Ross, A. M., & Hill, H. (Eds.). (1967). *Employment, race, and poverty: A critical study of the disadvantaged status of Negro workers from 1865 to 1965*. New York: Harcourt Brace Jovanovich.

Ross, A. R. (1973). *Negro employment in the south: Vol. 3. State and local governments*. Washington, DC: U.S. Government Printing Office.

Scribner, S., & Cole, M. (1973). Cognitive consequences of formal and informal education. *Science, 182,* 553–559.

Seagrim, G. N., & Lendon, R. J. (1980). *Furnishing the mind: A comparative study of cognitive development in central Australian Aborigines*. New York: Academic Press.

Sennett, R., & Cobb, J. (1972). *The hidden injuries of class*. New York: Random House.

Sexton, P. C. (1961). *Education and income*. New York: Viking Press.

Sexton, P. C. (1968). Schools: Broken ladder to success. In L. A. Ferman, J. L. Kornbluh, & J. A. Miller (Eds.), *Negroes and jobs*. Ann Arbor: University of Michigan Press.

Shack, W. A. (1970). *On black American values in white America: Some perspectives on the cultural aspects of learning behavior and compensatory education*. Paper prepared for Social Science Research Council: Sub-Committee on Values and Compensatory Education.

Shankoff, J. P. (1982). Biological and social factors contributing to mild mental retardation. *Placing children in special education: A strategy for equity*. Washington DC: National Academy of Sciences Press.

Sharp, D., Cole, M., & Lave, C. (1979). Education and cognitive development: The evidence from experimental research. *Monographs of the Society for Research in Child Development, 44*(1–2, Serial No. 178).

Shibutani, T., & Kwan, K. M. (1965). *Ethnic stratification: A comparative approach*. New York: MacMillan.

Sochen, J. (1972). *The unabridgeable gap: Blacks and their quest for the American dream, 1900–1930*. Chicago: Rand McNally.

Spear, A. H. (1967). *Black Chicago: The making of a Negro ghetto, 1890–1920*. Chicago: The University of Chicago Press.

Stanley, J. C. (Ed.). (1973). *Compensatory education for children, ages 2 to 8: Recent studies of educational intervention*. Baltimore, MD: Johns Hopkins University Press.

Stevenson, H. W. (1982). Influences of schooling on cognitive development. In D. A. Wagner & H. W. Stevenson (Eds.), *Cultural perspectives on child development*. San Francisco: W. H. Freeman.

Stone, C. (1948). *Black political power in America*. New York: Dell.

Thernstrom, S. (1973). *The other Bostonians: Poverty and progress in the American metropolis, 1880–1970*. Cambridge, MA: Harvard University Press.

Todd, D. M. (1977). Caste in Africa? *Africa, 47*(4), 398–412.

Travers, J. R. (1982). Testing in educational placement: Issues and evidence. *Placing children in special education: A strategy for equity*. Washington, DC: National Academy of Sciences Press.

U. S. District Court for Northern California. (1979). *Larry P. vs. Wilson Riles: Opinion.* (#C-71-2270 REP). San Francisco: Author.

van den Berghe, P. (1980). A review of "Minority Education and Caste." *Comparative Education Review, 24*, 126–130.

Vaughn, W. P. (1974). *Schools for all: The blacks and public education in the south, 1865–1877*. Lexington, KY: The University of Kentucky Press.

Vernon, P. E. (1969). *Intelligence and cultural environment*. London: Methuen and Co.

Warner, W. L. (1970). A methodological note. In St. C. Drake & H. R. Cayton (Eds.), *Black metropolis: Vol. 2. A Study of negro life in a northern city*. New York: Harper.

Warner, W. L., Havighurst, R. J., & Loeb, M. B. (1944). *Who shall be educated? The challenge of equal opportunity*. New York: Harper.

Weaver, R. C. (1948). *The Negro ghetto*. New York: Harcourt Brace Jovanovich.

Weinberg, M. (1977). *A chance to learn: A history of race and education in the United States*. New York: Cambridge University Press.

White, B. L. (1979). *The origins of human competence*. Lexington, MA: D. C. Heath.

White, S. H., et al. (1973). *Federal programs for young children: Review and recommendations: Vol. 1. Goals and standards of public programs for children*. Washington, DC: U.S. Government Printing Office.

Wigdor, A. K., & Garner, W. R. (Eds.). (1982a). *Ability testing: Uses, consequences, and controversies* (Part 1). Washington, DC: National Academy Press.

Wigdor, A. K., & Garner, W. R. (Eds.). (1982b). *Placing children in special education: A strategy for equity*. Washington, DC: National Academy Press.

Williams, R. L. (1972). *The Bitch Test (Black Intelligence Test of Cultural Homogeneity)*. St. Louis, MO: Black Studies Program, Washington University.

Williams, R. L. (1972). Scientific racism and IQ: The mugging of the black community. *Psychology, 101*, 32–41.

Williams, T. R. (1972). *Introduction to socialization: Human culture transmitted*. St. Louis, MO: Mosby Co.

Wilson, W. J. (1978). *The declining significance of race: Blacks and changing American institutions*. Chicago: University of Chicago Press.

Wilson, W. J. (1980). *Race, class and public policy in education*. Unpublished lecture prepared for the National Institute of Education Vera Brown Memorial Seminar Series, Washington, DC.

Yeakey, C. C., & Johnson, G. S. (1979). Review of minority education and caste. *American Journal of Orthopsychiatry, 49*, 353–359.

Reflections on the Concept of Risk for Developmental Retardation: A Summary

JAMES D. MCKINNEY

Assessing Risk

Much of the research on risk in intellectual development has been based on the assumption that accurate identification of children at risk will lead to effective primary prevention programs that reduce the prevalance of mental retardation and other developmental disorders. However, in order for intervention to be feasible and cost-effective, it must be targeted to that segment of the population that has the highest probability of actually developing the disorders one is trying to prevent. Unfortunately, as Haskins and Ramey and MacPhee point out in their chapters, one of the conclusions to be drawn from the research to date is that the methods used for assessing risk remain imprecise.

Early research on risk was guided by the hypothesis that biomedical factors associated with the birth process are directly related to later developmental outcomes. The "continuum of reproductive casualty" was advanced as a concept to describe a range of perinatal conditions that are correlated with a variety of intellectual and psychosocial disorders (Pasamanick & Knoblock, 1961). However, as illustrated in the chapter by Werner, the relationship between perinatal risk factors and later developmental problems is far from direct. Indeed, it is highly questionable beyond the first 2 years of life unless psychosocial risk factors (such as poverty status and/or an unstable family environment) are also present. Moreover, as Haskins and Ramey and MacPhee note in their chapters, the highest prevalence of mental retardation and other developmental problems occur in lower-SES (socioeconomic status) groups; the bulk of these negative outcomes cannot be attributed to serious biomedical complications during the perinatal period.

The failure of traditional biomedical risk models to account for the resistance of most children to perinatal stress, coupled with the need to account for the influence of SES, has stimulated research to identify psychosocial factors in the early childrearing environment that might place the child at risk. Based on their review of longitudinal evidence concerning the importance of biomedical risk factors, Sameroff and Chandler (1975) introduced the concept of a "continuum of caretaking casualty" to describe a range of developmental problems that could be attributed to poor parenting. In this volume, Haskins reviews research on a number of differences in the childrearing practices of lower and middle class parents that have been associated with subaverage intellectual development. Also, Werner cites evidence from her studies on the role of parental mental illness and family disorganization as risk factors.

The concept of caretaking casualty has resulted in a better understanding of the specific processes within families that produce the link between SES and inadequate development. However, when applied to the phenomenon of risk, it has suffered from many of the same limitations inherent in the concept of reproductive casualty. As Werner's chapter emphasized, many children who suffer environmental stresses, such as inadequate parenting and family disorganization, are nevertheless still resistant to these stresses, and display positive outcomes. Thus, neither the presence of biomedical risk factors alone, nor the presence of psychosocial risk factors alone, has been sufficient to account for the majority of deviant outcomes in a given study when each domain of risk factors has been considered singly.

The recognition of this limitation of early either–or main effect models has led investigators such as Sameroff and Chandler (1975) to hypothesize that outcome is the joint product or interaction of both sources of stress. Thus, a child may be considered to be vulnerable as the result of perinatal stress, but resistant to negative outcomes to the extent that his/her environment provides a compensating influence. This insight has led to the concept of "transactional processes" in which environmental factors are viewed as either maximizing or minimizing the effects of perinatal stress. However, the problem remains to specify how such transactions occur to either enhance or decrease the probability of unfavorable outcomes.

Transactional Processes

Considerable progress in understanding the nature of transactional processes was made by Werner and her colleagues' study of the children of Kauai. This study and others reviewed by Sameroff (1982) and Sameroff and Seifer (1983) suggest that the environment served to activate or suppress natural self-righting tendencies or coping strategies in the individual which offset early stress. They agree that this process is analogous to the way in which genetic forces regulate biological development. Thus, in conceptualizing developmental risk, the characteristics of the child must be considered in relation to factors in the environment that influence the course of his/her development. For example, in this volume, Werner observes that, independent of social class, infants with difficult temperaments, who are reared in unstable homes by distressed caretakers, are more likely to develop serious disorders than those who are rewarding to their caretakers and live in stable, supportive homes.

Accordingly, a major advance in the conceptualization of risk has come with the realization that the interaction between the child and the environment is bidirectional (Bell, 1968; Ramey, MacPhee, & Yeates, 1982; Sameroff, 1979). Thus, it has become apparent that the child modifies his/her environment at the same time the environment acts on the child.

In this regard, it is interesting to note that although interpersonal attributes, such as temperament, linguistic competence, self-esteem, and locus of control can be viewed as outcome variables, the evidence offered by Werner and by Ramey and MacPhee suggest that they may be important factors in the definition of the risk equation itself. In Werner's discussion of resilient children, she concludes that children who are successful in eliciting predominantly positive responses from their environment are stress-resistant, even when they experience severe perinatal stress and poverty. Thus, as Ramey and MacPhee persuasively argue, in order to understand, and thereby predict, *changes* in risk status, one must not only consider the sources and severity of the various stresses in the child's life, but also the built-in resistances of the individual as he/she interacts with supporting elements of the environment.

Complexities in Determining Risk

Finally, because it is generally recognized that the environment is an important variable in the assessment of risk, it is unfortunate that the environment has not been assessed more adequately in risk research.

Most of the research in this area has employed very global measures, such as SES level or poverty status, to assess the quality of the child's social environment. As both Haskins and Ogbu argue, drawing inferences about the quality of children's environment from gross measures of SES level can be very misleading, given the substantial variation that exists in the childrearing practices and cultural values of parents in this group. Nonetheless, it is evident that certain family factors and ecological processes are more likely to induce a state of risk for subnormal intellectual development than others. To the extent that these factors can be measured directly, as opposed to inferred from gross socioeconomic indexes, the assessment of risk status could be improved. Although many of the elements of the general systems theory proposed by Ramey and MacPhee remain unspecified, it is encouraging to note that they approach the issue of environmental variation in a comprehensive fashion that encompasses the child's larger social context as well as the immediate caretaking situation.

In sum, the concept of risk as we know it today is far more complex than was envisioned in the 1960s and 1970s. The chapters in this section imply that in order to understand the interplay of forces that produce developmental retardation, we must first describe the constitutional and biomedical integrity of the child and document fully whatever difficulties exist in his/her environment. Next, we must specify how these processes interact over development to influence the self-righting properities of the individual. Without operationalizing and understanding all of these processes, it is doubtful that we will achieve the ultimate goal of cost-effective primary prevention.

References

Bell, R. Q. (1968). A reinterpretation of the direction of effects in studies of socialization. *Psychological Review*, 75, 81–95.

Pasamanick, B., & Knoblock, H. (1961). Epidemiologic studies on the complications of pregnancy and the birth process. In G. Caplin (Ed.), *Prevention of mental disorders in children*. New York: Basic.

Ramey, C. T., MacPhee, D., & Yeates, K. O. (1982). Preventing developmental retardation: A general systems model. In L. A. Bond, & J. M. Joffee (Eds.), *Facilitating infant and early childhood development*. Hanover, NH: University Press of New England.

Sameroff, A. J. (1979). The etiology of cognitive competence: A systems perspective. In R. B. Kearsley & I. E. Siegel (Eds.), *Infants at risk: Assessment of cognitive functioning*. Hillsdale, NJ: Erlbaum.

Sameroff, A. J. (1982). Development and the dialectic: The need for a systems approach. In W. A. Collins (Ed.), *Minnesota symposium on child psychology (Vol. 15)*. Hillsdale, NJ: Erlbaum.

Sameroff, A., & Chandler, M. J. (1975). Reproductive risk and the continuum of caretaking casualty. In F. D. Horowitz, M. Hetherington, S. Scarr-Salapatek, & G. Siegel (Eds.), *Review of child development research (Vol. 4)*. Chicago: University of Chicago Press.

Sameroff, A. J., & Seifer, R. (1983). Familial risk and child competence. *Child Development, 54*, 1254–1268.

PART II

Risk in Psychosocial Development

6

Psychopathology and Preventive Intervention in Infancy: A Clinical Developmental Research Approach*

STANLEY I. GREENSPAN

Introduction

Mental health research is, in part, struggling with an appropriate scientific identity. One school of thought would see the appropriate role of research as the study of answerable questions—that is, the researcher's job is to select only those hypotheses that are testable with current methods. Another view, one that I believe is more in keeping with the historical values of our field, is that the appropriate starting point for research in mental health and illness are the clinically challenging questions, regardless of their complexity and the methods available to answer these questions. This view suggests an approach to research which does not start with an answerable question or a testable hypothesis, but at an earlier point in the development of knowledge—with the challenge of discovery to find the most relevant hypotheses and to develop the methods to test them. These different views are related to different traditions. One behavioral science tradition has focused on studying functional relationships between predefined groups of measurable variables. The value of this approach is that one knows in ad-

*Presented as the Edward A. Strecker lecture, November 12, 1982.

vance that one will clearly get a result. The functional relationship will or will not be demonstrated. As is well known, however, what is measurable may not always be meaningful and what is meaningful may not always be measurable. Therefore, the danger in this approach is that it either avoids areas of relevance to clinical practice or may study some problems in an oversimplified or even misleading manner.

The clinical descriptive and psychodynamic tradition, in contrast, begins not with preconceived notions of relevant or measurable variables, but seeks to describe complex naturally occurring phenomena. Then through a series of gradual approximations, it attempts to abstract meaningful patterns, to classify these patterns, and to describe their vicissitudes under natural and other conditions (e.g., intervention conditions). While a special asset of this approach is the opportunity it affords to discover phenomena relevant to challenging clinical problems (e.g., discovering and classifying new syndromes), it also has an important limitation. One is betting on the ingenuity of the investigator to describe the phenomena and recognize the patterns. There is no guarantee that useful descriptions, abstractions, patterns, and subsequent classifications will occur.

Both approaches are obviously necessary to study complex mental health problems. These approaches may be integrated through the following sequence:

1. Describe the complex natural, clinically relevant phenomena
2. Abstract relevant patterns (e.g., identify the relevant variables)
3. Develop useful classification systems (e.g., further modification, definition, and grouping of the relevant variables)
4. Develop instruments and protocols to recognize, measure, or quantify the aforementioned relevant variables and dynamics (Note: One should not avoid the challenge by developing instruments to measure factors less significant and relevant because they are easier to develop and validate.);
5. Describe variations in these classified patterns under natural and special (e.g., intervention) conditions
6. Develop new, special conditions (e.g., intervention) at a descriptive level that, on a case-by-case basis, appear to shift patterns toward more optimal configurations
7. Study the functional relationships between these new *clinically relevant*, predefined, measurable variables. (For example, studies would include such functional relationships as those between etiological variables and syndromes, treatment approaches and outcomes, and interrelationships among pathologic and adaptive patterns at biological, behavioral, experiential and environmental levels.)

The exploration of these functional relationships would be divided into two components:

1. **Basic Research** which looks at relationships among
   a. Etiological variables and syndromes
   b. Antecedent developmental patterns and disordered functioning
   c. Mechanisms responsible for disordered functioning at biological, behavioral, and experiential levels
   d. Mechanisms responsible for adaptive functioning at biological, behavioral, and experiential levels
   e. Approaches with and mechanisms of action of various therapeutic agents and improving adaptive functioning and reversing pathologic trends.
2. **Applied Treatment and/or Preventive Intervention Research**[1] (e.g., clinical trials), which looks at relationships among
   a. Defined interventions and clinically valid outcomes
   b. No intervention or hypothesized less-optimal intervention and outcomes
   c. Intervention process steps and outcomes
   d. Developmental level of patient's personality, diagnosis.

Clinical Mental Health Approaches to Infants and Their Families

As I approached the area of mental health problems in infancy and early childhood some 6 years ago, I was influenced by this framework. Where within these steps was I in my knowledge of clinical approaches to diagnosis, prevention, and treatment? Did I have sufficient knowledge of the way in which patterns were organized, and therefore could be classified and measured, in order to study functional relationships, or did I need to start at a descriptive level and immerse myself in complex clinical phenomena and bet that the clinical researcher's green thumb would lead to the extraction of meaningful patterns and techniques and the development of new methods? I was influenced by what I felt to be premature attempts at narrowing the field of observation in work with infants and their families. There were programs, for example, that intervened or that measured outcomes but looked at only one dimension of development. Often, sensorimotor or cognitive development, or aspects of social adaptation were the focus, and investigators ignored in-depth emotional and psychological features of development, as well as family

[1]See Greenspan and Sharfstein, 1981, for further discussion.

functioning. I reasoned that if the areas of development most sensitive to the preventive intervention concerned the formation of human relationships and the development of affective coping strategies, then assessments that looked only at cognition or limited aspects of social adaptation might be like the proverbial drunk looking under the street light for his wallet when he had left it in the dark across the street.

We were also struck by the fact that many programs seemed to be grouping participants, both infants and families, into pseudohomogeneous groups based on somewhat undifferentiated criteria. Parents and children might be grouped according to educational and economic status or other demographic variables, with little attention given to their clinical condition (i.e., the presence or absence of psychopathology) even though clinical status often accounts for much of the variance in most areas of functioning. In talking with front-line workers in such programs, it became clear that in some day care, or educational programs, they were aware of a subgroup that they "couldn't get to," who were "unmotivated," or "the mother seemed strange and would never come in and cooperate." This seemingly high, high-risk group within the general risk population would tend to pull down the group's scores and give the appearance that a particular intervention was ineffective. Not having used clinical dimensions to categorize the participants, it would then be difficult, after the fact, to subgroup the participants and include these high, high-risk individuals into a separate group. In fact, in many programs there have been no systematic ratings, even of the "difficult behavior they presented" (U.S. Department of Health, Education, and Welfare, 1979). Even more challenging was the common complaint: "We aren't trained or equipped to deal with some of these families. They need much more than we can offer." The difficult high, high-risk families not only received little help, but also tended to overwhelm the staff, leading to confusion, which compromised the staff's work with less-disordered families. Yet there was little planning on how to be helpful to these families or often even acknowledgment of their existence and clinical needs.

Even more compelling were the observations that are discussed later on, that these high, high-risk families often had multiple risk factors, had many children that evidenced impaired functioning quite early in life, were themselves the product of multiproblem families (suggesting an intergenerational pattern) and appeared to constitute the 5–10% of the population that were perhaps the biggest public health challenge, using 50–75% of all public health, mental health, and social services.

With some of these challenges in mind, my colleagues and I attempted to define an approach to infants and families which we called a

Clinical Developmental Approach. It was very important to define the scope and research agenda of a clinical development approach to infants and their families so that the range of variables we would need to attend to would be explicit from the beginning.

Clinical Development Approaches to Infants and Their Families[2]

This section summarizes the chief theoretical assumption underlying a clinical approach; demonstrates the ways in which these assumptions affect the approaches to diagnosis, prevention, and treatment of mental health problems in infants and their families; and sets forth an agenda for research designed to delineate adaptive and maladaptive patterns of development and potentially useful approaches to clinical services.

Theoretical Perspectives

The assumption that human development involves multiple, interrelated lines of development, rather than single unrelated sequences, forms the basis for a clinical approach. Included, for example, are physical and neurological growth, cognitive or intellectual development, the development of human relationships, and the capacity to organize and differentiate experience (coping and adaptive capacities).

An intervention strategy that takes into account the existence of multiple lines of development will approach a presenting problem in ways that will facilitate crucial development in all areas of the infant's life. For example, babies who have been nutritionally compromised improve physically and gain weight more efficaciously when nutrition is provided together with adequate social interaction. A baby born with an auditory and/or tactile hypersensitivity will tend to withdraw when held or talked to. A clinical approach would combine gentle exposure to the potentially noxious stimuli, in low doses with soothing experiences, such as rocking, and soothing sounds. At the same time, recognizing the youngster's tendency to withdraw, the clinical staff might formulate special patterns of care that would help the parents woo this baby into greater emotional relatedness.

In contrast, an approach that focused only on cognitive stimulation might attempt to enliven a withdrawn, seemingly slow baby through sensorimotor stimulation. Yet if a youngster actually has an undiagnosed sensory hypersensitivity, he or she could become even more irri-

[2]Much of this section may be found in Greenspan, 1980.

table and less available for human relationships as a consequence of this type of intervention.

Furthermore, failure to consider multiple lines of development in infancy may lead to impairment at a later age. In general, a youngster who responds to human stimulation with irritability, rigidity, and gaze aversion may very well be alert and show interest in the inanimate world with inanimate stimulation. From the point of view of physical and neurological development, such a youngster might develop adequate cognition during the first 12 to 18 months. However, the development of human relationships and the capacity to organize and differentiate animate experience (coping and adapting skills) might be severely impaired, although such impairments might not become clearly noticeable until the latter part of the second or early in the third year. It is during this period when relationships with peers become important, that complaints related to unsocialized behavior or patterns of withdrawal (refusal to play with others) are heard from parents.

The second assumption that forms the basis for a clinical approach views the infant in a context that includes not only his or her own developmental lines of development but also his or her mother, father, other family members, and relevant social structures. This might be termed an *interactional* (as opposed to an isolated) *approach*. An interactional approach would consider and work with, for example, the parents' predominant attitudes and feelings, with family relationships, and other crucial contextual factors, such as the system of health and mental health services and relevant community structures. More isolated intervention strategies, while working, for example, to stimulate an infant's cognitive capacities, may limit parental involvement to being auxiliary cognitive stimulators, or may limit intervention with parents to help only with issues such as food and housing.

Diagnosis and Treatment

The varying assumptions underlying clinical approaches to intervention and developmental facilitation result, not surprisingly, in differing diagnostic and treatment strategies. The complete diagnostic and comprehensive treatment approach contrasts sharply with the problem-oriented approach. The latter would formulate a diagnosis based simply on the clustering of symptoms or certain types of problems, whereas a complete diagnostic evaluation would include the assessment of each line of development in the context of an individual, family, and social system.

For example, a youngster who is regurgitating his or her feedings might be diagnosed from the purely symptomatic point of view as having an allergic reaction to certain foods or a congenitally spastic upper gastrointestinal (GI) tract. Medication to relax the tension in the tract, as well as a search for less allergenic foods, might be presented as a solution. A more complete diagnostic approach, however, would, in addition, study (1) the infant's physical and neurological development (including possible allergic reactions to feedings and/or anatomical or reactive differences in the upper GI tract); (2) the youngster's overall cognitive intellectual level of functioning; (3) his or her pattern of human relationships; (4) the way he or she organizes and differentiates experience (his or her coping capacity); and (5) his or her family and social context.

One might find, for example, that the youngster is generally tense, and although 6 months old, is not yet involved in a deep, rich, pleasurable attachment to his or her mother. She holds the infant rigidly and distantly, tension arises each time intimacy is tried, and feeding is experienced by both mother and infant as less than satisfying. During these times of enforced intimacy, there may be extraordinary rigidity of the child's entire voluntary musculoskeletal system, with occasional diarrhea and the noted regurgitation. If no specific difficulties were found in terms of allergic reaction, the therapeutic plan might focus on improving the overall nature of the infant's relationship to mother, and attempting to understand and alleviate the tension expressed through regurgitation. Even if a tendency toward spasticity of the GI tract were noted, this might be seen as a sensitivity that could be reversed by improving functioning along another line—that is, the development of positive human relationships and the capacity for organizing emotional experience, which, secondarily, might help this youngster regulate her- or himself, including relaxing his or her GI system.

In addition, if concrete issues around housing, food, employment, or the availability of appropriate health care were undermining the development of appropriate human relationships, these factors would require serious attention. While social and economic factors are often not quickly reversible, a clinical approach must seek to optimize the family's capacity to use available services.

The clinical approach thus translates its complex diagnosis into a comprehensive plan for treatment or preventive intervention. It includes working with the infant in the context of the social world of his or her family and the larger context, involving the collaboration of the health, mental health, social service, and often the legal systems.

An Agenda of Research

The assumptions that distinguish clinical from other approaches also suggest certain research strategies which, emerging from the context of clinical work, are likely to be (1) clinically useful (i.e., for interventive planning); (2) discriminative of subtle differences in the range of functioning observed (particularly in the high-risk, multiproblem population); and (3) sensitive to social and cultural differences.

Ideally, clinically relevant research concerning infancy should strike a balance between the comparatively easier-to-study problems that involve single (or even multiple), but readily identifiable risk factors and related conditions, and the more complicated situations that involve multiple risk factors in the context of complex developmental and social problems. For example, developing a research strategy to study the developmental patterns associated with prematurity, low birth weight, or early chronic medical illness, while challenging, may be relatively easy in comparison to developing research strategies for understanding developmental variations, clinical and service requirements, and the relative efficacy of preventive intervention strategies for the most high-risk groups of multirisk, multiproblem infants and their families.

An approach to studying these more complex questions involves a number of steps and a series of gradual approximations to tease out the relevant groups of variables and their potential relationships. Rather than attempting to acquire instant understanding of functional relationships between groups of variables (e.g., etiological variables and disordered functioning, or treatment variables and outcome), such an approach would try to obtain a greater understanding of (1) the nature of the disorders and their course during development, (2) the preventive and treatment strategies required, and (3) the ones most likely to be successful. More classical preventive studies would constitute a fourth stage of research.

Therefore, the first step would require investigators to understand the range in variation of adaptive and disordered functioning in infants, toddlers, young children, and their families along multiple developmental lines. It is especially important to obtain an understanding of the range and variation of these patterns in the most high-risk populations, including groups whose members traditionally do not come for services in routine settings and usually do not participate in research studies. Often, it is only possible to reach them by offering innovative services that will enlist their cooperation, and by providing a setting that will allow one to observe how development unfolds in an interactive service context. Even then, the challenge is great. Without understanding the ranges and variations in developmental patterns in these infants, toddlers, and their families, one has no way of knowing the natural history (in a relative sense) of an important host of disorders.

Step two would entail gaining an understanding of both the clinical techniques and the service system strategies required in relationship to the preceding developmental patterns and interactions. For example, what clinical strategies are required for the hyperactive or labile infant who has difficulty in focusing concentration, or for the infant who tends toward withdrawal and apathy and has difficulty alerting to routine auditory and visual stimuli, or for the infant with special tactile auditory or visual sensitivities, or for the infant who at 3 or 4 months is evidencing muscle rigidity and severe gaze aversion in relation to the human world? To complicate matters further, what clinical strategy is required to work with the aforementioned withdrawn infant with a similarly withdrawn and depressed mother, who feels helpless and inadequate, who interprets her baby's behavior as further evidence that she is worthless, and who therefore becomes immobilized and unable to try to find a way to reach out and interest her infant in her world? What clinical strategy is suggested for the hyperactive, unfocused infant whose father has paranoid ideation, views his baby's lability as an aggressive attack, and perceives anyone who is interested in his baby, such as a pediatrician or a clinical program for infants and their families, as his enemies?

At the service system level, what type of interagency collaboration and pattern of care is most useful for the recently discharged chronic schizophrenic mother who intermittently loses the capacity for reality testing and may not always be able to attend to the most basic needs of her infant for physical care and protection? How does one involve the protective service, social service, and/or foster care system in the context of a service system approach that is in the best interest of the infant? What type of service system approach is necessary for the youngster with early nonspecific lags in sensorimotor development, or for the neglectful and intermittently abusing family that has given up some children to foster care and is intermittently using the foster care system for their newest infant? Multiproblem families with infants or worrisome constitutional and early developmental patterns may involve a dozen or more agencies in ways sufficiently fragmented to parallel the fragmentation that already exists in the family.

A third step in research, once the developmental variations and the range of clinical and service requirements are identified, is the in-depth study on a case-by-case basis of optimal clinical and service system strategies and their relative efficacy. Case studies may often be thought to yield data of low reliability and generalizability. Yet, where the state of knowledge is such that the natural history of disordered functioning is not yet known, and only a handful of detailed, in-depth clinical studies exists in the literature, the case study becomes a crucial first step toward gaining an in-depth understanding of the nature of maladaptive and adaptive functioning in various multiple-risk families and toward developing reasonable hypotheses regarding the types of clinical and service system experience required and likely to work. Optimally, general principles would be abstracted from such in-depth studies to form the basis of a new clinical science of preventive intervention.

Those who argue that the state of knowledge has passed the case-study method have the obligation to provide a body of clinical literature that delineates from physical, cognitive, and social–emotional perspectives the variations in developmental patterns in multiproblem, multiple risk-factor (*multirisk*) families and the clinical and service system strategies found to be most successful. What, for example, is the course of development in the labile, distractible infant with an auditory hypersensitivity and a paranoid father? What types of clinical strategies have been found most successful? In how many cases? Such a collection of reported clinical experiences is not available. While there have been some studies of this population, by and large they have not included an in-depth understanding of the developmental patterns of infants along multiple lines. There is a great deal of fragmented clinical information (e.g., on the family but not on the infant development; or on one aspect of infant development, but not another). While hypotheses abound, the most relevant types of hypotheses and first-order constructs are still being formulated.

After the preceding three areas are more fully explored, it will become possible to conduct classical prospective studies that look for functional relationships between treatment, etiological, and developmental factors and outcomes at various stages of development. These types of studies, it must be emphasized, are only possible when a field has reached the point where there are useful functional categories. For example, categories of risk factors must be understood in the context of the range and variations of adaptive and disordered development. A typology of disordered functioning along multiple developmental lines must be formulated. Such a typology, which would be based on developmental patterns, is unlikely to fall along the lines of diagnostic classifications. Using existing classification schemes where such schemes are not applicable may only confuse rather than clarify functional relationships. Similarly, to conduct treatment assessment research, the most likely efficacious clinical and service strategies must first be clearly documented.

Therefore, a fourth level of study involves the more classically designed longitudinal studies of the efficacy of treatment and the relationship between the various etiological and developmental factors and outcome. There is a tendency to study only those problems that lend themselves to this fourth level, rather than to conduct the exploratory studies that will permit addressing the most compelling problems that occur in naturalistic settings.

New research approaches are required to assess capacities for the development of human relationships and for organizing and differentiating experience, especially in the affective sphere. These much needed approaches, however, are most likely to emerge from clinical research programs working with the populations that demonstrate the range and variations in functioning for which new assessment approaches are required. Approaches that emerge from relevant contexts are also likely (1) to prove clinically useful, as mentioned earlier; (2) to allow observation of subtle differences in functioning; and (3) to consider social and cultural differences.

While the types of studies relating to the preceding three issues are often thought of as exploratory, they constitute a most basic kind of clinical and service-relevant research. They are basic in a sense that they delineate, perhaps for the first time, the patterns of development in certain infants, children, and their families, and they describe clinical and service requirements related to these developmental patterns. The preceding approach is based on the assumption that one must begin to study a new field through a series of gradual approximations. It is a serious error to apply research designs that assume an understanding of relevant groups of variables, when we have not yet identified the most relevant variables from the perspective of etiology, developmental patterns, and prevention and treatment approaches.

The Clinical Infant Development Program

Using the preceding definitions, assumptions, and research agenda, my colleagues and I realized we were at the beginning of the research sequence discussed earlier. We therefore developed a study to describe the characteristics and to classify the patterns of a range of infants and their families. We wanted to examine on a case-by-case basis their service needs and the clinical techniques likely to be helpful, and to observe on a case-by-case basis which clinical techniques and service approaches worked best. Finally, we wanted to develop a data base that would also lend itself to looking at functional relationships between treatment, techniques, process, outcome etiological factors, and antecedent developmental patterns and subsequent adaptive and maladaptive functioning.

We decided to cast a wide net and work with a large population, including what we have called "multirisk" and others have called multiproblem families and their infants, as well as groups of relatively more competent infants and their families. While it is not possible to review the research in detail here (for an account of our theoretical and descriptive studies see Greenspan 1979, 1981; Greenspan, Nover, & Scheuer, 1984; Greenspan & Porges, 1984; and Greenspan & Wieder, 1984), I would like to touch on three aspects of the work. The first is what motivated this work, aside from the preceding research issues. While we wanted to focus on a wide range of infants and families, we were especially interested in including the multirisk and multiproblem families because of the major public health challenge they present. Therefore, there is a discussion of infant morbidity in the multiproblem family with some preliminary impressions about the compelling nature of the challenge these infants and families present. Based on clinical experience with a range of infants and families, a developmental model was formulated. There is a discussion of this model, which attempts to classify adaptive and disordered infant and family patterns for each phase of infancy and early childhood. Following this, there is a discussion of some of the principles of preventive intervention that have developed from our work (see Greenspan, 1981, for detailed discussion).

Infant Morbidity and the Multirisk
(Multiple Risk-Factor) Family[3]

The focus of this section is on the risk of infant morbidity in multirisk families, particularly psychological, social, and cognitive malfunction. My colleagues and I in the Clinical Infant Development Program (CIDP) at the Mental Health Study Center of the National Institute of Mental Health (NIMH) in Adelphi, Maryland, have been able to obtain an in-depth picture of the unfolding of infant morbidity in the multirisk family. Families are referred to the center because of severe interferences with their capacity to provide primary and secondary maternal functions for their children, as indicated by demonstrated difficulty in rearing an older child who is manifesting severe psychological, social, and cognitive problems.

[3]Much of the material in this section was presented at the National Health Policy Forum at The George Washington University on February 5, 1982.

We use the term *multirisk families* for those not only at risk of infant mortality and perinatal morbidity, but also for those in which the children appear to be at risk of developmental morbidity. Our clinical impression is that families at the high-risk end of the spectrum in respect to any single risk factor (e.g., substance abuse or poor nutrition) often evidence multirisk factors. Such families have also been described as "multiproblem," "hard to reach," "crisis-oriented," and so forth (Buell, 1952; Curtis, Simon, Boykin, & Noe, 1964; Geismar & La Sorte, 1964; Minuchin & Montalvo, 1967a, 1967b; Pavenstedt, 1967; Riessman, 1964; Riessman, Cohen, & Pearl, 1964; Zilbach, 1971). In addition, they have been classified by the way they use the service system and according to the kinds and number of problems they have. Results of the latter approach suggest that poverty or welfare status is not the only identifying characteristic, because families across the socioeconomic strata evidence the same multiproblem characteristics (Mazer, 1972).

In spite of definitional differences, there has been general consensus on the clinical characteristics of these families. They tend, for example, to think only in concrete terms, to be need oriented, and to have difficulty in anticipating the future and conceptualizing the consequences of their actions. The parents operate on a survival basis, often competing with their children for concrete, as well as psychological and social supports (Geismar, 1968; LaVietes, 1974; Levine, 1964; McMahon, 1964; Minuchin & Montalvo, 1967a, 1967b; Pavenstedt, 1967; Zilbach, 1971). Although most of the families have these characteristics, an individual family may differ in some respects. Some of the families evidence clearly diagnosable mental illness such as a psychosis, and some, a predominance of severe antisocial and asocial personality patterns. Others are characterized by passivity and inadequacy in coping with life's daily challenges. Individual clusters of symptomatic behaviors also characterize the families—psychotic symptoms, child abuse, spouse abuse, marital difficulties, crime, delinquency, alcoholism, physical illness, and suicide (Buell, 1952; Geismar & La Sorte, 1964; Mazer, 1972; Minuchin & Montalvo, 1967a; Pavenstedt, 1967).

While for the most part, these families have been thought of as a social problem, careful psychiatric and psychosocial evaluations of our population revealed a high incidence of psychiatric disturbance and history of impaired psychosocial functioning (Jasnow, Wieder, & Greenspan, 1982). Estimates vary regarding the use of health, social services, and welfare systems by these families. However, the significance of the challenge that they present is indicated by a study conducted some time ago (Buell, 1952), in which 6% of the study population was found to be using 45% of all public health resources and 55% of all social, psychiatric, and other auxiliary services. It has been estimated that this 6% uses approximately 70% of all public expenditures for health, social, and auxiliary services (report of the congressionally authorized Joint Commission on the Mental Health of Children, 1965). Moreover, the problem may be much greater now.

Children in Multirisk Families

Few in-depth studies have been conducted of the development of the children in multirisk families. In the classical descriptive study of Pavenstedt (1967), only 13 of such families (which had 40 to 50 children between the ages of $2\frac{1}{2}$ and 6 years) were studied. Nevertheless, the clinical impressions from the study were striking. Almost all the children showed social and psychological characteristics more consistent with $1\frac{1}{2}$ to 2-year-olds in their egocentricity and need orientation. Their ability to use a symbolic (or representational) mode to plan for their own needs and to consider the needs and actions of others was limited, and they had variable self-esteem. They tended to think in fragmented, isolated units rather than in cohesive patterns. They were not capable of goal-directed, organized action and were limited in their ability to socialize and interact appropriately for their age. The children already had an ingrained defeatist attitude and the core of an aimless (either asocial or antisocial) personality. The conclusion of the study was that there was a dire need to understand the developmental process in such children from the prenatal stage into later childhood.

Subsequently, no in-depth longitudinal studies have been done beginning with the prenatal period and following the children in multirisk families for 5 or more years, as is necessary to obtain information on how the behavioral patterns of these children develop and to gain insight into the repetitive, multigenerational nature of these families' problems. It seemed especially critical to identify the adaptive and maladaptive developmental patterns of such children and their families over time and to determine the clinical and service system techniques that are appropriate for preventive intervention. Therefore, my colleagues and I undertook a study of multirisk families. We provided periodic evaluations of the children in such families, based on standardized tests and naturalistic clinical and standardized recorded observations (for example, videotapes of interactions between the children and their caregivers). We have been able to study in depth for 2 or more years some 50 multirisk families with more than 200 children. Except for a few brief comments, details of the efforts made to recruit these families and of the clinical service approaches and assessments used are described elsewhere.

A family was referred to the program if it met three criteria: (1) a history of difficulty in providing basic nurturing for an older child and in facilitating that child's development, (2) evidence of disturbed development in that older child, and (3) limitations in the mother's current functioning that could be expected to interfere with the provision of care to a new infant.

In order to study these families, we recognized that the biggest challenge was involving multirisk families in a clinical services research effort. Historically, such families have remained outside the service system and have not volunteered for research studies. They rarely come for appointments and have learned to distrust traditional service providers. Therefore, extensive outreach approaches, including numerous home visits, clinicians stationed at prenatal clinics, work with protective service and other social service agencies, was a first step.

Agencies were alerted to send us their most difficult and challenging cases. We became known in the community as the group that would go anywhere to see anyone. Shortly, we were getting calls from prenatal clinics regarding mothers who had missed appointments, appeared confused, were not adequately following medical guidance, and who either where protective-service workers were involved with a family because of neglect of an older child, or in which the mother was pregnant again, evidenced a lack of interest in their yet unborn babies.

The key to recruitment and forming an alliance with these families was the staff's ability to deal with patterns of avoidance, rejection, anger, illogical and antisocial behavior, and substance abuse. Experienced clinicians were selected in part for their ability not to be frightened by such behavior. For example, in the early phases of the work it might be necessary for the primary clinician on a case to make 5–6 home visits, knock on the door, hear a very suspicious participant behind the door walking around, make a few comments through the door, not get an answer, and then return 3 days later and continue that pattern until the individual on the other side of the door would feel comfortable enough to open the door and let the primary clinician in. This pattern might repeat itself intermittently for a number of months. Even more difficult were participants who eagerly embraced the offering of services and who then would flee by missing 3 or 4 appointments, including not calling or returning telephone calls. The continual offering of an interested ear would in most cases eventually meet with success. Sometimes it could take a year, however, before a constant pattern of relatedness would evolve. The tendency to say "they're not interested in help," "they told us they don't want us," "they're not motivated," "we're being a burden to them," "we're making them more crazy," and so forth was one of the key challenges our staff had to overcome to work with individuals who in the past had not been offered services in a way that they could take advantage of them.

The second step in the approach was to develop a regular pattern of services including (1) organizing service systems on behalf of their survival needs such as food, housing, and medical care; (2) developing a constant emotional relationship with the family; and (3) most importantly, at pivotal junctures when the infant's development was in jeopardy, offering highly technical patterns of care including approaches to deal with the infant's and family's individual vulnerabilities and strengths. For example, a baby with a tactile hypersensitivity, with a hyperactive, suspicious mother who tended to deal with stress by hyperstimulating her baby, would require an approach in which the baby was provided with habituation and sensory integration approaches to overcome his or her special sensitivity. The mother was simultaneously helped through psychological treatment, counseling, or guidance (Fantl, 1958), to overcome her own tendency to undermine the baby's development.

All the families in the study were offered either comprehensive service approaches including either the preceding three elements or periodic evaluations with referral to community agencies. While participants were assigned randomly, the numbers of participants in the study were small and the attrition rates in the two groups different. It was also necessary to break the randomization in special cases. In addition, the techniques for preventive intervention, while outlined in the broad sense (in terms of coordinating the social service system, offering a constant affective human relationship and then offering special techniques based on the baby's, mother's, and family's individual differences) were not completely known in advance. Specific techniques, such as how to work with an auditory hypersensitivity in a baby or how best to work with a very depressed or suspicious mother and such an infant, had not been worked out or reported in the literature; nor were the patterns of psychopathology or even the framework for describing them reported in the literature prior to this study. It was expected that the study would lead to a more explicit definition of the appropriate clinical techniques and categories of disorders.

Nonetheless all the families did receive one or the other level of services and approximately 50 families were recruited into two groups. Systematic reports of the clinical, descriptive, and quantitative data will be reported in other publications, including the affective, social, cognitive, and familial patterns of these families, their relative response to intervention, and the relationship between various prenatal and developmental patterns.

It quickly became apparent to the staff at the center that we were dealing with families of various compositions, which were evidencing many risk factors such as psychiatric impairment, low educational and socioeconomic status (SES) (not only in the case of the parents who were the potential participants in our program, but also in the case of their own parents), high levels of social and psychological stress during the woman's pregnancy, and varying degrees of nutritional deficits and substance abuse.

It also became apparent that infant morbidity, infant mortality, and perinatal morbidity all may be related to the same common factors—incapacities of the infant's caregivers for self-care, care of another, planning around a pregnancy, or a child's developmental processes. In our group of multirisk families, successful prenatal intervention reduced the expected levels both of infant mortality and of immediate postnatal morbidity; few of the babies were born with physical or neurological handicaps. Yet we quickly observed that the next challenge, and in many respects the far more difficult one, was to reduce developmental morbidity.

Preliminary Report on Observed Trends

Because I am reporting in the middle of our study, I discuss only some preliminary trends observed in a child's development. These trends are presented in a theoretical framework in which the stages of a child's early development and the adaptive infant and family patterns that can be expected in each phase of the child's development—as revealed in our work—are conceptualized, (S. Greenspan, 1979, 1981; Greenspan, Lourie, & Nover, 1979). The trends described will not necessarily apply to every multirisk family, because different families and different infants apparently experience arrest at various levels of development. Intensive work with multirisk families, however, has shown us that they rarely are able to negotiate an infant's development into the second year of life without there being evidence of disruption in their infant's development and a need for specific services to overcome it. We have been able to identify the point at which the family fails to support the infant's development and at which the subsequent disordered development occurs. We also have gained a preliminary impression of a distribution in which the more disturbed families show difficulties early in the infant's first year, whereas in some of the less disturbed families, there is no evidence of the likelihood of morbidity until the second year of life. In general, none of the multirisk families studied has been totally free of the morbidity described in this section.

We have observed babies at the center who, during the first few days of life, are for the most part well in terms of weight, size, and overall physical health status, but who have difficulty in regulating social responsiveness, establishing habituation patterns, and organizing their motor responses. Some of them are withdrawn and unresponsive to animate stimuli; others are hyperlabile and overly responsive. Nevertheless, in contrast, a number of our babies also seem to be in optimal condition, even in terms of the soft neurological signs, and are appropriately adaptive in their initial capacity for homeostasis (self-regulation and an emerging interest in the world).

Yet, in general, babies in our program, most of whom were at risk prenatally but who had normal patterns of development perinatally (prenatal intervention having assured adequate nutrition and other supports, including appropriate medical care), show significantly less than optimal development as early as the first month of life. Pediatric, neurological, and Brazelton neonatal examinations at 1 month of age, for example, show developmental progression, but not the increased capacity for orientation characteristic of a normative population. Interestingly, the group receiving comprehensive intervention was similar to normal comparison infants at birth but slipped a little in their orientation capacity by 1 month. Our high-risk group, receiving only periodic evaluations, was significantly worse in a number of areas, including orientation, habituation, and motor organization (even with some of the most-disturbed families having left the program—that is, those with the greatest risk) than both the normal and intervention groups at 1 month of age (Hofheimer, Poisson, Strauss, Eyler, & Greenspan, 1983).

By 3 months of age, instead of a capacity for self-regulation, organization, and an interest in the world, a number of our babies showed increased tendencies toward lability, muscle rigidity, gaze aversion, and an absence of organized sleep–wake, alert, and feeding patterns. Their caregivers, instead of having an overall capacity for offering the babies comfort, protection, and an interest in the world, either withdraw from them and avoid them or overstimulate them in a chaotic and intermittent fashion.

At about the ages of 2 to 4 months, we expect to find in the infant the beginnings of a deep, rich, emotional investment in the human world, especially in his or her primary caregivers. We also expect a human environment that will fall in love with the child and will woo that child to fall in love in turn, in an effective, multimodal, pleasurable manner. Instead, a significant number of these children exhibit a total lack of involvement in the human world or an involvement that is nonaffective, shallow, and impersonal, and we see caregivers who are emotionally distant, aloof, impersonal, and highly ambivalent about their children.

Between 3 and 9 months of age, we expect an infant's capacity for interacting with the world in a reciprocal, causal, or purposeful manner to further develop and form a foundation for his or her later organized causal behavior or thinking (reality orientation and testing). Instead, in the multiproblem families, the child's behavior and affect remain under the control of his or her internal states in random and chaotic or narrow, rigid, and stereotyped patterns of interaction. The child's environment, instead of offering the expected optimal contingent responsiveness to the child's varied signals, tends to ignore or misread them. The child's caregivers are overly preoccupied, depressed, or chaotic.

Toward the end of the first year of life and the beginning of the second, a child in a multirisk family, instead of showing an increase in organized, complex, assertive, and innovative emotional and behavioral patterns (for example, taking the mother's hand and leading her to the refrigerator to show her the kind of food wanted) tends to exhibit fragmented, stereotyped, and polarized patterns. These toddlers may be withdrawn and compliant or highly aggressive, impulsive, and disorganized. Their human environment tends to be intrusive, controlling, and fragmented. The toddler may have been prematurely separated from her or his caregivers, or the caregivers may exhibit patterns of withdrawal instead of admiringly supporting the toddler's initiative and autonomy and helping him or her to organize what are now more complex capacities for communicating, interacting, and behaving.

As the toddler's potential capacities continue to develop in the latter half of the second year and in the third year (18–36 months), profound deficits can be more clearly observed. The child, instead of developing capacities for internal representations (imagery) around which to organize behavior and feelings, and for differentiating ideas, feelings, and thoughts pertaining to the self and the nonself, either develops no representational or symbolic capacity, or if the capacity develops, it is not elaborated beyond the most elementary descriptive form, so that the child's behavior remains shallow and polarized. The child's sense of the emerging self, as distinguished from the sense of other people, remains fragmented and undifferentiated. The child's potentially emerging capacities for reality testing, impulse regulation, and mood stabilization are either compromised or become extremely vulnerable to regression. In other words, we see patterns either consistent with later borderline and psychotic personality organization or severe asocial or antisocial, impulse-ridden character disorders.

At this stage, the underlying impairment manifests itself in the child's inability to use a representational or symbolic mode to organize his or her behavior. In essence, the distinctly human capacity of operating beyond the survival level, of using internal imagery to elaborate and organize complex feelings and wishes and to construct trial actions in the emotional sphere, and of anticipating and planning ahead are compromised. In many of our families, the parents simply do not have these capacities. Even when they are not under emotional distress or in states of crisis or panic, they do not demonstrate a symbolic mode, as evidenced in the lack of verbal communication (only one aspect of symbolic communication) and in the lack of symbolic play. Such families tend to be fearful and to deny and fail to meet needs in their children that are appropriate for their ages. They engage the child only in nonsymbolic modes of communication, such as holding, feeding, and administering physical punishment, and at times they misread or respond unrealistically to the child's emerging communication, thus undermining the development in the child of a sense of self and a flexible orientation to reality.

Needless to say, the mastery by the children in these families of higher-level developmental tasks is even more difficult. At each new level of development, the infants and toddlers, who for a variety of reasons have survived earlier developmental phases intact, invariably challenge the multirisk environment with their new capacities, for example, with their capacity for symbolic communication. The healthier the toddler, the more challenging and overwhelming he is likely to be to the people around him. In a pattern that we have frequently observed, the child moves ahead of the parent (engaging, for example, in symbolic play around themes of dependency or sexuality), and thus the parent becomes confused and either withdraws from, or behaves intrusively toward the child. Shortly, unless other, more skillful caregivers are available, the child begins to regress to presymbolic modes of behaving. The child may be able to consolidate higher-level capacities when she or he begins to receive support from other systems, such as the school, and is capable of understanding his or her parents' limitations. These capacities, however, can only develop when the child is a little older. The youngster who experiences developmental failures, including the failure to develop a full representational or symbolic capacity (the basis for formal school experience later on), will unquestionably be handicapped in all subsequent opportunities for learning and coping.

Clinical and Service System Approaches

On the encouraging side, we have found that in most of the families we work with, the maladaptive trends just described can be reversed. By carefully pinpointing the area in which a child's development first begins to go awry and by using organized and comprehensive clinical techniques and service system approaches, we have been able to effect significant reversals in the direction of more adaptive patterns. Many parents in our population began their childrearing as teenagers and have commonly experienced further deterioration in their own functioning and that of their infants with each subsequent birth. In most instances, however, even when a woman has had four or more children, we have been able to reverse this pattern of deterioration by means of appropriate clinical methods and services. In a number of these multi-risk families, we have observed that after they enter our program, a gradual improvement takes place in the mother and a modest but positive change in the first baby born thereafter. Then, if the family remains in the program and a second baby is born, the change in the family is dramatic and is reflected in the new baby's more optimal development.

For example, Mrs. E. was pregnant when she came to our attention. At first glance, she appeared to the team social worker to be beyond help after she was found sleeping on the street. All of her children had been removed from her care by the County Department of Protective Services after she had severely abused and neglected them. Mrs. E. appeared unable to think except in concrete terms, at times was psychotic, could not communicate her thoughts and plans, and seemingly lived by impulse only and a talent for survival. Shortly before the birth of her child a few months later, however, she entered our program, prompted by our outreach efforts. All of our collective efforts to induce Mrs. E. to use a support structure (for example, to obtain housing, food, or clothing) failed. Nevertheless, subsequently, of her own accord, she requested foster care for the new infant before severe trauma could be inflicted on the child. Mrs. E. maintained contact with this child and made a great deal of progress in treatment over a 2-year period. When she became pregnant again, not only could she care for the newest baby, but she was also able to work and to support an apartment. Thus far with therapeutic support, she has nurtured a competent 11-month-old and also has become constructively involved with her older children.

Even when improvement was not so dramatic, the expected patterns of deterioration often did not take place in our families, and some of them became capable of adequately supporting the growth and development of their children. Many mothers, for example, who previously had children taken away and put in foster care became able to care for a new infant as well as for their older children. Also, some mothers, who had been recurrently hospitalized for psychiatric illness in the past developed the ability to function appropriately with a new baby and have not been rehospitalized for psychiatric illness for 2 or more years.

We found that the babies in our families had a surprising capacity to recover from early developmental deviations. Even when an infant's development had deteriorated during the first 3 months of life (as evidenced by gaze aversion, muscle rigidity, and a state of lability), intervention with appropriate patterns of care (including special clinical techniques) could lead to adaptive homeostatic and attachment capacities within 1 to 2 months. Infants would become apathetic and withdrawn and begin to show delays in sensorimotor development when no one would read their signals or respond to them. However, with patient, clinically informed care, they would begin interacting with people and, within 2 to 3 weeks of intensive intervention, would begin to catch up developmentally.

Implications for Clinical Services

I can discuss only briefly some of the principles on which a clinical and service system approach to multirisk families should be based. Although services for this population have been the subject of much study, (Argles & Mackenzie, 1970; Berstein, 1964; Buell, 1952; Edelstein, 1972; Fantl, 1958; Gunter & MacCorquodale, 1975; Lang, 1974; La Vietes, 1974; Levine, 1964; Minuchin & Montalvo, 1967; Powell & Monahan, 1969; Reid & Shyne, 1969; Sperebas, 1974; Suarez & Ricketson, 1974; Zilbach, 1971), I will try to present some perspective on the organization and service challenges for the child and family, related to the child at each stage of development.

A comprehensive approach, as indicated earlier, requires that a number of elements be combined: (1) services that respond to concrete needs for survival (food, housing, and so forth), (2) a planned effort to meet the need of the family and the child for an ongoing, trusting human relationship, (3) specific clinical techniques and services that focus on the many lines of a child's development and that are specific to the child's tasks at each developmental subphase, and (4) a special support structure to provide at one site partial or full therapeutic day care for the child, innovative outreach to the family, and ongoing training and supervision of the program staff.

To respond to the family's concrete needs, various community agencies need to be organized to build a foundation for the family's survival. However, this approach alone will not ensure a family's survival, because many of the families, for a variety of reasons, are adept at circumventing offers of traditional supports.

The second component of a comprehensive effort, and one that is absolutely necessary for these families, is a human relationship with one or more workers. Such a relationship, however, is not easy to establish, because distrust is often ingrained in each parent as well as in the family as a unit. This human relationship needs to grow in ways paralleling the infant's development, and needs to help the parents facilitate that development. To provide this human relationship, we have used both a team and a single primary clinician.

Organizing to respond to a family's concrete needs and offering the family a human relationship, however, are not enough. That human relationship must be able to help the parents understand some of their maladaptive coping strategies and teach them how to deal with their own primary needs and those of their infant. In addition, special clinical techniques and patterns of care (Greenspan, 1981) to reverse maladaptive developmental patterns in the areas of affect and social interaction, sensorimotor development, and cognition must be available at the appropriate time. Moreover, the intervention must occur over a sufficiently long period to allow the family's own strengths to take over and sustain it. We are speaking here then not of a crisis intervention approach over a few months but an approach that will be available to the families for several years at a minimum. We have found that after working with many of these families for some 2 years, the mother's capacity to nurture and facilitate the development of a new baby is significantly more advanced than when she entered the program pregnant with an earlier child. In other words, when the helping relationship is offered over a period of time, the frequently observed trend of multiproblem families to deteriorate further upon the birth of each subsequent baby begins to be reversed.

In addition, the approach to the multiple needs of these infants and their families must be integrated. Simply offering nutritional advice, (Cravioto, 1980) or educational counsel, providing cognitive stimulation, or taking an entirely infant-centered or entirely family-centered approach is not sufficient. The infants have individual differences that dictate special patterns of care; at the same time, the concerns of their caregivers and other family members have to be addressed. Each stage in the infant's and the family's development requires specialized clinical services and service system approaches (Greenspan, 1981).

Although the costs of offering programs of intervention are great, the costs of not offering them are even greater. The estimated 6% of the U.S.

population that use 50% of all health, mental health, and social services account for economic and social costs that are compounded by the additional loss to society that these people might have contributed to the labor force and to other creative endeavors (Buell, 1952).

Programs of prevention are expensive, but they are not so costly as might be imagined, because even when services are offered to an entire high-risk community, only a small percentage of the families in that community will actually need the most intensive help. Selma Fraiberg, as director of a Michigan infant mental health program, found that in a program offering a range of preventive services, including intensive individual clinical services, the average yearly cost per family participating was $850.[4] In terms of providing screening and backup for an entire community, the cost per family for such preventive services would average out to a significantly lower amount.

Perhaps we need to look at the cost–benefit ratio. Using cases from our own study to project the probabilities (based on observed family patterns and clinical assumptions) of different outcomes with and without preventive intervention, we found that benefits outweighed costs by five or six to one (depending on the degree of risk). Interestingly, in the cases at greater risk, in which initial costs might be high, the benefit–cost ratio was often better than in less severe cases, because the benefits of preventive intervention were relatively greater (Greenspan, 1981).

A Clinical Developmental Model for Diagnosis and Preventive Intervention in Infancy and Early Childhood[5]

Work with the multirisk families and their infants and other risk groups (i.e., low-birthweight babies), as well as competent infants and families, provided us with a range of experiences that led to a conceptual framework to categorize adaptive and maladaptive infant and family patterns. Ideally, a diagnostic framework would encompass all of the clinically relevant lines of human development. These include physical, neurologic, and cognitive lines, human relationships, and capacities for organizing and differentiating experience (adaptive and coping strategies). This framework would lend itself to an understanding of the range and variation in human functioning, from the normal to the pathologic.

Several existing developmental frameworks have provided enormous understanding of individual lines of development in infancy and early

---

[4]Personal communication with Selma Fraiberg, December, 1980.
[5]Much of this section may be found in Greenspan and Lourie, 1981.

childhood, for example, Erikson (1959), Anna Freud (1965), Sigmund Freud (1905, 1953), Kernberg (1975), Kohut (1971), Mahler, Pine, and Bergman (1975), Piaget (1972), and Sander (1962); in addition, there has been empirical research. These foundations, together with the rapidly growing body of clinical experience with infants and their families, provide direction for a much needed integrated approach encompassing the multiple lines of development in the context of adaptive and disordered functioning.

These contributions have led to an integrated clinical approach based on a developmental structuralist framework (Greenspan, 1981) and to the classification of adaptive and pathologic personality organizations and behaviors in infancy and early childhood. This in turn provides a basis for understanding adaptive and maladaptive environments and principles of preventive and therapeutic intervention.

Traditional approaches to the classification of adaptive functioning, disordered functioning, and intervention are based on the clustering of certain symptoms and/or on an understanding of the etiologic basis of the disorder. However, while necessary, the etiologic and symptom-complex approaches to classification and diagnosis are in themselves insufficient. For example, the same etiologic factor can result in different behavioral outcomes or symptoms; as an illustration, a reaction to a given allergen or stress may differ depending on individual differences in response proclivity. One individual may become dizzy or develop peripheral neuropathy, another may develop hives, and yet another may develop a gastrointestinal disorder. Conversely, several different etiologic agents may result in the same symptoms; for example, a given allergen, infectious agent, or series of external events can all produce a similar gastrointestinal disturbance.

In considering adaptive and maladaptive personality development, we do not yet have a complete framework for delineating the pathogenic and adaptive processes. There is, therefore, a need for another classification, which would focus on the organism's individual way of processing, organizing, integrating, and differentiating experience—that is, the pathways that lead to certain behavioral outcomes. This final common pathway connects the influence of multiple etiologic factors with varying outcomes and suggests something fundamental about the individual organism's manner of organizing its experience of its world, internal and external, animate and inanimate.

In applying this concept to psychopathology in infants, one can start with the manner by which experience is organized at each developmental stage, according to the characteristics that define the particular organization. Each organizational level may be viewed as a structure (Piaget,

1968/1970, 1972). The developmental structuralist approach defines these experiential organizations (structures) at each developmental stage in terms of a given infant's emotional and cognitive experience (Greenspan, 1979). A few examples for early infancy will help illustrate the point. One of the infant's first tasks is to establish and maintain a state of internal regulation in the face of external environmental changes. This regulation includes basic neurophysiologic processes reflected in such rhythms as sleep and hunger cycles (Brazelton, Koslowski, & Main, 1974; Sander, 1962). This capacity may be viewed as a stage-specific structural capacity to achieve homeostasis (Greenspan, 1979; Greenspan et al., 1979). Depending on individual constitutional differences and environmental influences, some infants can remain alert and engage the world in a multisensory affective manner in the context of internal regulation and regular cyclic patterns. They are able to console themselves or are easily consoled by caregivers. However, when other infants are on their own, they can only remain regulated or calm by shutting out the external world (e.g., by sleeping if their internal disregulation allows it). When they are unable to regulate their internal processes, they remain hyperexcitable and irritable, with varying degrees of engagement with the external world, depending on the capacity of their caregivers to find ways to help them achieve a steady state.

Another illustration pertains to the infant's capacity for forming a human attachment—another early and important developmental task. Infants between 2 and 4 months of age clearly begin to demonstrate a unique investment in the animate as opposed to the inanimate world. Typically, they develop a special interest in their permanent caregivers, as evidenced by the social smile (Emde, Gaensbauer, & Harmon, 1976; Spitz, Emde, & Metcalf, 1970). In addition, they show individual differences in communication patterns and affects expressed and experienced in their special dyadic attachments (Brazelton, Koslowski, & Main, 1974; Stern, 1974a, 1974b). This capacity for attachment may also be viewed as a stage-specific structural achievement and considered in terms of a number of parameters, including the range, depth stability, and personal uniqueness of the experience evidenced and tolerated. In assessing a given infant's response to this most fundamental developmental step, one looks to whether it is a warm, loving dyad in which infant and mother both experience a range of affects from deep, rich pleasure to assertiveness and protest, or whether it is a shallow, mechanical attachment, devoid of affect, behavioral richness, and flexibility. What is the range of sensory modalities used by the infant and the mother? Are they visually, audibly, vocally, and tactilely connected, or are only one or two of these modalities used? What is the range of motoric involvement? Do these experiential organizations exist only intermittently or are they the usual mode of involvement? Can the dyad re-engage after a disruption? Are unique personal characteristics beginning to express themselves? Are there special games or preferred affects and sensorimotor patterns that characterize this relationship?

Additional areas to observe in determining the spectrum from adaptability to pathology include the basic parameters of (1) range and depth of age- and phase-appropriate experiences, (2) stability of experiential organization, which includes integrative capacity and resilience to stress, and (3) unique, individual characteristics.

In such a pattern of assessment, beginning with infancy, initial organizing capacities are observed as development proceeds. One looks at the enlarging structural capacity of the developing child in order to monitor the patterns of emergence of higher level integrating and synthesizing capacities (Greenspan, 1979; Piaget, 1972).

The degree to which an individual experiences the full range of stage- and age-appropriate experiences in stable, stress-resilient personal configurations is an indicator of progression in a particular stage of development. It also indicates readiness for progressing to those experiential realms that emerge from the earlier ones and become integrated into the next developmental stage. The optimally adaptive structure at each developmental stage facilitates further development. For example, an infant who begins warding off affectionate, intimate behavior is unlikely, without a reversal of that trend, to learn those skills that involve personal intimacy. If the reversal takes place after the optimal period for its development, resolution can be less than optimal. On the other hand, the infant who adequately organizes experiences of physical closeness and interpersonal affection is likely to have an opportunity to better learn intimate exchanges. This is not to suggest that catch-up learning does not occur—it does. Such learning, however, may have a different developmental sequence and final configuration.

The developmental structuralist approach to assessment is consistent with, and partially derived from, current empirical research on early development. It is now well documented that the infant is capable, even at birth or shortly thereafter, of organizing experience in an adaptive fashion. The infant can respond to stimulation with apparent pleasure and displeasure (Lipsett, 1966), change behavior as a function of its consequences (Gerwirtz, 1965, 1969), form intimate bonds and make visual discriminations (Klaus & Kennell, 1976; Meltzoff & Moore, 1977), organize sleep–wake and alertness cycles and rhythms (Sander, 1962), and demonstrate organized social responses in conjunction with increasing neurophysiologic organization (Emde et al., 1976). This empirically documented view of the infant is, in a general sense, consistent with Freud's early hypotheses (Freud, 1958) and Hartmann's postulation (Hartmann, 1939) of an early undifferentiated organizational matrix. Empirical data (Brazelton et al., 1974; Emde et al., 1976; Escalona, 1968; Murphy & Moriarty, 1976, Sander, 1962; Sroufe, Waters & Matas, 1974; Stern, 1974a, 1974b), also support earlier theories suggesting that the organization of experience broadens during the early months of life, to reflect increases in the capacity to experience and tolerate a range of stimuli. This capacity includes responding to social interaction in stable and personal configurations. In addition, there is evidence that capacities to organize experience reflect individual differences in infants and their caregivers, which are present early in life (Bergman & Escalona, 1949; Parmelee, 1972; Thomas, Chess, & Birch, 1968; Wolff, 1966).

A detailed developmental structuralist classification scheme for infancy and early childhood has been described according to stage-specific tasks (Greenspan, 1979; Greenspan et al., 1979). The capacities described by these stages are all present in some rudimentary form in very early infancy. The sequence presented suggests not when these capacities begin, but when they become relatively prominent in organizing behavior and furthering development. In this classification, the first stage is the achievement of homeostasis, as described earlier. Once the infant has achieved some capacity for regulation in the context of engaging the world, and central nervous system (CNS) maturation is increasing (between 2 and 4 months of age), he or she becomes more attuned to social and interpersonal interaction. The infant is more able to respond to the external environment and to form a special relationship with the significant primary caregivers.

Thus, described earlier, a second, closely related stage is that of forming a human attachment. If an affective and relatively pleasurable attachment (an investment in the human, animate world) is formed, then with growing maturational abilities the infant develops complex patterns of communication in the context of this primary human relationship. Parallel with development of the infant's relationship to the inanimate world, where basic schemes of causality (means–ends relationships [Piaget, 1972] are being developed, the infant becomes capable of complicated human communications (Brazelton et al., 1974; Charlesworth, 1969; Stern 1974a; Tennes, Emde, Kisley, & Metcalf, 1972).

When there have been distortions in the attachment process (e.g., if a mother responds in a mechanical, remote manner and/or projects some of her own dependent feelings onto her infant), the infant may not learn to appreciate causal relationships between people at the level of compassionate and intimate feelings. This can occur even though causality seems to be developing in terms of the inanimate world and the impersonal human world. We have observed infants who are differentiated in the assertive impersonal domain of human relationships, but who are relatively undifferentiated in the intimate, pleasurable domain.

Causal relationships are established between the infant and the primary caregiver, as evidenced in the infant's growing ability to discriminate significant primary caregivers from others. He or she also becomes able to differentiate her or his own actions from their consequences, affectively, somatically, behaviorally, and interpersonally. Usually by 8 months of age or earlier, the process of differentiation begins along a number of developmental lines (e.g., with sensorimotor integration, affective relationships). A third stage therefore may be formally termed somatopsychologic differentiation, to indicate processes occurring at the somatic (e.g., sensorimotor) and emerging psychological levels. (In this context, *psychologic* refers to higher-level mental processes characterized by the capacity to form internal representations or symbols as a way to organize experience.) While schemes of causality are being established in the infant's relationship to the interpersonal world, it is not at all clear whether these schemes exist at an organized representational or a symbolic level. Rather, they appear to exist mainly at a somatic level (Greenspan, 1979), even though we do observe the precursors of representational capacities. Some are perhaps even prenatally determined (Lourie, 1971).

With appropriate reading of cues and systematic differential responses, the infant's or toddler's behavioral repertoire becomes complicated, and communications take on more organized, meaningful configurations. By 12 months of age, the infant is connecting behavioral units into larger organizations as she or he exhibits complex emotional responses such as affiliation, wariness, and fear (Ainsworth, Bell, & Stayton, 1974; Bowlby, 1969; Sroufe & Waters, 1977). As the toddler moves farther into the second year of life, in the context of the practicing subphase of the development of individuation (Mahler et al., 1975), there is an increased capacity for forming original behavioral schemes (Piaget, 1972) and imitative activity and intentionality.

A type of learning through imitation evidenced in earlier development now seems to assume a more dominant role. As imitations take on a more integrated personal form, it appears the toddler is adopting or internalizing attributes of his or her caregivers. To describe these new capacities, it is useful to consider a fourth stage, that of behavioral organization, initiative, and internalization.

As the toddler moves into the end of the second year, with further CNS maturation, we notice an increased capacity to form and organize mental representations. Internal sensations and unstable images become organized in a mental representational form that can be evoked and is somewhat stable (Bell, 1970; Gouin-Decarie, 1965; Piaget, 1972). While this capacity is initially fragile (i.e., between 16 and 24 months), it soon appears to become a dominant mode in organizing the child's behavior, and a fifth stage can be documented—that of forming mental representations. As a clarification of related concepts, it should be pointed out that the capacity for *object permanence* is relative and goes through a series of stages (Gouin-Decarie, 1965); it refers to the toddler's ability to search for hidden inanimate objects. *Representational capacity* refers to the ability to organize and evoke internal organized multisensory experiences of the animate object. The capacities to represent animate and inanimate experiences are related and depend on both CNS myelination and appropriate experiences. The process of internalization may be thought of as an intermediary process. Internalized experiences eventually become sufficiently organized to be considered representations.

At a representational level, the child again develops his or her capacities for elaboration, integration, and differentiation. Just as causal schemes previously were developed at a somatic and behavioral level, now they are developed at a representational level. The child begins to elaborate and eventually differentiate those feelings, thoughts, and events that emanate from self and those that emanate from others. He or she begins to differentiate what she or he experiences and does from the impact of his or her actions on the world. This gradually forms the basis for the differentiation of self representations from those that embody the external world, both animate and inanimate.

The capacity for differentiating internal representations becomes consolidated as object constancy is established (Mahler et al., 1975). In middle childhood, representational capacity becomes reinforced, with the child's ability to develop derivative representational systems tied to the original representation and to transform them in accord with adaptive and defensive goals. This permits greater flexibility in dealing with perceptions, feelings, thoughts, and emerging ideals. Substages for these capacities include representational differentiation, the consolidation of representational capacity, and the capacity for forming limited derivative representational systems and multiple derivative representational systems (structural learning [Greenspan, 1979]).

At each of these stages, in varying degrees, pathologic as well as adaptive formations are possible. These may be considered as relative compromises in the range, depth, stability, and/or personal uniqueness of the experiential organization consolidated at each stage. The infant can form adaptive patterns of regulation in the earliest stages of development. Internal states are harmoniously regulated and he or she is free to invest in the animate and inanimate world, thereby setting the basis for rich emotional attachments to his or her primary caregivers. On the other hand, if regulatory processes are not functioning properly and she or he cannot maintain internal harmony in the context of being available to the world, the infant may withdraw. From relatively minor compromises such as a tendency to withdraw and/or be hyperexcitable under stress, to a major deviation such as an overwhelming avoidance of the animate world, we can observe the degrees to which the infant, even in the first months of life, achieves a less-than-optimal adaptive structural organization.

Thus, the early attachments can be warm and engaging, or shallow, insecure, and limited in their affective tone. In the early reciprocal relationships, we can observe differences between an infant who reads the signals of the caregivers and responds in a rich, meaningful way to multiple aspects of the communications (with multiple affects and behavioral communications), and one who can respond only within a narrow range of affect (e.g., protest) or who cannot respond at all in a contingent or reciprocal manner (e.g., the seemingly apathetic, withdrawn, and depressed child who responds only to his or her own internal cues). As the toddler, optimally, becomes behaviorally more organized, and complex patterns appear which reflect originality and initiative in the context of the separation and individuation subphase of development, we can observe those toddlers who manifest this full adaptive capacity. They may be compared with others who are stereotyped in their behavioral patterns (reflect no originality or intentionality), who remain fragmented (never connect pieces of behavior into more complicated patterns), or who evidence polarities of affect, showing no capacity to integrate emotions (e.g., the chronic negativistic aggressive toddler who cannot show interest, curiosity, or love).

As a capacity for representational organization is reached, we can distinguish the child who can organize, integrate, and differentiate a rich range of affective and ideational life from one who remains without representational capacity, or who may form and differentiate self and object representations only at the expense of extreme compromises in the range of tolerated experience (e.g., the schizoid child). Similar adaptive or maladaptive structural organizations can be observed in later childhood (the triangular phase), latency, and adolescence.

A more detailed discussion of this framework, including principles of prevention and intervention, is available (Greenspan, 1979). It should also be pointed out that through videotaped analyses of infant–caregiver interactions (Greenspan & Lieberman, 1980; Hofheimer et al.,

1983), these patterns can be reliably rated, and new raters can be trained to achieve and maintain high levels of reliability. In addition, these patterns are stable over time. Principal component analyses of the rating scales are underway.

Principles of Preventive Intervention; Application of Developmental Structuralist Classification to Diagnosis and Treatment

Using the stage of somatopsychologic differentiation as an example of a clinical approach to infants and families, the following description illustrates the types of patterns that result from inappropriate resolutions and the clinical strategies that can be applied.

Patterns Resulting from Inappropriate Resolutions

When the stage of somatopsychologic differentiation is not appropriately achieved, there can be degrees of defects in somatopsychologic differentiation. An extreme defect is illustrated by the infant who does not develop differential reactions to behavioral, emotional, or inanimate environmental events. If the primary caregiver ignores or withdraws from the infant's assertive and/or protest behaviors, or if the infant's signals are weak and therefore not perceived, a sense of causality and differentiation around this particular spectrum of affect and behavior may not become consolidated. When frustrated, such an infant may evidence either disorganized aggressive responses (e.g., biting, flailing) or apathy, passivity, and withdrawal, rather than assertive, organized protest behavior.

A variety of symptoms may be seen in relation to disorders of somatopsychologic differentiation. They include sensorimotor developmental delays, apathy, intense chronic fear, clinging, lack of explorativeness and curiosity, lack of (or nonresponsive) emotional reactions to significant caregivers, specific maladaptive patterns of relatedness such as biting, chronic crying and irritability, and difficulties with sleeping and eating.

A number of somatic, emotional, and behavioral symptoms may emerge as a consequence of more fundamental disturbances in differentiation. If emerging capacities for contingent interactions in sensorimotor and affective areas are not systematically responded to, developmental progress (differentiation) in the most vulnerable areas may slow down or cease simply because there is no opportunity for repetitive action sequences or practice (i.e., there is a lack of the repetitive minimal stimulus nutriment necessary to consolidate these capacities), and we may observe cognitive or interpersonal delays. Secondary apathy, withdrawal, disorganization, and/or other regressions may follow. An infant who receives no response or an inappropriate one (e.g., is misread) to his or her reaching-out cues may mobilize negativistic responses to achieve a reaction from the environment. Instead of reaching out, this infant may cry and refuse to respond. This may elicit a quick response from the environment, and chronic patterns of negativism may be established. If this negativism expands, development in important motoric and sensory areas may be compromised, as opportunities for practicing action patterns will be missed. Even such basic functions as eating may be caught up in a pattern of negativism. The pleasurable component of using negativism as an organizer of individuation can also be bypassed if it is allowed to become a method of expressing aggression, such as in chronically oppositional children.

If, secondary to the lack of differentiated patterns, there are compromises in the infant–primary-caregiver relationship (e.g., the infant becomes frustrated and irritable as new capacities for contingent interactions are ignored or misread), the basic comforting and soothing function that supports the sense of security and makes it possible for the infant to achieve homeostasis and attachment may also falter. We may then see compromises in attachment and homeostatic patterns (e.g., physiologic disorders, interferences in already achieved rhythms and cycles such as sleep and hunger).

To further illustrate the use of the concept of a somatopsychologic differentiation, we can briefly consider its implication for understanding disordered environments and for approaches to prevention and intervention. The disordered environment does not engage the infant in a reciprocal manner, either because of the caregiver's inability to read the infant's signals or because of the infant's inability to respond differentially. For example, the mother may be depressed and unavailable for "reading" or responding to signals; she may project her own needs onto the infant and therefore misread cues; or she may read the cues but, instead of responding appropriately, may try to control or manipulate the infant. In addition, either because of the infant's own constitutional makeup or because of earlier developmental problems, the infant may be a weak sender, unable to make his or her own needs known (e.g., she or he may fell asleep when interested in being held or fed). Under any of these circumstances, development may be seriously delayed and a number of the symptoms mentioned earlier may occur. Obviously, no environment is perfectly responsive, and this should not be expected.

An infant must learn to tolerate frustration in balance with support for his or her own maturational thrust toward differentiation.

Prevention and Treatment

Understanding the ordinarily expected structural capacity at each stage of development helps to focus prevention and intervention efforts. Regardless of symptoms, if we observe a fundamental deficit in somato-psychologic differentiation and can diagnose the contributing problems (i.e., in the environmental system and/or in the makeup of the infant), an approach is immediately suggested. For example, if homeostatic capacities and attachment patterns seem to be well established and yet there seems to be difficulty in the stage of somatopsychologic differentiation, the effort can be aimed at strengthening the specific missing components that would lead to differentiation. If the infant is passive and a weak sender, the mother, the father, or another family member can be taught to read the otherwise difficult signals and to work with the infant toward increasing the strength of the signals. For example, the infant who puts his or her hand forth only very slowly in order to make contact can initially be met by the mother three-fourths of the way; slowly, by finding novel stimuli, she can encourage the infant to begin meeting her halfway. Similarly, through providing other satisfying experiences, she can gradually encourage the increased use of a number of communication modalities, affects, and behaviors.

If the difficulty is in the environment (e.g., with the primary caretakers), the caretakers can be worked with in a psychotherapeutic and educative setting. If necessary, someone else (e.g., an older sibling) can be encouraged to provide the missing reciprocal interactions. In working with the primary caretaker, the developmental structuralist approach helps formulate specific goals. For example, the mother who tends to project her own feelings and therefore is suspicious and guarded may continually misread her infant. Because she may read the infant's press for emotional closeness as "being angry at her," she may decide to "teach him a lesson" and "not spoil him." In a therapeutic relationship with such a mother, the mother may quickly come to feel that the therapist "is [also] angry at her." As the distortion in the relationship to the therapist is highlighted, the comment can be made that perhaps she also sees her infant as angry with her, particularly when his or her signals are ambiguous. Those situations in which she feels "attacked" by her infant may then be reviewed in detail. The meanings and feelings a mother attaches to her infant's communications are often quite complex and may require sensitive exploration.

In addition, the therapist may suggest techniques to her for making the infant more comfortable. As she learns that she can calm her infant, her underlying feelings of helplessness and rage may diminish, and the infant may become less a target of her projections than other individuals whom she cannot deal with as effectively. Thus, her husband, the therapist, and others may remain targets of her anger, but the infant may be relatively free from malevolent projections. After a time, therapeutic progress should occur so that the mother can relate to the important people in her life in a more positive manner. The developmental structuralist approach alerts us to those unhealthy mother–infant interactions we might be able to modify quickly.

The developmental structuralist concepts can be applied for each phase of early development. The features that characterize the infant's and the environment's functioning at each of these early phases may be defined as a basis for effective preventive or corrective intervention.

Conclusion

In conclusion, first I have attempted to present a theoretical perspective on mental health research, with a special focus on the challenges confronting clinical approaches to infants and their families. It was emphasized that it may be an error to begin studying functional relationships prior to the adequate understanding of how phenomena group themselves in natural situations and prior to developing appropriate methods to classify and measure naturalistically occurring phenomena. Second, I attempted to present a definition of clinical approaches to infants and their families, which begins at the descriptive level and takes into account the complexity of challenging clinical infant developmental problems. Third, I presented an overview of our work with multirisk families and their infants. And finally, I presented our developmental structuralist model for classifying adaptive and maladaptive infant and family patterns for each developmental stage and discussed the associated principles of diagnosis and preventive intervention.

In this discussion, the concepts of adaptive and maladaptive functioning and risk are viewed in the context of a clinical developmental framework. The way in which the infant and family organize and integrate multiple dimensions of experience (e.g., affective, cognitive, physical, familial) at each phase of development determines the relative degree of adaptation or maladaptation at that particular phase and suggests the risk or probability of successful engagement of the challenges at the next developmental stage. While the degree of recovery as well as the balance between nature and nurture may differ for different dimensions of development, it is likely that only an integrated frame of reference for studying the multiple dimensions of experience at each developmental phase will significantly advance our understanding of the relationship between individual differences, risk, normality, or pathology.

References

Ainsworth, M., Bell, S., & Stayton, D. (1974). Infant–mother attachment and social development: Socialization as a product of reciprocal responsiveness to signals. In M. Richards (Ed.), *The integration of the child into a social world*. Cambridge, England: Cambridge University Press.

Argles, P., & Mackenzie, M. (1970). Crisis intervention with a multi-problem family: A case study. *Journal of Child Psychology and Psychiatry, 11*, 187–195.

Bell, S. (1970). The development of the concept of object as related to infant–mother attachment. *Child Development, 41*, 219.

Bergman, P., & Escalona, S. (1949). Unusual sensitivities in very young children. *Psychoanalytic Study of the Child, 333*, 3–4.

Berstein, B. (1964). Social class, speech systems, and psychotherapy. *British Journal of Sociology, 15*, 54–64.

Bowlby, J. (1969). *Attachment and loss*. New York: Basic Books.

Brazelton, T. B., Koslowski, B., & Main, M. (1974). The origins or reciprocity: The early mother–infant interaction. In M. Lewis & L. Rosenblum (Eds.), *The effect of the infant on its care giver* (pp. 49–76). New York: Wiley.

Buell, B. (1952). *Community planning for human services*. New York: Columbia University Press.

Charlesworth, W. R. (1969). The role of surprise in cognitive development. In E. Elkind & J. H. Flavell (Eds.), *Studies in cognitive development: Essays in honor of Jean Piaget*. London: Oxford University Press.

Cravioto, J. (1980, May) *Malnutrition in infants: A developmental perspective*. Paper presented at the scientific meeting of the Mental Health Study Center of the National Institute of Mental Health, Adelphi, MD.

Curtis, J. L., Simon, M., Boykin, F. L., & Noe, E. R. (1964). Observations on 29 multi-problem families. *American Journal Orthopsychiatry, 34*, 510–516.

Edelstein R. I. (1972). Early intervention in the poverty cycle. *Social Casework, 53*, 418–424.

Emde, R. N., Gaensbauer, T. J., & Harmon, R. J. (1976). Emotional expression in infancy: A biobehavioral study. *Psychological Issues* (Monograph No. 37). New York: International Universities Press.

Escalona, S. K. (1968). *The roots of individuality*. Chicago: Aldine.

Erikson, E. H. (1959). Identity and the life cycle. *Psychological Issues* (Monograph No. 1). New York: International Universities Press.

Fantl, B. (1958). Integrating psychological, social, and cultural factors in assertive casework. *Social Work, 3*, 37.

Freud, A. (1965). Normality and pathology in childhood. In *The Writings of Anna Freud* (Vol. 6). New York: International Universities Press.

Freud S. (1953). Three essays on the theory of sexuality *Standard Edition, 7*, 135–242. London: Hogarth Press. (Original work published in 1905.)

Freud, S. (1958). Formulation on the two principles of mental functioning *Standard Edition,* *12,* 218–226. London: Hogarth Press. (Original work published in 1911.)

Geismar, L. L. (1968). The results of social work intervention: A positive case. *American Journal Orthopsychiatry, 38,* 444–456.

Geismar, L. L., & La Sorte, M. A. (1964). Understanding the multiproblem family: A conceptual analysis and exploration in early identification. New York: Association Press.

Gewirtz, J. L. (1965). The course of infant smiling in four child-rearing environments in Israel. In B. M. Foss (Ed.), *Determinants of the infant behavior* (Vol. 3) (pp. 205–260). London: Methuen.

Gewitz, J. L. (1969). Levels of conceptual analysis in environment–infant interaction research. *Merrill-Palmer Quarterly, 15,* 9.

Gouin-Decarie, T. (1965). *Intelligence and affectivity in early childhood: An experimental study of Jean Piaget's object concept and object relations.* New York: International Universities Press.

Greenspan, N. (1981, October 28–31). *Funding and cost–benefit analysis for a preventive intervention program.* Paper presented at Pediatric Round Table on High-Risk Parenting sponsored by Johnson & Johnson Baby Products Company, Key Biscayne, FL.

Greenspan, S. I. (1979). Intelligence and adaption: An integration of psychoanalytic and Piagetian developmental psychology. *Psychological Issues* (Monograph No. 47–48). New York: International Universities Press.

Greenspan, S. I. (1981). Psychopathology and adaption in infancy and early childhood: Principles of clinical diagnosis and preventive intervention. *Clinical Infant Reports* (No. 1). New York: International Universities Press.

Greenspan, S. I., & Lieberman, A. F. (1980). Infants, mothers, and their interaction: A quantitative clinical approach to developmental assessment. In S. Greenspan & G. Pollock (Eds.), *The Course of Life: Psychoanalytic Contributions toward Understanding Personality Development; Vol. 1. Infancy and Early Childhood* (pp. 271–312). Washington, D.C.: U.S. Government Printing Office.

Greenspan, S. I., & Lourie, R. S. (1981). Developmental structuralist approach to the classification of adaptive and pathologic personality organization: Application to infancy and early childhood. *American Journal of Psychiatry, 138*(6) 725–735.

Greenspan, S. I., Lourie, R. S., & Nover, R. A. (1979). A developmental approach to the classification of psychopathology in infancy and early childhood. In J. Noshpitz (Ed.), *The basic handbook of child psychiatry* (Vol. 2) (pp. 157–164). New York: Basic Books.

Greenspan, S. I., Nover, R. A., & Scheuer, A. Q. (1984). A developmental, diagnostic approach to infants, young children, and their families. *Journal of Early Child Development and Care, 16,* 85–148.

Greenspan, S. I., & Porges, S. W. (1984). Psychopathology in infancy and early childhood: Clinical perspectives on the organization of sensory and affective–thematic experience. *Child Development, 55* (1), 49–70.

Greenspan, S. I., & Sharfstein, S. S. (1981). The efficacy of psychotherapy: Asking the right questions. *Archives of General Psychiatry, 38* (11), 1213–1219.

Greenspan, S. I., & Wieder, S. (1984). Dimensions and levels of the therapeutic process. *Psychotherapy: Theory, Research, and Practice, 1,* 5–23.

Gunter, B. G., & MacCorquodale, D. W. (1975). Informal role strategies of outreach workers in family planning clinics. *Journal of Health and Social Behavior, 15,* 127–135.

Hartmann, H. (1939). *Ego psychology and the problem of adaptation.* New York: International Universities Press.

Hofheimer, J. A., Poisson, S. S., Strauss, M. E., Eyler, F. D., & Greenspan, S. I. (1983).

Prenatal and behavioral characteristics of neonates born to multi-risk families. *Developmental and Behavioral Pediatrics, 4,*(3), 163–170.

Jasnow, M., Wieder, S., & Greenspan, S. I. (1982). Multi-risk families: Prenatal characteristics and family patterns.

Jasnow, M., Wieder, S., Greenspan, S. I., & Strauss, M. (1984). Identifying the multi-risk family prenatally: Antecedent psychosocial factors and infant developmental trends. *Infant Mental Health Journal, 4*(3), 165–201.

Kernberg, O. F. (1975). *Borderline conditions and pathological narcissism.* New York: Aronson.

Klaus, M., & Kennell, J. H. (1976). *Maternal–infant bonding: The impact of early separation or loss on family development.* St. Louis: Mosby.

Kohut, H. (1971). *The analysis of self: A systematic approach to the psychoanalytic treatment of narcissistic personality disorders.* New York: International Universities Press.

Lang, J. (1974). Planned short-term treatment in a family agency. *Social Casework, 55,* 369–374.

La Vietes, R. (1974). Crisis intervention for ghetto children. *American Journal of Orthopsychiatry, 44,* 720–727.

Levine, R. A. (1964). Treatment in the home: An experiment with low income multiproblem families. In F. Reissman, J. Cohen, & A. Pearl (Eds.), *Mental health of the poor* (pp. 329–335). New York: Free Press.

Lipsett, L. (1966). Learning processes of newborns. *Merrill-Palmer Quarterly, 12,* 45.

Lourie, R. S. (1971). The first three years of life: An overview of a new frontier of psychiatry. *American Journal of Psychiatry, 127,* 11.

Mahler, M. S., Pine, F., & Bergman, A. (1975). *The psychological birth of the human infant.* New York: Basic.

Mazer, M. (1972). Characteristics of multi-problem households: A study in psychosocial epidemiology. *American Journal Orthopsychiatry, 44,* 720–727.

McMahon, J. T. (1964). The working class psychiatric patient: A clinical view. In F. Reissman, J. Cohen, & A. Pearl (Eds.), *Mental health of the poor.* New York: Free Press.

Meltzoff, A. N., & Moore, K. M. (1977). Imitation of facial and manual gestures by human neonates. *Science, 198,* 75.

Minuchin, S., & Montalvo, B. (1967a). *Families of the slums.* New York: Basic Books.

Minuchin, S., & Montalvo, B. (1967b). Techniques for working with disorganized low socioeconomic families. *American Journal of Orthopsychiatry, 37,* 880–887.

Murphy, L. B., & Moriarty, A. E. (1976). *Vulnerability, coping, and growth.* New Haven, CT: Yale University Press.

Parmelee, A., Jr. (1972). Development of states in infants. In C. Clemente, D. Purpura, & F. Mayer (Eds.), *Sleep and the maturing nervous system* (pp. 199–228). New York: Academic Press.

Pavenstedt, E. (1967). *The drifters.* Boston: Little Brown.

Piaget, J. (1970). *Structuralism.* New York: Basic Books. (Original work published in 1968).

Piaget, J. (1972). The stages of the intellectual development of the child. In S. I. Harrison & J. F. McDermott (Eds.), *Childhood psychopathology.* New York: International Universities Press.

Powell, M. B., & Monahan, J. (1969). Reaching the rejects through multifamily group therapy. *International Journal of Psychotherapy, 19,* 35–43.

Reid, W. J., & Shyne, A. W. (1969). *Brief and extended casework.* New York: Columbia University Press.

Riessman, F. (1964). Role playing and the lower socioeconomic group. *Group Psychotherapy, 17,* 36–48.

Riessman, F., Cohen, J., & Pearl, A. (Eds.). (1964). *Mental health of the poor.* New York: Free Press.

Sander, L. (1962). Issues in early mother–child interaction. *Journal of American Academy of Child Psychiatry, 1,* 141.

Sperebas, N. B. (1974). Home visiting in family therapy. *Family Therapy, 1,* 171–178.

Spitz, R. A., Emde, R., & Metcalf, D. (1970). Further prototypes of ego formation. *Psychoanalytic Study of the Child, 25,* 417.

Sroufe, L., & Waters, E. (1977). Attachment as an organizational construct. *Child Development, 48,* 1184.

Sroufe, L., Waters, E., & Matas, L. (1974). Contextual determinants of infant affective response. In M. Lewis & L. Rosenblum (Eds.), *The origins of fear.* New York: Wiley.

Stern, D. (1974a). Mother and infant at play: The dyadic interaction involving facial, vocal, and gaze behaviors. In M. Lewis & L. Rosenblum (Eds.), *The effect of the infant on its caregiver.* New York: Wiley.

Stern, D. (1974b). The goal and structure of mother–infant play. *Journal of the American Academy of Child Psychiatry, 13,* 402.

Suarez, M. L., & Ricketson, M. A. (1974). Facilitating casework with protective service clients through use of volunteers. *Child Welfare, 52,* 313–322.

Tennes, K., Emde, R., Kisley, A., & Metcalf, D. (1972). The stimulus barrier in early infancy: An exploration of some formulations of John Benjamin. In R. Holt & E. Peterfreund (Eds.), *Psychoanalysis and contemporary science* (Vol. 1). New York: Macmillan.

Thomas, A., Chess, S., & Birch, H. G. (1968). *Temperament and behavior disorders in children.* New York: New York University Press.

U.S. Department of Health, Education, and Welfare. (1979). *Clinical Infant Intervention Research Programs; Selected Overview and Discussion* (DHEW Publication No. ADM 78-748; Stock No. 017-024-00914-8). Washington, DC: Superintendent of Documents, U.S. Government Printing Office.

Wolff, P. H. (1966). The causes, controls, and organization of behavior in the neonate. *Psychological Issues* (Monograph No. 17). New York: International Universities Press.

Zilbach, J. J. (1971). Crisis in chronic problem families. *International Psychiatry Clinics, 8,* 87–99.

Age-Specific Manifestations in Changing Psychosocial Risk

RICHARD Q. BELL

Introduction

Despite draconian reductions in federal outlays for support of the social and behavioral sciences, research on the prevention of child and adult mental disorders remains a high priority of the alcohol, drug abuse, and mental health programs of the federal government (Mayer, 1982). Up until the early 1980s, most scientists would say that prevention first requires early identification and then intervention. However, it is no longer generally accepted that the earliest point in development is most important in affecting later development, and that any intervention is better than no intervention at all.

Prediction from the newborn period has proven to be inconsistent and of low order, even with the best of instruments (Sameroff, 1978) and with assessments that were repeated often enough to achieve measurement stability (Bell, Weller, & Waldrop, 1971). Nancy Bayley's (1949) discovery that childhood and adult cognitive functioning were predicted poorly from early infancy has been rediscovered (Lewis & McGurk, 1972). The thesis that development in early infancy is critical for later development has been attacked, and increasing evidence for resiliency or recoverability of functioning has been reported (Clarke & Clarke, 1976). It now appears that all periods of development are important. The developmental process may take an unfortunate turn toward mental illness at any phase. Middle-class parents who have done what would ordinarily be considered an excellent job of childrearing find that their

169

children become dropouts or drug abusers when they are exposed to a peer group with values different from that of the family. Thus, it is apparent that infancy is not an exclusively critical period, and that interventions might be needed at other times.

While it would not be surprising that an intervention would be ineffective, four reports of adverse results from well-intentioned efforts in the area of antisocial behavior (Elliot, 1978; Gersten, Langner, & Simcha-Fagan, 1979; Klein, 1975; McCord, 1978) suggest the need for caution until a disorder is well enough understood to provide the basis for positive effects of intervention. Whereas it has been considered by many review committees on human subjects that intervention was an ethical imperative for any research contact with a population at risk, the burden of proof should now be on those who claim that an intervention should be undertaken whether or not the disorder is well understood.

At this time, it appears that early identification should mean detection prior to the emergence of symptoms that would make a disorder difficult to prevent or treat, and that intervention should not be undertaken until the developmental course of a disorder has been established on the basis of replicable, well-agreed-upon findings. Once this developmental course or history has been identified, including related changes in the family, peer, and community context (DCFPC), the optimal time and mode for intervention can be selected on rational grounds. Interventions should not be launched until this basic information on the developmental pathway is known.

Determining Developmental Pathways

The next question is how DCFPC can be determined for the various child and adult mental disorders. As far as research on etiology is concerned, the disorders that pose the least formidable problems in following their developmental course are those that show a short latency and a high base rate, such as substance abuse. It is quite feasible to carry out a customary longitudinal study of a cross-section of the population over a period of 4 years, identify those who became extreme substance abusers, and then scan the longitudinal data to determine the early precursors, turning points, and contextual influences. While feasible, this kind of study is inefficient, nonetheless, because most of the sample will emerge as not showing abuse.

The most difficult categories to track through time are the schizophrenia spectrum disorders and affective psychoses. With a latency of 25 to 30 years, and an incidence of 1% over that time, a longitudinal study of the general population is not practical. It is for this reason that investigators turned to retrospective reports from identified patients or parents. However, it is now widely accepted that events of the life history are imperfectly recorded and recalled by both classes of informants. These reports offer interesting hypotheses, but little more.

It is for this reason that investigators turned to what might be called the reconstituted longitudinal approaches. There are two such reconstituted longitudinal approaches. One approach involves following those seen in child clinics early in life into adult status. This line of research offers rich and intensive data, though not easily quantified, on the earliest phases of development. However, it is now well recognized that few children seen in clinics become schizophrenics or delinquents (Neale & Oltmanns, 1980, p. 384).

Whereas the follow-up approach has its richest data at a point in development when differentiation is not complete, as far as individual differences are concerned, another approach entitled the "follow-back" approach starts with records from later childhood or adulthood, when the disorder has evolved, a point in time when differentiation is much greater. The disadvantage to following back is that this approach has to rely on sketchy school and other records to construct the course of development. This second approach achieves salience by having the precise population of interest under study, but lacks good information on early phases of the disorder (Bell, 1959–1960).

The Risk Approach

Because of the limitations in the retrospective and reconstituted longitudinal studies, as well as the difficulties of conducting the customary longitudinal studies on long-latency, low-incidence disorders, Mednick and McNeil (1968) introduced the risk approach from medicine into the study of behavior disorders. Basically, the risk approach concentrates the outcome population in some way, so that one is studying the smallest possible number of individuals who will not emerge with the disorder. The bases of determining risk status must be factors that show an association with the disorder. These factors must be strong enough to override specific developmental phases and situational changes that also occur over time. A risk group consists of individuals, on the average, who do not show a disorder at Time 1, or only show it in partial form, but who will very possibly show a complete form of the disorder at Time 2. The concept is only applicable to groups, not to individuals, as is the case in most applications to behavioral and social science problems.

The risk approach differs from a prediction study in that individuals are selected to increase the frequency of certain outcomes. Typically, a prediction study selects a cohort that is thought to be representative of a larger population of interest, follows it up until its members can be characterized dependably, then relates early measures to later outcome. Often, a risk group can be formed after the follow-up, then tested for outcome, turning the predictive study into a risk study after the fact.

Studying children at risk permits investigators to study a disorder as it unfolds and without the complicated effects of labeling (provided the identification of risk exists only in the files of the investigators). High-quality data can be gathered at each developmental phase being studied, as the risk group is contrasted with the nonrisk group. Presumably, the differences uncovered between the two groups are related to the eventual outcome. However, this may come about through complex developmental changes that may not be traceable over many phases of development in which considerable change in the form of behavior has occurred.

The risk approach has been applied primarily to the schizophrenia-spectrum disorders, despite their low incidence in the general population, because government agencies and foundations recognize that these disorders take so long to develop, are so difficult to treat, and are such a costly caretaking burden. The application of the risk approach to this area was made possible by information from genetic studies that the risk for individuals who had one parent with schizophrenia was 10%, in contrast to the risk of only 1% in the general population. Schizophrenia in the parents could be present at any phase of development for their offspring, even including early pregnancy, and could be counted on to override all the developmental and situational changes that might affect other possible risk bases. Thus, a risk group and its nonrisk contrast group or series of such groups, could be constituted at any phase of development including the period just before outcome. From these contrasts it should be possible to determine what the characteristic phenomena of the risk group were at each time, as well as carry out limited follow-ups short of a full-scale longitudinal study. Theoretically, it should even be possible to reconstruct the developmental history segment by segment, each age segment being studied by a different team in a collaborative effort, or by having one team study three age groups simultaneously. In the latter case, it may be possible to articulate data from risk groups representing different ages, provided the terminal assessment of age Group 1 is at the same age and using the same instruments as the initial assessment of Group 2, and so on for Groups 2 and 3, as in the University of Rochester Child and Family Study (Wynne, 1984).

By itself, results from a single-risk study should not be used as a basis for intervention. Interventions should be launched only after sufficient studies have been carried out whose results can be integrated into stable, well-agreed-upon findings on the DCFPC. The fact that a difference exists between a risk and nonrisk group at a single age or phase of development does not imply that an intervention should then be launched to wipe out this difference. The reason why this reflexive type of intervention is not defensible is detailed later in this chapter, though I have already pointed out that it is no longer an ethical imperative that any research contact with a risk population should be accompanied by an intervention effort.

Although the most extensive applications of the risk approach have been to the schizophrenia-spectrum disorders, using the genetic basis, other nongenetic bases can be used, providing their effects are sufficiently persistent across maturational and situational fluctuations, as well as the interactions between these that can be expected in all but the most short-term follow-ups. For example, in the case of risk for antisocial behavior, a large family, lower SES status, and parental criminality can be used as bases for determining risk status.

Applications of The Risk Approach

Table 1 provides a list of disorders classified by latency and base rate, including some to which the risk approach has already been applied with reasonable success, and others for which the groundwork has been laid and which are on the threshold of active research (substance abuse, hyperactivity, and major depressive episodes). Incidence or prevalence figures commonly cited for the disorders are listed first, followed by commonly accepted estimates of latency. In the case of child abuse, learning disability, and substance abuse, the latency simply represents the time from identification of the risk group to the follow-up, each latency being taken from one of the most recently cited studies. In one case—major depressive episodes—the latency cannot be cited because of controversy over whether true childhood forms of depression exist and belong in the same category as the adult disorder. It would go beyond the purpose of this chapter or the need for accuracy to document the sources of incidence, prevalence or latency data, but in the case of disorders discussed in more detail in material to follow, the references provide relevant data.

It has already been mentioned that the traditional longitudinal study can be applied to disorders such as substance abuse, which show a short latency and high base rate. Smith and Fogg (1979) have carried out such a study, which provided predictions of substance abuse in grades 9 to 12, based on grades, peer ratings of obedience, self-reports of rebellious-

Table 1

Classification of Risk Groups

| | Risk groups | |
Latency	Low base rate	High base rate
Long	Schizophrenia (1%: 25 years)	Antisocial behavior (15%–30%: 9 years)[a]
	Affective psychoses (1%: 30 years)	Major depressive episodes (9%–21%: various)[a]
Short	Child abuse (3%: 3 years)	Substance abuse (11%–28%: 4 years)[a]
	Cultural–familial retardation (3%: 3–6 years)	
	Hyperactivity (4%: 3 years)[a]	
	Learning disability (3%: 3 years)[a]	

[a]Prevalence figures.

ness, cigarette smoking, and attitudes toward cigarette smoking 2 years earlier. The next step would be to form a risk group from a new sample on the basis of multiple cutoffs or regression, then follow the risk group and its nonrisk contrast with more frequent assessments in order to determine the pathways followed by the risk children in reaching the status of substance abuse 2–3 years later. The important thing is to determine the DPFPC in sufficient detail from several risk studies so that clues to timing and mode of intervention will become apparent.

Child abuse, cultural–familial retardation, hyperactivity, and learning disability are readily accessible to risk research, just as is substance abuse, though in this case the low base rate makes it imperative to concentrate risk in order to avoid only having 3 to 4 individuals out of 100 reaching the expected outcome at the end of 3 to 6 years. Despite a long history of clinical retrospective studies, comparisons of medications, as well as longitudinal studies in which the interest was in the nature of the individual in later childhood and adulthood, the field of hyperactivity has not reached the point of actually carrying out studies of risk groups. As in the case of substance abuse, at present the stage appears to be set by research for the risk approach to hyperactivity. The findings that set the stage have been reported by Waldrop, Bell, McLaughlin, and Halverson (1978), who showed that a brief examination for minor physical anomalies at the newborn period made it possible to predict distractible, fast-moving, impulsive, and aggressive play 3 years later in a nursery school. The minor physical anomalies were linked to aberrant development of the central nervous system (CNS), because both were a product of chromosome breakdowns or teratogenic agents affecting early fetal development. The visible minor physical anomalies permitted an inference about the invisible CNS disorders. In males, a high level of prediction and a low rate of false positives was achieved.

Just as in genetic risk for schizophrenia disorders, it is possible to assess minor physical anomalies at many times in early and later development. From the newborn period through the early school-age period, assessments have an equal likelihood of being associated with a later tendency toward hyperactivity. The prediction study used a nonclinical sample, but other research cited by the authors documents the same relationship with clinical hyperactivity. From research done to date, it appears that the first year would be the earliest that a risk group could be formed, both on the basis of the minor physical anomalies and a behavioral precursor of hyperactivity. Schexnider, Bell, Shebilske, and Quinn (1981) have shown that 1-year-olds with a high number of minor physical anomalies show a more rapid habituation of visual attention to human and geometric forms when fatigued, but habituate more slowly when not fatigued.

In the case of all other short latency, low base rate disorders, actual risk research has been carried out and, in the case of cultural-familial retardation and learning disability, there have been several studies. These studies have been reviewed by Bell and Pearl (1982).

The next classification of disorders in Table 1 poses still more difficulties for research on DCFPC. This comprises the long latency, high base rate disorders of antisocial behavior and major depressive episodes. Research on these disorders is still less difficult than that on schizophrenia and affective psychoses, however, because of the relatively high base rate. There have been many longitudinal studies of antisocial behavior directed to the determination of risk for delinquency, but very few have selected risk groups in advance. Just as in the case of the previous category, research on antisocial behavior has been reviewed previously from the standpoint of the risk approach (Bell & Pearl, 1982).

Major depressive episodes are listed as an area in which risk research could be carried out because the strong genetic contribution that is found in affective psychoses is also found in the less severe depressions. Children who have a parent with an affective psychosis have been included as a contrast risk group for children who have a parent with schizophrenia (Weintraub, Prinz, & Neale, 1978; Wynne, 1984), as have children with parents who have had major depressive episodes (Sameroff & Zax, 1978), but the latter disorders warrant much more research in their own right, considering their prevalence and the accessibility of the disorders to longitudinal and risk designs. The term "various" is used with respect to latency, because there is some question about whether a classification of childhood depression is defensible, as advocated by Cytryn and McKnew (1972).

As mentioned earlier, the long latency, low base rate disorders of schizophrenia and affective psychoses pose the most difficult research problems. The long latency itself poses considerable difficulty for risk research, as advanced here. For example, the first follow-up of an adolescent risk group that would possibly be near the point of outcome for schizophrenia would take 5 years.

To summarize, active research using the risk paradigm exists in the case of five disorders that range from infancy to adulthood in outcome, while in two disorders the risk research is a by-product of studying risk on another disorder. Two other disorders, hyperactivity and substance abuse, are on the threshold of more concerted efforts.

Problems in the Risk Approach

CONCEPTUAL

Up to this point in the chapter, I have discussed the basis for risk but have not examined its meaning closely. In one sense, the fact of schizophrenia in a parent is a fixed risk, even if not an established risk in the sense of blindness, deafness, or paralysis. However, in another sense this risk is not fixed. For example, a blind child functioning in a nursery school in which the other children have been trained to accommodate its limitations, and whose parents are also functioning well to facilitate its adjustment at home, is not at risk for social maladjustment. Nothing needs to be done further to avert undesirable consequences, and the child is doing as well as one might expect, given the handicap. A deaf infant may not encounter any serious difficulties in adaptation during the early sensorimotor period, being able to manipulate objects and maintain a bond with its parents in the ways most infants do but, as localization problems become apparent, parental expectations are upset and their concerns affect interactions. The change may move the infant from a nonrisk to a risk status until a diagnosis is made and counseling becomes available. Thus, even infants who have a basis not only for fixed risk, but also established risk, may not be at risk in a given period, due to their own development, situational changes, or interactions between the two.

METHODOLOGICAL

One puzzling problem in risk research arises out of the assessment methods used. In the field of developmental retardation, sometimes referred to as cultural–familial retardation, the basis for risk is low IQ in the mother and poverty level of the home. It has not been difficult to obtain differences between risk and nonrisk infants in behavioral development scores as early as 18 months, but the scores that differentiate these two groups in this phase show little relationship to IQ scores in the first grade. If the infant tests cannot predict IQ at school entry, how can they differentiate two groups that are very likely to differ in average IQ at the time of school entry?

Still another problem for risk research is the number of false positives in the prediction. Despite three decades of active research on antisocial behavior, the most recent large-scale study (West & Farrington, 1973) obtained over 50% false positives in predicting delinquency at age 16 from family and child characteristics at age 8 to 10 years. Granted that more sophisticated psychometric procedures such as multiple-gating might reduce these false positives somewhat, the puzzling fact remains that a concerted effort by many disciplines to establish risk in this disorder that shows a long latency and high base rate has revealed quite disappointing results.

One further puzzle in risk research involves shifts in those who are considered to be at risk. This problem has emerged from a comprehensive diagnostic and assessment survey of health, neurological, sensory, developmental, and psychological components at 2 weeks of age, and at 3 and 6 months, as a part of the Brookline Early Education Project (Levine, Palfrey, Lamb, Weisberg, & Bryk, 1977). This project starts with young infants and follows them up to kindergarten. Even though the criteria for risk were very generous, resulting in 73% being considered at risk at 2 weeks, 39% at 3 months, and 52% at 6 months, most of the children who were at risk in one period were not at risk in the next. The investigators were puzzled by what they called the "shifting sands effect."

Fluid Risk and Age-Specific Manifestations

The problems we have been discussing become more comprehensible if we make a distinction between risk basis, age-specific manifestations (ASM), and outcome behavior. Risk basis may be fixed, as in the case of sensorimotor limitations that we have discussed, or at least persistent in effects so that these effects override developmental phases and situational changes. However, as far as ASM are concerned, individuals move in and out of risk in any given period. Furthermore, we can assume that ASM may change from one developmental period to the next, even though the individuals may remain at risk as far as the fixed or overriding basis for risk is concerned.

ASM are behaviors that characterize a risk group versus a nonrisk group in a single phase of development, but are not necessarily a basis for risk themselves or similar to outcome characteristics of the risk group. Nor are ASM necessarily specific to one group. Both children at risk because of schizophrenia in a parent, and children at risk because of affective psychosis in a parent, have been differentiated from nonrisk groups, though it has been difficult to find differences between the two risk groups (Neale & Oltmanns, 1980, p. 376).

Individuals traversing the developmental terrain toward risk outcome may or may not show ASM in each phase or period. The risk group may contain a much larger number of individuals who have difficulties in adjustment at different times, while only a small number have problems throughout most of the phases of development and reach the outcome behavior that characterizes the risk group. In the case of congenital or genetic risk basis (e.g., hyperactivity, schizophrenia) all individuals may remain at risk as far as outcome is concerned, but the group will change in composition with respect to ASM. In the case of other disorders, such as developmental retardation, delinquency, and substance abuse, individuals may move in and out of risk basis, as well as ASM, in certain developmental phases.

Fluid Risk and Transactions

Sameroff (1977) has maintained that risk does not exist in the child, but rather is a transaction between the child and the situation. The basis for this implication of the transactional model is the general inability to demonstrate direct relationships between genetic or congenital factors and longitudinal outcome. However, since this viewpoint was announced, Waldrop et al. (1978) have demonstrated a strong predictive relationship between a congenital condition assessed in the newborn period and behavior 3 years later, a relationship that has already been discussed in detail. Furthermore, in the case of infants with sensory and motor handicaps, it is clear that risk does exist in the child. The infant or child is more than the sum of its interactions. Core characteristics of the individual have been underestimated because of research in which situations appeared to overpower individual characteristics when, in fact, inadequate measurement of characteristics of the individual, rather than situational specificity, was the problem (Epstein, 1980). Perhaps a better restatement of the implications from the transactional model for risk would be that risk basis may exist in the child, or in the situational context, but that transactions may be seen much more clearly in the ASM. What is seen in any one phase of development will be a transaction between the basis for risk, the developmental phenomena characterizing the phase, and the family, peer, or community context.

Factors Affecting ASM

General developmental change shown by most children in most societies will modify the form in which risk is manifest within any given phase. We should not expect that risk in a 1-year-old infant would take the same form as hyperactivity in a 3-year-old. The 1-year-old has neither the sensory, the motor, nor the cognitive capabilities of a 3-year-old. Thus the risk basis will be manifest through the filter of the particular developmental phase. It may be the case that certain laboratory procedures or tests so constrain behavior that parallels can be found between child and adult behavior pathology (Neale & Oltmanns, 1980, p. 372). However, in the case of behavior occurring in the natural setting, it verges on the ridiculous to look for literal or isomorphic continuities between infant or child and adult, considering that each is engaged in such different developmental tasks. The infant may be primarily engaged in generating stimulation by its own action and developing means–end schemas, the toddler in attaining control over its space by movement, the young child in playing with its peers, and the young adult in trying to achieve an identity. Thus, there is little reason to expect continuity between manifestations of a disorder in an early and a later period when major phases of development intervene.

In addition to the effects of general developmental change, there are interactions of that change with supports or demands by family and society at different times. An example of this kind of interaction has already been cited: the fact that a deaf child might function quite adequately in the early sensorimotor period, but would have difficulty meeting the expectations of his or her parents when problems with localization become obvious.

Situational changes may affect ASM whether or not there are any parallel or interacting general developmental changes. A new baby in the family, starting in a day-care center or preschool, and movement of the family from an apartment to a home are examples of frequent events in the history of a family, which are capable of modifying the form of ASM.

Although general developmental and situational changes will affect the form of ASM in any given period for most children at risk, the movement of some children in and out of ASM will be further determined by individual differences and specific variations in these factors. These unpredictable heterogeneous influences will show their effects in weaker and weaker cross-time correlations in longitudinal studies, as the interval between assessments increases. A relative may come to live with a family and provide support and stimulation for an otherwise neglected infant, thus deflecting its downward course relative to norms for behavior development. A learning disabled child may cease to show an attentional deficit after the mother and father are reunited and the mother begins reading with him or her, helping on homework, and providing emotional support. A family may move into a neighborhood with a high crime rate or a child may be transferred to a school that has a higher risk for delinquency, and thus the child's manifestations of risk will change. On the other hand, the family may move out of an area in which substance abuse is a common means by which peers cope with adjustment problems. An individual who is at risk for depression may form a relationship with a confidante who provides emotional support, and this may offset depression (Brown & Harris, 1978).

The possibility of obtaining meaningful negative or positive results in the long-latency disorders is much greater if the longitudinal study involves the last segment of risk including outcome, and no major phases of development occur in the follow-up period. For example, Mednick and Schulzinger (1968) in Denmark, and Rodnick, Goldstein, Lewis, and Doane (1982) in Los Angeles, have carried out 5- to 10-year follow-ups of adolescents at risk for schizophrenia to the earliest phase of the maximum risk, young adulthood. Although there are some questions as to whether early breakdown cases will be similar to later breakdown cases, a number of significant and theoretically useful findings have emerged from both studies.

With the problems of risk research in mind, and an indication of the need for a model of fluid or changing risk, resulting from the developmental and situational factors, we can return to the problem of early identification and intervention. Particularly in the case of the long-latency disorders, the risk approach is needed, and this involves (1) locating some overriding factor(s) that maintain(s) individuals at risk, (2) then contrasting risk and nonrisk groups to identify ASM, and finally (3) studying final segments of the developmental continuum when risk groups are followed to outcome. The objective is to obtain the information that is needed to form a coherent picture of the history of the disorder. From this history, a rational choice of an optimal time and mode of intervention should be possible.

Explanation of Problems in Risk Research

It is now appropriate, also, to return to the conceptual and methodological problems of risk research and to evaluate the extent to which the distinction between risk basis, ASM, and outcome behaviors is useful. First of all, congenital sensory and motor handicaps constitute a basis for fixed risk, but as far as the manifestations of the disorder in a particular phase are concerned, the infant can be described as moving in and out of risk.

How do we explain the large number of false positives in antisocial behavior? While there may be no change in the age range from 8 to 17 in risk basis (e.g., large family, criminality in parents, low SES), children are likely to be moving in and out of risk as far as ASM are concerned. Put in terms of scaled behaviors, the child may be at the first, second, third, or last position in the sequence of disobedience, running around, lying, stealing, and fire-setting which Patterson (1982, p. 250) has identified. Consider that this sequence probably can occur within the short age range of 2 to 3 years, and that in such a scalable series, there still might be little correlation between rank order for intensity of disobedience in the beginning of the sequence and fire-setting in the end. Then, what are the chances of finding strong predictive relations between rank orders on this sequence, (or several other yet-to-be discovered sequences) at age 8 and the ultimate criterion of self-reported or adjudicated delinquency at 17? Unlike the scaling procedure used by Patterson, Time 1–Time 2 correlations in a longitudinal study are based on relationships between such rank orders. The implication for research strategy based on the concept of a fluid risk model would be that this age span should be divided up into developmentally and ecologically meaningful segments, risk-group contrasts carried out within each segment, with a final segment followed up to the criteria mentioned. Because it seems quite likely that children are moving in and out of ASM, the research segments should be adjusted to the fact of fluidity.

The "shifting sands effect" reported from screening carried out in the Brookline Early Education Project is not difficult to see as a function of children moving in and out of ASM because of developmental, situational, and interactional change, just as in the case with the infant, child, and adult behavior disorders. Because the screening team identified quite different numbers of infants at risk in the different assessment periods (and quite reasonably, considering the many aspects of physiology that must be orchestrated in the neonatal period), it is evident that they had already adjusted to developmental differences. When the salient (and quite likely different) features at risk, in their judgement, at each period are considered, only a small percentage of children remain at risk through all periods (21%). The predictive basis for this 21% might be sought to provide risk bases for the next such survey. The study as it stands is entirely a study of ASM.

With respect to developmental retardation, the ability to distinguish risk and nonrisk groups with developmental tests, and the inability of the latter to correlate with early school-age IQ can be explained as the result of the rapid and metamorphic change in perceptual and cognitive functions from early infancy up to the point at which language emerges. The tests are testing these different processes at different times, and thus a child may be advanced on object permanence during Stage 3, but not advanced in IQ at kindergarten or first grade, despite the fact that she or he remains at risk throughout as far as the mother's IQ and SES level of the home are concerned. Because of the latter, the group remains at risk on whatever test items are appropriate for that age range, although individual children from the risk and nonrisk groups may be moving in and out of ASM (such as deficits on particular items, or a general decline relative to norms from 18 months of age on).

Summary

At one time, it might have seemed that the objectives of prevention would be best served by locating the earliest point in time at which some manifestations of a disorder can be detected, then carrying out an intervention that would alter the apparent precursor behavior. The credo could well be described as "the earlier the better, and any intervention is better than no intervention." Now that we have found prediction from earliest infancy to be tenuous at best, and that interventions may actually have adverse consequences rather than simply be effective or ineffective, it may be necessary to turn to a more rational solution to the problem. This involves selecting the optimal time and mode of intervention, based on knowledge of the developmental course of life history, including changes in the family, peer, and community context.

The longitudinal study is the method of choice for determining such pathways, and it can be applied to those disorders that develop within a short time and have a high frequency in the population, such as substance abuse. However, the longitudinal study is inefficient even in application to such short latency, high base rate disorders. It is quite inapplicable to categories such as the schizophrenia-spectrum disorders and affective psychoses, which do not reach full form for 25 to 30 years and only involve a 1% incidence in the general population. Retrospective reports and reconstituted longitudinal studies (such as follow-ups from child clinic records, or follow-backs from adult clinical populations) have proved to be useful sources of hypotheses, but inadequate in themselves for identifying sources of risk. For this reason, the risk-group approach has come into wide use. At the present time it is being applied actively to seven behavior disorders, and is at the threshold of application in two other disorders.

The risk approach requires a basis for risk that overrides developmental phases and situational changes, thus making it possible to distinguish a risk and nonrisk group in any given period. Although the most frequent application of the approach has been to the schizophrenia spectrum disorders, using the genetic linkage to the disorders as the basis for risk, it is also possible to use other bases, such as congenital contributors, SES, large family size, and problem behavior in parents. It is necessary to distinguish the basis for risk, ASM, and outcome before we can account for such anomalies as: (1) ability to distinguish risk and nonrisk groups even though the number of individuals in the risk group that will reach the outcome criteria is very small, (2) the ability to distinguish risk and nonrisk groups with tests that fail to correlate with outcome, and (3) infants or children with fixed or established risk who are, nonetheless, not at risk during certain periods and under certain circumstances. The distinctions make it possible to accommodate the likelihood that children move in and out of risk as far as ASM are concerned, though they may not necessarily change in the basis by which their risk was defined. Although risk basis may exist in the child (in the family or other situations), the transactions between the child's developmental status and situations may cause the child to move in and out of risk as far as ASM are concerned.

References

Bayley, N. (1949). Consistency and variability in the growth of intelligence from birth to eighteen years. *Journal of Genetic Psychology, 75,* 165–196.

Bell, R. Q. (1959–1960). Retrospective and prospective views of early personality development. *Merrill-Palmer Quarterly, 6,* 131–144.

Bell, R. Q., & Pearl, D. (1982). Implications for early identification of changing risk status in seven categories of risk. *Journal of Prevention in Human Services, 1.*

Bell, R. Q., Weller, G. M., & Waldrop, M. F. (1971). Newborn and preschooler: Organization of behavior and relations between periods. *Monographs of the Society for Research in Child Development, 36,* 1–2.

Brown, G. W., & Harris, T. (1978). *Social origins of depression: A study of psychiatric disorder.* New York: Free Press.

Clarke, A. M., & Clarke, A. D. B. (Eds.). (1976). *Early experience: Myth and evidence.* New York: Free Press.

Cytryn, L., & McKnew, D. (1972). Proposed classification of childhood depression. *American Journal of Psychiatry, 129,* 149–155.

Elliott, D. S. (1978). *Diversion: A study of alternative processing practices.* Final report to Center for Studies of Crime and Delinquency, Division of Special Mental Health Programs, NIMH, USPHS, Department of HHS.

Epstein, S. (1980). The stability of behavior: II. Implications for psychological research. *American Psychologist, 35,* 790–806.

Gersten, J. C., Langner, T. S., & Simcha-Fagan, O. (1979). Developmental patterns of types of behavioral disturbance and secondary prevention. *International Journal of Mental Health, 7,* 132–149.

Klein, M. (1975, June 30). *Alternative disposition for juvenile offenders: An assessment of the Los Angeles County Sheriff Department's "Juvenile Referral and Resource Development Program".* Social Science Research Institute, University of Southern California.

Lewis, M., & McGurk, H. (1972). Evaluation of infant intelligence. *Science, 178,* 1174–1177.

Levine, M. D., Palfrey, J. S., Lamb, G. A., Weisberg, H. I., & Bryk, A. S. (1977). Infants in a public school system: The indicators of early health and educational need. *Pediatrics, 60* (suppl.), 579–587.

Mayer, W. E. (1982, May). Anticipated impact of block grants. Paper presented at the annual meeting of the American Psychiatric Association, Toronto, Canada.

McCord, L. (1978). A thirty year follow-up of treatment effects. *American Psychologist, 33,* 284–289.

Mednick, S. A., & McNeil, G. S. (1968). Current methodology in research on the etiology of schizophrenia: Serious difficulties which suggest the use of the high risk approach. *Psychological Bulletin, 70,* 681–693.

Mednick, S. A., & Schulzinger, F. (1968). Some premorbid characteristics related to the breakdown of children with schizophrenic mothers. In M. D. Rosenthal & S. Kety (Eds.), *The transmission of schizophrenia* (pp. 267–292). New York: Pergamon.

Neale, L. M., & Oltmanns, T. S. (1980). *Schizophrenia.* New York: Wiley.

Patterson, G. R. (1982). *Coercive Family Process.* Eugene, OR: Castalia Press.

Rodnick, E. H., Goldstein, M. L., Lewis, L. M., & Doane, L. A. (1984). Parental communication style, affect and role as precursors of offspring schizophrenia spectrum disorders. In N. Watt, E. J. Anthony, L. Wynne, & J. Rolf (Eds.), *Children at risk for schizophrenia: A longitudinal perspective.* New York: Cambridge University Press.

Sameroff, A. J. (1977). Concepts of humanity. In G. W. Albee & J. M. Joffe (Eds.), *Primary prevention of psychopathology: Vol. I. The issues* (pp. 42–64). Hanover, MA: New England University Press.

Sameroff, A. J. (1978). Organization and stability of newborn behavior: A commentary on the Brazelton Neonatal Behavior Assessment Scale. *Monographs of the Society for Research in Child Development, 43,* (Nos. 5–6).

Sameroff, A. J., & Zax, M. (1978). In search of schizophrenia: Young offspring of schizophrenic women. In L. C. Wynne, R. L. Cromwell, & S. Matthysse (Eds.), *The nature of schizophrenia: New approaches to research and treatment* (pp. 430–441). New York: Wiley.

Schexnider, V. Y. R., Bell, R. Q., Shebilske, W., & Quinn, P. (1981). Habituation of visual attention in infants with minor physical anomalies. *Child Development, 52,* 812–818.

Smith, G. M., & Fogg, C. G. (1979). Psychological antecedents of teenage drug use. In R. G. Simmons (Ed.), *Research in community and mental health* (Vol. 1) (pp. 87–102). Greenwich, CN: JAI Press.

Waldrop, M. F., Bell, R. Q., McLaughlin, B., & Halverson, C. F. (1978). Newborn minor physical anomalies predict short attention span, peer aggression, and impulsivity at age 3. *Science, 199,* 563–564.

Weintraub, S., Prinz, R. L., & Neale, L. M. (1978). Peer evaluations of the competence of children vulnerable to psychopathology. *Journal of Abnormal Child Psychology, 6,* 461–473.

West, D. J., & Farrington, D. G. (1973). *Who becomes delinquent.* London: Heineman.
Wynne, L. (1984). The University of Rochester child and family study: Overview of research plan. In N. Watt, E. J. Anthony, L. Wynne, & J. Rolf (Eds.), *Children at risk for schizophrenia: A longitudinal perspective.* New York: Cambridge University Press.

8

Psychosocial Risk: Which Early Experiences Are Important for Whom?

DALE C. FARRAN AND DAVID H. COOPER

Introduction

The concept of risk is a difficult one and becomes more difficult as our understanding of developmental processes deepens. It is clear that risk for a particular disorder is an interactive phenomenon influenced by characteristics of the organism as well as of the environment. (Rubella, as a classic example, only has its devastating effects on the developing fetus at a particular period of the fetus's growth.) In this chapter, we review the factors in childhood which place children at risk for psychosocial problems. We have developed a model that describes the interaction between certain child characteristics, particular environmental contributions, and aberrant psychosocial outcomes. All the studies reviewed here are (1) longitudinal in nature—children followed for at least 1 year, but most frequently from childhood into adolescence; (2) studies of prediction and not just stability—that is, early experiences or characteristics are linked to later, different outcomes; and (3) concerned with psychosocial *outcomes*—something about the child's later social and emotional functioning should have been measured.

A word should be said about the last point. We have many studies in the developmental literature of the relation between psychosocial predictors and later intelligence. One major problem we have in looking at the same connections for psychosocial outcomes is that we do not have a

187

yardstick for measuring psychosocial development comparable to the IQ test. That lack may seem to be a major drawback to this line of research. Studies are not comparable because their outcomes and methods for measuring outcomes are different. Psychiatric definitions of normalcy, neurosis, and psychosis are notoriously unreliable. There is no standardly accepted paper and pencil or self-report measure of psychosocial development. Given these problems, how is a review in this area possible?

We would like to argue that the lack of a common yardstick measuring increments of psychosocial adjustment is not a drawback at all. In fact, the existence of such a yardstick in the study of intelligence has been a detriment to that realm of research because, among other things, it reduces complex cognitive processes to a single number. The demarcation line we would like to draw between good and poor psychosocial adjustment is one defined by the larger society. Poor psychosocial adjustment is present in people who have a history of occupational and marital instability, who have been institutionalized for a mental breakdown, who have been classified as antisocial personalities or who have received prolonged treatment for other severe emotional disorders. It is also present in adolescents who are rated as having difficulty interacting with peers and teachers or who are referred to child guidance clinics for behavior problems. In other words, in this chapter we are not focusing on subtle psychosocial adjustment problems. We are interested in outcomes that are universally agreed upon as being out of the normal variation range, problems that require the society to make special provisions for that person.

The following chapter first outlines methodological issues involved in studying risk, particularly risk for negative psychosocial outcomes. Next, we present our model for predicting who is at risk, and then the bulk of the chapter develops the model from existing studies.

Methodology

In this section, we discuss some of the methods employed in risk research. What is apparent from this discussion is that no consensus has been reached with regard to scientifically sound designs or procedures. Perhaps the variety of methods is a result of the difficult task faced by investigators desiring to demonstrate causal links without benefit of either experimental manipulation or the kind of evidence that emerges from studies in which subjects are randomly assigned to groups. Often the risk research is carried out using existing data from previously constituted groups, and the investigator must attempt to make sense of someone else's definitions, measurements, and analyses. The net result is confusion in definitions of risk, and often idiosyncratic and unvalidated assessments of outcome. Before turning to substantive findings, and to provide a context in which to evaluate the extant literature on risk, we address the issues of definition, measurement, and research design.

Definitions of Risk

The earliest use of the term *risk* that we found was by Robinson and Robinson (1965): "There appears to be relatively little agreement as to whether low birth weight (or prematurity) itself carries any particular *risk* to the child" (p. 425, emphasis added). Elsewhere, the priority was attributed to Mednick and Schulsinger as being the first to identify their subjects as being high-risk (Neale & Weintraub, 1975; Rosenthal, 1974). However, the Mednick–Schulsinger study did not appear in press until 1968, a year after Mednick (1967) first discussed the high-risk group method, and 3 years after the appearance of the Robinson's article in *Pediatrics*. Without making too much of the priority question, suffice it to say that use of the term *risk* as applied to research in behavioral sciences is a relatively recent occurrence, one contributor perhaps to the uncertainty about its exact definition.

UNCERTAINTY

The Webster (1984) dictionary defines *risk* as the "possibility of loss or injury." Inherent in the word "possible" is the uncertainty of outcome, along with some speculation as to the *probability* that exposure to an agent will have an adverse effect. It seems that risk research has as its aims and responsibilities, the identification of an agent, specification of an effect, and an estimate of the probability that they will be associated. We could add other burdens, such as defining the population at risk, specification of the time frame of the association, and the demonstration of a causal link. But at the minimum, we should expect risk researchers to provide us with an agent, an effect, and a probability estimate of their association. Surprisingly, few studies self-identified as being concerned with risk meet these minimal criteria.

STABILITY

Many studies purporting to assess risk are in fact studies of stability. To understand the distinction, it is necessary to separate risk agents from their effects, and to accept the uncertainty of their association. Exposure to the risk agent and subsequent adverse outcome are not the same phenomenon, but are two phenomena observed together. When a phenomenon is observed on two or more occasions, it would be incorrect to conclude that subsequent occurrences were the adverse effects of the earlier occurrence; if they are the same outcome, observed at different times, they are therefore stable to some degree. An example from the temperament literature may be helpful. Repeated measures of children's temperament have been used to assess the *stability* of various dimensions of temperament as well as clusters formed of these dimensions (Feiring & Lewis, 1980; Thomas & Chess, 1977; Torgerson, 1982). In contrast, assessments of early negative temperament have been associated with later psychiatric illness (Graham, Rutter, & George, 1973; Thomas & Chess, 1982). In the first case, the temporal stability of the phenomenon is studied. In the second, it is the risk of a specified adverse outcome that is associated with an antecedent factor: negative temperament.

RELATIVITY

Adverse psychosocial outcomes do not lie at the end of a single, one-way street. People travel multiple routes to the same end: some are exposed to one risk factor, others to different ones, some to none at all. If we want to assess the risk associated with a particular route, then comparison of the risk relative to other routes gives meaning to our findings. Thus, in risk research, control groups are employed to test the hypothesis that control subjects who are traveling a different (less risky) route arrive at a different endpoint. Some of the controls arrive at the adverse destination, but usually more at-risk subjects get there. Inferential statistics, such as *F*-tests or multiple regression analyses, are employed to confirm the observation that groups formed on the basis of where they began, then wound up at different destinations (prospective), or groups formed by where they wound up had started at different places (restrospective, e.g., Mellsop, 1972). The obtained p values reveal the probability that the findings are a result of sampling error, *not* the probability of an effect associated with a risk factor. For that probability level, a different type of statistic, called relative risk, is required. The concept of relative risk is used by epidemiologists to measure the strength of a risk factor and is defined as the ratio of the incidence of a specified outcome in an at-risk group to the incidence in a risk-free group. The extent to which this ratio deviates from unity makes it a meaningful index of the association between the risk factor and the outcome (MacMahon & Pugh, 1970). In a later section, we suggest appropriate designs for obtaining the relative risk of one or more risk factors.

Measurement

OPERATIONAL DEFINITIONS OF VARIABLES

Measurement of risk factors and outcomes begins with clearly operationalized definitions. Studies vary considerably in their attention to clarity of definition. Lack of replication and failure to progress toward answering questions by risk researchers are attributed by Birch (1974) to heterogeneity of definitions:

> If we are still in the stage of arguing that what you describe as schizophrenia and what somebody else describes as schizophrenia in his studies are not the same and you find different findings, this is parallel play. What is required is some uniform definition of the entity, operational definitions that can be effectively applied; in the absence of this, any kind of variations can occur. (p. 20)

VERIFICATION OF DATA

Risk research, especially long-term longitudinal studies, often depends on existing data, such as school records, mental health registers, or hospital rolls. This presents investigators with special problems related to the technical issues of reliability and validity. When data have been collected for one purpose, such as administrative monitoring, and used for different purposes, such as measurement of incidence in a population study, the researcher has an obligation to account for biases introduced by the lack of control over the data collection procedures (Rutter & Quinton, 1977). Study subjects who, on follow-up, fail to appear in a given registry, may appear on one not available to the researcher; thus underestimating the incidence at follow-up (e.g., Mellsop, 1972, p. 92). In school records, teachers, not blind to the comments of previous teachers, may perpetuate reports of misbehavior that has actually diminished or ceased (Chess, 1974, p. 209), thus overestimating the incidence. For example, one follow-up study of adult adjustment relied on military service records to differentiate among neurotics, bad conduct cases, and controls (Roff, 1974), although these diagnoses may have come about to serve particular institutional requirements of the military and therefore may have introduced bias into the data. Without some independent verification (validity data), the findings from such a study are most difficult to interpret.

BLIND ASSESSMENT

Longitudinal research that employs psychiatric outcome as a dependent measure must be particularly sensitive to the need for blind assessment. Because an integral part of the diagnostic process is taking a history of the subject, it may be impossible to sort out current functioning from earlier conditions. The diagnosis becomes in part at least an artifact of the history and thereby inflates the apparent association between the antecedent risk condition and subsequent outcome (e.g., Watt, 1974). Another aspect of blind assessment is knowledge by the examiner of the hypothesis under investigation. Awareness that the study is of schizophrenia, for example, may influence the examiner to inflate the prevalence of the disorder under investigation. In a study of adopting parents of schizophrenics, the dependent measure, prevalence of schizophrenia, was assessed by interviews in which "particular attention was directed towards detecting minimal 'soft signs' of schizophrenic dysfunction" (Wender, Rosenthal, Rainer, Greenhill, & Sarlin, 1977, p. 779). Keeping the examiner blind both to hypotheses and to the risk-status of the subjects is exemplified by a report of the effects of early malnutrition on later school behavior:

> Every teacher of every child was interviewed with respect to the behavior of all male children in her class, so that she did not know that we were interested in any particular case and did not know that we were interested in the relation of behavior to nutrition. (Birch, 1974, p. 13)

Another approach to preserving the blindness of the examiner to the risk status of subjects is deception. In a study of the school behavior of children of schizophrenic parents, teachers were asked to complete brief ratings of all children, then longer ratings of three children "selected randomly" (Neale & Weintraub, 1975, p. 105). The three were, of course, not randomly selected; one was the offspring of a schizophrenic parent and one was a matched control. The decision to employ deception of this type must not be undertaken lightly for several reasons. First, the deception may prove ineffective, because some teachers (or other professionals) may find out or figure out the actual methods for selecting subjects. Second, the deception, if discovered during the study, may threaten the relationship of the teachers and the researchers and jeopardize the commitment of teachers to provide reliable data. Third, teachers who have been deceived once, or who know of deceptive practices, may hesitate to participate in subsequent studies not only by the offending researchers but also by others.

STATISTICAL VERSUS PRACTICAL SIGNIFICANCE

Earlier, it was asserted that risk research has an obligation to specify an effect of a risk factor. Choosing how that effect is to be measured involves decisions regarding how the effect is to be conceptualized and what magnitude of the effect is of interest.

Conceptualization of the outcome variable is often inferred from the operationalization of dependent measures. For example, the concept of criminality was indicated in one study by a record of one or more criminal convictions (Mitchell & Rosa, 1981). This type of all or nothing conceptualization precludes the assessment of relative extent of outcome; in the example given, no estimate of more or less criminality is possible. However, this type of all or nothing definition is common in psychosocial risk research (e.g., is the person schizophrenic or not), and reflects both the medical model of disease present–disease absent, as well as the popular categorizations of people into those kinds of groups (for employment, for military service, etc.).

Effect size can be a difficult issue, especially when the outcome of interest is conceptualized as a continuum of subjectively determined points. For example, rating scales are a popular technique for assessing psychosocial outcome, and statistically significant differences in ratings are often used to confirm hypotheses about differences between groups constituted on the basis of the presence or absence of a putative risk factor (Baldwin, Cole, & Baldwin, 1982; Rolf, 1976; Weintraub, Neale, & Liebert, 1975). With large enough samples, fractional differences in mean ratings can attain statistical significance although the practical significance of even a one-point difference in ratings may be nil. Cook and Campbell (1979) recommend the use of magnitude estimates (e.g., "a reduction in prison recidivism of 20%," p. 40) along with statistical significance levels.

A final concern in the conceptualization of the outcome is to distinguish between gross abnormality and variability within the normal range. We touched on this issue in the earlier discussion of all-or-nothing classifications of outcome. While most psychosocial outcomes can be scaled and measured across a range from extremely negative to extremely positive, the factors that influence variability may themselves vary depending on which segment of the outcome distribution is considered. Given the possibility of this type of nonlinear association, initial steps in risk research should be to identify appropriate cutting points in the distribution of an outcome variable and to assess risk factors for the extremes separate from normal outcomes. Then, more fine-grained analysis of the effect of risk factors within these groups could produce more-precise data on these relationships.

Studies of risk tend to be one of two types: those that seek to identify risk factors and those that study known high-risk groups for purposes of describing the etiology or natural history of disorder. In subsequent sections, we specify designs, analyses, and approaches to interpretation appropriate to these types and their respective goals. No attempt will be made either to cover the full spectrum of methodological approaches or to undertake a highly technical treatment of statistical procedures. Rather, we present illustrations of innovative attempts to answer the question, Who is at risk for what?

Research Designs

In their early study of low birth weight, the Robinsons (1965) asked the prototypic risk question, "What is the general prognosis of a child whose birth weight was 2500 gm. or less compared with a child of comparable social background whose birth weight was over 2500 gm?" (p. 426). The design for the Robinsons' study is characteristic of most risk research published subsequently: two or more groups, constituted on the basis of the putative risk factor (in this case, birth weight) are followed over time, and tested for group mean differences on some outcome (in this case, cognitive and social development). Mean differences between the groups, when statistically significant, typically are interpreted as arising from the initial difference on the risk factor. This design has utility in the exploratory stage of risk studies. In subsequent sections, we present some techniques of sampling and design that have helped to clarify and extend the interpretation of observed mean differences.

SELECTIVE SAMPLING

Perhaps the most frequently studied high-risk population is the group of children of schizophrenic parents, particularly mothers. In an effort to identify the risk agents and to put the outcomes of these children in perspective, Rolf (1972) formed and assessed four target groups: children of schizophrenic mothers, children of depressed mothers, children with disturbed behavior directed toward themselves (internalizers) but healthy mothers, and children with disturbed behavior directed toward others (externalizers) but healthy mothers. In addition, each child was matched with two normal children; one control matched on sex, age, and psychosocial variables, the other matched only on sex and age. This

stratified sampling allowed Rolf to rank order the variables that contributed to observed group differences in social competence. For eample,
the nature of the mother's illness, more so than the fact that she was ill,
seemed to help differentiate among more or less socially competent
children. However, this study by Rolf nicely illustrates a dilemma, discussed by Fisher and Jones (1978), that when samples are so well defined as to be homogeneous, variables that in the general population
contribute little to the variance in the criterion variable "may appear to
have exaggerated importance" (p. 225). On the other hand, less well-
defined samples, in addition to being difficult to replicate, often lead to
ambiguous findings.

INNOVATIVE USE OF CONTROL GROUPS

The inclusion in a research design of multiple control groups demonstrates an awareness of the multivariate nature of most risk–outcome
relationships. Weintraub et al. (1975), studying children at-risk due to
having mentally ill parents, employed controls both matched on SES,
race, sex, and IQ and randomly selected: "The two control groups are
necessary since, on the one hand, matching is desirable to control for
potential confounding . . . while, on the other hand, variables that are
matched may not be merely peripheral correlatès of schizophrenia" (p.
840).

In a series of studies of the biological and adoptive parents of schizophrenic children, differences among the parent groups were examined,
to attempt to disentangle the genetic and environmental influences on
the development of schizophrenia (Wender et al., 1977): "We chose a
second comparison group to control for the effects of the child on the
parents. . . . The best compromise we could devise was to study the
biological parents of non-genetically produced severe retardates who
had been reared by their parents" (p. 778).

ADOPTION STUDIES

The work by Wender et al. (1977) not only illustrates the innovative
use of control groups, but also a creative variation on the use of adoptive
families in differentiating genetic from environmental risk factors. The
results of such adoption studies and the theoretical as well as practical
issues involved have been thoroughly explicated by Plomin, DeFries,
and McClearn (1980). It is sufficient to add here that because of the
consistently found implication of genetic risk in the development of
various psychosocial disorders (e.g., Mendlewicz & Rainer, 1977;

Wender et al. 1977), present and future risk researchers are advised to account for genetic factors in their work.

The probabilistic nature of risk research is evidence that adverse outcomes are not found in every case of exposed individuals; some are spared. One approach to improving prediction of outcome is to define narrowly the characteristics of the individual at the time of exposure, or, as Birch (1974) said, "In short, what we really have to begin to know is what were the antecedent circumstances to the exposure to risk—namely, what was the organism that came into the condition of risk" (p. 16). Further refinement of the relationship can be attained if the events are known that intervene after the risk event but before the outcome is assessed. This is the missing component of most longitudinal research, and quite possibly accounts for much of the unexplained variance. If, as Bell (this volume) has asserted, "individuals move in and out of risk status," then there are naturally occurring developmental cross-over experiments waiting to be studied—experiments in which, for example, some high-risk subjects become controls and vice versa. Figure 1 depicts the design of a longitudinal cross-over study. Various contrasts at the several assessment times can shed light on different issues. For example, comparison of the EEE, EEC, and ECC groups outlined in Figure 1 can be used to test hypotheses regarding the effect of persistence of the risk factor. Comparison of the CCE, CEE, and EEE groups can answer questions regarding effects of time of onset of the risk condition. Comparison of the EEC and ECC groups can address the question of the optimal time to intervene, if that is appropriate. Examples of risk conditions for which this design may be useful are unemployment of the parent, hospitalization of the child or parent, malnutrition (see Birch, 1974), parental–marital discord, et cetera.

The limitations on the use of such a design are not inconsiderable. First, the initial sample size required to fill all the cells and allow for attrition may be enormous. Second, the lack of random assignment at each branching point (including T_0, see Figure 1) introduces bias into the design, if the selection factors cannot be assessed and controlled statistically. Finally, and because of the many contrasts that can be analyzed, care should be taken not to capitalize on chance variation.

In our earlier discussion of uncertainty, it was asserted that one essential result of risk research is an estimate of the probability that a putative

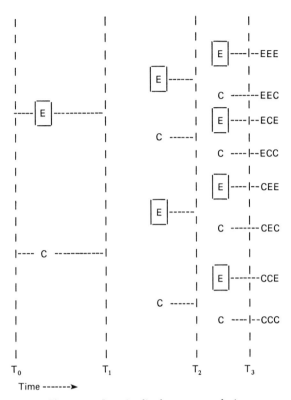

Figure 1. Longitudinal cross-over design.

risk factor will be associated with a specific adverse outcome. Case-control designs provide such estimates (Kleinbaum, Kupper, & Morgenstern, 1982). Before presenting this design, a word on measurement is needed. To estimate probability, the design of a study must depart from the standard comparison of group means on a continuous variable. Probability estimates require the enumeration of discrete events or categorically measured variables. For psychosocial outcomes, dichotomous variables are often appropriate, such as hospitalized or not, emotionally disturbed or not, arrested or not, et cetera. While it was argued earlier that such dichotomization may obscure an underlying continuum, in practical terms, the real-life consequence of quantitative differences in, say, criminality, may be insignificant, whereas, a categorical diagnosis of being a criminal carries an array of consequences. We agree that it is important not to lose sight of the underlying continua, especially when wrestling with definitions of conditions such as emotional disturbance

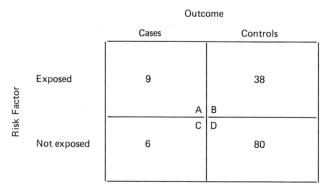

Figure 2.   A simple case-control design.

and criminality, but need also remember that for now the practical significance of continuously measured psychosocial outcomes is limited.

Returning to our discussion of case-control designs, we find them well suited to handling categorical and especially dichotomous measures. In this context, a *case* is an individual subject suffering from the adverse outcome of interest. A *control subject* is one who has been spared that outcome. A similar distinction is made for the putative risk factor: exposed or not exposed. The simplest case control design is then, a two-by-two table as shown in Figure 2. The entries in each cell will be the totals of individuals meeting each of the four conditions, and are assumed to represent the totals for each cell in a defined population, or an unbiased sample drawn from the population of interest.

RELATIVE RISK COMPUTATION

The purpose of this section is to call attention to a potentially productive approach to statistical treatment of data from risk studies: estimation of relative risk. Defined earlier as an incidence ratio, relative risk is a handy index of the strength of a risk factor. An example demonstrates the simplicity with which the relative risk can be determined. In a hypothetical study of the risk for developing schizophrenia (the outcome), the risk factor to be evaluated is exposure to (living with) a schizophrenic parent. When reported in conjunction with the confidence interval, the relative risk summarizes data concisely and yet meaningfully (Kleinbaum et al., 1982). Its computation is trivial. For the simple case–control design, and assuming either a 100% sample or a representative sample of the population of interest (see Figure 2), the relative risk is equal to the product of boxes A and D, divided by the product of boxes C and B, or $(9 \times 80) \div (38 \times 6) = 3.16$.

Translation of relative risk into common parlance is possible without gross distortion of its technical definition. In the example, the relative risk in this small sample is observed to equal 3.16, and the 95% confidence interval extends from 1 to 9; one can say then with 95% confidence that the risk of schizophrenia associated with exposure to a schizophrenic parent is from 1 to 9 times that of the unexposed numbers of that population.

INTERACTING FACTORS

What about multiple risk factors? The interaction of two risk factors, A and B, can be tested by comparing the relative risk estimates for A in the presence and in the absence of B. Examples of this procedure are to be found in Breslow and Day (1980, p. 108–109). Interactions are suggested by "appreciable variations in the odds ratio" (p. 108). Statistical tests for differences in the odds ratio may be found in Fleiss (1981). Procedures are available for estimating confidence intervals around an observed relative risk (see Miettinen, 1970).

INTERPRETATION

The interpretation of relative risk, or odds ratio, differs substantially from that of statistical test values and p levels reported in most psychosocial research. Because the odds ratio itself is not tied to sample size, only sampling accuracy, observed values can be compared across replications of a study, regardless of differences in sample sizes. In contrast, large samples can make slight differences or weak associations appear to be highly significant if p levels are relied on too heavily. Sample size, however, will affect the size of the confidence interval around a relative risk, with small samples such as in the previous example resulting in large (and therefore, difficult to interpret) confidence intervals around an observed relative risk value.

SUMMARY

In this brief treatment of methodological issues, we tried to establish standards of scientific rigor against which to evaluate both the research reviewed subsequently as well as future work in the area of psychosocial risk. The obstacles presented to risk researchers by the unavailability of "true" experimental methods should not be viewed as insurmountable. Cook and Campbell (1979) have written in great detail on the conduct of quasi-experiments, including how and when their results may be used in drawing conclusions regarding cause and effect. Epidemiology and biostatistics provide solid methods for quantifying risk. And finally, we can turn to the extant literature (e.g. Birch, 1974; Rutter, 1977) for excellent reviews of the issues and suggestions for ways to answer tough questions.

In the following sections, we present a model that may prove helpful in understanding current available evidence of psychosocial risk and that may help in the conceptualization of future research. The organization of our literature review is guided by this proposed model.

Psychosocial Risk Model

The model we propose is an interactive one. Garmezy (1974), Rutter (1981), and Werner (1982) have written about "invulnerable children"—children who are exposed to risky conditions but who do not succumb to them. A great deal of work has gone into identifying which characteristics or environmental factors serve to protect these children from adversities and their consequences. The implicit presumption in this approach is that all children are equally vulnerable but that for some children their vulnerability is shielded by external factors (extended kin network, particular talents, and so forth). We argue that some children, by virtue of certain characteristics, are more *vulnerable* than others. We believe that children do not enter the world equally at-risk for reactivity to a negative environment; children have predispositions which make them allergic, in a sense. Only a small proportion of children who undergo risk experiences develop the predicted, negative outcome. It is possible that they do so because they are particularly vulnerable due to individual characteristics that predispose them to react poorly to certain environmental conditions.

The next part of our psychosocial risk model is concerned with identifying the intervening environmental experiences that interact with child characteristics to produce deviance. We believe those intervening experiences to be of a particular type; not all aberrant environments produce deviance, even in vulnerable children. We believe discordant, stressful, and chaotic environments, with exposure to multiple caregivers, to be ones that produce problems for children who are vulnerable.

The kinds of problems we believe this combination of child characteristics and discordant intervening experiences produces involve problems adjusting to societal norms and difficulties in interacting socially with peers. Adjustment problems to the demands of society can be extreme (incarceration, antisocial personality) or moderate (financial and occupational instability). Problems with peers can also range in their level of manifestation (from low popularity as an adolescent to inability to form a stable marriage or relationship as an adult).

The rest of this chapter describes in detail the first two components of the model: characteristics that make children vulnerable and then the kinds of intervening experiences. Included within the section on intervening experiences is a discussion of the various psychosocial risk outcomes.

Child Characteristics

In this section, risk factors evident early in the lives of children are discussed. Studies are divided according to whether the nature of the risk factor is primarily familial or constitutional or related to gender. Rutter (1982) has suggested that variability within the normal range may be traced to factors other than those associated with gross abnormality. The organization of this review acknowledges that distinction. Risk factors for mild or subclinical behavioral deviance are discussed separately from those associated with moderate to severe clinical disorders.

Familial Risk Factors: Parental Mental Illness

It has been established that children of schizophrenic parents, especially if the mothers are schizophrenic, are at risk themselves of becoming schizophrenic (Mednick, Schulsinger, Teasdale, Schulsinger, Venables, & Rock, 1978). In an effort to chart the developmental course of the disorder, investigators have studied the high-risk, yet premorbid, offspring of schizophrenics. Sons of schizophrenic mothers were rated lower than controls on social competence by their elementary school peers, while sons and daughters of schizophrenic mothers were rated by teachers as more aggressive than controls (Rolf, 1972). These findings are generally supported by more recent studies. Peer-rated social competence of high-risk boys and girls was lower than controls (Fisher, Harder, Kokes, & Schwartzman, 1982). Deviant behavioral ratings (as compared to controls) were noted for high-risk children in two additional studies (Hanson, Gottesman, & Heston, 1976; Weintraub et al., 1975). Weintraub et al. obtained similar results for children of depressed mothers.

Also, efforts to partition genetic from environmental risk factors have been reported. Studies of high-risk children reared by their mentally ill parents (e.g., Hanson et al., 1976; Rolf, 1972), have been inadequate to explain how the risk is transmitted across generations. Support for genetic transmission has come from adoption studies. In the basic adoption design, subjects adopted at birth or within their first year are studied, along with their adoptive and biological families. Resemblances between adoptees and their biological parents are assumed to be entirely explained by genetics, because environments were not shared. Similarly, resemblances between adoptees and adopting parents are assumed to be entirely explained by environment because genetic similarity is assumed to be near zero (Plomin et al., 1980). One study of this type compared the incidence of parental schizophrenia in biological and adopting parents of adoptees who become schizophrenic as adults (Wender et al., 1977). A comparison group of parents of severe retardates was included to control for the effect on adopting parents of raising a severely impaired child. Adopting parents had a significantly lower incidence of schizophrenia than biological parents of schizophrenic adoptees. The authors conclude that (1) adopting parents, while admittedly subject to screening by adoption agencies, were nonetheless representative (Evidence in support of this conclusion is the reported equal incidence of schizophrenia in the adopting and retardates' parent groups.); (2) genetics play the major role in the etiology of schizophrenia.

In a similar study, support for genetic transmission of manic depressive disorder was found (Mendlewicz & Rainer, 1977). An additional feature of this study was the inclusion of a sample of non-manic-depressive (normal) adoptees and their biological and adopting parents. These biological and adopting parents' incidence of psychopathology was equivalent to that of the adopting parents of manic-depressive adoptees and they were, therefore, considered to be representative rather than inordinately healthy.

Constitutional Risk Factors

Evidence is accumulating that supports the predictability of childhood behavioral disorders from early assessments of temperament. As Plomin (1983) has pointed out, the predictability referred to is more in the sense of statistically significant associations than clinically useful prognoses. In two studies, temperament ratings in the first year of life were associated with children's later need of treatment for mild behavioral disorders (Cameron, 1978) or acute behavioral crisis (Huttenen & Nyman, 1982). Mothers' retrospective ratings of their elementary school children's temperament in infancy predicted pervasive, nonorganic hyperactivity (Lambert, 1982). Dunn and Kendrick (1982) obtained temperament ratings for firstborn 2-year-olds at the time of their mothers' second pregnancy. Extreme temperaments, especially high intensity and negative mood, were associated with marked increases in problem behaviors after the birth of the younger sibling. Temperament ratings of

3- and 4-year-olds were related to their later adjustment in school (Thomas & Chess, 1982).

From the biological side, Mednick (Mednick et al., 1978) provides evidence that differences in the autonomic nervous system of high-risk children are not only associated with, but also integral to the development of schizophrenia. According to Mednick's theory, escape from a discomforting or fear-producing experience into irrelevant thought is rewarded by a rapid autonomic recovery from the discomforting arousal. The model is given stronger support from the data on males than on females. Direct effects (i.e., not mediated) on high-risk males who developed schizophrenia were noted for rapid autonomic nervous system recovery and early separation from the schizophrenic parent—an event that could qualify as a fear-producing experience.

Gender

Several thorough reviews have concluded that the risk of adverse psychosocial outcome for males is greater than for females. Boy babies are more susceptible to pre- and postnatal damage than girls (Eme, 1979; Maccoby & Jacklin, 1974). Early in life, boys display more aggression than girls (Maccoby & Jacklin, 1974) and encounter less tolerance for their behavioral deviance from adults than do girls (Eme, 1979). Possibly as a result of these and other differences, there is a "greater male prevalence in . . . adjustment reactions, antisocial disorders, gender identity disorders, learning disorders" (Eme, 1979, p. 591), as well as infantile autism and hyperactivity (Schwarz, 1979).

Beyond the age of early biological vulnerability, male children are also more susceptible to the effects of a disruptive family environment (Rutter, 1970, as cited in Eme, 1979). Rutter reports finding that the association between family discord and antisocial behavior is stronger for males than for females. Evidence for both the biological and environmental vulnerability of males suggests that maleness is not simply a neutral characteristic, but deserves consideration as one risk factor in the development of psychosocial deviance.

Summary: Risk Factors in Early Childhood

In this brief review, we have pointed to studies representative of the exploratory nature of most risk research. Relationships have been reliably demonstrated between early biological or behavioral factors and later behavioral deviance. However, the implications of these findings are more encouraging for researchers than for practitioners. First of all, samples of cases and controls have been generally small and not representative of general population incidence, either for the putative risk factors or for the later outcomes. Second, for the subclinical samples, differences between risk and nonrisk groups' outcomes have not been expressed in terms of practical significance. Third, with few exceptions (e.g., Mednick et al., 1978), the psychological mechanisms underlying continuity from risk status to later deviance have yet to be explored systematically. Finally, multivariate approaches may be the most productive. By allowing multiple risk-factors to vary simultaneously, one has the potential for testing more complex models of behavioral development.

Intervening Experiences and Outcomes

In this section, we discuss both outcomes and what we have termed *intervening experiences*—those experiences that appear to be linked to a variety of outcomes for children who possess the predisposing characteristics described in the preceding section. We have not separated outcomes into a separate section because they are difficult to talk about apart from their likely causes and because in many cases the outcomes appear to be interchangeable. For example, what makes one individual with the same vulnerabilities and experiences an alcoholic while another becomes an antisocial personality are probably accidental and uncontrollable turns of fate.

The various types of intervening experiences described range from mild to more extreme. We begin with variations in typical parent–child interactions.

General Mother–Child Interactions

EFFECTS OF PARENT ON CHILD

Despite Bell's (1968) admonition that development was a reciprocal process, with each member of the dyad both influencing and reacting to the other, studies continue to appear, which assess rather small variations within the broad band of normal parent–child interactions for their effect on the child's development. There is a body of literature that addresses the effects of these variations on intellectual development (see Haskins, this volume); in this chapter, we have restricted ourselves to social development.

The impetus for this kind of research has come from several sources, not the least of which is a psychodynamic approach to the study of personality development, an approach which assumes that variations among children are due almost solely to differences in parental interactions with them. In 1964, Bettye Caldwell summarized efforts to associate various parental socialization techniques (weaning, toilet training, and so forth) with children's personality characteristics. Despite a great deal of research, little association could be established.

Since then, studies of other aspects of maternal behavior confirm Caldwell's earlier conclusion about specific socialization techniques. A quick review suggests that we cannot say with any certainty that particular parenting styles are linked to child behaviors. Martin (1981) described a research study founded on the following premises: if at 10 months the infant and his or her mother were mutually responsive, then the dyad could be thought of as well-functioning; if the dyad functioned well when a child was young, then it would function well later; and finally, a well-functioning dyad would be associated with child-competence, socially. Unfortunately, only 35 of the original 49 infant–mother pairs were followed longitudinally to 42 months, and the hypothesis was upheld weakly only for boys.

Several larger studies have assessed similar kinds of interactions. In a brief report, Grow (1980) describes a 3-year longitudinal study of 448 mothers (of whom more than a third were unmarried) and their first-borns. She concludes that contented mothers, who used little corporal punishment and whose children were in good physical health were most likely to have well-adjusted 3-year-olds. Also dealing with a heterogeneous sample is a study by Jones, Rickel, and Smith (1980) of 72 preschoolers and their mothers. They linked maternal nurturance and lack of restrictiveness (scored from a paper and pencil assessment) to the child's scores on Shure and Spivak's problem-solving test, where the child had to think of different solutions or strategies related to social situations. Both of these studies have the serious problem of dealing with heterogeneity in their samples. The Grow study is too briefly reported to provide enough information, but it does appear as though the married and unmarried mothers (who likely came from different social and economic circumstances) were treated as a single group. In the Jones et al. study, the point is more clearly made. It is clear that subgroups differ in parents' reliance on authority and their ability to report their values in a paper and pencil format. It is also known that children in some subgroups are less verbal in responding to testing situations (even interviews). Maternal behaviors could, in fact, be unrelated to children's problem-solving strategies; the underlying connection may be social class or ethnic differences in both variables.

By observing only white middle-class infants, Matas, Arend, and Sroufe (1978) avoided the problems of heterogeneity in the sample. They were assessing the relationship between variations in security of attachment and maternal responsivity. The contribution of the mother was presumed to be her sensitivity to infant cues during the first year of life, which was thought to be linked to security of the attachment relationship at 18 months, which in turn was linked to the child's level of play and problem solving at 24 months. The assumption behind this line of research is that the infant is a constant and that any individual differences are due to environmental input. For example, to be rated high on quality of assistance, mothers had to provide help "in a way the child can understand it and at a time when he/she can use it" (pg. 555). Thus, the rating of the mother was greatly dependent on the child; the child had to use the mother's help for the mother to get a high score. (An oppositional toddler would likely also be uncooperative on problem-solving tasks.) It is important in studies like this one to find a way to study maternal behavior and child characteristics separately. (See Yoder, 1985, for one of the few examples of such an approach.)

CHILD'S CONTRIBUTION TO DYADIC FUNCTIONING

The child's contribution to the functioning of the dyad and thus perhaps to his or her own later development has been uncovered in a number of studies. Clarke-Stewart's (1973) initial work investigated the relationship between maternal and infant emotional expression across a set of 7 home visits. She found a strong relationship between signs of the child's attachments to his or her mother (looking at her, smiling, following and so forth) and the frequency of the mother's social behaviors toward the child. Through cross-lagged correlations, she determined that the child's positive emotion toward her or his mother caused the mother to express positive emotion toward the child later. In an ambitious attempt to replicate these and other findings from this study, Clarke-Stewart, VanderStoep, and Killian (1979) studied four other cohorts of children and found *no* general sociability factor. In fact, "sociability variables were not intercorrelated nor were they related to the same maternal variables" (pg. 791) across the four groups.

In a very comprehensive study of possible early mother–child interaction influences on sociability, Bakeman and Brown (1980) followed low-income black children over the first 3 years of life. They concluded that from birth, the only predictor of later social behavior was the rating of infant responsiveness and not any behaviors of the mothers. Bakeman and Brown believe that infant social responsiveness is a temperament factor and not one resulting from interaction experiences, and that their research gives evidence for a stable social disposition.

If Bakeman and Brown are correct, parental contribution to the infant's social development (within a broad normal range of parental behavior) would be very hard to deduce. Infants are likely to vary in this social orientation, and parents vary in their practices. Some parental variation is related to infant characteristics, while the rest of it is likely due to the orientation of the parents. However, these two sources of variation are not separable for individual investigation.

SUMMARY

Both Dunn (1976) and Kagan (1979) conclude that there is little support from all the research effort for the proposition that variations in child development are related to early handling by parents. As Dunn argues, "A system which enables an organism to learn from a wide range of possible environmental situations is clearly more biologically useful than one which specifies a restricted range" (pg. 485). In fact, the Baldwins (1973) conclude from their series of observational studies of different samples that there really are rather small variations among families in their play behavior with their children.

It is well established that these small variations are consistent differences in the behaviors of middle- and low-SES mothers (e.g., Farran & Haskins, 1980). However that these differences *within* an SES level are related to any outcome, cognitive or social, is not established. It may be that SES has a direct effect on the child separate from its transmission through the mother. Children may be more affected by the stability of their larger environment and what their parents model and actually do with their lives than they are by the amount and quality of parent–child play. Also, their perceptions of their parents and the rightness of their upbringing is dependent on the milieu in which they live. Where polymatry is the normal life style, for example, children do not feel deprived of mothering if they are separated from their biological mothers for large parts of the day (Leiderman & Leiderman, 1974).

Family Stress and Discord

MULTIPLICITY OF STRESSES

Stress in the family, both within and from without, is associated with greater behavior problems evidenced by children and subsequent difficulties in adaptation when those children are adults. Whether family stress has an effect on the children through its effects on the behaviors of the parents or whether the stress itself (e.g., financial worries, difficulties with father's work, chronic alcoholism of a parent) has a general

impact on the child is unclear and probably cannot be absolutely determined. Several major studies (Robins, 1966; Werner, this volume) and
reviews (Rutter, 1981) have concluded that the *number* of risk factors to
which a child is exposed is the critical factor in his or her adaptation and
subsequent social development. When children are exposed to three or
more risk factors in their backgrounds, no matter which particular ones
they are, the likelihood of future serious adjustment problems is very
high. (In Robins's 1966 study, for example, 84% of the adults who were
less antisocial as children but who later became adult sociopaths were
predictable by accumulating the risk factors in their childhood, factors
such as the father's being sociopathic, the child's having a history of
running away, and so forth.)

Richman, Stevenson, and Graham (1982) have conducted a major longitudinal study following 828 preschoolers through school entry, inves-
tigating the effects of various stresses on the presence of behavior problems in the children before school entry and afterwards. Those children
who appeared to have behavior disturbances at age 4 years came from
families in which there was a great deal of stress. These families, despite
being similar to a nondisturbed group on age and education of parents,
were under more housing, medical, and financial stress. (They may
have been poorer managers of their finances.) They showed major differences from families with nondisturbed children in the areas of family
relationship—the marital situation was less harmonious; children were
more subject to criticism and hostility, and the mothers were more likely
to show psychological disorder.

Two predisposing factors were suggested in this study: (1) Males were
more likely to continue the behavior disorder into school functioning;
and (2) cognitive delay was more characteristic of the disturbed group at
ages 4 and 8 years. Slower cognitive development could have been a
consequence of the family discord and stress or it could have been a
contributor to the child's vulnerability to family stress. The general finding of Richman et al. (1982) is that these families whose children were
behavior disordered were subject to more acute and chronic stresses
over the years of the study, a finding similar to Robins (1966), Rutter
(1981), and Werner (this volume).

Acute stress was associated with poor-quality maternal care in a study
of 275 primiparous, low-SES mothers by Egeland and Brunnquell (1979).
Mothers whom they characterized as offering inadequate care to their
children experienced stresses over the first 20 months of their infants'
lives of a chaotic and disruptive nature. They were also least able to cope
with stress. When compared to a group Egeland and Brunnquell characterized as being good mothers, fewer of the inadequate mothers had a

high school diploma; they were 5 years younger than the other group at the birth of this first child, and most had not attended the childbirth preparation classes.

A final note about family stress involves its greater negative potential if it occurs in an urban environment rather than a rural one (Rutter, Cox, Tupling, Berger, & Yule, 1975) and if it occurs in conjunction with the child's attending a school marked by high levels of discord compared to attending low-discord schools (Rutter & Quinton, 1977). This set of relationships reinforces the idea of multiple stresses. Thus, if a child encounters stress both at home, in the neighborhood, and in school, the chances for behavioral disturbance increase dramatically.

TEMPERAMENTAL VULNERABILITY TO FAMILY STRESS

It appears that family stress is a particularly potent, intervening experience for those children who may be vulnerable because of genetics, gender, or their temperamental characteristics. The contribution of temperament to adult adaptation has been explored by the Thomas and Chess group (1982), as they continue to follow their longitudinal sample. The preliminary reports for the sample in adulthood suggested that about 35% of the variance in adult adaptation could be accounted for by a combination of temperamental characteristics in the first or second year of life, parental conflict at age 3 years, and experiences of permanent separation from parents through divorce or death.

Another example of the interactive effects of temperament and family characteristics can be found in a study by Graham et al. (1973). They looked at adverse temperamental characteristics (such as negative mood, activity level, intensity of reactions) evidenced by children in families where one parent was mentally ill and found children with negative temperament to have more behavior disorders in school. In reviewing the alternative explanations for the association between temperament, parental mental illness, and behavior disorder, they were persuaded that the adverse temperamental characteristics rendered "the child more vulnerable to the adverse effects of family discord and other 'stress' factors." (pg. 337). Transient disturbances in these children may have become permanent problems because of temperamental patterns that made it difficult for parents with few resources to deal effectively with the child.

Also, negative temperamental characteristics can have an adverse effect on vulnerable parents. Thus, in the Graham et al. (1973) study, family discord might have been heightened to an intolerable level by the presence of a difficult child in a family already beset by mental illness.

Wolkind and DeSalis (1982) followed 106 mothers prenatally and for 42 months after the child's birth. They found that maternal depression at 42 months was strongly related to the possession of negative temperamental traits in their infants. The loss of self-esteem began for the mothers when their babies were difficult at 4 months. Mothers became tired and anxious; when their children were older, the mothers were depressed, suggesting an interactive, cyclical effect.

MATERNAL PSYCHOSIS

One particular type of family stress that has been studied extensively is the presence of mental illness in the mother prenatally and during the preschool years of her children. It is beyond the scope of this chapter to present a summary of the large number of connected studies in this area. The reader is referred to reviews by Garmezy (1974) and by Watt, Anthony, Wynne, and Roff (1982) for more detailed information.

One report has special relevance to the issue of family stress. Sameroff, Seifer, and Zax (1982) have summarized the Rochester study of children of schizophrenic mothers and other mentally ill mothers through 30 months. They conclude that their 3-year work "confirms the obvious. The poorest social adaptation (was) found for children coming from the worst social, psychological and financial circumstances." (pp. 64–65). They found no single effect on the children's social and intellectual development for having a schizophrenic mother. Rather, they found that SES had a pervasive effect and that its effects were profound in conjunction with mental illness of the mothers. Thus, in their sample, children of schizophrenic mothers who were also of low SES and who were black had the worst developmental pattern—they showed more maladjustment at home, and the lowest test scores, and were less responsive in the laboratory. High-SES white children performed the best, with low-SES white children performing intermediately.

A series of hierarchical multiple regressions directly compared the relative prediction from SES and severity of illness. In this study, it was clear that at 30 months, SES was a greater risk factor than any of the mental illness measures. Among the mental illness categories, though, neurotic depression was associated with more difficulties evidenced by the children than schizophrenia in the mothers.

Another longitudinal study (Mednick, 1973) of 207 children of schizophrenic mothers has followed them for a much longer period of time. Of the 207, 20 became seriously mentally ill over the course of the study. These were matched to 20 subjects for age, sex, and SES, who had not become mentally ill to determine other factors that might have played a role. Neither the mother's length or number of hospitalizations nor age of onset nor subtype of schizophrenia differentiated the breakdown group from the matched controls. However, mothers of the breakdown group tended to become ill within a year after the child's birth, while mothers of the controls tended to become ill several years later. Therefore, significantly more breakdown subjects had neither a mother nor a mother substitute from birth through age 10 years.

It appears then that the mere presence of mental illness in the parent may not have a direct effect on the child (save through its possible genetic transmission). Rather, it is an additional stress that may be the final factor in moving a vulnerable child in a multiproblem family toward pathology and behavioral disturbance. In fact, the *separations* of mother and child that are a by-product of the illness may be more difficult than living with mental illness itself. (A review in the *American Psychological Association Monitor* [Wolinsky, 1982] would appear to confirm this notion; a follow-up study of Israeli children of schizophrenic mothers showed that a much higher percentage became mentally ill if they were raised in a kibbutz than if they were home with their mentally ill mothers.)

SUMMARY

These various studies illuminate the potency of stressful family situations in tipping the balance for a child whose gender, genetic background, or temperament makes her or him vulnerable to later behavioral disturbance. No factor was shown to have a unique and major effect on producing child deviance, not even the most extreme—schizophrenia of the mother. However, various stress factors working in conjunction were shown to be highly related to problems in some children.

The following sections address experiences that happen to the child outside the family, which may also be potent interveners in producing deviance.

Separation Experiences

HOSPITALIZATION

The experience of a hospital admission for a young child is often particularly difficult because it is a result of trauma, frequently accompanied by pain as well as the indignities of being treated by unfamiliar adults. Also, in the past, it involved separation from one's family for a prolonged period. Although earlier work had described young children's immediate response to this abrupt and difficult experience (Schaffer & Callender, 1959; Spitz, 1945), there was little evidence to suggest that this experience may have a more lasting effect. Since then, however two large-scale studies have suggested that it does.

Douglas (1975) studied a cohort of 958 children born in 1946 who had hospital admissions. Detailed interviews with their parents were conducted from the time the children were 4 years old and every 2 years thereafter (a portion of these were checked against hospital records for accuracy; recall was quite good, perhaps because this sort of dramatic event is relatively easy to recall accurately). The children were assessed on other measures at ages 13, 15, and 17 years: teacher ratings, reading test scores, records of delinquency, and job changes.

Douglas found that troublesome behavior, (as rated by teachers), poor reading, delinquency, and an unstable job history increased with the number and length of hospital stays before age 5 years. Troublesome behavior and poor reading scores occurred more frequently in children with early, long, or repeated admissions, whether or not there were later admissions after age 5 years, while delinquency and job changes were associated with admissions before and after age 5. First hospital admissions after age 5 were not associated with any problems. Hospitalizations that were repeated admissions or were of more than a week's duration had the strongest consequences. (The median stay for these children was 8.5 days and 20% had readmissions.)

From interviews with the parents, Douglas determined the degree of disruption in the child's behavior associated at the time with the hospital admission. Excluding those children whose mothers reported deteriorated behavior after discharge removed the association between hospital admission and ratings of troublesomeness in adolescence. Children were more likely to suffer if (1) they were only children (Douglas argues that there was an intense mother–child bond greatly disrupted by separation); (2) there was a recent birth of a sibling or (3) there was a sibling 2–5 years older (Douglas argues that these latter situations may be associated with ambiguity in the child's relationship with her or his mother). The correlations among the different outcome measures in adolescence were quite low, suggesting that individual children may show different long-term effects.

Because the poor are hospitalized more frequently and have more troubles in adolescence, Quinton and Rutter (1976) argued that the Douglas findings were merely a product of poverty's continuing and long-lasting effect on children's health and behavior. They attempted to replicate the Douglas findings on a sample of children born in 1969, this time controlling for SES effects. Quinton and Rutter found also that a single hospital admission of more than a week or repeated admissions were associated with disturbance in adolescence. These findings were more pronounced in disadvantaged homes, but were found in all types of homes. They conclude that "while the evidence is necessarily circumstantial, the strong suggestion is that repeated admissions to hospital may well play some part in the causation of some cases of psychiatric disorder or emotional behavioral disturbance in later childhood" (pg. 455).

These two major studies have confirmed that radical separation from home before age 5 years is associated with later problems, especially in peer adjustment in adolescence. It is important to remember that hospital practices have changed a great deal since the 1970s. The Douglas cohort would have been hospitalized in the late 1940s, while Quinton and Rutter's group would have been admitted in the early 1960s. For the Douglas group, for example, 47% were allowed *no* visitation; only 3 of 958 mothers were allowed to stay with their child. Hospital stays for young children now frequently involve parental participation and are of shorter duration.

Maternal Disruption or Loss

A series of British studies has investigated "adult emotional capacity in relation to childhood experience" (Frommer & O'Shea, 1973b, pg. 159). These studies have assessed the mothering abilities and marital stability of women who themselves had experienced maternal separation or loss in childhood. The question addressed here is very similar to that studied by Harlow and Harlow (1969) with primates and broadens the idea of psychosocial risk. It is possible that one of the outcomes that should be studied with risk populations is their capability at performing the parental role years later.

Frommer and O'Shea (1973a) posed the hypothesis that maternal separation before age 11 years would result in later difficulties for these women in their own marriages. They interviewed 89 women shortly after the birth of their firstborns and every 3 months thereafter until the babies were 13 months. Initially, more separated-mothers were severely depressed, and by the time the babies were 6 to 7 months old, more separated-mothers were leaving their babies to feed themselves by propping the bottle. More of these mothers were pregnant again at the child's first birthday, and more had marital problems resulting in separation.

In an observational study designed to investigate the same hypothesis, Wolkind, Hall, and Pawlby (1977) also found a greater distancing of

separated mothers from their firstborns. Observed in the home, separated-mothers spent significantly more time out of sight than mothers
from nonseparated backgrounds; they spent less time holding their
babies in a face-to-face position. Even controlling for the greater distance
between them and their babies, the separated-mothers vocalized, touched, and looked less than the others. A follow-up of the children of these
mothers when the children were 27 months (Pawlby & Hall, 1980) revealed lower scores on the Reynell language scales, especially for girls.

While this line of research is extremely interesting, there are problems
with these studies. Frommer and O'Shea (1973a) used a different definition of separation from the one used by Wolkind et al. (1977); they
defined separation as occurring before age 11 years, whereas Wolkind et
al. defined separation as before age 16. (If the hospitalization studies are
a model, separation before 5 years could be the more useful demarcation.) Also, it appears from a follow-up study conducted by Frommer
and O'Shea (1973b) that many of their original nonseparated group had
indeed experienced separation, resulting in considerable overlap in the
childhood experiences of the two groups. One could argue that separation for the original group was more meaningful because they remem-
bered it initially and the other group did so only after being probed. The
critical aspect of a separation experience could be feeling abandoned or
bereaved rather than the actual experience. Nonetheless, further work
in this area would do well to standardize the age of separation, perhaps
including only those with younger separation experiences, and would
be advised to probe very carefully before assigning women to groups.

RADICAL SEPARATIONS: FOSTER CARE AND INSTITUTIONALIZATION

Some children are removed from their homes and experience not only
disruption of maternal caretaking, but also the loss of the family and
everything that is familiar for an extended period of time. Foster care
involves the placement of these children into homes with potential parent surrogates, while institutionalization involves placing them in a situation with numerous caregivers and little chance for the establishment
of an alternate parental relationship. The data suggest that separation
may be associated with long-term problems in peer adjustment and in
marital stability and security in the later parenting role, but that attachment to another adult (a parental replacement) is possible even if placement in an adoptive or foster home is late in the child's life.

Rathbun, McLaughlin, Bennett and Garland (1965) followed children
who had been adopted cross-nationally. These children had left not only
their families, but also their culture and their language. Following an

initial period of upset, these children showed adequate to superior personal competence and adjustment 6 years later. The children were all placed in above-average homes with families who must have been committed to easing their transition.

Low-income children in an urban environment who were placed by the courts in foster care (whose home situations therefore would have to be most inadequate) actually improved in intellectual functioning after placement (Fanshell & Shinn, 1978) and showed a 30% rate of emotional impairment. Fanshell and Shinn argue that this rate is the same as other low-income children. Children who remained in care after the 90-day mandatory, emergency-placement period fared better than children who were returned home.

While Fanshell and Shinn (1978) followed foster-care children for 5 years after placement, Meier (1965) found information on 82 adults who had been in foster care for 5 or more years when they were children and who had not returned to their own families. She concluded that there was a higher incidence of marital breakdown and illegitimate births among this group than in the general population, although on the whole the women in the group were faring relatively well. Disrupted marital relationships were much more common among the men. Many of the married former foster-care adults were using their in-laws as parent surrogates; they found this new family to be extremely important and turned to them for advice and help. Apparently, the ability to form a strong relationship with a parent surrogate is present through adulthood.

Tizard's series of studies of institutionalized children (Tizard & Hodges, 1978; Tizard & Joseph, 1970; Tizard & Rees, 1975) provide solid evidence of young children's ability to form strong attachment relationships with surrogate parents even after the extremely distressing experience of separating from parents and living in an institution with multiple caregivers. When seen at age 8 years, children who had been adopted (at whatever age) had a much closer relationship with their adoptive parents than children who had left the institution to be restored to their families. It seemed as though once having relinquished their children, no matter how pressing and unavoidable the reasons, the families had no emotional room for them. The later the child was restored to his or her family, the less likely it was that a good relationship could be established. This was not true of the adopted children; even the older adoptees appeared to have a very secure relationship with their new parents. Of course, there was a strong SES difference between the two sets of families to which children went when they left the institution. Adopting families tended to be older and more middle class and may have devoted much effort to establishing a good relationship with the child (similar to the cross-national adopting parents studied by Rathbun et al., 1965).

All of the institutionalized children, however, showed some effects of their previous experiences. These effects were particularly marked in their relationship with adults outside the family and in their interactions with peers. They showed as a group "an almost insatiable desire for adult attention, and a difficulty in forming good relationships with their peer group" (Tizard & Hodges, 1978; pg. 114). Tizard and Hodges assert that the experience of multiple and ever-changing caregivers had led to the development of overfriendly and attention-seeking behaviors, which once established were hard to modify. The children were not "affectionless" as evidenced by their solid relationships with adults who made an effort to establish one. Overfriendliness and attention-seeking, in fact, often have the opposite effect to the one desired, placing the child at an even greater disadvantage for learning appropriate social behaviors in a group.

Wolkind (1974) also studied the effects of institutionalization; however, he observed children of varying ages who were still in the institution. Wolkind believed that behavioral patterns he observed were secondary to the family situation and not so much a direct consequence of the institution. In this study, he did not have the opportunity to observe behavior outside the context of the institution once children were in other placements. Wolkind's data indicated that institutionalization maximized deviant behaviors, but that the form of the deviance was determined by the prior family situation. One-third of his group showed such severe problems in relating to peers and authority that they were diagnosed as conduct-disordered. This diagnosis was shown by children who had intermittently present or absent fathers and who came from a large family. Disinhibition was shown by 19 of the 92 children, and it was almost exclusively seen in those admitted to care at less than age 2 years. It may be linked to a lack of formation of an affectional bond with an adult; if Tizard and Hodges' data provide an example, these problems may be modified by a subsequent good adoptive placement.

SUMMARY

Radical separation of the child from her or his family when the child is under age 5 years does appear to be associated with poor psychosocial outcomes, most especially in the area of peer relationships, later marital stability, and the interactions with non-family-related adults. The extent of the influence seems highly dependent on the situation to which the child goes after separation and what happens subsequently. Children placed in hospitals for an extended period, with all the attendant trauma and pain, have problems in adolescence, even though they are returned to their natural families. Children placed in institutions by their families—given up, as it were—do very poorly both within the home and outside it if they are returned to the family that released them. All children who experienced large-group care with multiple caregivers (hospitals and institutions), no matter what else happened to them appeared to have developed inappropriate social skills for interacting with other children or authoritative adults.

The Utility of the Psychosocial Risk Model

Specific Example

Robins' series of studies (1966, this volume; Robins, Murphy, & Woodruff, 1971) have focused on the outcome in adulthood of sociopathology, a serious disturbance associated with job and marital instability, criminal behavior, alcoholism and drug abuse. Although many adult neuroses are not predictable from childhood symptoms or early experiences in the home, the predictability for this serious problem is alarmingly high. A clinic population followed into adulthood (Robins, 1966) revealed that at age 44 years, 61% of the childhood sociopathic group were still seriously antisocial. In fact, the most common age for improvement for those 39% who had improved was between ages 30 and 40. The best single predictor of later antisocial behavior was the degree of childhood antisocial behavior, including the variety, number, and severity of the symptoms shown.

Robins' work suggests that this serious malady is predicted by a combination of child characteristics and subsequent experiences and appears to be an apt demonstration of the utility of our risk model. She found that there seemed to be a genetic predisposition to childhood antisocial behaviors—two-thirds of the presociopaths had fathers who were sociopathic or alcoholic. She also found that males were especially vulnerable. From the Robins's work, it appears that two types of intervening experiences were related to later disturbance. The first involves family discipline: where there was very little or it was inconsistent, children acted out more. The second involves an early childhood experience involving defiance of authorities. This one is particularly troublesome to describe because the more instances there are of these kinds of behaviors, then the greater the likelihood that the child will be defined as suffering the disorder. (One cannot explain a disorder by its definition.) It is possible, however, that the *first* act of being truant, of acting out in school severely enough to be expelled or of theft is the trigger for subsequently similar behavior. Thus, there might be males, with a genetic predisposition to sociopathy, with lax discipline in the home, who never commit the first challenge to authority and who therefore never set in motion the series of antisocial instances typical of the Robins' sample. Protection from committing that first act may come from the presence of an extended family of conforming relatives (Robins, West, & Herjanic, 1975; Rutter, 1981) or a positive strong relationship with a single parent (Rutter 1981; Werner, this volume). Evidence suggests that if vulnerable children reach age 10 years without committing a serious antisocial act, their adult status will not be marked by sociopathy (Robins et al., 1971).

Process Explanation

The previous sections have demonstrated an interaction between certain *child characteristics:* negative temperament, being male, cognitive delay, genetic background; certain *intervening experiences:* multiple stresses on the family or radical, early separations from the family; and certain *outcomes:* greater aggression, conduct disorder, behavioral disturbance with peers, inability to relate appropriately to adult authority. This interactive model is depicted in Figure 3. What the model delineates in a simplified form is what we believe to be the major route toward developing severe psychosocial adjustment problems in adolescence and adulthood. If one were going to target intervention efforts, for example, to those truly at risk, one would focus on a population with the predisposing characteristics listed, who are likely to undergo a subset of the intervening experiences listed. We believe that the more characteristics of the model that fit a particular individual, the more the child is at risk. We have left the model with spaces to be completed because we are aware that more factors may be added as research in this area develops.

In this section, we would like to pursue an explanation for why the association between the three components of the model exists. If we are right (that it takes the first two of these components, but neither alone, to produce the outcomes listed), why should that be so? We are not simply re-identifying the transactional model Sameroff and Chandler (1975) proposed—we are not saying solely that development is an interaction between the organism and her or his environment at any one moment. While that is likely true, the model we are presenting is much

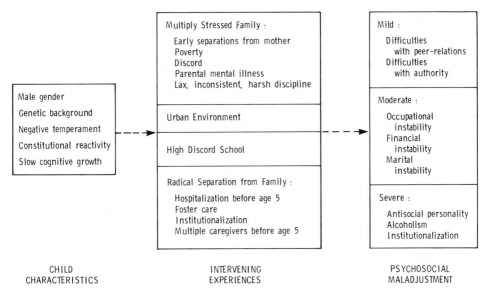

CHILD   INTERVENING   PSYCHOSOCIAL
CHARACTERISTICS   EXPERIENCES   MALADJUSTMENT

Figure 3. Psychosocial risk model.

more specific and limited to the psychosocial outcomes we have listed. Serious difficulties in psychosocial functioning can be predicted from the combination of the particular child characteristics that make the children vulnerable, and exposure to any of the intervening experiences we have described. (There may be additional vulnerability factors and additional intervening experiences to add to the list as more work is done; the discovery of these will make the model more precise.)

We would like to suggest that the process uniting these factors is the child's formation of internalized standards and an understanding of regularities in behavioral expectations. Certain children may find it more difficult to internalize rules. For some, temperamental characteristics such as activity level or negative mood or lack of malleability may make it necessary for them to experience more instances of reinforcement for standards or may elicit inconsistent, sometimes harsh punishment from impatient adults. Males, for example, tend to be more active, as well as more impulsive (Maccoby & Jacklin, 1974); they also tend to be much more vulnerable. Slow cognitive development could also be associated with slower internalization of rules and standards, and the need for more instances or demonstrations of rules and regularities before they are understood. Genetic predisposition (a family history of sociopathology, schizophrenia, or alcoholism) may be nothing more than the inheritance of negative temperamental characteristics that are the underlying factors for these specific disorders *or* it may provide a unique contribution to vulnerability.

Characteristics of the situations we have termed intervening experiences seem to link them and create their precipitating nature. The first set of experiences relating to family functioning—multiple family stress, discord, the presence of a psychotic parent—all have in common the likelihood of less regularity in expectations being presented to the child. These kinds of families are marked by periodic, extreme crises, leading to disruption in the flow of predictable events day to day. The parents in these families are coping not only with childrearing but also with the exigencies of poverty, occupational instability, and medical difficulties. There is evidence to suggest (Zussman, 1980) that when secure, affluent parents are taxed and under stress, their behavior toward their children changes; they become much less warm. They continue to control their children but without warmth. Baumrind (1967) noted that control without warmth is associated with dependent, preneurotic symptoms in nursery school children, even of middle-class parents.

The other kinds of situations producing these outcomes for vulnerable children involve a radical separation. Here, the child experiences an abrupt break in the expectancies and regularity of his or her environment. That break may be accompanied by physical pain and emotional upset. It appears that if the child radically separates from her or his family, but subsequently is placed in another orderly environment (a foster or adoptive home), he or she adjusts to these new standards and shows little long-term effect. If however, the child goes into a situation with multiple caregivers (and thus multiple, sometimes conflicting standards for behavior), or with large numbers of peers and few adults, then vulnerable children appear to develop the problems in peer relations and relating to society which we have described.

Why these outcomes? What is it about orderly environments that promotes internalization of standards and the suppression of aggression? Developmental psychology offers hints about the process. Zahn-Waxler, Radke-Yarrow, and King (1979) have demonstrated that children learn to be prosocial through very intense interactions with their mothers, where a rule for social behavior is presented by the mother immediately following a violation in an emotionally charged one-to-one interaction with the child. Collins, Sobal, and Westby (1981) have shown that second graders do not understand motivations for aggressive behavior and consequences for unmotivated aggression unless an adult points out the implicit relations between events. The more complicated the causal sequence is, the more explanation and interpretation the adult is going to have to make. Learning motivation and consequences for aggression is important, because research (Dodge, 1980) suggests that children later labeled as aggressive are ones who make no distinction between situations when aggression is clearly called for and situations where motivation is unclear or the consequences are uncertain. Finally, work by Chandler, Koch, and Paget (1977) shows that young children, when placed in situations where they do not have the organizational skills to cope, become "more affectively labile, behaviorally disorganized [and] motorically driven" (pg. 121). It is possible that radical placement in hospitals or institutions (or perhaps large-group daycare) exposes children to a situation where the organization is too difficult for them to grasp, resulting in anxiety and behavioral disorganization.

Summary

Robins (this volume) demonstrates that the rate of adult deviance is increasing, and moreover, increasing at an alarming rate. Our model would suggest that this would be so either because (1) more children are vulnerable—that is, there are more negative-temperament children being born or something similar, or (2) children who are vulnerable are being exposed to more-adverse environmental situations, which maximize the likelihood that they will have psychosocial adjustment problems later. The first possibility does not seem very likely; there is no reason to suspect the genetic pool has recently been altered or that early infant characteristics are any different from years past. The second possibility is extremely likely. With the divorce rate nearing 50%, with an increasing urbanization of the population, with the multiplicity of stresses that face families today, the chances of a vulnerable child being exposed to an intervening experience that could trigger psychosocial maladjustment are greatly increased.

If we conclude that psychosocial maladjustment is on the increase, and understandably so, given our model, and if the root cause appears to lie in societal change, is there essentially nothing that can be done? We are not doomsayers, pessimists bewailing the loss of the next generation. The most important part of the chapter may be this last section and our initial attempts to explain the process by which these particular experiences affect vulnerable children. If we could understand the process, we could construct compensating experiences for children who are at risk in order to minimize the negative environmental effects. What we have to learn is not how to avoid the negative intervening experiences but how to provide alternative sources of support for the child. To do that, we need more focused research on the features of those experiences that are truly critical and more research directed toward intervention.

References

Bakeman, R., & Brown, J. (1980). Early interaction: Consequences for social and mental development at three years. *Child Development, 51,* 437–447.

Baldwin, A. L., & Baldwin, C. P. (1973). The study of mother–child interaction. *American Scientist, 61,* 714–721.

Baldwin, A., Cole, R., & Baldwin, C. (Eds.). (1982). Parental pathology, family interaction, and the competence of the child in school. *Monographs of the Society for Research in Child Development, 47* (5, Serial No. 197).

Baumrind, D. (1967). Child care practices anteceding three patterns of preschool behavior. *Genetic Psychology Monographs, 75,* 43–88.

Bell, R. (1968). A reinterpretation of the direction of effects in studies of socialization. *Psychological Review, 75,* 81–95.

Birch, H. (1974). Methodological issues in the longitudinal study of malnutrition. In D. Ricks, A. Thomas, & M. Roff (Eds.), *Life history research in psychology* (Vol. 3). Minneapolis: The University of Minnesota Press.

Breslow, N., & Day, N. (1980). *Statistical methods in cancer research: Vol. 1. The analysis of case-control studies.* Lyon, France: International Agency for Research on Cancer.

Caldwell, B. (1964). The effects of infant care. In M. L. Hoffman & L. L. Hoffman (Eds.), *Review of child development research* (Vol. 1). New York: Russell Sage.

Cameron, J. (1978). Parental treatment, children's temperament, and the risk of childhood behavioral problems: I. Initial temperament, parental attitudes and the incidence and form of behavioral problems. *American Journal of Orthopsychiatry, 48*(1), 140–147.

Chandler, M., Koch, P., & Paget, K. (1977). Developmental changes in the response of children to conditions of crowding and congestion. In H. McGurk (Ed.) *Ecological factors in human development.* Amsterdam, Holland: North Holland Publishing Company.

Chess, S. (1974). Commentary. In D. Ricks, A. Thomas, & M. Roff (Eds.), *Life history research in psychopathology* (Vol. 3). Minneapolis: The University of Minnesota Press.

Clarke-Stewart, K. A. (1973). Interactions between mothers and their young children: Characteristics and consequences. *Monographs of Society for Research in Child Development, 38* (6–7, Serial No. 153).

Clarke-Stewart, K. A., VanderStoep, L. P., & Killian, G. (1979). Analysis and replication of mother–child relations at two years of age. *Child Development, 50,* 777–793.

Collins, W. A., Sobal, B. L., & Westby, S. (1981). Effects of adult commentary on children's comprehension and inferences about a televised aggressive portrayal. *Child Development, 52,* 158–163.

Cook, T., & Campbell, D. (1979). *Quasi-experimentation: Design and analysis issues for field settings.* Boston: Houghton Mifflin.

Dodge, K. A. (1980). Social cognition and children's aggressive behavior. *Child Development, 51,* 162–170.

Douglas, J. W. B. (1975). Early hospital admissions and later disturbances of behaviour and learning. *Developmental Medicine and Child Neurology, 17,* 456–480.

Dunn, J. (1976). How far do early differences in mother–child relations affect later development? In P. P. G. Bateson & R. A. Hinde (Eds.), *Growing points in ethology*. Cambridge, England: Cambridge University Press.

Dunn, J., & Kendrick, C. (1982). Temperamental differences, family relationships, and young children's response to change within the family. In R. Porter & G. Collins (Eds.), *Temperamental differences in infants and young children (CIBA Foundation Symposium 89)*. Pitman Books Ltd.

Egeland, B., & Brunnquell, B. A. (1979). An at-risk approach to the study of child abuse. *American Academy of Child Psychiatry, 18*, 219–235.

Eme, R. (1979). Sex differences in childhood psychopathology: A review. *Psychological Bulletin, 86*(3), 574–595.

Fanshell, D., & Shinn, E. (1978). *Children in foster care: A longitudinal investigation*. New York: Columbia University Press.

Farran, D. C., & Haskins, R. (1980). Reciprocal influence in the social interactions of mothers and 3 year old children from different socioeconomic backgrounds. *Child Development, 51*, 780–791.

Feiring, C., & Lewis, M. (1980). Temperament: Sex differences and stability in vigor, activity, and persistence in the last three years of life. *The Journal of Genetic Psychology, 136*, 65–75.

Fisher, L., Harder, D., Kokes, R., & Schwartzman, P. (1982). School functioning of children at risk for behavioral pathology. In A. Baldwin, R. Cole, & C. Baldwin (Eds.), Parental pathology, family interaction, and the competence of the child in school. *Monographs of the Society for Research in Child Development, 47* (5, Serial No. 197).

Fisher, L., & Jones, F. (1978). Planning for the next generation of risk studies. *Schizophrenia Bulletin, 4*(2), 223–235.

Fleiss, J. L. (1981). *Statistical methods for rates and proportions*. (2nd ed.) New York: Wiley.

Frommer, E. A., & O'Shea, G. (1973a). Antenatal identification of women liable to have problems in managing their infants. *British Journal of Psychiatry, 123*, 149–156.

Frommer, E., & O'Shea, G. (1973b). The importance of childhood experience in relation to problems of marriage and family building. *British Journal of Psychiatry, 123*, 157–160.

Garmezy, N. (1974). Children at risk: The search for the antecedents to schizophrenia: Part II. Ongoing research programs, issues, and intervention. *Schizophrenia Bulletin, 9*, 55–125.

Graham, P., Rutter, M., & George, S. (1973). Temperamental characteristics as predictors of behavior disorders in children. *American Journal of Orthopsychiatry, 43*(3), 328–339.

Grow, L. J. (1980). Follow-up study of early child rearing. *Child Welfare, 59*, 311–313.

Hanson, D., Gottesman, I., & Heston, L. (1976). Some possible childhood indicators of adult schizophrenia inferred from children of schizophrenics. *British Journal of Psychiatry, 129*, 142–154.

Harlow, H. F., & Harlow, M. K. (1969). Effects of various mother–infant relationships on rhesus monkey behavior. In B. M. Foss (ed.), *Determinants of infant behavior* (Vol. 4). London: Methuen.

Huttenen, M., & Nyman, G. (1982). On the continuity, change and clinical value of infant temperament in a prospective longitudinal study. In M. Porter & G. Collins (Ed.), *Temperamental differences in infants and young children* (CIBA Symposium 89). London: Pitman Books, Ltd.

Jones, D., Rickel, A., & Smith, R. (1980). Maternal child-rearing practices and social problem-solving strategies among preschoolers. *Developmental Psychology, 16*, 241–242.

Kagan, J. (1979). Family experience and the child's development. *American Psychologist, 34*, 886–891.

Kleinbaum, D., Kupper, L., & Morgenstern, H. (1982). *Epidemiologic research: Principles and quantitative methods*. Belmont, CA: Lifetime Learning Publications.

Lambert, N. (1982). Temperament profiles of hyperactive children. *American Journal of Orthopsychiatry, 52*(3), 458–467.

Leiderman, P. H., & Leiderman, G. F. (1974). Affective and cognitive consequences of polymatric infant care in the east African highlands. In A. Pick (Ed.), *Minnesota Symposia on child psychology* (Vol. 8). Minneapolis: The University of Minnesota Press.

Maccoby, E., & Jacklin, C. (1974). *The psychology of sex differences*. Stanford: Stanford University Press.

MacMahon, B., & Pugh, T. (1970). *Epidemiology: Principles and methods*. Boston: Little, Brown and Co.

Martin, J. A. (1981). A longitudinal study of the consequences of early mother–infant interaction: A microanalytic approach. *Monographs of the Society for Research in Child Development, 46*, (3, Serial No. 190).

Matas, L., Arend, R., & Sroufe, L. A. (1978). Continuity of adaptation in the second year: The relationship between quality of attachment and later compliance. *Child Development, 49*, 547–556.

Mednick, B. R. (1973). Breakdown in high-risk subjects: Familial and early environmental factors. *Journal of Abnormal Psychology, 82*, 469–475.

Mednick, S. (1967). The children of schizophrenics: Serious difficulties in current research methodologies which suggest the use of the ''high-risk group'' method. In J. Romano (Ed.), *The origins of schizophrenia*. Amsterdam, NY: Excerpta Medica Foundation.

Mednick, S., Schulsinger, F., Teasdale, T., Schulsinger, H., Venables, P., & Rock, D. (1978). Schizophrenia in high-risk children: Sex differences in predisposing factors. In G. Serban (Ed.), *Cognitive defects in the development of mental illness*. New York: Brunner/Mazel.

Meier, E. G. (1965). Current circumstances of former foster children. *Child Welfare, 44*, 196–206.

Mellsop, G. (1972). Psychiatric patients seen as children and adults: Childhood predictors of adult illness. *Journal of Child Psychology and Psychiatry, 13*, 91–101.

Mendlewicz, J., & Rainer, J. (1977). Adoption study supporting genetic transmission in manic-depressive illness. *Nature, 268*, 327–329.

Miettinen, O. (1970). Estimation of relative risk from individually matched pairs. *Biometrics, 26*, 75–86.

Mitchell, S., & Rosa, P. (1981). Boyhood behavior problems as precursors of criminality: A fifteen year follow-up study. *Journal of Child Psychology and Psychiatry, 22*, 19–33.

Neale, J., & Weintraub, S. (1975). Children vulnerable to psychopathology: The Stony Brook High-Risk Project. *Journal of Abnormal Child Psychology, 3*(2), 95–113.

Pawlby, S., & Hall, F. (1980). Early interactions and later language development of children whose mothers come from disrupted families of origin. In T. Field, S. Goldberg, D. Stern, & A. Sostek (Eds.), *High-risk infants and children*. New York: Academic Press.

Plomin, R. (1983). Childhood temperament. In B. Lahey & A. Kazdin (Eds.), *Advances in clinical child psychology* (Vol. 6). New York: Plenum.

Plomin, R., Defries, J., & McClearn, G. (1980). *Behavioral genetics: A primer*. San Francisco: W. H. Freeman and Co.

Quinton, D., & Rutter, M. (1976). Early hospital admissions and later disturbances of behaviour: An attempted replication of Douglas' findings. *Developmental Medicine and Child Neurology, 18*, 447–459.

Rathbun, C., McLaughlin, H., Bennett, C., & Garland, J. (1965). Later adjustment of children following radical separation from family and culture. *American Journal of Orthopsychiatry, 35*, 604–609.

Richman, N., Stevenson, J., & Graham, P. J. (1982). *Pre-school to school: A behavioural study.* London: Academic Press.

Robins, L. (1966). *Deviant children grown up.* Baltimore, Maryland: The Williams & Wilkins Company.

Robins, L., Murphy, G., & Woodruff, R. A. (1971). Adult psychiatric status of black school boys. *Archives of General Psychiatry, 24,* 338–345.

Robins, L., West, P., & Herjanic, B. (1975). Arrests and delinquency in two generations: A study of black urban families and their children. *Journal of Child Psychology and Psychiatry, 16,* 125–140.

Robinson, N., & Robinson, H. (1965). A follow-up study of children of low birthweight and control children at school age. *Pediatrics, 35,* 425–433.

Roff, M. (1974). Childhood antecedents of adult neurosis, severe bad conduct, and psychological health. In D. Ricks, A. Thomas, & M. Roff (Eds.), *Life history research in psychopathology* (Vol. 3). Minneapolis: The University of Minnesota Press.

Rolf, J. E. (1972). The social and academic competence of children vulnerable to schizophrenia and other behavior pathologies. *Journal of Abnormal Psychology, 80*(3), 225–243.

Rolf, J. E. (1976). Peer status and the directionality of symptomatic behavior: Prime social competence predictors of outcome for vulnerable children. *American Journal of Orthopsychiatry, 46*(1), 74–88.

Rosenthal, D. (1974). Issues in high-risk studies of schizophrenia. In D. Ricks, A. Thomas, & M. Roff (Eds.), *Life history research in psychopathology,* (Vol. 3). Minneapolis: The University of Minnesota Press.

Rutter, M. (1977). Prospective studies to investigate behavioral change. In J. Strauss, H. Babigian, & M. Roff (Eds.) *The origins and course of psychopathology: Methods of longitudinal research.* New York: Plenum.

Rutter, M. (1981). *Maternal deprivation reassessed.* Middlesex England: Penquin Books Ltd.

Rutter, M. (1982). Epidemiological–longitudinal approaches to the study of development. In W. Collins (Ed.), *The concept of development* (Minnesota Symposium on Child Psychology, Vol. 15). Hillsdale, NJ: Erlbaum.

Rutter, M., Cox, A., Tupling, C., Berger, M., & Yule, W. (1975). Attainment and adjustment in two geographical areas I: The prevalence of psychiatric disorder. *British Journal of Psychiatry, 126,* 493–509.

Rutter, M., & Quinton, D. (1977). Psychiatric disorder—ecological factors and concepts of causation. In H. McGurk (Ed.), *Ecological factors in human development.* Amsterdam: North-Holland Publishing Co.

Sameroff, A., & Chandler, M. (1975). Reproductive risk and the continuum of caretaking casualty. In F. D. Horowitz, M. Hetherington, S. Scarr-Salapatek, & G. Siegel (Eds.), *Review of child development research* (Vol. 4). Chicago: University of Chicago.

Sameroff, A., Seifer, R., & Zax, M. (1982). Early development of children at risk for emotional disorder. *Monographs of the Society for Research in Child Development, 47*(7, Serial No. 199).

Schaffer, H. R. & Callender, W. M. (1959). Psychologic effects on hospitalization in infancy. *Pediatrics, 24,* 528–539.

Schwarz, J. C. (1979). Childhood origins of psychopathology. *American Psychologist, 34,* 879–885.

Spitz, R. (1945). Hospitalization: An inquiry into the genesis of psychiatric conditions in early childhood. *Psychoanalytic Study of the Child, 1,* 53–74.

Thomas, A., & Chess, S. (1977). *Temperament and development.* New York: Bruner/Mazel.

Thomas, A, & Chess, S. (1982). Temperament and follow-up to adulthood. In R. Porter & G. Collins (Eds.), *Temperamental differences in infants and young children* (CIBA Foundation Symposium 89). London: Pitman Books Ltd.

Tizard, B., & Hodges, J. (1978). The effects of early institutional rearing on the development of eight-year-old children. *Journal of Child Psychology and Psychiatry, 19,* 99–118.

Tizard, B., & Jospeh, A. (1970). The cognitive development of young children in residential care. *Journal of Child Psychology and Psychiatry, 11,* 177–186.

Tizard, B., & Rees, J. (1975). The effect of early institutional rearing on the behaviour problems and affectional relationships of four-year-old children. *Journal of Child Psychology and Psychiatry, 16,* 61–73.

Torgerson, A. (1982). Influence of genetic factors on temperament development in early childhood. In R. Porter & G. Collins (Eds.), *Temperamental differences in infants and young children* (CIBA Foundation Symposium 89). London: Pitman Books Ltd.

Watt, N. (1974). Childhood and adolescent routes to schizophrenia. In D. Ricks, A. Thomas, & M. Roff (Eds.), *Life history research in psychopathology, Vol. 3.* Minneapolis, MN: The University of Minnesota Press.

Watt, N., Anthony, E. J., Wynne, L., & Roff, J. (1982). *Children at risk for schizophrenia: A longitudinal perspective.* Cambridge, MA: Cambridge University Press.

Webster's Ninth New Collegiate Dictionary. (1984). Springfield, MA: Merriam Webster, Inc. Publishers.

Weintraub, S., Neale, J., & Liebert, D. (1975). Teachers' ratings of children vulnerable to psychopathology. *American Journal of Orthopsychiatry, 45*(5), 838–845.

Wender, P., Rosenthal, D., Rainer, J., Greenhill, L., & Sarlin, B. (1977). Schizophrenics' adopting parents. *Archives of General Psychiatry, 34,* 777–784.

Werner, E. (1982). *Vulnerable but invincible.* New York: McGraw Hill.

Wolinsky, J. (1982, November). Israeli schizophrenia study surprises NIMH. *APA Monitor,* p. 1.

Wolkind, S. N. (1974). The components of "affectionless psychopathy" in institutionalized children. *Journal of Child Psychology and Psychiatry, 15,* 215–220.

Wolkind, S. N., & DeSalis, W. (1982). Infant temperament, maternal mental state, and child behavior problems. In R. Porter & G. Collins (Eds.), *Temperamental differences in infants and young children.* London: Pittman Books Ltd.

Wolkind, S., Hall, F., & Pawlby, S. (1977). Individual differences in mothering behavior: A combined epidemiological and observational approach. In P. J. Graham (Ed.), *Epidemiological approaches in child psychiatry.* London: Academic Press.

Yoder, P. (1985). *Maternal attributions of communication in dyads with handicapped and nonhandicapped 11-month-olds.* Unpublished doctoral dissertation, University of North Carolina, Chapel Hill.

Zahn-Waxler, C., Radke-Yarrow, M., & King, R. A. (1979). Child rearing and children's prosocial initiations toward victims of distress. *Child Development, 50,* 319–330.

Zussman, J. U. (1980). Situational determinants of parental behavior: Effects of competing cognitive activity. *Child Development, 51,* 792–800.

9

Changes in Conduct Disorder over Time*

LEE N. ROBINS

Introduction

Beginning in the 1920s, a series of studies have supported the conclusion that conduct problems in childhood have important implications for later outcomes. Originally the interest was concentrated on formal adjudications of delinquency. Juvenile delinquents were found to have high risks of adult arrest (Glueck & Glueck, 1940). But it soon became clear that by the time of first court appearance, the offender typically had already had a long history of school and social maladjustment, and that children with these school and social predictors of delinquency had elevated arrest rates as adults, even if they never became official delinquents (Robins, 1966). These predictive behaviors of early childhood were not limited to illegal acts, but involved a set of signs of resistance toward authority, hostility toward peers and adults, impulsiveness, and

*The Epidemiologic Catchment Area Program is a series of five epidemiologic research studies performed by independent research teams in collaboration with staff of the Division of Biometry and Epidemiology (DBE) of the National Institute of Mental Health (NIMH). The NIMH Principal Collaborators are Darrel A. Regier, Ben Z. Locke, and Jack D. Burke, Jr.; the NIMH Project Officer is Carl A. Taube. The Principal Investigators and Co-investigators from the five sites are Yale University, U01 MH-34224—Jerome K. Myers, Myrna M. Weissman, and Gary Tischler; Johns Hopkins University, U01 MH-33870—Morton Kramer, Ernest Gruenberg, and Sam Shapiro; Washington University, St. Louis, U01 MH-33883—Lee N. Robins and John Helzer; Duke University, U01 MH-35386—Dan Blazer and Linda George; University of California, Los Angeles, U01 MH-35865—Marvin Karno, Richard L. Hough, Javier Escobar, Audrey Burnam, and Diane Timbers. This work acknowledges support of this program as well as Research Scientist Award MH-00334.

precocious assumption of behaviors reserved for adults: drinking, sexual relations, running away from the parental home, and leaving school. This configuration of behaviors, now summed up in the psychiatric nosology under the title of conduct disorder,[1] seems to be the basic predictor of later arrest, with delinquency only one striking part of the set of childhood behaviors.

It also became clear that what delinquency or this set of associated behaviors predicted was not crime alone, but a set of intercorrelated adult behaviors, which, like the children's constellation, reflected an inability to obey social norms and difficulty in maintaining responsible interpersonal relationships. The adult constellation included excessive drinking; failure to hold a job because of absenteeism, arguments with co-workers, and poor performance; marital breakups; child neglect; vagrancy; failure to pay debts; and fighting. In adults, this constellation of behaviors carries an official designation of antisocial personality in the psychiatric nomenclature (American Psychiatric Association, 1980).

While only about half the children with conduct disorder develop this constellation, it virtually never appears in adults who lack a history of conduct disorder. The latter observation has been made so regularly that conduct disorder before age 15 years is now a required criterion for antisocial personality in the third edition of the *Diagnostic and Statistical Manual* (DSM-III) of the American Psychiatric Association (APA, 1980). The predictive power of conduct problems in childhood for adult antisocial behaviors has led to a broad acceptance of the conclusion that antisocial behavior is the most stable of all childhood behavioral and psychological problems (Kohlberg, LaCrosse, & Ricks, 1972).

The studies that convinced researchers of the stability of antisocial behavior of childhood were follow-up studies. A follow-up design has three advantages: (1) the report of childhood problems cannot have been influenced by the later outcome, and thus there is no danger of retrospective bias; (2) the reports of child problems and adult outcomes are each made close to the time at which the events occurred, so that there is relatively little forgetting; and (3) premature death is one of the outcomes that can be studied. One of the findings of those follow-up stud-

---

[1]This constellation of childhood behaviors has no universally accepted name. In some studies it is referred to as aggression. This term can be misleading, because it seems to imply that the core symptom is fighting. There is no evidence that fighting is uniquely predictive; indeed stealing and truancy have been found to be better predictors, although the diversity of behaviors (i.e., a count of the number of different types of antisocial acts) or their frequency has been found a better predictor than the presence of any individual behavior.

ies that continued into adulthood is that conduct disorder does predict early violent deaths, both by accident and by homicide.

Most follow-up studies have selected as their probands children identified as delinquents or child-guidance-clinic patients, to guarantee sufficient cases with serious behavior problems. However, this design carries within it the danger that the true cause of the later problems was not the childhood behavior but rather factors that led to referral to court or treatment. Later extension of similar studies to general populations showed that this was not a problem; studies of general populations of children confirmed the initial finding that antisocial behavior in childhood was a stable and powerful predictor of later outcome (Farrington, in press; Gersten, Langner, Eisenberg, Simcha-Fagan, & McCarthy, 1976; Robins, 1978b; Rutter, 1972).

General population studies designed to investigate consequences of conduct problems or predictors of crime usually selected a sample largely or entirely male and urban lower class, to maximize the number of affected children. When conduct disorder was included in the context of studying all pathological conditions of childhood, as in the Isle of Wight study (Rutter, 1970), there was no such selection. In the Isle of Wight study, the same predictive power appeared: antisocial behavior was more stable at follow-up 4 years later than were other children's problems. Further, the Isle of Wight study, by covering all disorders of childhood, was able to show that conduct disorder was the most common of all childhood psychiatric problems.

Studies of the distribution of conduct disorder in the community have noted its concentration in boys (Eme, 1979) and in lower-class urban areas (Rutter, 1980). Variation in rates within urban lower-class areas has stimulated an interest in identifying schools that seem able to keep delinquency levels low even in a lower-class student body (Power, Alderson, Phillipson, Shoenberg, & Morris, 1967; Rutter, 1981).

Although there has been great attention to the geographical distribution of delinquency and conduct disorder in the community, there has been surprisingly little attention to variation in rates of conduct disorder over time. Nonetheless, it is generally believed that children's behavior problems have been increasing. Yet, without better data, one wonders whether we are merely witnessing a traditional complaint by the elders in each generation that youth has gone to the dogs—a complaint that dates at least from the days of Socrates. One cannot infer that the prevalence of conduct disorder is stable from the fact that it continues to predict later psychopathology with approximately the same power in samples studied in different eras. The strength of correlations between conduct problems and drug addiction appears to remain reasonably stable even when the prevalence of addiction increases as dramatically as it did among Vietnam soldiers (Robins, 1978a). While one could treat the well documented rise in juvenile delinquency rates as an indirect indicator of an increase in conduct disorder, a rise in official delinquency may reflect only increased police activity or administrative decisions to refer a higher proportion of youngsters picked up by the police to court, or a growing concentration of young people in cities, where police surveillance is greater than in small towns and rural areas, rather than a rise in illegal behavior.

Follow-up or cross-sectional studies done in different eras could in theory provide an estimate of changes over time, but unfortunately the studies in existence do not use common sampling strategies or common evaluation instruments, and therefore rates are not comparable. Nor are estimates of change available from single longitudinal or cross-sectional studies of children. In longitudinal studies, the cohort is often defined in terms of a narrow age range, to give all members an approximately equal number of years at risk of having engaged in the indicator behaviors before time of intake, and having had an equal number of years at risk of having carried out the adult behaviors being forecast by the time of follow-up. Cross-sectional studies of children, by definition, study a single generation, because otherwise not all subjects would be children at the time of study. Of course, samples all chosen from one generation provide no information about historic change.

Despite the absence of relevant survey data, there are indications other than the rise in juvenile delinquency that a true recent increase in the rate of conduct disorder may have occurred. The best evidence may be that while death rates have been declining overall since 1950, that decline has not been shared by youth. Death rates in the 15–24 age bracket were as high in 1970 as in 1950 (National Center for Health Statistics, 1983). Deaths from the major natural causes, cardiovascular and cancer, *did* decline among youths as they did in other age groups, but violent deaths, which account for three-fourths of all deaths in this age range, increased. While deaths in auto accidents in this age group peaked in 1970, homicide and suicide rates were still rising through the most recent reported year, 1983. Violent deaths are known to be predicted by conduct disorder (Robins, 1968).

There has been no dearth of theories as to *why* rates of conduct disorder have risen, even in the absence of compelling evidence that they have. Among popular theories are increasing secularization, with concurrent decline in the power of religious fear; increased parental permissiveness; working mothers; restrictions on corporal punishment in schools; high-rise apartment buildings that make supervision difficult; loss of a sense of community responsibility for children's rearing; and a general deterioration of moral values. An increase in conduct disorder could also have genetic causes. Because a number of studies have shown that the offspring of alcoholic and antisocial persons have an increased risk of conduct disorder, any factor that differentially affects the reproductive rate of these persons will affect the relative size of the high-risk cohort. If, for instance, young alcoholic and antisocial persons are less affected by the general trend toward postponed pregnancy and smaller families than their age peers, they will be at a reproductive advantage. Additionally, if the changes in social norms related to women's working and going into recreational places previously reserved for men results in more assortative mating between alcoholic or antisocial persons, the size of the pool of offspring bearing the genetic liability will be altered (Gershon, Dunner, Sturt, & Goodwin, 1973).

Not only may the rate of conduct disorder change over time, but there can also be changes in its manifestations. Some behaviors previously considered highly deviant became less so in the 1970s—premarital sex for women and illicit drug use for both sexes are prime examples. Such changes would lead us to expect that the order of popularity of deviant behaviors would change in the direction of a rise in the frequency of these behaviors relative to those whose status has not changed, for example, fighting and stealing. There also seems to be a trend toward decreased sexual differentiation in the traits parents try to instill in children. Thus, one might expect patterns of deviance for girls and boys to have become more similar. Because the changes are reported to be in the direction of increased freedom for girls to act in ways previously reserved for boys, the expected change should be in the direction of girls' deviance increasing more than boys', and taking on a more masculine pattern.

How can we test these hypotheses? The solution I explore is based on the observation that in a cross-sectional study of adults, each age group was reared in a different historical period. Because all groups were sampled in the same way and all were administered the same instrument measuring childhood conduct disorder, comparing histories of childhood behavior that occurred in different eras allows inferring historical change. But are there sufficient problems in using a cross-sectional study for this purpose so as to invalidate our conclusions?

The cross-sectional design lacks the advantage of studying conduct disorder during childhood, when there is no danger that the reporting of behavior will have been influenced by the adult outcomes that the childhood behaviors forecast. Studies in childhood also overcome the problem that recall is expected to decline the farther back in time the behaviors occurred. Although these seem substantial arguments for studying conduct disorder in children rather than by adult recall, there is some indication that these problems are not necessarily overwhelming. I have found approximately the same strength of relationships between conduct disorder and later behavior problems when I compared retrospective with prospective studies (Robins, 1978b), suggesting that retrospective reporting was not seriously biased or impaired. Interview responses concerning antisocial behavior have been found to be reliable and valid when tested by repeat interviews or verification in objective records (Hindelang, Hirschi, & Weis, 1979; Robins, 1966, 1974; Robins, Helzer, Croughan, & Ratcliff, 1981). Apparently deviant acts are memorable and will be reported honestly, so long as there is no danger that the respondent will suffer adverse consequences from such confessions.

If conduct problems can be recalled and reported reasonably accurately long after their occurrence, retrospective reports by adults of varying ages can rapidly give evidence for historical change and its effects. A cross-sectional retrospective study is very attractive in terms of cost and rapidity of data collection, compared with the only alternative that appears to be really error proof: a series of prospective studies taking in a new cohort of children every 10 years or so and follow-up of each cohort through the age of risk of the outcomes of interest. Not only is there a tedious waiting period, but also it is difficult to keep standardized the methods of assessment, both of conduct problems and of outcomes, as the development of new methods and interests change scientific practice over this long period.

However, there are clearly risks involved in drawing inferences about historic change from a cross-sectional study. Not only must the ability to recall childhood behavior and early adult behaviors not be seriously affected by the number of intervening years, so that older people are able to give as complete accounts as younger people, but also older people must be equally willing to report both childhood and adult deviant behavior, so that what is recalled is as fully reported for one age group as for the other. Next, we must assume that the disappearance of potential respondents through death, mobility, or institutionalization has not been more influenced by childhood or adult behaviors for one age cohort than for another. If any of these assumptions is incorrect, conclusions as to whether conduct disorder has increased over time may be erroneous.

Because members of the youngest cohort are closest in time to their childhoods and to their young adult problems, they should have better recall for both. Because they grew up in an age of decreased inhibition about discussing sex and perhaps also other formerly private matters, they may be more honest about the socially disapproved behaviors that constitute both conduct disorder and its consequences. Also, they have lived through fewer years at risk of migration, institutionalization, and the types of deaths that are consequences of the antisocial life styles predicted by conduct disorder.

In the face of these potentially biasing factors, we need to exercise whatever checks we can on our interpretations. One check on bias will be to see whether those behaviors which from common knowledge should have increased over time have actually done so more than other behaviors. If drug abuse has risen more than, for instance, stealing, it becomes more plausible that different answers from different age cohorts are not entirely artifacts of differential forgetting, inhibition, or mortality. A second check is to look at whether correlations between reported childhood behaviors and recent events are similar for young and old. Recent events should be no more likely to have been forgotten by the older than by the younger group, since they are the same distance in the past. If correlations between childhood behaviors and recent events are not diminished for the older cohorts, then we would infer that their reports of childhood behaviors have not suffered excessive random forgetting, which would reduce their predictive power.

These tests do not protect us entirely against the false inference that conduct disorder has increased. The younger cohort has not yet been through the risk period for deaths attributable to conduct disorder and its adult consequences. However, deaths yet to appear could only account for a very small error according to our estimates. For instance, let us assume that 20% of children have conduct disorder, that half of those with conduct disorder will develop adult antisocial behavior, that all cases of adult antisocial behavior began with conduct disorder in childhood, and that 20% of those who develop adult antisocial behavior will die violently in young adulthood. These deaths would reduce the correct estimate of 20% with conduct disorder to 18% for those beyond the age of risk of deaths due to conduct disorder, an underestimate of only 2%. (That is, deaths due to conduct disorder would have occurred in 20% of the 10% who represent those conduct disorder cases followed by adult antisocial behavior, or 2% of the sample.) An estimate of 20% of those with adult antisocial behavior dying of attributable causes in their youth is probably generous, and therefore a cross-sectional study of older adults would probably underestimate the true prevalence of conduct disorder because of mortality by less than 2%. If attributable mortality *were* a major source of error, the error should be constant in cohorts past the age of risk of these deaths—that is, those over 40. Therefore, if conduct disorder rates are not uniform among cohorts over 40 years of age, premature deaths in the older cohorts cannot explain the apparent increase in conduct disorder in the younger cohorts.

While early deaths create a bias in favor of finding higher rates of conduct disorder in cohorts under 40 years, loss of prospective respondents through institutionalization does the opposite. The type of institutionalization best predicted by conduct disorder is incarceration, and the prison population is extremely young. In the random sample of prisoners included in a St. Louis sample, 73% were under the age of 30. Thus a cross-sectional household sample will miss some of the most severe young cases of conduct disorder, who are in jail or prison, whereas equally severe older cases will have served their terms and reentered the household population.

The expected loss of respondents due to migration is not so clearly from either younger or older cohorts. Mild male cases of conduct disorder often enlist in the military, probably because their adolescent problems have so restricted their education and eligibility for jobs that they cannot find employment (Robins, Hesselbrock, Wish, & Helzer, 1978). More severe cases are likely to be found ineligible by the services on the basis of their criminal histories. These enlistees are often such unsatisfactory soldiers that they are not encouraged to re-enlist. Thus, their service period is likely to remove them only from the youngest cohort.

Our follow-up of ex-child-guidance-clinic patients (Robins, 1966) showed that migration was more common among antisocial adults than others, but was usually over shorter distances. If this finding applies generally, to recent as well as to earlier cohorts, persons with a childhood history of conduct disorder are likely to still reside somewhere in the general geographic area in which they grew up and thus will still be accessible for interview as adults if one is surveying an exporter area like Missouri, but will be relatively absent if one is surveying an importer area like California.

A final source of potential bias in identifying persons with conduct disorder in a cross-sectional area survey comes from the sampling strategy typically used. From a specified geographic area, a sample of blocks is randomly selected; then dwelling units on those blocks are selected, using a random start, and selecting every Nth dwelling unit thereafter; and finally, a respondent is randomly selected from among the residents of selected dwelling units. A consequence of this sampling strategy is that persons unattached to a dwelling unit have no opportunity to be selected.

Although the current study tried to minimize this loss by including group quarters such as transient hotels as dwelling units and enumerating roomers and those away from home along with resident family members of the dwelling units surveyed, persons with no home address at all were missed. Their number is unknown because they are also missed by the U.S. Census. However, special studies of consecutive censuses has shown that those missed are principally young males, who reappear in later censuses when they become reattached to a household. Because conduct disorder predicts transiency, losing the transients should bias results of a cross-sectional survey *against* finding an increase in conduct disorder over time, because the youngest cohort will be the one most likely to include missed transients.

Because bias can occur in both directions, and because we do not know in which direction it is likely to be stronger, we need to be cautious in our interpretations and check for evidence for bias when we can.

Data Source and Methods

My colleagues and I have completed a survey of 3004 adults residing in households in the St. Louis Metropolitan Area. The households were selected from three mental-health catchment areas, one in the inner city, one suburban, and one that covers three counties made up of a mix of small towns and rural areas. Together, these three areas resemble the total U.S. population with respect to age and sex distributions; as compared with the United States, the area is somewhat more urban (85% vs. 74%) and has a somewhat higher proportion of black adults (19% vs. 12%).

Sample selection followed a typical area sampling strategy, beginning with a random selection of U.S. census enumeration districts, blocks within those districts, and dwelling units within those blocks. One person over 18 was randomly selected for interview from each dwelling unit that fell into the sample. There was no upper age limit. Interviews were completed with a resident of 80% of the selected households.

The sample was weighted to equal 1980 census counts in the area, in order to compensate for sample design factors (e.g., we selected only one person per household, regardless of the number in the household, and we oversampled blacks) and for nonresponse. Thus, the results I report should be representative for the household population living in these geographic areas. It is uncertain to what extent they are also representative for the country as a whole.

The study reported here is part of a large project known as the Epidemiology Catchment Area (ECA) project, which is being carried out in four other locations as well. The ECA project has as its chief goal ascertaining the prevalence and incidence of the major adult psychiatric diagnoses in DSM-III of the American Psychiatry Association (APA, 1980). This is accomplished by use of the Diagnostic Interview Schedule (DIS), which covers DSM-III criteria for 32 diagnoses (Robins et al., 1981). Criteria for one of those diagnoses, antisocial personality, includes having had at least 3 of 12 childhood behavior problems before age 15 years. Because those 12 problems are similar to the criterion behaviors for conduct disorder in DSM-III, the study provides an opportunity to compare the frequency of conduct disorder and each of its elements across age cohorts, and so to infer what historical changes in rates may have taken place in the disorder and its criterion behaviors.

In addition to diagnostic information, the study inquires about recent utilization of health services, recent life events, current health status, current living arrangements, and current occupational status. Thus, we can see whether conduct disorder's ability to predict these adult events has changed over time.

The 12 conduct disorder symptoms covered in the interview are stealing, sexual intercourse, fighting, discipline problems at school, chronic lying, repeated truancy, expulsion or suspension from school, getting drunk or using illicit durgs, vandalism, doing poorly in school despite adequate intelligence (underachieving), getting arrested or sent to juvenile court, or running away overnight. The specific questions used to elicit them appear in the Appendix. Persons who reported having 3 or more of these behaviors before age 15 are considered to have had conduct disorder as a child. This arbitrary choice of three behaviors reflects the rules in DMS-III:3 such behaviors before age 15 are required for the diagnosis of antisocial personality.

We restrict our report to the 2955 household residents who answered questions about at least 9 of the 12 childhood behaviors inquired about to ensure that a failure to meet criteria for conduct disorder was not due to lack of information. Those omitted because of incomplete information were largely ($N = 31$) elderly persons so ill or demented that they were unable to answer coherently. Seventeen (0.6% of the respondents) terminated the interview before reaching this group of questions. No one refused to answer these specific questions.

Results

As Figure 1 shows, the proportion qualifying as having had conduct disorder is greater in each successive birth cohort than it was in the

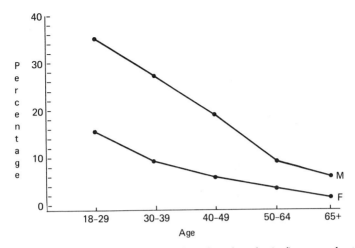

Figure 1.   Male versus female rates of conduct disorder in five age cohorts.

preceding one. This pattern holds for both males and females. Because the increase occurs for each successive cohort rather than beginning at age 40 or younger, it is unlikely that the failure of the youngest group to have survived the age of risk of excessive violent deaths is the full explanation. In addition, the increase in rates is too large for early deaths to be the sole explanation.

Rates of conduct disorder in the cohort over 65 are 6% for males and 0.5% in females; in the cohort under 30, rates are 36% for men and 13% for women ($p < .001$).

The curves in Figure 1 show male rates consistently higher than female rates. There is a larger difference between male and female rates in the youngest and next-youngest cohorts than in the older ones, the contrary of what we had expected given the general observation that sex-role differences had diminished. Deciding whether sex differences are actually increasing rather than decreasing as I would have predicted is not simple. A calculation of differences shows a widening gap, but if one considers ratios rather then differences, one can argue that women's rates have increased more than men's, because rates for women have increased 26-fold as compared with 6-fold for men. (Of course the higher rate for men than women in the oldest cohorts results in a lower maximum ratio for men than women: 100%:6% = a maximum of 16.7 for men; 100%:0.5% = a maximum of 200.0 for women.)

A look at the specific behaviors making up conduct disorder (Table 1) shows that each behavior is reported more frequently by the younger cohorts than the older ones, with one exception: Among women, a histo-

Table 1

Frequency of Specific Childhood Behavior Problems by Sex and Age Cohorts

	Percentage by age in years and by sex (Group N)									
	18–29		30–39		40–49		50–64		65+	
Behavior problems	F (517)	M (359)	F (385)	M (263)	F (206)	M (127)	F (324)	M (216)	F (350)	M (208)
Truancy	10.2	12.9	2.3	13.0	2.1	8.5	1.4	5.6	0.4	5.5
School expulsion	10.2	16.5	3.3	12.1	2.6	5	1.7	5.3	0.2	2.5
Arrest	1.8	9.2	1.6	7.8	0.2	2.9	0.1	2.5	0.0	1.3
Runaway overnight	3.6	2.6	1.3	4.6	0.5	0.7	0.1	1.1	0.3	0.1
Chronic lying	15.3	23.0	11.9	15.8	5.1	12.2	3.6	5.1	3.3	14.8
Sexual intercourse	11.5	27.9	5.1	21.1	5.5	24.0	2.9	12.0	2.0	8.1
Substance abuse	6.0	16.8	1.5	7.0	0.7	5.2	0.9	2.1	0.0	1.0
Stealing	19.4	37.1	13.3	26.0	8.4	26.5	6.1	16.2	5.7	7.4
Vandalism	1.1	11.3	2.1	11.4	0.0	4.8	0.5	0.9	0.0	5.4
Underachievement	4.6	7.9	3.9	9.7	1.8	6.3	3.2	4.6	1.1	6.2
School discipline	11.9	25.2	6.4	17.8	1.5	15.3	1.8	7.5	2.0	5.5
Fighting	8.0	20.1	4.4	18.3	10.8	14.4	5.3	10.4	3.8	12.2
Mean M:F difference	9.6%		9.0%		7.9%		3.6%		4.3%	
Mean M:F ratio	2.8		3.7		—		5.2		—	

ry of fighting in childhood is most commonly reported by the 40–49-year-old cohort. Although the perfectly consecutive increase in each successively younger cohort found for the summary measure, conduct disorder, is not found for every one of its component behaviors, it is found for school expulsion and arrests for both sexes, for truancy and lying for women, and for substance abuse and school discipline problems for men.

Our failure to find clear evidence for increasing similarity between boys' and girls' behavior in the younger cohorts is echoed when we look at individual behaviors. In the youngest cohort, males exceed females with respect to every behavior except running away, just as they did in the oldest cohort. Furthermore, the average difference between the proportions of each sex showing particular behaviors increases in each successively younger cohort. Nor can we find any single behavior in which there has been a regular and consistent narrowing of differences between the sexes. Ratios, on the other hand, tell a different story, as they did for the summary measure. Although average sex ratios cannot be calculated for two age cohorts because of the zero positive responses by women for some behaviors, they clearly seem to have fallen in the youngest cohort. However, we can identify no single behavior in which sex ratios have declined consistently in successive cohorts. Thus, given these inconclusive results as to convergence of female to male patterns of behavior, we need to apply other tests.

If such a convergence has occurred, as well as a narrowing gap in prevalence, we would also expect to find higher correlations between the frequency ranks of these behaviors in males and females for the younger than for the older cohorts, and we would expect the traditionally more exclusively masculine behaviors such as fighting, arrests, vandalism, and stealing to have gained in popularity with females and so to have moved upward in their frequency ranks for females, but not necessarily for males.

We in fact found only modest evidence for the first of these expectations, and none for the second. Table 2 shows that although the rank order correlation between the sexes with respect to the frequency of the 12 conduct problems has always been high, it has indeed increased slightly in the younger two cohorts, peaking at .89 in the cohort aged 30–39 at interview. However, we find little evidence for an upward movement in the ranks of the more traditionally masculine behaviors in girls. For both sexes, the most common behavior problems in each cohort have been lying, stealing, fighting, sex, and discipline problems. For women, lying has been more common than sex in every cohort, while for men the reverse has been true (see Table 1). In each cohort,

Table 2

Correlations between the Sexes
in Each Cohort with Respect
to Rank Order of Frequency
of 12 Conduct Problems

Age in years	r	z
18–29	.85	2.82
30–39	.89	2.95
40–49	.81	2.69
50–64	.68	2.26
65+	.84	2.78

arrests and vandalism have been among the behaviors least frequently reported by women, while running away has been the behavior least frequently reported by men.

We have not found, therefore, that traditionally masculine behaviors have gained ground with girls more than with boys. While the youngest cohort of women report as much lying as do men only 10 years their seniors, and as much truancy, school expulsion, and substance abuse as do men 20 years their seniors, their rate of arrest is comparable to that of men 40 years their seniors, and their childhood fighting is still lower than that reported by any male cohort. Thus, we see no evidence that the undoubted convergence of the sexes with respect to many aspects of their lives has been accompanied by girls' rushing to adopt the particularly aggressive and daring behavior of boys. Instead, their deviance has increased by more freely practicing the behaviors that do least violence to females' traditional roles.

Despite this overall coherence of patterns, Table 3 shows that in the youngest cohort as compared with the oldest, four behaviors have risen in frequency rank relative to others for both sexes: substance abuse, sexual intercourse, school discipline problems, and school expulsion or suspension. In addition, truancy and lying have risen among women, stealing among men.

Finding general stability of rank orders across cohorts for both sexes except for behaviors widely believed to have increased markedly among the young (drug abuse and sex) is consistent with the belief that even older cohorts provided meaningful self-reports about their childhood behavior. If forgetting plays a major role in their lower rates of these behaviors, their forgetting appears to be proportional to the relative frequencies of these behaviors. While forgetting strictly proportional to

Table 3

Change in Ranks of Specific Behaviors
between Oldest and Youngest Cohorts

Behaviors	Ranks moved up from oldest to youngest cohort	
	Women	Men
School expulsion	3.5	2.0
Substance abuse	3.0	5.0
School discipline	1.5	3.5
Truancy	1.5	−1.5
Lying	1.0	−3.0
Sexual intercourse	0.5	1.0
Stealing	0.0	3.0
Arrest	0.0	0.0
Vandalism	−1.0	−1.0
Runaway overnight	−2.0	0.0
Underachievement	−3.0	−6.0
Fighting	−5.0	−3.0

the actual frequencies is logically possible, it seems more probable that, like other sources of error, it would have been random and so have reduced the clarity of sex differences in older as compared to younger cohorts.

A more trenchant argument for the validity of recalled deviance than the stability of its patterns and its reflection of known social changes would be its ability to continue to predict adult outcomes. However, if we were to use outcomes covering the whole adult history, a problem would arise: early adult outcomes would be more likely to be forgotten by older than by younger cohorts, along with their childhood behavior, and therefore correlations would be found between childhood behavior and adult outcome for older cohorts if only because those with good memories recall both periods of their lives and those with poor memories forget both. To overcome this problem we confine our analyses to more recent outcomes, so that each respondent has the same risk of forgetting or recalling them. If recent events are predicted by conduct disorder for younger but not for older cohorts, that would suggest that inaccuracy in the older cohorts' recall of the childhood behaviors has masked the true relationship, although one might also expect that the longer interval between the childhood behaviors and the recent events for older than for younger cohorts might have weakened the predictive power of the childhood behavior.

Table 4

Power of Conduct Disorder to Predict Recent Events: Odds Ratio Comparing 3+ Behaviors before Age 15 vs. 0–2 Behaviors

	Men			Women		
	Young (<30)	Middle-aged (30–49)	Older (50+)	Young (<30)	Middle-aged (30–49)	Older (50+)
Years since age 15:	3–14	15–34	35+	3–14	15–34	35+
N with 3+ conduct problems before 15:	124	105	45	84	47	16
N with 0–2 conduct problems before 15:	235	285	379	433	544	658
A. Health Status and Care						
Ability to work restricted	2.1	2.0	1.3	1.9	2.7	1.3
Health care *not* private	1.2	2.4	2.2	2.2	1.3	5.8
No health insurance	1.4	2.1	1.2	3.5	1.1	2.2
Mental health services in last 6 months	3.0	1.7	2.8	2.5	4.1	3.1
B. Residence						
Moved in last 6 months	2.1	1.0	1.1	3.4	0.8	1.2
Lives in inner city	0.8	1.6	2.9	2.5	6.2	1.4

C. Job						
Not employed full-time	1.8	2.9	0.9	2.5	1.0	1.5
Lost job in last 6 months	1.4	1.9	1.0	2.1	3.1	5.8
Unemployed 6+ months in last 5 years (not retired or housewife)	3.8	2.1	3.1	3.7	2.2	14.4
D. Interpersonal						
Broke up with spouse/lover in last 6 months	2.0	4.2	1.1	2.3	2.3	5.2
Broke up with best friend in last 6 months	1.3	1.7	0.9	4.0	2.5	60.5
E. Antisocial						
Sued or suffered repossession in last 6 months	0.6	3.8	1.7	7.1	5.1	13.7
Arrested in last six months	2.1	4.0	24.0	1.8	6.3	193.5
Any antisocial behavior in last 3 years[a]	9.1	5.7	2.8	6.8	5.7	22.8
Mean	2.3	2.7	3.4	3.3	3.2	23.7
Median	1.9	2.1	1.5	2.5	2.4	5.5
Number of behaviors with odds ratio of 2 or higher:	7	9	6	12	10	10

[a]Includes arrest, illegal income, fighting, wife or childbeating, job problems, desertion, child neglect, frequent lying, transiency, prostitution or pimping.

Table 4 compares odds ratios across cohorts for all recent behaviors investigated that were predicted with an odds ratio of 1.5 or higher for *any* age–sex group. Odds ratios were chosen to compare the similarity of association because they are independent of variations in the proportions with a history of conduct disorder in the age–sex groups. The 5 cohorts have been compressed into 3 for this table because of the small number of conduct disorders in the older cohorts. As before, we define conduct disorder as reporting having ever done 3 or more of the 12 specified behaviors before age 15. At the bottom of the table are found the mean and median odds ratios and the number of odds ratios of 2 or greater.

For young women, 12 outcomes were predicted by childhood conduct disorder with an odds ratio of 2 or higher, compared with 10 for the older cohorts. This is the only summary comparison that indicates that associations between childhood behavior and adult outcomes are stronger for the younger than for the older cohorts. Indeed, the youngest group of both sexes has the lowest mean odds ratio, and their median odds ratio is lower than that of middle-aged men and older women. Therefore, we clearly do *not* find less powerful prediction of later outcomes for older than for younger cohorts, further evidence that the reporting by the elderly is reasonably accurate.

It is interesting that according to each of the summary criteria, conduct disorder predicts women's outcomes more efficiently than men's. Although rare in girls, conduct disorder appears to be particularly ominous when it does appear.

Table 4 also confirms earlier findings (Robins, 1966) that childhood conduct disorder predicts a wide variety of adult problems. The range includes mobility, health status and care, social status of the area lived in, job loss, and interpersonal relationships, as well as behaviors conventionally thought of as antisocial—not paying bills, being arrested, or any of the behaviors used to diagnose antisocial personality.

Use of mental health services, serious unemployment, arrests, and the presence of any type of antisocial behavior are predicted by childhood conduct disorder across all age-sex groups as are rupture of relationships with spouse, lover, or best friend, and credit problems for women of all age groups.

Two outcomes are predicted for other groups, but *not* for young men: living in the inner city and repossession of something purchased for failure to keep up payments. Inner-city residence of older men with a history of conduct disorder may be a drift phenomenon. As they repeatedly lose jobs and fail to pay the rent, other residential locations may become unavailable to them. This interpretation is supported by the finding that recent moves are predicted by conduct disorder only for the young. Their frequent moves may be steps toward residence in a poor area. An alternative possibility is that antisocial men were not financially able to participate in two massive movements from the city into the suburbs, one in the 1960s brought about by St. Louis' large urban redevelopment, and one in the 1970s with the razing of St. Louis' infamous Pruitt Igoe housing project. During these periods, those in the youngest cohort with a history of conduct disorder were not yet living on their own, and therefore moved to the suburbs or stayed in the city as part of their parents' household, independently of their own behavior problems.

The second result—that credit problems are not associated with conduct disorder in young men—echoes my finding in previous studies, that young men with a severe history of conduct problems are not at risk of bankruptcy or repossession because no one is willing to extend credit to them in the first place.

There are a few behaviors that were predicted by conduct disorder for young and middle-aged but not for the oldest group of men, for example, current unemployment, recent job loss, and recent break-up with spouse, lover, or best friend. However, because all of these *are* predicted for older women, there is no reason to believe either that conduct disorder actually has little impact on such events for the elderly or that the lower association found for elderly men is caused by forgetting. Lack of health insurance and current unemployment are predicted for younger and older women but not for the middle-aged. These few exceptions to the rule that conduct disorder before 15 continues to have a striking impact on a variety of recent life situations of persons of all ages may well be explained by the effects of aging itself on health and job status, making the long-term effects of conduct disorder in these realms difficult to discern in older persons. Overall, given the striking effects for all age groups, we can conclude that conduct disorder in childhood appears to predict many important aspects of life throughout the adult lifespan.

Among the recent adverse life situations explored, many were found most frequently in the youngest cohort. These include having no private physician; job loss; moving; breaking off with spouse, lover, or best friend; credit problems; arrests and other forms of antisocial behavior. We asked whether these extra stresses experienced by young adults might be entirely explained by a rising rate of conduct disorder. Table 5 shows that while the increase in conduct disorder probably helps to explain their high rate in the young, young people *without* conduct disorder were still more susceptible to each of these events than their elders.

Table 5

Effect of Conduct Disorder on Those Recent Events Most Common in the Youngest Cohort

	Men			Women		
	Young (<30)	Middle-aged (30–49)	Older (50+)	Young (<30)	Middle-aged (30–49)	Older (50+)
Ns						
Total	359	390	424	517	591	674
3+ Conduct Problems[a]	124	105	45	84	47	16
0–2 Conduct Problems[a]	235	285	379	433	544	658
Events in the last 6 months	%	%	%	%	%	%
Job loss						
Total	22.4	13.4	4.6	13.3	12.5	2.6
3+ Conduct problems	26.5	19.4	4.7	22.3	29.1	13.0
0–2 Conduct problems	20.0	11.5	4.6	11.9	11.6	2.5

Moved						
Total	17.8	9.9	1.5	23.3	7.9	4.7
3+ Conduct problems	24.8	9.7	1.6	45.4	6.7	5.5
0–2 Conduct problems	13.8	10.0	1.5	19.7	7.9	4.7
Arrested						
Total	9.3	4.1	0.3	1.9	0.8	0.4
3+ Conduct problems	13.6	9.2	2.8	3.0	3.9	19.7
0–2 Conduct problems	6.9	2.5	0.1	1.8	0.6	0.1
Broke up with spouse or lover						
Total	13.5	5.6	1.1	10.7	5.0	0.7
3+ Conduct problems	18.7	12.9	1.2	19.3	10.1	3.4
0–2 Conduct problems	10.6	3.4	1.1	9.4	4.7	0.7
Broke up with best friend						
Total	5.6	2.3	0.5	7.3	1.8	0.7
3+ Conduct problems	6.6	3.4	0.5	18.8	4.0	20.5
0–2 Conduct problems	5.0	2.0	0.5	5.5	1.6	0.4

[a]Before age 15.

Youth is in itself a time of change, which may involve loss of residence, interpersonal relationships, and jobs, and a time at which violence and other forms of antisocial behavior are most likely to be expressed. Today's young adults appear to carry an extra liability to
✓ change and antisocial activities, compared with their elders' experience at the same age, because of their greater frequency of histories of conduct disorder. Together, these account for the fact that within 6 months before interview, 22% of the young men had lost their job, 18% had moved, 9% had been arrested, 14% had broken up with a spouse or lover, and 6% had broken up with their best friend. Parallel figures for young women were 13% with job loss, 23% moved, 2% arrested, 11% broke up with spouse or lover, and 7% broke up with a best friend.

Conclusions

This report has explored a method for detecting historical change in the level of conduct disorder: comparing childhood histories reported retrospectively by a random sample of adults of all ages, who represent a succession of historical cohorts. In each successive cohort, conduct disorder appeared to have increased as compared with the preceding cohort. This pattern was found for both men and women, and terminated in a 6-fold increase in men's rates, from 6% to 36%, and a 23-fold increase in women, from 0.5% to 13%.

I considered the possibility that the increase was only apparent, perhaps a spurious effect of the briefer period at risk of exposure to deaths and mobility associated with conduct disorder in each successively younger cohort, but it seemed unlikely that these factors could account for an increase of the magnitude observed.

I then considered the possibility that the increase could be attributed to progressive forgetting of childhood behavior as respondents age. The most persuasive arguments against this interpretation were the stability of the ranking by frequency of the specific childhood behaviors across cohorts, the high correlation in this ranking between the sexes for old as well as for younger cohorts, and a greater increase in reports by the younger cohort of sex and substance abuse, behaviors known to have increased among youth in recent years, than of other behaviors. These patterns of frequencies showed that if older persons were forgetting their childhood behaviors, their forgetting was approximately proportional to the actual events, a regularity not known to characterize patterns of forgetting. Finally, there was the equally strong prediction of recent events by childhood behaviors for older and younger cohorts.

Thus, we found no grounds for discrediting the memory of older respondents, and so we cannot discount the finding of a striking increase in conduct disorder over this historical period.

If marked growth in the rate of conduct disorder has taken place, we are challenged to understand why it has happened. One possible explanation is the increasing urbanization over the era covered by the childhoods of these respondents, which provided younger cohorts with increased opportunities for deviant behavior and provided the anonymity that may have made it feasible to take those opportunities. This possibility will be exlored by limiting cohort members to those who grew up in cities, to see whether this markedly reduces differences between cohorts. Another possibility is that the progressive secularization of values during that period reduced the internal barriers against acting in a socially disapproved way. Unfortunately, this study provides no information on values with which to test this hypothesis.

A second challenging question is whether a large increase in the frequency of socially disapproved acts necessarily leads to a change in their meaning and a weakening of their consequences. It might be expected that when "everyone is doing it," "doing it" no longer has the same implications in terms of long-term outcome. Unfortunately, there is no evidence that the consequences of conduct disorder are any less dismal for the younger generation than for the older ones. The predictive power for a large series of recent adverse experiences, including arrest, interpersonal conflicts, and job loss, was much the same across age groups.

This study provided older groups than I have previously studied. The extension into a sample now over 65 leads me to the awesome conclusion that the effects of conduct problems in childhood can last a lifetime. In all, the findings of this study only serve to underscore and extend the conclusions of my own and others' previous research that finding ways of interrupting the development of conduct disorder in children and preventing its transmission from antisocial parent to child is a vital concern for our society. Not only do effects of conduct disorder last even longer than we knew previously, but if as this suggests, there is a rising rate among the young, increasing proportions of each age group will suffer its consequences over the next 50 years, as members of each age bracket are replaced by a more-affected, later birth cohort.

Finally, the present chapter confirms the impression of others that conduct disorder in women is a rare but a particularly serious problem. Although less often arrested, women with the disorder showed even more severe and long-lasting adult consequences of other kinds than did men.

References

American Psychiatric Association. (1980). *Diagnostic and statistical manual of mental disorders* (3rd ed.). Washington, DC: American Psychiatric Association.

Eme, R. F. (1979). Sex differences in childhood psychopathology: A review. *Psychology Bulletin, 86,* 574–595.

Farrington, D. P. (in press). Stepping stones to adult criminal careers. In D. Olweus, M. R. Yarrow, & J. Block (Eds.), *The development of antisocial and prosocial behavior.* New York: Academic Press.

Gershon, E. S., Dunner, D. L., Sturt, L., & Goodwin, F. K. (1973). Assortative mating in the affective disorders. *Biological Psychiatry, 7,* 63–74.

Gersten, J. C., Langner, T. S., Eisenberg, J. G., Simcha-Fagan, O., & McCarthy, E. D. (1976). Stability and change in types of behavioral disturbance of children and adolescents. *Journal of Abnormal Child Psychology, 4,* 111–127.

Glueck, S., & Glueck, E. (1940). *Juvenile delinquents grown up.* New York: The Commonwealth Fund.

Hindelang, M. J., Hirschi, T., & Weis, J. G. (1979). Correlates of delinquency: The illusion of discrepancy between self-report and official measures. *American Sociological Review, 44,* 995–1014.

Kohlberg, L., LaCrosse, J., & Ricks, D. (1972). The predictability of adult mental health from childhood behavior. In B. B. Wolman (Ed.), *Manual of child psychopathology* (pp. 1217–1284). New York: McGraw-Hill.

National Center for Health Statistics. (1983). *Health, United States 1983* (DHHS Pub. No. PHS 84-1232. Washington, DC: U.S. Government Printing Office.

Power, M. J., Alderson, R. R., Phillipson, C. M., Schoenberg, R., & Morris, J. N. (1967). Delinquent schools? *New Society, 264,* 542–543.

Robins, L. N. (1966). *Deviant children grown up: A sociological and psychiatric study of sociopathic personality.* Baltimore: Williams & Wilkins.

Robins, L. N. (1968). Negro homicide victims—who will they be? *Trans/action, 5*(7), 15–19.

Robins, L. N. (1974). *The Vietnam Drug User Returns* (Special Action Office Monograph, Series A, No. 2). Washington, DC: U.S. Government Printing Office.

Robins, L. N. (1978a). Interaction of setting and predisposition in explaining novel behavior: drug initiations before, in, and after Vietnam. In D. Kandel (Ed.), *Longitudinal research in drug use: Empirical findings and methodological issues* (pp. 179–196). Washington, DC: Hemisphere.

Robins, L. N. (1978b). Sturdy childhood predictors of adult outcomes: replications from longitudinal studies. *Psychological Medicine, 8,* 611–622.

Robins, L. N., Helzer, J. E., Croughan, J., & Ratcliff, K. S. (1981). The NIMH Diagnostic Interview Schedule: Its history, characteristics, and validity. *Archives of General Psychiatry, 38,* 381–389.

Robins, L. N., Hesselbrock, M., Wish, E., & Helzer, J. E. (1978). Polydrug and alcohol use by veterans and nonveterans. In D. E. Smith et al. (Eds.), *A multicultural view of drug abuse* (pp. 74–90). Cambridge: Schenckman.

Rutter, M. L. (1970). Psycho-social disorders in childhood and their outcome in adult life. *Journal of the Royal College of Physicians London, 4*(3), 211–218.

Rutter, M. L. (1972). Relationships between child and adult psychiatric disorders. *Acta Psychiatrica Scandinavica, 48,* 3–21.

Rutter, M. L. (1980). School influences on children's behavior and development. *Pediatrics, 65*(2), 208–220.

Rutter, M. L. (1981). The city and the child. *American Journal of Orthopsychiatry, 51,* 610–625.

**Appendix: Conduct Disorder Questions
from the Diagnostic Interview Schedule (DIS)**

Substance Abuse

1. Now I am going to ask you some questions about using alcohol. How old were you the *first* time you ever drank enough to get drunk? (NEVER = 00; BABY, INFANT = 02)

   ENTER AGE: ☐☐

   INTERVIEWER: IF 15 OR OLDER, SKIP TO Q. 2.
           IF LESS THAN 15, ASK B.
           IF "DK", ASK A.

   A. Do you think it was before or after you were 15?

   Before 15 ...... (RECORD 01 ABOVE & ASK B)
   15 or older ... (RECORD 95 ABOVE & SKIP TO Q. 2)
   Still DK .... (RECORD 98 ABOVE & SKIP TO Q. 2)

   B. Did you get drunk more than once before you were 15?

   No 1
   Yes 5

2. Now I'd like to ask about your experience with drugs. (HAND CARD A[a]) Have you ever used any drug on this list to get high or without a prescription, or more than was prescribed—that is, on your *own*?

   No .... (ASK A) 1
   Yes .... (SKIP TO Q. 3) 5

   A. Have you taken any other drugs on your own either to get high or for other mental effects? IF R SAYS ONLY ALCOHOL, TOBACCO OR COFFEE, CODE 1.

   No .... (SKIP TO Q. 4) 1
   Yes .... (ASK Q. 3) 5

[a]See last page of the Appendix.

3. How old were you when you first used (this drug/any of these drugs) on your own?

ENTER AGE: ☐☐

> INTERVIEWER: IF YOUNGER THAN 15, SKIP TO Q. 3B.
> IF 15 OR OLDER, SKIP TO Q. 4.
> IF "DK", ASK A.

A. Were you younger or older than 15?

Younger than 15 .... (RECORD 01 ABOVE AND ASK B)
15 or more .... (RECORD 95 ABOVE AND ASK Q. 4)
Still DK .... (RECORD 98 ABOVE AND ASK Q. 4)

B. Had you tried any of these drugs more than once before you were 15?

No 1
Yes 5

Underachievement

4. Now I'd like to ask about your life as a child. Let's begin with some questions about school. Did you ever repeat a grade?

No .... (SKIP TO Q. 5) 1
Yes .... (ASK A) 5

A. Did you get held back more than once?

No, only once 2
Yes, more than once 5

5. How were your grades in school—better than average, average, or not so good?

Better than average .... (SKIP TO Q. 6) 1
Average .... (SKIP TO Q. 6) 2
Not so good .... (ASK A) 5

A. Did you teachers think you did about as well as you could or did they think you had the ability to do much better?

Did as well as could .... (SKIP TO Q. 6) 3
Could have done much better .... (ASK B) 5

B. How old were you when your teachers first felt that way?

ENTER AGE & GO TO Q. 6 □□

> INTERVIEWER: IF R SAYS "DK": ASK C.

C. Do you think it was before you were 15 or later than that?

Under 15 ...... (RECORD 01 ABOVE)
15 or more ... (RECORD 95 ABOVE)
Still DK .... (RECORD 98 ABOVE)

School Discipline

6. Did you frequently get into trouble with the teacher or principal for misbehaving in school? (ELEMENTARY, JUNIOR HIGH, OR HIGH SCHOOL)

No .... (SKIP TO Q. 7) 1
Yes .... (ASK A) 5

A. How old were you when you first got into trouble for misbehaving in school?

ENTER AGE & GO TO Q. 7 □□

> INTERVIEWER: IF R SAYS "DK": ASK B.

B. Do you think it was before you were 15 or later than that?

Under 15 ...... (RECORD 01 ABOVE)
15 or more ... (RECORD 95 ABOVE)
Still DK .... (RECORD 98 ABOVE)

School Expulsion

7. Were you ever expelled or suspended from school? (ELEMENTARY, JUNIOR HIGH, OR HIGH SCHOOL)?

No .... (SKIP TO Q. 8) 1
Yes .... (ASK A) 5

A. How old were you when you were first expelled or suspended?

ENTER AGE & GO TO Q. 8   ☐☐

┌───┐
│ INTERVIEWER: IF R SAYS "DK": ASK B.   │
└───┘

B. Do you think it was before you were 15 or later than that?

Under 15 ...... (RECORD 01 ABOVE)
15 or more ... (RECORD 95 ABOVE)
Still DK .... (RECORD 98 ABOVE)

Truancy

8. Did you ever play hooky from school at least twice in one
   year?

No .... (SKIP TO Q. 9) 1
Yes .... (ASK A) 5

A. Was that only in your last year in school or before that?

Last year only ..... (SKIP TO Q. 9) 2
Before last year .... (ASK B AND C) ... 5

B. Did you play hooky as much as 5 days a year in at least
   two school years, not counting your last year in school?

No 1
Yes 5

C. How old were you when you first played hooky?

ENTER AGE & GO TO Q. 9   ☐☐

┌───┐
│ INTERVIEWER: IF R SAYS "DK": ASK D.   │
└───┘

D. Do you think it was before you were 15 or later than that?

Under 15 ...... (RECORD 01 ABOVE)

15 or more ... (RECORD 95 ABOVE)
Still DK .... (RECORD 98 ABOVE)

Fighting

9. Did you ever get into trouble at school for fighting?

No .... (SKIP TO Q. 10) ... 1
Yes .... (ASK A) 5

A. Did that happen more than once?

No .... (SKIP TO Q. 10) ... 1
Yes .... (ASK B AND C) 5

B. Were you sometimes the one who started the fight?

No 1
Yes 5

C. How old were you when you first got into trouble for fighting at school?

ENTER AGE & GO TO Q. 10   □□

INTERVIEWER: IF R SAYS "DK": ASK D.

D. Do you think it was before you were 15 or later than that?

Under 15 ...... (RECORD 01 ABOVE)
15 or more ... (RECORD 95 ABOVE)
Still DK .... (RECORD 98 ABOVE)

10. Before age 18, did you ever get into trouble with the police, your parents or neighbors because of fighting (other than for fighting at school)?

No .... (SKIP TO INSTRUCTIONS BEFORE Q. 10E) 1
Yes .... (ASK A) 5

A. Did that happen more than once?

No .... (SKIP TO C) 2
Yes .... (ASK B) 5

B. Were you sometimes the one who started the fight?

No 1
Yes 5

C. At what age did you first get into trouble because of fighting (away from school)?

ENTER AGE & GO TO Q. 11   ☐☐

INTERVIEWER: IF R SAYS "DK": ASK D.

D. Do you think it was before you were 15 or later than that?

Under 15 ...... (RECORD 01 ABOVE & SKIP TO Q. 11)
15 or more ... (RECORD 95 ABOVE & SKIP TO Q. 11)
Still DK .... (RECORD 98 ABOVE & SKIP TO Q. 11)

INTERVIEWER: ARE BOTH Q. 9 AND 10 CODED 1?
HH   No .... (SKIP TO Q. 11) ... 1
            Yes .... (ASK E) 5

E. Even though you didn't get into trouble for fighting, did
you start fights more than once before you were 15?

No 1
Yes 5

Runaway

11. When you were a kid, did you ever run away from home
overnight?

No .... (SKIP TO Q. 12) ... 1
Yes .... (ASK A) 5

A. Did you run away more than once?

No, just once 2
Yes, more than once 5

B. How old were you when you first ran away from home
overnight?

ENTER AGE & GO TO Q. 12   ☐☐

> INTERVIEWER: IF R SAYS "DK": ASK C.

C. Do you think it was before you were 15 or later than that?

> Under 15 ...... (RECORD 01 ABOVE)
> 15 or more ... (RECORD 95 ABOVE)
> Still DK .... (RECORD 98 ABOVE)

Lying

12. Of course, no one tells the truth *all* the time, but did you tell a lot of lies when you were a child or teenager?

> No .... (SKIP TO Q. 13) ... 1
> Yes .... (ASK A) 5

A. How old were you when you first told a lot of lies?

> ENTER AGE & GO TO Q. 13   ☐☐

> INTERVIEWER: IF R SAYS "DK": ASK B.

B. Do you think it was before you were 15 or later than that?

> Under 15 ...... (RECORD 01 ABOVE)
> 15 or more ... (RECORD 95 ABOVE)
> Still DK .... (RECORD 98 ABOVE)

Stealing

13. When you were a child, did you more than once swipe things from stores or from other children or steal from your parents or from anyone else?

> No .... (SKIP TO Q. 14) ... 1
> Yes .... (ASK A) 5

A. How old were you when you first stole things?

> ENTER AGE & GO TO Q. 14   ☐☐

> INTERVIEWER: IF R SAYS "DK": ASK B.

B. Do you think it was before you were 15 or later than that?

> Under 15 ...... (RECORD 01 ABOVE)
> 15 or more ... (RECORD 95 ABOVE)
> Still DK .... (RECORD 98 ABOVE)

Vandalism

14. When you were a kid, did you ever intentionally damage someone's car or do anything else to destroy or severely damage someone else's property?

> No .... (SKIP TO Q. 15) ... 1
> Yes .... (ASK A) 5

A. How old were you when you first did that?

> ENTER AGE & GO TO Q. 15   □□

> INTERVIEWER: IF R SAYS "DK": ASK B.

B. Do you think it was before you were 15 or later than that?

> Under 15 ...... (RECORD 01 ABOVE)
> 15 or more ... (RECORD 95 ABOVE)
> Still DK .... (RECORD 98 ABOVE)

Arrest

15. Were you ever arrested as a juvenile or sent to juvenile court?

> No .... (SKIP TO Q. 16) ... 1
> Yes .... (ASK A) 5

A. How old were you the first time?

> ENTER AGE & GO TO Q. 16   □□

> INTERVIEWER: IF R SAYS "DK": ASK B.

B. Do you think it was before you were 15 or later than that?

> Under 15 ...... (RECORD 01 ABOVE)

15 or more ... (RECORD 95 ABOVE)
Still DK .... (RECORD 98 ABOVE)

Sex

16. How old were you when you first had sexual relations?

ENTER AGE ☐☐

INTERVIEWER: IF R SAYS "NEVER": CODE ∅∅
IF R SAYS "DK": ASK A

A. Do you think it was before you were 15 or later than that?

Under 15 ...... (RECORD 01 ABOVE)
15 or more ... (RECORD 95 ABOVE)
Still DK .... (RECORD 98 ABOVE)

Card A

Marijuana, hashish, pot, grass
Amphetamines, stimulants, uppers, speed
Barbiturates, sedatives, downers, sleeping pills,
    Seconal, Quaaludes
Tranquilizers, Valium, Librium
Cocaine, coke
Heroin
Opiates (other than heroin: codeine, Demerol,
    morphine, Methadone, Darvon, opium)
Psychedelics (LSD, mescaline, peyote, psilo-
    cybin, DMT, PCP)
Other

Problems and Perspectives for the Concept of Risk in Psychosocial Development: A Summary

DALE C. FARRAN

Introduction

All of the chapters in this book have dealt with the issue of risk, and most have focused on longitudinal populations, either the authors' own or ones they have summarized. Longitudinal populations are truly appropriate for assessing risk because the concept of risk implies prediction, predictors from a state of not having a certain condition to developing it. We have contended that one of the confusing aspects to conclusions currently possible about which populations are truly at risk (and therefore in need of preventive, proactive services) is that we have not properly attended to longitudinal studies of the phenomena. Bell's chapter provides a model for summarizing existing data about certain risky outcomes, but this model has rarely been followed by others in the field.

Although the chapters cover different kinds of outcomes, similarities among them exist. We have developed seven major issues germane to research in the area of risk. The rest of this chapter is devoted to talking about those issues and to drawing from the chapters on psychosocial risk information relevant to these issues.

Definition of Outcome

The first major issue relates to the definition of outcome; the concerns in this area are somewhat different for intellectual and psychosocial risk. In the area of psychosocial development, there are no standardly accepted positive outcomes, and although there is likely a continuum of adjustment from severely maladjusted to mildly neurotic to well-adjusted, we have no means of discriminating the middle points of that continuum. Most of the chapters in this section of the book dealt with well-defined negative psychosocial outcomes. Bell describes the predictive factors associated with later substance abuse, schizophrenia, hyperactivity, and major depressive episodes. Robins' chapter deals with the prediction of psychosocial disorders listed in DSM-III. Greenspan's work is less specific as to outcome; instead, this line of research concentrates on risk conditions that could be associated with a number of different, poor outcomes—criminality, ill health, teenage pregnancy. Some of these outcomes may be determined more by the fact of living in a poor environment generally rather than any traceable pathway from specific antecedent experiences.

In order to understand risk, we must be more precise about the possible negative outcomes, for example, what a given population or subgroup is at risk for. Individuals live in poor and undesirable conditions, conditions that most people would find deplorable and unacceptable. Despite our concern about the daily lives of people in these conditions, these conditions alone are not sufficient to place an individual at risk for a poor psychosocial outcome.

Part of the problem in defining who-is-at-risk-for-what stems from the conflict between a public-health model of risk and a medical / psychological notion of risk. Determining risk in a public health model involves identifying areas of a city, state, or country as having certain negative characteristics: high unemployment, high crime rates, poor housing, high infant mortality rates, and so forth. These areas are also more likely to have other negative characteristics, which could be thought of as outcomes, associated with them: greater truancy, more school failure, more delinquency, more aggression among the children. Thus, we can identify a whole cluster of characteristics that can be found in certain areas, and we can possibly sort those characteristics into ones that appear to be mediators and those that seem to be outcomes (though the relationship is likely highly reciprocal). What we cannot do with any certainty is to pick out who among the children in that area will develop these negative outcomes.

Most of our screening endeavors have been based on the idea that individuals carry within them (or in their immediate families) signals or characteristics, which if we could only read them well enough, would indicate who is going to develop those negative outcomes later. Those screening endeavors have not been successful. Their lack of success may be due to the fact that they are based on an incorrect model for predicating the kind of outcomes in which they have been interested, outcomes associated in large part with poverty and ones for whom we do not know how to trace individual risk.

The medical or individual-risk model may be most suitable for more precise and severe psychosocial adjustment categories, the kinds of outcomes Bell and Robins are describing. But that model may not be very good for determining who is going to show outcomes that are associated in large part with poverty and disorganization, outcomes like early pregnancies, ill health, and school failure.

Which model one uses may be related to the kinds of outcomes in which one is interested, as well as one's philosophical attitude toward those outcomes and how they emerge. One can look at the presence of psychosocial disturbance in a number of individuals in a particular area as symptomatic of a broad level of disarray and disorganization within the community. Which disorders are manifested by certain individuals could be viewed as happenstance, an accident of coinciding circumstances. When a community is disorganized and barely surviving, individuals are going to manifest disorder in a number of interchangeable ways. This view would equate various outcomes and group them into broad categories. The alternative point of view is to treat the condition as being almost exclusively within the province of the individual. Different pathways would be proposed for each condition; outcomes would not be interchangeable, and each would be investigated individually. Under this model, individuals would be treated, not geographic areas. The important distinction between a medical model and a public health approach affects the other issues in this chapter as well.

Specification of Risk Conditions

Greenspan argues forcefully for the need to define better the risk groups with which research and intervention are dealing. Risk is frequently taken to mean something like lower socioeconomic status (SES) in general, without any attention being paid to the variation within such designations. Greenspan's research and clinical program both deal with multiple-risk families, those families showing several factors that would indicate they are functioning poorly.

Bell, and Farran and Cooper seem to be treating those multiple risk factors as being intervening variables that place only certain individuals at risk. Both Bell and Farran and Cooper are arguing for predisposing characteristics of the child, which make him or her more vulnerable to the negative impact of the multiple risk factors. Bell contends that risk in the child is not constant, but is a result of the interplay among genetic predisposition, the developmental capabilities of the child at this stage of his or her growth, and the family context. Risk conditions, in other words, would change as a function of changes in the childs' abilities to deal with situations around him or her.

Farran and Cooper portray the interaction somewhat differently. They see several characteristics as making the child more vulnerable and several intervening variables as being possible triggers for the development of negative psychosocial outcomes. The greater the number of predisposing characteristics a child possesses, the fewer interim experiences would be needed to create the outcome. Likewise, the more intervening negative experiences present, the less important it would be to have all the predisposing risk conditions. Thus, there is an interplay between risk factors within the child and risk factors with the family and larger environment.

Robins, on the other hand, describes one of the few diagnostic populations in which there is good continuity from childhood to adulthood. Children showing conduct disorder before age 4 years are 50% more likely to be adults with antisocial personalities. The risk associated with their particular genetic predisposition is so overwhelming in these children that it dwarfs any risk status singly associated with family, neighborhood, or community. Very few other disorders are like that.

Measuring the Environment

The next area in terms of risk is related to measurement. None of the chapters adequately addresses the issue of how to measure those aspects of the environment that are endangering children. For Robins, *environment* is taken to mean large-scale changes in society, which could account for an increase in conduct disorder among young adults—increasing urbanization, secularization of values. As she acknowledges, there is no way to measure these sorts of environmental changes, though they may well be the most important.

Greenspan's conception of the environment is much narrower. To him, what is important to the child is the family. Other forces might affect the child but only as they are mediated by the family. However, even with this more limited focus, measurement is a problem. Greenspan emphasizes a more clinical approach to the families; to be accurately characterized, each family would receive a psychiatric diagnosis. Perhaps it is the case that psychiatric descriptions are the only truly adequate way of describing the family environment. If that is true, then the concept of risk with that form of measurement as its premise will not generalize very easily to larger-scale work.

In his DCFPC, Bell labels the FPC as the family, peer and community context. This context is presumed to interact with the child's characteristics to account for his or her risk status at the time. Bell, however, does not provide guidance as to how these areas are to be measured. What factors in the larger environment have the negative effect? Farran and Cooper have begun to try to delineate these aspects of the environment, at least for young children, which may have effects on psychosocial adjustment, but their list is by no means exhaustive, and all of their factors should be tested empirically.

All of the chapters recognize the importance of the environment for the child, and most conceive of the environment as being tiered, including family, neighborhood, community, and larger society. Measurement, however, is a trickier problem. One way of measuring the environment is simply to count the occurrence of certain major experiences, for example, divorce, desertion, child abuse, hospitalization. Another way is to try to specify qualitative differences in environments, for example, pathology in the families. This latter approach is much more time consuming and expensive. Before determining that so much effort must go into this description, it might be worthwhile to try the counting-occurrences approach first. If it appears that the presence of these broad variables is associated with greater risk, one could then develop more precise and qualitative measurement of particular ones.

As research psychologists and other practitioners interested in the welfare of children, we have done a rather poor job of describing the phenomenon in which we are interested. Accurate measurement is the hallmark of good science; it is at the beginning of the scientific process, and without it, not much can be accomplished. We can barely measure good or appropriate psychosocial development in the child. We seem to be many years away from qualitatively describing the various environments in which the child functions. We need to work on this problem immediately or else abandon the notion of risk as a testable entity.

Designs to Specify Intervening Processes

Design issues permeate the area of risk research; they are important for the selection of a disorder, the selection of a population, the length of time to follow the population and what factors to measure. Various approaches have been used to look at the continuity of disorders or the early predictors of outcomes already manifested. Accounting for behavior seen today, by looking at the past, has always been a popular endeavor. When done on a large scale, these studies are called follow-back approaches. Outcomes such as adult psychopathology, criminality, or the like are identified and the histories of the people showing these symptoms are studied for clues as to common factors among them. The reconstituted longitudinal approach involves identifying a group of people who had a presumed risk condition as children (usually identified through the case records of a clinic or through the schools or courts) and then attempting to locate them as adults to determine how they have fared.

Either approach is flawed. The more-recent preferred model for studying risk—in fact, what is often termed the *risk approach*—involves choosing a group of children who have not manifested the disorder but who are experiencing factors associated with developing the disorder. These children are then followed for some time period to determine if a substantial portion of them develop the disorder. *Relative risk* is a term indicating the greater risk for the disorder given the associated factors compared to a group of children who do not experience these factors. *Relative risk* is an important concept, indicating as it does the fact that some children who are exposed to the risk conditions will not develop the disorder, while others who are not exposed will develop the disorder. Prediction is nowhere close to perfect.

Bell argues that the risk design is most appropriate and cost effective for disorders that have a short latency and a high base rate, such as substance abuse. The most difficult are disorders such as schizophrenia and affective syndromes where the latency is 25–30 years and the incidence is less than 1%. These conditions are often ones for which we are the most eager to account. When these long-latency disorders have a strong genetic component, one can do as Bell suggests and first identify the risk group of children from the status of the parents, and second begin the study at a time shortly before the disorder is most commonly developed.

Some disorders have a moderately high incidence, but in order to gather a sample large enough to do an adequate longitudinal study, the risk researcher would be restricted to certain geographic areas—for example, large urban settings. That restriction itself may be a risk condition. We have known for some time that urban areas are associated with a higher manifestation of disorders than rural areas. Low birthweight research is a good example of this problem. In order to have enough low birthweight babies to follow longitudinally (allowing for attrition and with attempts to control for SES), one would need to recruit samples from large urban hospitals. One could never be certain whether the risk concomitant with low birthweight would be the same in a less stressful environment. In other words, is the risk a result of the interaction between low birthweight and urban stress or is there a main effect for low birthweight? This kind of question is crucial to answer in research on risk factors.

Greenspan has argued that our efforts in risk research are so nascent that we are not even at the level of an adequate design. He believes that we have not generated the hypotheses that need testing yet, and that we need now to do more careful and detailed case studies of families living in risk conditions. These case studies should generate the hypotheses we need to test. In some sense, Greenspan may be correct. The troubles with case studies are many, including the danger of one's theoretical viewpoint coloring and even determining what is seen as significant in a particular problem family. It is also difficult to generalize across case studies to make testable hypotheses.

Thus, we seem to be in the position outlined by Farran and Cooper, where no particular design will handle all the problems associated with prediction. It could be that the problem lies with the search for the perfect risk design. Different disorders may be at different levels of etiological understanding. Some may be in the position where what is needed is Greenspan's case-study approach. Others may be closer to the designs recommended by Bell or advocated by Robins.

Forms of Intervention

Intervening with children who are at risk for developing a psychosocial disturbance is relatively new, concentrating as we have on the prevention of school failure and mental retardation. We may be more hesitant about the effects of labeling on a child who is at risk for social and emotional problems. Greenspan is the only researcher in that group of chapters who is advocating a complete intervention approach, and it appears that the intervention itself may be part of the research. His case studies include the intervention component.

Bell makes a persuasive argument for divorcing intervention from research. His point is that we should not have to justify research efforts by virtue of their implications for intervention, that we are forced into hasty interventions because of funding pressures. He argues that research on the manifestation of major psychosocial disorders is important. Once we understand the process, we can design intervention research. Doing the two together only creates confusion.

Without a clearer understanding of the kinds of experiences that place one at risk for psychosocial disorders, it does seem premature to think about what type of intervention to propose. For example, early-stimulation day care is an intervention often used with children at risk for mental retardation. Yet if Farran and Cooper's model is correct, this may be a very poor form of intervention to propose for children who are at risk for conduct disorder. A multiple-caretaker, early-rearing situation may be one of the risk factors for this disorder, which causes vulnerable children actually to develop conduct disorder and later antisocial personality.

Responsiveness to Intervention

One of the problems with intervention efforts is that we are often unable to specify what dosage a particular individual received. For example, if the intervention is stimulating experiences provided through day care, records need to be kept of absenteeism and of the amount of time children actually interacted with the teachers or participated in a curriculum even when they were present. Another facet to this problem is that these dosage differences may not be random. They may be associated with certain characteristics of the child. For instance, it could be that more passive, quiet children are interacted with less by the adults in the day care program or that more aggressive children have more frequent but negative interactions with teachers. Thus, both the quality and the quantity of the intervention may vary in conjunction with other factors also placing the child at risk for developing the disorder.

For psychosocial problems, we are in somewhat of a dilemma. We cannot yet specify the interventions appropriate to preventing disorders because we do not know the pathways by which those disorders are developed. It is likely that as our understanding becomes clearer and our interventions more precise, we will find that individuals differ in their responsiveness to interventions even when the dosages are equivalent. At that point, we should do the relevant research.

Conclusion

This book is devoted to a very important and timely topic. The chapters in the psychosocial risk section help to suggest where the research efforts should go next. In the next section, we consider policy implications of these studies. Kaye's chapter and the one by Keogh, Wilcoxen, and Bernheimer are important contributions to the area of public policy for both intellectual and psychosocial risk. Policies are being implemented without adequate research to support them. The danger is that researchers and practitioners will give up this endeavor because of confusing results. The confusion may lie more in our approach to risk; once we are more certain about that, intervention policies for later may become quite clear.

PART III

Risk Assessment
and Public Policy

A Four-Dimensional Model of Risk Assessment and Intervention

KENNETH KAYE

Much of what has been written about the concept of risk is based on concepts of assessment and intervention that I believe are extremely problematic. One reason these two concepts are problematic is that they are usually discussed independently. The other reason is that each is viewed unidimensionally.

It is the thesis of this chapter that (1) the assessment of any sort of developmental risk, and (2) the availability of interventions to reduce it, are two dimensions of the same problem, and furthermore that each of those dimensions has to be viewed two-dimensionally. Therefore, all meaningful discussion of "risk," whether from a research or a policy point of view, requires a four-dimensional model.

Assessment and Intervention Are Inseparable Concepts

For some reason, clinicians and researchers alike often try to separate these two aspects of the same problem. They have tended to deal with assessment without regard to what interventions might be available—without regard to the question, "Assessment for what?" Or they have tried to evaluate intervention strategies with inadequate attention to the question, "Intervention with whom?" I illustrate these tendencies with three examples below. At this point, we need to see the problem of

Risk in Intellectual
and Psychosocial Development

273

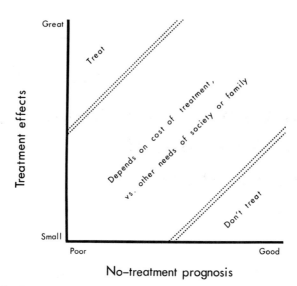

Figure 1. The decision to intervene, viewed two-dimensionally as the intersection of (1) the prognosis if no treatment is attempted and (2) the expected effects of the treatment.

developmental risk as portrayed two-dimensionally in Figure 1. I suggest that the phrase "at risk" really means "should be treated." The patient and society take a risk by failing to take advantage of some available intervention. Clinically, human beings are at risk when two things can be said about them:

1. They can be clearly identified as having a poor developmental prognosis, compared to the rest of the population, if left untreated.
2. A treatment exists that has been shown to improve that prognosis significantly when offered to this segment of the population. (In this context, *significantly* means not just a statistically significant difference, but to a significant extent.)

We all have a chance of getting cancer, but we do not say we are at risk for cancer. Smokers are at risk for lung cancer, not just because they have a higher likelihood of inducing it, but because there is something they can do to reduce that likelihood: quit smoking.

So not everyone with a poor, untreated prognosis is at risk: just those whom we have reason to believe an intervention can help. Similarly, not everyone who might gain from an intervention is at risk: just those whose prognosis is poor without it. The important implication, reiterating a crucial monograph by Cronbach and Gleser (1965), is that an assessor should always be looking for the individuals who need and will profit from an existing intervention program or one that can be designed, and an intervener should always be designing a program for individuals who can be identified as needing it. This is why the two concepts are inseparable.

Assessment: A Signal-Detection Problem

A fundamental misconception in the field of behavior assessment is that classification is based on measurement theory. Instead, it has to be based upon decision theory (Cronbach & Gleser, 1965, Chapter 11). The measurement-theory approach assumes that people can be located along any given dimension, subject to the precision of available instruments. My assertion that assessment is usually unidimensional may seem strange in view of the fact that most research is clearly aimed at analyzing the multiple factors that put people in a risk category. The instruments themselves, including the neonatal assessment scales and the IQ tests discussed here subsequently, are indeed multifactorial. But the idea of what it means to classify someone along the abscissa of Figure 1 has been seen unidimensionally instead of as a two-dimensional problem in signal detection.

The decision process inherent in assessment (no matter how many factors are involved in the prognosis itself—one, two, or many) is conceptually a two-dimensional problem (Figure 2). The more reliable an instrument is for detecting nearly every instance of a given category (e.g., the category of all newborns at risk for failure-to-thrive and treatable by intervening with their families), the more the instrument can be expected to err in the direction of false positives, misclassifying as risk cases some individuals who do not really belong in that category. Conversely, the more reliable an instrument is in the sense that nearly every case selected will really belong in the category, the more it can be expected to err in the direction of false negatives, by failing to identify some cases that also belong in that category. These two kinds of reliability have been defined as r_β and r_α, respectively (Kaye, 1980).

Figure 1 indicated that the question of whether to intervene would often depend on the cost to society, or to the family itself, of doing so versus not doing so. Now we can see this as having an extra dimension, because the assessment has to consider the likelihood and cost of an alpha error (false positive) versus the likelihood and cost of a beta error (false negative). A single validity coefficient, such as a correlation between the assessment instrument and some outcome criterion, is almost meaningless in this context. In the first place, there are the two kinds of

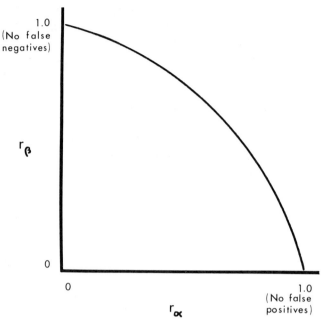

Figure 2. Risk assessment, viewed two-dimensionally. When false positives are eliminated (high r_β), there are more false negatives (low r_α), and vice versa.

reliability, with a trade-off between them that has to be evaluated anew
in any particular application. Secondly, the shape of Figure 2 will vary at
different points along the abscissa of Figure 1: the reliability of any test is
greater, the smaller the selection ratio. For example, the same test can
select the top or bottom 10% of a normally distributed sample much
more reliably than it can select the top or bottom 25%, and it can do the
latter more reliably than it can classify cases as belonging in the top or
bottom half. It is not an exaggeration to say that any assessment scale
that merely reports a linear validity coefficient has oversimplified the
problem to such an extent as to be practically useless.

Intervention: A Cost–Benefit Problem

Even if the untreated prognosis can be stated with certainty, and an
intervention exists, there is still a cost–benefit decision to be made. A
coma patient with no brain wave may be regarded as at risk if one
believes that the costs of continuous intravenous life support are outweighed by the moral or scientific benefits, or may be regarded as legally

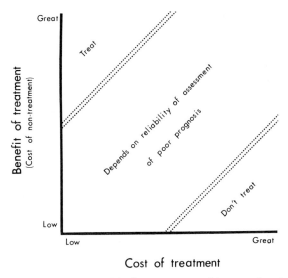

Figure 3. A four-dimensional model of assessment and intervention: benefit, cost, and the two dimensions (shown in Figure 2) of reliability of assessment of poor prognosis.

dead if one does not. Figure 3 needs to be substituted for the ordinate in Figure 1.

Now, we have a four-dimensional model—r_α, r_β, cost, and benefit—which I suggest is really at the root of all policy discussions about intervention as well as all methodological discussions about assessment. Sometimes the issues seem less complex only because we make certain assumptions that simplify the model. For example, we know that all rational people should refrain from smoking. The assessment is easy—you smoke or you don't—and so is the intervention: quit. But the problem becomes this simple only if we ignore the benefits many people apparently believe they get from smoking (relaxation, image enhancement) and only if we accept a high false positive rate in our assessment (the many smokers whose health does not suffer). Smokers themselves have an intuitive understanding of these oversimplifications, so they ignore the surgeon general's warnings. More sophisticated assessments, involving how much of what kind of cigarettes can be smoked by which people at precisely what costs to their health, would give people a more convincing basis for deciding whether the benefits of quitting are worth the physical, mental, and emotional cost of doing so.

The Johnson administration's Project Head Start presented a good example of the cost–benefit question. The real question was not "How much can we boost IQ and scholastic achievement?" (Jensen, 1969), but "What is the cost of boosting it by any given amount?" and "In what terms should the benefits be evaluated?" It should be obvious that these were not questions that psychologists, educators, and other human development experts could answer. They were political questions as much as technological ones. All questions about intervention are inherently political questions, as are all questions about assessment.

We can turn now to a few examples of how researchers and practitioners concerned about developmental risk have failed to include all four dimensions in their thinking. (Note that I am merely advocating this four-dimensional model conceptually; from a mathematical point of view, more than four factors will often be required.)

IQ Testing: Assessment with Confusion about "Why?"

We have developed in the United States, and continue to maintain despite all the controversy of the 1970s, a system in which nearly every school child is administered an average of four nationally standardized aptitude and achievement tests per year, or about 50 over the course of Grades 1 through 12. At most, 2 or 3 of those 50 tests will be used to track a child through programs loosely designed (but inadequately evaluated) for children of different cognitive capacities; for a small number of children, another couple of testings may be used as part of a diagnostic battery aimed at identifying learning disabilities for which specific interventions may or may not exist. For most children, all such tests—and for all children, most such tests—are administered without any purpose except the perpetuation of a multi-million-dollar industry and the statistical comparison of different demographic groups (Kaye, 1973).

When the justification for a test is supposed to be selection—that is, when it is a placement test—then there ought to be research matching the program into which a group of children are to be placed with the criteria on which they are selected. Let me limit the argument to IQ tests, though much of this applies to standardized achievement tests too. IQ tests usually constitute *mensor gratia mensoris*, measurement for its own sake. They certainly are not tests for risk, unless it can be shown that children of a certain age with IQs in a certain range have a poor prognosis in normal classes and a *better* prognosis—considering all social, emotional, and cognitive costs and benefits—in special school programs. That was the subject of many lawsuits against local and state school authorities in the 1970s and 1980s: the burden of proof fell upon those who purport to assess ability, and that assessment process has repeatedly been ruled inseparable from the question of what interventions are available (Jensen, 1980, Chapter 2).

In the cost–benefit analysis, a crucial issue is the cost of the assessment itself. And the benefit of the assessment must be measured in the value of whatever information it provides beyond what would already have been known without it. Sechrest (1963) called this the "incremental validity" of a test. For example, the so-called validity coefficient of IQ, .80 to .85, gives an indication of how much better the tests predict school achievement than a random throw of dice would predict it. We tend to forget that the previous year's school performance will predict this year's performance very well; IQ only raises the multiple correlation by about 5%. How much is that incremental validity worth? It depends how specifically the information can be used in tracking children into more effective special programs. The reality is that IQ scores, as actually used in schools, give teachers no worthwhile information that could not be more usefully derived from each year's actual school achievement. Even Jensen (1980) takes this position at the same time that he defends the reliability, validity, and lack of bias in IQ tests.

Behavioral Assessment of Newborns

Now, let us extend these same considerations to the high-risk infant. When are newborns at risk? When their developmental prognosis is relatively poor, and when a cost-effective intervention exists that can significantly improve that prognosis. One of the most important factors that can make an intervention cost-effective is selecting all and only the babies and parents who need the program, so that its resources are not wasted on those who do not need it or cannot profit from it. Hence, the assessment of newborns, or of newborn–parent interaction, should be conceptualized as the development of placement tests for actual or feasible intervention programs.

That was one of the explicit aims of Brazelton's (1973) scales: to be a clinical instrument for decisions about the treatment of young infants and their parents. (The other goal was a research instrument.) However, exactly as was the case with general-ability or IQ scales, the clinical uses of newborn assessment—that is, the specific intervention programs for which it could be regarded as a placement test—were not explicitly involved in the creation of the assessment instrument. Perhaps Brazelton and his colleagues felt that not enough was yet known about psychological treatment of high-risk infants and parents, or perhaps they naively believed that an all-purpose assessment could be possible. Consequently, I argue, the Neonatal Behavioral Assessment Scales (NBAS) have extremely limited utility for clinicians concerned with neonatal risk.

One possible use in this area would be a source of research evidence that a population thought to be at risk—because of medical history, socioeconomic status (SES), obstetric medication, and so forth—does or does not show deficits at birth. Among 31 published studies of different samples of newborns using the NBAS (Sostek, 1978), 60% were studies of this kind. (That proportion is even higher, I suspect, among the much larger number of unpublished NBAS studies.) Sometimes the known risk does lead to NBAS deficits as predicted; sometimes it does not. For example, Aleksandrowicz and Aleksandrowicz (1974) found effects of obstetrical medication upon NBAS performance; Tronick, Wise, Als, Adamson, Scanlon, and Brazelton (1976) did not. More important, however, is the fact that even consistent results in this type of study tell us nothing about the risk for such populations. Infants may show severe deficits in the first month of life, yet have a perfectly good developmental prognosis, or they may show no deficits on the NBAS, yet have a terrible prognosis.

A better use of such assessments is to identify which individual infants within a presumed high-risk population are the ones actually at risk. For example, premature infants are considered at risk because samples of premature infants tend to differ significantly from full-term infants on several long-term measures (Sameroff & Chandler, 1975), but this is only because some premature infants have serious neurological deficits and/or cumulative transactional deficits with caretakers. Only that subpopulation is really in need of intervention, so a function of newborn assessment would be to select those babies out of the total premature population. (If all premature infants needed intervention, the assessment scales would be superfluous.) Of the studies reviewed by Sostek, only four, or 13%, tested the NBAS's predictiveness (incremental validity) over and above the known risk factors. The NBAS helped to predict 12-month Bayley developmental scores, whether infants were premature, full-term, or postmature (Field, Hallock, Ting, Dempsey, Dabiri, & Shuman, 1978). Tronick and Brazelton (1975) showed that the NBAS produced fewer false predictions of neurological deficit over a 7-year follow-up than did standard neonatal neurological tests. In terms of Figure 2, the NBAS's r_β was as good as, and its r_α was better than, the neurological test. This is the only published study of which I am aware that treats newborn assessment as a two-dimensional decision problem rather than a unidimensional measurement problem.

Unfortunately, the studies just mentioned had to do only with assessment, not with all four dimensions that are necessarily involved in the concept of risk. Only three, or 10% of the published studies up to the time of Sostek's 1978 bibliography, looked at the intervention question.

Two of those had very short-term follow-ups, simply showing that the NBAS itself was sensitive to the results of extra stimulation with low-birthweight infants. The only study with a 12-month follow-up showed significant Cattell IQ score effects for a stimulated group of low-birth-weight infants, regardless of NBAS performance. In other words, the intervention was successful with the presumed high-risk group, but the newborn behavioral assessment was completely superfluous.

That, I think, is a fair summary of the status of newborn assessment as a clinical tool: the cost of administering the scales would often be greater than the cost of giving treatment (for example, greater vestibular stimulation in the nursery) to all infants in a presumed high-risk group. Only where there might be great cost, danger, or a social stigma attached to the treatment would it be worth developing newborn assessment procedures, and then the question in need of research is the four-dimensional one that has barely been broached.

Until then, perhaps our presumption should be that *every* newborn is at risk. Devoting limited research funds to improving the way society as a whole, and families in general, prepare new human organisms for personhood makes more sense than devoting those funds to assessment tools that lack any specific utility for treatment.

The fields of IQ testing and newborn behavioral assessment have in common the fact that far too much energy was wasted on the development of instruments with insufficient attention to the question of what they were going to be used for. We have in IQ a fairly good predictor of school achievement, but equally good political, moral, economic, and pedagogical reasons for ignoring that predictor and giving children the opportunity to disconfirm it. The treatment choices for which Binet's assessment was originally designed—whether to leave children in the Paris school system or to remove them—have been replaced with a larger and slightly more sophisticated range of alternatives, each of which requires its own set of placement tests based on the four-dimensional considerations. As intervention programs for the parents or caretakers of young infants become more sophisticated, they too will each require their own placement tests, for which the NBAS will not serve.

Child and Family Therapy: Intervention with Vagueness about "Whom?"

We can also point to areas of research in which more or less the opposite error has prevailed: concentration on intervention techniques for children known to be at risk, with inadequate attention to the problem of precisely when a given treatment is indicated. This complaint has been leveled against much psychotherapy research (Epstein & Vlok, 1981; Kauffman, 1977), for example, where different ways of treating schizophrenia are evaluated as though the disease were a precise and unitary phenomenon as unvarying and as well understood as a physical illness, like scurvy. Scurvy is a hemorrhaging condition that results from a vitamin C deficiency. When it is suspected, biochemical diagnostic methods are available, of which the ultimate and best test is whether the symptoms respond to vitamin C. There are few mental or psychosomatic illnesses for which that kind of specific biochemical and/or trial-and-error drug test is possible. Instead, we have diagnostic categories based on a combination of symptomatology and etiology. Like schizophrenia, many of our categories undoubtedly confuse several different underlying causes, which we hope eventually to distinguish from one another. The way to make scientific progress in that direction is to be constantly differentiating types and subtypes. A general principle, as valid in relation to disorders of psychological development as it is in medicine, is that progress in the refinement of diagnostic categories is inseparable from progress in methods of treatment. They must always be two facets of one and the same research program.

This has not always been clear to psychotherapy researchers, who sometimes accept diagnostic categories like hyperactive, autistic, psychotic, depressed, or acting-out as though they were labels for integral entities rather than convenient, conventional, often arbitrary and always blurry dividing points along multidimensional continua. Once the category has been reified, the investigator proceeds to compare different treatment models in terms of their efficacy with this type of patient. Suppose that a sample of children with diagnosis D are randomly assigned to two treatment conditions. If one model is effective with 60% of the patients treated, and its competitor helps only 40%, this should not make the first method the treatment of choice for all future patients with that particular diagnosis. Among the other possibilities, it may mean that 60% of the children classified as D really have a different problem than the other 40%.

To take a specific example, a group of family therapists has reported success in treating the families of children with chronic severe asthma (Liebman, Minuchin, & Baker, 1974). The alternative to family therapy was individual child therapy, attempting to address the emotional problems that seemed to contribute to the severity and chronicity of the asthma, and continued dependence upon steroids, allergic desensitization, and bronchodilation exercises. The authors presented a theoretical rationale for structural family therapy and reported seven case studies.

Each child had visited the emergency room frequently and had been hospitalized at least three times in the previous year. After 5 to 10 months of family therapy, the symptoms went into remission, and at the time of publication, having been followed for another 10 to 22 months subsequent to this therapy, none of the seven cases had suffered acute attacks.

These were impressive results. No competing therapeutic model has been as successful, to date. Similar results have been reported for structural family therapy with anorexia nervosa, intractable diabetes, and severe chronic gastric disorders in children (Minuchin, Baker, Rosman, Liebman, Milman, & Todd, 1975). However, the applicability of their work is severely limited by the lack of any systematic research on when family therapy is actually indicated for chronic psychosomatic illness. The Minuchin group implies that it is always indicated, but proponents of other forms of therapy (e.g., psychodynamic approaches to anorexia) will not be convinced by the published studies, in which the way the test samples were selected is not discussed. It appears likely that the family therapists had some excellent intuitions about which cases would respond to their preferred mode of treatment. Before others can achieve the same success, we need some assessment tools to help predict which children's illnesses have been caused, maintained, or exacerbated by the kinds of dysfunctional family interactions that respond to family therapy.

Although it is too sweeping a generalization, I believe that as crude as our treatment methods are in clinical child psychology, they have been developed to a technical level that far outstrips our methods of assessment. Yet every treatment plan entails a diagnosis. It can ultimately be no more effective than the diagnosis is accurate. Most importantly, we cannot make much improvement in the efficacy of therapy without simultaneous advances in the classification of illnesses. Those advances, in turn, cannot be on some arbitrary descriptive or even etiological basis alone: they have to be on the basis of what is treatable. (It is more important to subdivide hyperactive children, for example, according to what interventions they will respond to than according to the consequences of their hyperactive behavior in the classroom, or according to the prenatal traumas that may have induced it.) Etiology, in fact, is of clinical importance only because it may provide clues as to some deficit—whether vitamin C or a nurturant parent—that can still be made up for. A theory about the cause can sometimes, but not necessarily, lead to a treatment plan.

Furthermore, the research that we require, basing diagnostic categories upon treatment models, and evaluating treatment in terms of more refined classifications of behavioral disorders, will have to involve all of the preceding four dimensions. (See Sroufe, 1975, for a similar critique of drug therapy with hyperactive children.)

It may occur to the reader that I have made no distinction between the diagnosis of a childhood behavior disorder and the concept of risk. Indeed, I can think of no difference. When we diagnose a child as requiring treatment, we are saying, "There is a high risk that these problems will not go away with the passage of time, that they will have a negative impact on the child's education and social development, that the parents' relationship with this child will suffer, or that the family as a whole will develop dysfunctional patterns of interaction." We are also saying that a treatment exists, with a reasonable likelihood of improving that prognosis. On the other hand, even if there is something wrong with a child, if it does not present a developmental risk for the child or family, either because it is a passing phase (like the "terrible twos") or because it is untreatable (like tone deafness), then it is unnecessary and unethical to pretend to intervene.

Discussion

Thinking about the problem of developmental risk four-dimensionally leads to some criticism of much work, both in the field of risk assessment and in the field of intervention. I have tried to argue that there is no justification for creating and routinely administering assessment scales, at any age, unless the scores on those tests are known to predict a "differential payoff" (Cronbach & Gleser, 1965) in different economically and politically feasible treatment conditions. On the other hand, no intervention can be defended without addressing precisely whom it can help, by how much, and what their fate would be without it. A treatment of a high-risk sample cannot be evaluated simply in terms of significant before–after differences, or even treatment–control group differences. Proper evaluation must be in terms of a cost–benefit payoff matrix. That, in turn, becomes more than just an evaluation of the specific program. Program evaluation is, in fact, a phase in the evolution of theories about the problem itself (Cronbach & associates, 1980).

A final point concerns the concept of assessment and intervention conceived of as society's tampering with its own internal variance. When a group is selected from the lower end of the distribution of predicted developmental outcomes and given special treatment, the goal is not so much to increase the population mean or median as it is to reduce the variance. On the other hand, there are circumstances in which we select individuals for special treatment from the upper end of the distribution, as in college placement examinations and in elementary school programs for gifted children. Their aim is actually to increase the population variance. The concept of risk can be inverted somewhat to apply here: The untreated prognosis for the brightest students is better than for any other students, but still not as superior as it can be made to be with extra investment of society's resources. So the parents of those children regard them as at risk in regular school classes: at risk of not remaining superior.

Suppose, instead, that we were to consider the goal of public programs to be not necessarily decreasing or increasing the variance among children's developmental attainments, but raising the mean or median for the whole population. Alternatively, suppose we decide that it is more important to help certain demographic groups than it is to help others. Such considerations would add even more dimensions to the model. We would need to weigh the relative value of an intervention aimed at one group compared with the value of all other interventions that the same money could buy for some other groups. That may seem, and indeed is, far more complex than the way developmental psychologists have thought about these issues in the past. Yet it is inevitably the way politicians, bureaucrats, and even private philanthropists have to make decisions.

Does this mean that a scientific approach to the issues addressed in this book is impossible? No, but I think it means that a model strictly based in our own disciplines, those concerned with human development, is impossible. The concept of developmental risk, as something that can be identified and ameliorated, involves economics, history, sociology, and political science: It is about as interdisciplinary as a concept can be.

References

Aleksandrowicz, M., & Aleksandrowicz, D. (1974). Obstetrical pain-relieving drugs as predictors of infant behavior variability. *Child Development, 45*, 935–945.

Brazelton, T. B. (1973). *Neonatal behavior assessment scale*. Philadelphia: Lippincott.

Cronbach, L., & Associates. (1980). *Toward reform of program evaluation*. San Francisco: Jossey-Bass.

Cronbach, L., & Gleser, G. (1965). *Psychological tests and personnel decisions* (2nd ed.). Urbana: University of Illinois Press.

Epstein, N., & Vlok, L. (1981). Research on the results of psychotherapy: A summary of evidence. *American Journal of Psychiatry, 138*, 1027–1035.

Field, T., Hallock, N., Ting, G., Dempsey, J., Dabiri, C., & Shuman, H. (1978). A first-year follow-up of high-risk infants: Formulating a cumulative risk index. *Child Development, 49*, 119–131.

Jensen, A. (1969). How much can we boost IQ and scholastic achievement? *Harvard Educational Review, 39,* 1–123.

Jensen, A. (1980). *Bias in mental testing.* New York: Free Press.

Kauffman, J. (1977). *Characteristics of children's behavior disorders.* Columbus, OH: Merrill.

Kaye, K. (1973). I.Q.: A conceptual deterrent to revolution in education. *Elementary School Journal, 74,* 9–23.

Kaye, K. (1980). Estimating false alarms and missed events from inter-observer agreements: A rationale. *Psychological Bulletin, 88,* 458–468.

Liebman, R., Minuchin, S., & Baker, L. (1974). The use of structural family therapy in the treatment of intractable asthma. *American Journal of Psychiatry, 131,* 535–539.

Minuchin, S., Baker, L., Rosman, B., Liebman, R., Milman, L., & Todd, T. (1975). A conceptual model of psychosomatic illness in children. *Archives of General Psychiatry, 32,* 1031–1038.

Sameroff, A., & Chandler, M. (1975). Reproductive risk and the continuum of caretaking casualty. In F. Horowitz, M. Hetherington, S. Scarr-Salapatek, & G. Siegel (Eds.), *Review of child development research* (Vol. 4). Chicago: University of Chicago Press.

Sechrest, L. (1963). Incremental validity: A recommendation. *Educational Psychological Measurement, 23,* 153–158.

Sostek, A. (1978). Annotated bibliography of research using the neonatal behavioral assessment scale. In Sameroff, A. (Ed.), Organization and stability in newborn behavior: Commentary on the Brazelton neonatal assessment scale. *Monographs of the Society for Research in Child Development, 43,* No. 177.

Sroufe, L. A. (1975) Drug treatment of children with behavior problems. In F. Horowitz, M. Hetherington, S. Scarr-Salapatek, & G. Siegel (Eds.), *Review of child development research* (Vol. 4). Chicago: University of Chicago Press.

Tronick, E., & Brazelton, T. B. (1975). Clinical uses of the Brazelton Neonatal Behavioral Assessment. In B. Friedlander, G. Sterritt, & G. Kirk (Eds.), *Exceptional infant 3: Assessment and intervention.* New York: Brunner/Mazel.

Tronick, E., Wise, S., Als, H., Adamson, L., Scanlon, J., & Brazelton, T. B. (1976). Regional obstetric anesthesia and newborn behavior: Effect over the first ten days of life. *Pediatrics, 58,* 94–100.

12

Prevention Services for Risk Children: Evidence for Policy and Practice*

BARBARA K. KEOGH, ANNE G. WILCOXEN, AND LUCINDA BERNHEIMER

Introduction

This chapter is focused on preventive services for children at risk. By *risk*, we mean children with a higher than average probability of problems in development. Negative developmental outcomes are viewed as ranging from life-threatening or handicapping conditions to school failure. Our emphasis is on prevention because this aspect of services is frequently neglected and because the policies that lead to preventive services are too often ambiguous and controversial. The chapter is organized in several major sections. The first contains a brief rationale for the need for preventive services and pinpoints assumptions about development and risk which provide a framework for policy and services. A second section relates prevention strategies to various risk conditions. In the third section, we illustrate the complexities of policy and service delivery systems using as an example the Medicaid program of Early and Periodic Screening, Diagnosis, and Treatment (EPSDT). A final section contains recommendations for policy which link risk and services.

*This research was supported in part by Contract #300-77-0306 between the University of California and the Bureau of Education for the Handicapped, U.S. Office of Education, Washington, D.C.

Rationale and Assumptions

Preventive services for children at risk for intellectual and psychosocial development receive support from a number of perspectives. The importance of early experience for subsequent development, the spiraling and often negative impact of child-risk on family and interpersonal dynamics, and the relatively low cost of prevention as opposed to treatment or remediation have been well described. However, despite both theoretical and empirical support, comprehensive prevention programs aimed at children with developmental risks are, for the most part, lacking. Children with developmental delays or specific learning or emotional problems may go unserved until the problems become so acute that major interventions or treatment regimens are required. Even basic health needs are often not attended to. Figures collected by the Select Panel for the Promotion of Child Health (1981, Vol. 3) indicate that 25% of women giving birth receive late or no prenatal care before delivery, that 7% of the nation's children lack routine immunizations against major childhood diseases prior to entering school, and that 16% of children under age 6 have not seen a physician within the past 12 months. While the importance of prevention is increasingly recognized, programs aimed at children's health and developmental needs have been slow to develop and too often are fragmented and inconsistent. This is both troubling and puzzling, and it raises serious questions about the policy basis for health services for children, especially for children at risk for developmental problems. Questions of prevention are also troubling for professionals, and we agree with Albee (1982) that adoption of a prevention perspective may require reconsideration of widely held models of causation.

In our view, the lack of consistent policy on which to build programs stems in part from economic and political influences. However, policy is also affected by the somewhat uncertain nature of risk and of its consequences. Developmental risk is an ambiguous term which may vary in operational definition and in implications for services. Thus, before considering the relationship of risk condition and preventive services, it is necessary to specify our assumptions about risk.

Four major assumptions about development and risk have directed the arguments presented in this chapter. First, we view development as embedded within a broad health context. Second, we assume that many child and extrachild influences contribute to developmental status. Third, we suggest that developmental risk may be evidenced in different problems and in varying degrees of severity. Fourth, we assume a link between risk and services, such that early risk status can be identified, lessened, sometimes even ameliorated. As these assumptions provide a basis for policy relating to services for risk children, each deserves brief elaboration.

Development and Health

Changing views of the nature of development have led to recognition that developmental status and other aspects of health are highly related, perhaps synonymous. Prolonged severe malnutrition is often associated with developmental delay and emotional apathy. Unrestricted diet in cases of PKU (phenylketonuria) may lead to cognitive deficits. Undetected hearing impairments may affect language acquisition and educational achievement. Children with chronic respiratory problems or allergies may lack the energy and vigor necessary for full participation in social and educational activities. As biological and psychological integrity are related and interactive, we assume that both must be considered in planning services for children with developmental risks.

Development is Multidetermined

Development is not a function of biological *or* environmental adequacy. Genetics, nutrition, caregiver attitudes, and opportunities for social experiences are among the many contributors to children's physical and psychological health. The complex interplay between biological and experiential factors has been conceptualized by Sameroff (1975) in an important theoretical paper. His transactional perspective led to further insights into the course of developmental risk (Sameroff & Chandler, 1975) and to better understanding of issues of identification, treatment, and intervention with risk children (Keogh & Kopp, 1978; Ramey, Trohanis, & Hostler, 1982; Ramey, Zeskind, & Hunter, 1981; Siegel, 1982). Empirical support for considering many contributors to developmental status comes from the extensive studies of infants at risk by Parmelee and his colleagues (Kopp & Parmelee, 1979; Parmelee, Kopp, & Sigman, 1976; Sigman & Parmelee, 1979), as well as from the work of Hunt (1981), Werner, Bierman, and French (1971), and Werner and Smith (1982).

The complex factors that affect children's health and development are illustrated by Bronfenbrenner's ecological model. This model is well described (Bronfenbrenner, 1977) and need not be presented in detail here. Important to the present discussion, however, is the clear delineation within the model of four levels of influences (micro, meso, exo, and macro) that converge around an individual child and family. As noted by Young (1980), the ecology of handicap or risk can be systematically described using Bronfenbrenner's model. It is possible to identify what kinds of services are needed, to determine where services are missing, and to assess the degree of coordination of services within and among levels. Examination of service delivery programs for risk and handicapped young children using this framework (Young, 1980) suggests major limitations, even gaps, in services, such that many children are at continuing risk for a variety of developmental problems. The multideter-mined nature of development and risk carries many implications for programs of service.

The Nature of Risk

A third assumption that provides direction for policy is that develop-mental risk is not a single, unitary condition but rather subsumes a broad range of conditions and degrees. Ramey et al. (1982) note that an infant might be called at risk, suspect, high priority, vulnerable, or at developmental risk; others have conceptualized risk in terms of time (e.g., prenatal, perinatal, or postnatal). Tjossem (1976) proposed three likely overlapping risk types: established, environmental, and biolog-ical. Tjossem's categories are similar to those of Keogh and Kopp (1978), who suggest that one risk category includes children with identifiable, usually organically based, in-child conditions, which frequently have negative developmental consequences (e.g., visual impairment, Down's syndrome). In this chapter, we refer to these children as evidencing *biologic risk*. In-child conditions are frequently apparent at birth or early on in a child's life, and often have well described, long-term effects. Keogh and Kopp's second category, referred to in this chapter as *suspect risk*, identifies children whose health and developmental status are asso-ciated with conditions which have documented relationships to subse-quent problems (e.g., perinatal anoxia, prematurity, low birthweight). Both the biologic and suspect risk categories identify biosocial factors included in Lilienfeld and Parkhurst's (1951) continuum of reproductive wastage, and both call for therapeutic interventions that are directed at relatively specific child conditions.

A third risk group identified by Keogh and Kopp relates developmen-tal risk to extrachild conditions within the broader environment. This category of risk subsumes conditions included in Sameroff and Chan-dler's (1975) continuum of care-taking casualty, and identifies threats to development that are associated with social–interactional influences. In this chapter, we call this category *environmental risk*. Clearly the condi-tions of risk are interactive, possibly transactive, so that biological risk may have different consequences, depending on the context in which it appears. However, the three conditions of risk carry somewhat different prevention and treatment implications.

Risk and Services

A fourth assumption that has direct implication for policy relates to the links between risk and services. Despite recognition of the complex nature of risk and the dangers inherent in prediction for individuals, there is increasingly powerful evidence to suggest that early risk-status can be identified and ameliorated by appropriate and timely services. It would be naive and inaccurate to argue that all risk or handicapping conditions can be cured or obviated. It is important to recognize, however, that the long-term outcomes of many risk conditions have been dramatically improved by medical and social–educational interventions. To illustrate, PKU screening and subsequent dietary modifications have effectively reduced the incidence of mental retardation due to that metabolic disorder. Surgical shunts have prevented or reduced abnormal physical and intellectual growth in cases of hydrocephalus. Improved neonatal procedures have reduced the mortality rates for premature infants and have increased the chances of normal development for suspect risk babies. Educational and social interventions have increased the achievement and school competence of environmentally at-risk children.

From an actuarial perspective, children in poor economic conditions are at risk for low educational and vocational accomplishment, as well as for a variety of health conditions. Yet, a report of early educational interventions with children from low economic backgrounds (Lazar & Darlington, 1982) documents long-term effects of intervention programs on school competence, on developed abilities (intelligence and achievement), on attitudes and values, and on the family. The point to be emphasized is that there is extensive and solid evidence to support the impact of services on risk conditions. In our view, these links between risk and services are well enough defined to direct policy aimed at prevention programs.

Risk, Prevention, and Treatment

A number of policy and service implications follow from the four assumptions about development and risk. As risk has both physical and psychosocial components, services must be broad based. The development of high-risk infants and children has been shown to be related to the attitudes, resources, and strength of their caretakers and the social environments in which they live, as well as to the biological condition of the child. Thus, effective programs for risk children must include medical, educational, and psychosocial components. In addition, services must have continuity over time, and must change in specific content, according to developmental period and individual need. Recognition of the transactional nature of growth and of the many influences on individual development clearly increases the complexity of the prevention and intervention task.

It should be noted, too, that the distinction between treatment and prevention is sometimes blurred. Indeed, the same procedures or services might be viewed as therapeutic or preventive, depending on the context in which they are administered and the timing of their administration. A nutritional supplement, for example, might correct a problem for one child, prevent a problem for another. From the perspective of needed services for children at risk, it seems reasonable to view treatment and prevention as a continuum, not as discrete entities. The determination of whether a particular service is treatment or prevention relates to the nature of the risk condition, as well as to the content of the service itself. Authors in other chapters in this volume have focused on treatment. We emphasize the prevention aspect of services for risk children, drawing on definitions of prevention useful in public health programs.

Levels of Preventive Services

Public health professionals frequently define three levels of prevention: primary, secondary, and tertiary. The goal in primary prevention is to enhance development of all individuals, to prevent the development of disease by protecting all group members. Secondary prevention is selective, aims at individuals or particular groups, and involves early diagnosis and treatment of problems before they develop into potentially handicapping or life-threatening conditions. Tertiary prevention is also referenced to the individual or to specific groups of individuals, and is intended to reduce the effects of irreversible illness, to limit handicapping conditions, and/or to promote rehabilitation. With regard to risk children, within each level of prevention the content of services may be medical, educational, psychosocial, or combinations thereof.

To illustrate, at the level of primary prevention, medical services might include PKU screening and follow-up, immunization, or water fluoridation; educational services might focus on community-wide programs of home safety, nutrition, and developing intellectually stimulating environments; and psychosocial services might subsume a broad constellation of services such as assisting heads of households in finding employment or in financial planning. These primary prevention services are important for all children. Secondary prevention services are concerned with early identification, diagnosis, and treatment of specific children who evidence conditions that might lead to risk or handicapping conditions if left untreated, and concerned with help for families with incipient pathology. Medical services might involve diagnosis and treatment of children with chronic ear infections, anemia, or nutritional deficiencies; educational services might target poor school progress or specific learning problems; and psychosocial services might be directed at reduction of potential child abuse. In the case of tertiary prevention, the individual is identified as having a problem or a handicapping condition, and prevention services are directed toward limiting and/or remediating the effects of the condition. Services such as restorative surgery, speech therapy, vocational rehabilitation, and family counseling programs fall into this category of prevention services.

The focus of services changes from a prevention emphasis at the primary level to a remediation emphasis at the tertiary level. From a prevention perspective, the overriding goal is to reduce the need for extensive services at the tertiary level by providing effective services at the primary and secondary levels. Although all levels of prevention and types of services are to some degree applicable across risk categories, there do appear to be differences in emphases according to risk category. In this regard, we reiterate that *all* children profit from primary prevention programs, and large numbers of children can benefit from effective secondary level services. Children with biologically based, in-child conditions typically require tertiary-level services, while children with suspect conditions require secondary-level services, including careful monitoring and prompt intervention as needed. Children in the third category, risk by virtue of environmental conditions, are most likely to profit from comprehensive primary and secondary prevention programs. An increasingly extensive data base argues for the effectiveness of services within the three levels. A brief discussion of prevention strategies according to risk category follows.

Biologic Risk and Prevention Services

One category of risk defined by Keogh and Kopp (1978) includes infants and young children with identified problems likely to interfere with development (e.g., Down syndrome, vision or hearing impairment, cerebral palsy). Appropriate services for these children and families may be medical, educational and/or psychosocial and are usually at a tertiary level. Services are designed to minimize the impact of a limiting or handicapping condition, to promote development as possible, and to prevent the occurrence of compounding physical or psychosocial problems. In many cases of biologic risk, the handicapping condition itself may not be directly treatable but the associated problems are.

Tertiary prevention services can reduce the effect of a disability and promote rehabilitation. As example, educational and social services for Down's syndrome children have been shown to have powerful effects and to reduce associated problems. The historical advice to parents of Down's syndrome infants was to institutionalize; indeed, many of these infants went directly from the newborn nursey to the institution. Since then, research (Clunies-Ross, 1979; Hanson, 1981; Rynders & Horrobin, 1975) has led to reassessment of the developmental potential for Down's syndrome children, particularly to the recognition of the impact of experience on their development. Ongoing work by Hayden and associates at the University of Washington (Hayden & Dmitriev, 1975; Hayden & Haring, 1976, 1977), for example, has shown that many Down's syndrome children can perform at remarkably high levels of competence, given early and comprehensive services. Data from the University of Washington programs provide convincing evidence of the effectiveness of early intervention.

While the work of Hayden and her colleagues demonstrates improved development for a specific population, educational interventions have also been effective in reducing the effects of other identified disabilities. As example, Fraiberg (1975) developed techniques to teach blind infants to compensate for their lack of vision through adaptive hand behavior. Horton (1976) and Simmons-Martin (1981) have shown the impact of early intervention for deaf children on second-grade reading ability and language, respectively. Bricker and Sheehan (1981) described significant progress in a group of normal, at-risk, mildly, moderately, and severely handicapped children enrolled in a University of Oregon intervention program, making the important point that the absence of significant decline in the most severely handicapped children was particularly encouraging. In spite of an ongoing and healthy controversy surrounding the best outcome measures selected, and what constitutes an indication of acceptable change in these children (Garwood, 1982a, 1982b; Sheehan & Keogh, 1982), it is clear that early education is an effective form of tertiary prevention for children with biologic risk conditions. In addition, delaying intervention frequently means that children require more services later, and that fewer children enter regular education. Thus, early intervention is cost-effective, both developmentally for the child, and financially for the family and taxpaper (Colorado Department of Education, 1983; Garland, Stone, Swanson, & Woodruff, 1981; Karnes, Schwedel, Lewis, Ratts, & Esry, 1981).

For the most part, medical and educational services have been directed primarily at the handicapped child. Increasingly, however, the need for ongoing psychosocial support for families of handicapped children has been recognized. Eloquent testimony about the stresses associated with raising a handicapped child is available from parent reports (Bernheimer & Keogh, 1982; Featherstone, 1980; Roskies, 1972; Turnbull & Turnbull, 1985). In addition to confronting their feelings, frustrations and disappointments, parents of handicapped children need to acquire certain knowledge not required of other families (Ireys, 1981). They must learn about medications, diets, financial resources and how to obtain them, and strategies for dealing with the special-education maze (Cutler, 1981). As noted by Young (1980), successful management or coordination of the many needed services is a complex and demanding task for parents of handicapped children. Unfortunately, the task is complicated because of the fragmentation of services (Ireys, 1981; Smith, 1984) and the well-documented problems in parent–professional interaction (Anderson & Garner, 1973; Bernheimer, Young, & Winton, 1983; Bobath & Finnie, 1970; Brock, 1976; Keirn, 1971; Roos, 1977; Solnit, 1976; Tarran, 1981; Young, 1980). Lacking adequate resources and support services, caregivers of handicapped children may be hard pressed to provide the amount of support necessary for their child to attain his or her potential. Clearly, reduction of family stress through psychosocial services is an important prevention strategy.

While most of the appropriate prevention services for the biologic risk group are tertiary in nature, it is important to emphasize that there are primary prevention strategies that can reduce the number of children in this risk category. Examples of primary level services include prenatal care, genetic counseling, and prevention of alcohol and drug abuse during pregnancy. In addition, there are a number of conditions identifiable early on in an infant's life which carry implications for subsequent developmental status and which are amenable to secondary level prevention. As example, Ireys (1981) notes that mentally retarded children have frequent medical problems distinct from their retardation: convulsions, recurrent bronchitis, higher frequency of major diseases, and more frequent hospital admissions than nonretarded children. Down's syndrome children are prone to upper-respiratory infections and have a high incidence of other medical problems ranging in severity from dental caries to congenital heart defects (Connaughton, 1978). If undetected or untreated, these conditions may complicate or exacerbate the primary handicapping condition. Given the assumption cited earlier in this chapter that development is embedded in a broad context of health, it becomes particularly important that children with biologic risk have access to ongoing comprehensive health services which can prevent the occurrence of significant secondary problems or handicaps. While primary and secondary strategies of prevention have demonstrated effectiveness, their implementation is unfortunately closely tied to economic and social conditions, a point to be elaborated in subsequent sections of this chapter.

Suspect Risk and Prevention Services

A second category of risk defined by Keogh and Kopp (1978) identified infants and young children with pre- or perinatal stress conditions associated with subsequent problems in development. Such conditions include low birthweight, perinatal anoxia, and prematurity. While it is true that many of these conditions had been associated with high rates of infant mortality and problem development, advances in neonatal medicine and in care for high-risk newborns have resulted in dramatic changes in survival rates, as well as in reduction of associated problems. The link between risk conditions and secondary prevention efforts is well established in these cases. As noted by Hunt (1981), "If the very small infant is born without congenital anomalies or primary diseases, the likelihood of handicaps (like that of mortality) may depend primarily on the quality of perinatal care" (p. 331).

The medical technology necessary to ensure anoxic or premature infants' survival is an obvious example of the link between risk and services. Less obvious, however, is the link between risk and continuous comprehensive health care after birth. We know, for example, that low birthweight is associated with increased health problems in the early years, particularly bronchiolitis and pneumonia (Fitzhardinge, 1976). In addition, there is evidence that significant medical problems during the first year are correlated with developmental status in the second year for preterm populations (Littman, 1979). It is well recognized that pregnancy, labor, delivery, and the first month of life are periods of risk. According to Littman, however, "What happens to the infant at ages beyond the fetal and neonatal stages takes on greater importance. In the area of medical events, those complications occurring later in infancy demand more careful study. This is especially so if we are to determine what children are at risk for developmental handicaps and possibly in need of intervention" (p. 56).

Although appropriate and immediate medical response to perinatal and neonatal problems has clearly been effective in reducing handicapping conditions, evidence from a number of studies suggests that children of suspect risk may continue to be vulnerable for a variety of psychosocial and educational problems. As example, analysis of data from a subgroup of children with perinatal anoxia from the Collaborative Perinatal Project revealed that the probability of retardation at age 7 years was six times as high for the anoxic than for the nonanoxic infants (Broman, 1979). Kopp (1983) has noted the sleeper effect imposed by early risk, suggesting that perinatal stresses may not influence generalized sensorimotor repertoires, but may impose constraints on the growth of specific abilities required for school. Children in the suspect risk category may require regular monitoring during their elementary school years. The few studies that have separated perinatal risk and low socioeconomic status (SES) provide unsettling evidence that suspect risk infants have a higher incidence of problems at school in the language and perceptual motor areas than do nonrisk children, despite IQs within the normal range (Caputo, Goldstein, & Taub, 1979, 1981; Ehrlich, Shapiro, Kimball, & Huttner, 1973; Hunt, Tooley, & Harvin, 1982). Indeed, the Hunt et al. data suggest that assessment at ages 2–3 and 4–6 years underidentified children who would have specific learning disabilities at the age of 8. This continuing risk raises serious questions as to the adequacy and timeliness of services, and suggests that medical response to pre- or perinatal stress may be only one of a set of necessary services.

Finally, premature birth and/or vulnerable conditions of infants in this risk group put stress on parents that may negatively affect future parent–child interactions. The impact of child behavior on parent response (Bell & Harper, 1977) and the importance of a goodness of fit between child and caretaking environment (Thomas & Chess, 1977) are well established. Several researchers have noted the importance of assisting parents in interpreting weak or distorted signals from their at-risk infant (Bromwich, 1981; Kass, Sigman, Bromwich, & Parmelee, 1976; Kopp, 1979). Such signals may lead to a breakdown in the parent–child interaction, which in turn can create self-reinforcing consequences (Field, 1979, 1983; Field, Hallock, Ting, Dempsey, Dabiri, & Shuman, 1978). Support for parents of suspect risk infants in the first months of life may present a "compounding of problems that occur all too early when the environment cannot adjust appropriately to the infant at risk" (Kass et al., 1976, p. 325).

In summary, prevention for infants and children in the suspect risk category may be primary, secondary, or tertiary. Primary level services include adequate prenatal and perinatal care. Secondary prevention may be appropriately directed toward parent or child, and includes counseling and support for the parent as well as comprehensive health and educational services for the child. If secondary prevention is successful, there is no need for tertiary level services. Without access to a range of secondary services, however, children in the risk group may require costly medical and educational treatments, and their families may need psychosocial interventions. The continuing vulnerability of children in this category of risk underscores the need to extend services beyond the infant and preschool years.

Environmental Risk and Prevention Services

We have already argued that development and risk must be viewed within a broad context of health. It is clear that, in part at least, health and social–educational achievement are associated with economic status. Poor children are at high risk for a variety of health-related developmental problems. At birth, they are at increased risk for prenatal and postnatal trauma. According to the 1972 National Natality Survey (Placek, 1977), low-income mothers were less likely than middle-income mothers to receive prenatal care in the first trimester of pregnancy. They also had fewer prenatal care visits and they were more likely to have low birthweight babies. Data from a landmark study of all births in New York City in 1968 (Kessner, Singer, Kalk, & Schlesinger, 1973) revealed that approximately 460 infants died as a result of inadequate prenatal care. In a foreword to this study, Robert Coles commented that "such children were not the victims of a profession's intellectual or scientific inadequacies. They were not boys and girls born too soon—because certain fatal diseases have yet to be understood and made responsive to medical treatment. They were boys and girls who, with their mothers, of course, needed only what millions of others received: adequate medical attention. Their deaths were, by and large, utterly avoidable" (p. viii).

Evidence from a number of sources confirms the health problems of children in low-SES families. As summarized in the Select Panel report (1981, Vol. 3), low-income parents were $3\frac{1}{2}$ times as likely to report that their children were in fair or poor health than were high-income parents. Results of medical examination of adolescents in Harlem (Brunswick & Josephson, 1972) revealed that $\frac{2}{3}$ had at least one medical condition (excluding dental) requiring treatment and $\frac{1}{3}$ had two such conditions. Vision problems were found in $\frac{1}{5}$ of the group, and $\frac{1}{6}$ had heart or blood pressure abnormalities. Poor nutrition, particularly iron deficiency, is more common in poor families and contributes to the health problems of children in these families (Birch & Gussow, 1970).

In addition to a high incidence of illness and poor nutrition, poverty children suffer from a lack of medical attention for their health problems. As summarized in the Select Panel report (1981, Vol. 3), children from low-income families are less likely to receive medical services than are children from high-income families. Relative to children from more economically advantaged homes, poor children are hospitalized for twice as many days per year, lose more days per year at school due to illness, and are twice as likely to have limitations of major activities. Primary prevention services are too often lacking in this population. In 1976, 62% of the children under the age of 4 years living in urban poverty areas were not fully immunized against polio.

Problems are not limited to childhood. As reported by the Children's Defense Fund (1977), a Selective Service study in 1966 revealed that more than 15% of 18-year-olds examined for military duty were rejected because of medical, developmental, and emotional problems; a disproportionate number of these young men were from low-SES families. An HEW task force reviewed these data and estimated that 62% of the serious conditions identified by the Selective Service could have been prevented or corrected with adequate primary and secondary prevention services.

There is little dispute that primary prevention services in the area of health care are effective deterrents of later health problems. Adequate prenatal care, improved immunization status, and living conditions free of environmental hazards are only a few of many medical and health services that reduce death, disease, and disability. Figures on lead poisoning reported in the *New England Journal of Medicine* (Berwick & Komaroff, 1982) provide a good example of the consequences of inadequate primary prevention services among low-income populations. The national incidence of lead poisoning is 7%, but in some inner city areas it exceeds 15%. Based on the national figure of 7%, lead poisoning causes an additional 13 cases of learning disability and 1.4 cases of mental retardation in every thousand children. Lead-abatement and lead-screening programs reduce these figures to 7 cases of learning disability and 0.6 cases of mental retardation. Corresponding figures for inner city areas would be approximately double, given the incidence figure of 15% for these areas.

Providing preventive health services only in selected situations (e.g., lead poisoning), however, is not sufficient. Children need access to continuous health care. Secondary prevention strategies involving early diagnosis and treatment of health problems can prevent many serious illnesses and handicaps. For example, there is consensus that if strep (streptococcus) throat were detected and treated adequately, the incidence of rheumatic fever and rheumatic heart disease would be dramatically reduced (Halfon & Davies, 1980). Yet, in 1972, approximately 68,000 children suffered from these conditions (National Center for Health Statistics, 1974); many of these children were from poor families. These findings are consistent with those of Birch and Gussow (1970), who found that the Watts area of Los Angeles contained only 17% of the city's population, but 43% of the cases of rheumatic fever were reported there. When comprehensive health care programs have been available in low-income communities, the incidence of rheumatic fever has been shown to be reduced by as much as 60% (Gordis, 1973).

In addition to increased risk for health, poor children are at risk for low educational success (Nichols & Chen, 1981). The correlation between SES and intellectual and educational risk has been well documented (see Ramey & Finklestein, 1981, for review). Virtually every study that has included standard intellectual measures has shown that middle-class children perform better than children from lower SES groups on cognitive and achievement measures. Importantly, these differences are found within ethnic groups (Lesser, Fifer, & Clark, 1963).

The health and educational findings linking poverty and risk are particularly disturbing when it is recognized that a significant number of American children are in low-SES families. According to the Select Panel report (1981, Vol. 3), in 1978 16% of the children and youth under the age of 18 in the United States (approximately 10 million children) lived in poverty. Obvious effects of poverty are lack of financial resources for adequate housing, clothing, food, and medical care. Other factors associated with low SES compound the problems. A disproportionate number of nonwhite children are included in this group—41% of all black children and 27% of Hispanic children live in poverty, compared to 11% of white children. The linguistic and cultural differences of children from many nonwhite ethnic groups may exacerbate risk conditions related to economic status when these children enter school. Further, poverty status is often a characteristic of young, single mothers who may be ill equipped physically and emotionally to care for a child, especially a child with problems. Finally, poverty is associated with limited education. Poorly educated parents may not be aware of the need for health or developmental services or of where to obtain them.

Although the impact of preventive services in the domains of social and educational development may not be as dramatic or as easy to document as those involving medical services, there is increasing evidence to support the effects of early intervention programs. Preliminary evaluations of intervention services by Abt Associates (Stebbins, St.

Pierre, Proper, Anderson, & Cerva, 1977) and Westinghouse (1969) tended to be negative, and serious questions were raised about the effectiveness of early education programs. Hodges and Buzelli (1984) and Hodges, Sheehan, and Carter (1979) suggest, however, that these evaluations were limited because they focused exclusively on cognitive outcomes, devaluing affective, motivational, and attitudinal changes. The importance of social competence, rather than IQ, as an outcome criterion of program effectiveness has been persuasively argued by Zigler and Trickett (1978). Fox (1982) suggests that accumulating evidence from a number of different programs demonstrates the effects of early education on social and emotional factors, which in turn have likely effects on school performance.

This interpretation receives support from the Society for Research in Child Development monograph by Lazar and Darlington (1982), which summarizes outcome findings from 11 different early education programs serving low-SES children. Data from the individual programs were integrated and analyzed, taking into account subjects' family backgrounds and initial ability estimates. Findings were in general positive, and deserve brief summary. In terms of school performance, program graduates were less likely than control children to be retained in grade or to be placed in special education. The percentage of children in special education was 5.3 for program graduates and 29.4 for controls in the program ranked at the median in effectiveness. Grade-retention data were not as striking, but all projects reported a lower rate of repeated grades for program than control children.

Results of intelligence and achievement test scores were somewhat less definitive, although there was a significant effect of program on IQ for the first 4 years after the end of the program. Program graduates also performed somewhat better on achievement tests, evidence from the Perry Project (Weikert, Bard, & McNeil, 1978) suggesting more powerful achievement effects over time. Positive attitudes toward school and achievement were also found to favor program graduates at the time of long-term follow-up. Family effects, as evidenced in mothers' attitudes and aspirations for their children, were found in many of the projects. Taken as a whole, the consortium findings are encouraging.

As noted by Ramey (1982), however, a number of goals were not achieved, the most obvious being permanent change in intellectual performance. At the long-term follow-up, the mean IQ for program graduates was still below the national average, leading Ramey to observe that "this represents a group of children who are likely to experience major hardships in an increasingly technological and sophisticated culture" (p.

149). While Ramey's observation is sobering, it should come as no surprise. We have already outlined the complexity of risk, its many contributors, its health context, and its transactional character. The educational programs begun in the 1960s were effective in bringing about changes in children and families, and demonstrated a direct link between risk condition and services. Yet, these programs were for the most part limited in depth and scope, and lasted a relatively short time in the children's and families' lives. In a sense, it is surprising that they were able to accomplish as much as they did. We can only speculate at the possible long-term effects if these educational programs had been supported by effective medical and social programs, and if the interventions had continued over longer periods of time.

The limited scope of many early intervention programs leads to recognition of the need for more comprehensive services to families and children. Head Start research and development projects, such as the Child and Family Resource Program, now often include medical, educational, and psychosocial components for disadvantaged children and their families from birth through the early school years. Longitudinal evaluation data from these projects are not yet available, but promising follow-up evidence is beginning to emerge. Data from one small-sample, comprehensive intervention project, the Yale Child Welfare Research Program (Rescorla & Zigler, 1981), is illustrative.

The Yale project was designed to help disadvantaged families improve their quality of life and foster the healthy development of their children. Services provided depended on individual family needs and preferences and included a home visitor, regular medical care, developmental examinations, and an optional day care program. The home visitor offered assistance in dealing with social service agencies, psychological and emotional support, child care advice, and therapeutic counseling. Although the program offered services only from birth to 30 months of age, a follow-up evaluation when the children were 7 to 8 years old indicated that the program had a long-term impact on the children's intellectual and academic development. Compared to control children from their original neighborhoods, the children in the Yale project scored higher on measures of IQ, school achievement, and school attendance. A striking finding was the impact of the program on the families. Program families at the time of follow-up showed significant improvements in their housing, educational status, economic self-sufficiency, and general quality of life. Rescorla and Zigler (1981) conclude that significant long-term effects can be obtained by offering a range of services that support family aspirations for parents and their children.

The Links between Risk and Services

Taken as a whole, there is considerable evidence to support the implementation of prevention programs for risk children. Tertiary services to children with biologic condtions and their families can lessen the impact of handicap and can reduce the human and economic costs of continuing care. Timely and appropriate secondary prevention for children with suspect risk conditions has been shown to reduce the frequency of subsequent developmental problems and the incidence of handicap. Early educational and social interventions with children at risk because of environmental conditions, along with primary prevention programs of comprehensive health services, lead to better physical, social, and educational outcomes.

Given the established links between risk and services, it is puzzling that so few comprehensive service delivery programs have been implemented. A number of programs for risk and handicapped children have been articulated at the Federal level. These include programs of Maternal and Child Health, Crippled Children's Services, Head Start, PL 94-142 (the Education of All Handicapped Children Act of 1975), as well as the Medicaid program of EPSDT. Although the programs have somewhat different emphases, they are all directed at services for children at risk or with problems. They also have in common limited implementation, and in some cases, continuing controversies. We use EPSDT to illustrate the complexities.

Early Periodic Screening, Diagnosis, and Treatment[1]

A benchmark in Federal commitment to health services to mothers and children is represented in a 1967 amendment to the Medicaid legislation, Title XIX of the Social Security Act. The 1967 amendment provides for preventive and treatment health care services for children under the age of 21. EPSDT requires that every state operating a Medicaid program ensure the provision of EPSDT to all Medicaid-eligible children. The breadth of the EPSDT mandate for services was clear in the Congressional statement that EPSDT was to provide "such early and periodic screening and diagnosis of individuals who are eligible under the plan and are under the age of 21 to ascertain their physical or mental defects, and such health care, treatment, and other measures to correct or ameliorate defects and chronic conditions discovered thereby" (PL 90-248, Sec. 302[a]).

---

[1]Specifics of the organization, scope, and implementation of EPSDT may have changed subsequent to the preparation of this chapter.

EPSDT contains three major components: (1) *outreach,* in which states must identify all eligible children and ensure that their families are informed of EPSDT services and where and how these services may be obtained; (2) *screening,* to include health and developmental history, unclothed physical examination, developmental assessment (mandated 1979, effective in 1981), assessment of immunization and nutrition status, vision screening, hearing screening, laboratory procedures appropriate for age and population (TB, anemia, diabetes, sickle-cell anemia, lead poisoning, etc.), direct referral to dentists; and (3) *treatment,* requiring that health problems identified in the screening must be referred for detailed diagnosis and treatment. EPSDT also mandates that assistance be offered to families on obtaining services, the assistance to include transportation, follow-up, and the like. In short, EPSDT is a comprehensive health care program directed at physical and developmental problems; it contains both preventive and treatment capabilities.

Administratively, EPSDT is housed at the Federal level within the Health Care Financing Administration (HCFA of the Department of Health and Human Services). At the state level, the Medicaid agency is charged with the responsibility for administering EPSDT, and eligibility is determined according to Medicaid requirements. Eligibility status varies from state to state, although minimum requirements have been established by the Federal government. One of the problems with the use of Medicaid assistance roles as a source of child find is that there are children who would be eligible for Medicaid services whose families have not requested public assistance. Also, many families are inconsistently eligible for Medicaid services. Outreach and service requirements apply only to children of families whose Medicaid eligibility has been established.

Medicaid and EPSDT are essentially reimbursement systems. Direct services are not provided; rather, the state Medicaid agency pays vendors for services rendered. Questions as to appropriate vendors, monitoring and evaluation of services, and the like, have been troublesome. As with eligibility criteria, Medicaid payment schedules vary from state to state, although most states pay a set fee for EPSDT screening. Monies for direct services reimbursement come from Federal and state funds via the state Medicaid agency. Finally, Federal matching funds are available for costs of outreach, case management, follow-up services, training, resource development, and local administrative costs.

Despite a clear need for services and Congressional mandate, EPSDT has been plagued with problems. EPSDT was to become operational in 1969, yet reports by the Children's Defense Fund (1977) based on 1974–1975 data revealed that only about 25% of Medicaid-eligible children were screened and that only about 60% of those referred for services received diagnosis and treatment. Ineffective programs of outreach, limited numbers of vendors to provide screening, inability of clients to get to services, and lack of follow-up services to ensure treatment were among the reasons cited by the Children's Defense Fund in explaining the failure of EPSDT to meet its Congressional intent. To understand the difficulties encountered in the implementation of EPSDT, it is important to recognize that EPSDT called for a major change in program management—that is, from a vendor payment system focusing almost entirely on the treatment of diagnosed medical problems to the development of a case management and service delivery system covering the entire outreach, screening, diagnosis, and treatment continuum. In addition, the sheer magnitude of the program (there were over 2 million Medicaid recipients under the age of 21 in fiscal year 1979) presented complex problems in developing an effective health care delivery program for children.

A number of administrative problems at both Federal and state levels have limited implementation of this legislation (Children's Defense Fund, 1977; Wilcoxen & Keogh, 1982). Since its inception, EPSDT has been plagued by a series of delays in the development and publication of the regulations that guide the operation of the program. General regulations were first available in November, 1971, 4 years after the passage of the legislation. More detailed guidelines followed in 1972, but final guidelines for the developmental assessment component were not published until 1981. The regulations governing the penalty provision (1% of Aid for Dependent Children [AFDC] funds), enacted by Congress in 1972, mandated fewer services than did original regulations. Not surprisingly, many states responded only to the penalty regulations, thus restricting services. Monitoring of compliance has been almost nonexistent, and where states have failed to meet the minimum regulations, penalties have not been assessed. In 1982, the penalty provision was withdrawn, and monitoring and compliance activities have virtually ceased.

Eligibility and services covered under EPSDT vary geographically, as the services are tied to Medicaid, and Medicaid criteria differ according to states. There are minimum eligibility and service requirements, but states differ in Medicaid coverage beyond the minimum. As example, statistics collected by the Children's Defense Fund in 1977 indicated that the Georgia Medicaid program covered only categorically needy families (families eligible for AFDC) or Supplemental Security Income [SSI] funds) while the Maryland program covered categorically and medically needy families, families with unemployed fathers, and all financially needy children under 21. In the area of services, physical therapy was a treatment provided in many areas, but was not covered by 22 state Medicaid programs. It seems likely that there are children in some states who need but do not receive services because their families do not meet specific state criteria, their parents are unaware of the program, or because the state plan does not cover the services. To add to the complexity, families may lose Medicaid eligibility and, thus, be intermittently eligible for EPSDT services for their children. Continuity of services is obviously threatened by loss of eligibility and by the range and availability of services. Although services are mandated, states may be negligent in providing them in the absence of vigorous Federal enforcement policies. Statistics on EPSDT screenings, for example, vary greatly from state to state. A Children's Defense Fund study (1977) of five states revealed that the number of screenings performed (compared to the state's own periodicity schedule) ranged from 3.8% in New Jersey to 63.6% in South Carolina in fiscal year 1975.

An additional problem in implementation relates to inconsistencies in administrative responsibility for the program. There is overlap and sometimes confusion with programs operated through Maternal Child Health, Crippled Children's Services, Head Start, Education for All Handicapped Children's Act (PL 94-142), and other Federal programs concerned with services to risk or handicapped children. Even within the EPSDT program, there is confused responsibility. A program with major medical focus, EPSDT is often administered through a state social service agency. The State Health Department, Head Start, local public schools, or private physicians or clinics may be vendors. State Departments of Education, mandated to seek and serve all handicapped children under PL 94-142, are often totally independent or even ignorant of EPSDT. Children and families may be referred from agency to agency, and there is little coordination of follow-up diagnosis and treatment. The result is that many families with children who need services are unable or unwilling to seek help when faced with "a maze of poorly coordinated public services" (Wilcoxen & Keogh, 1982, p. 8).

Budget decisions at the federal level have also affected implementation of EPSDT. Medicaid payments to states have been reduced; as a consequence there have been cuts in services and/or increased patient responsibility for medical expenses. One major area of services affected by budget reduction has to do with prevention. As noted in the *Congressional Quarterly* (Wehr, 1982), hospitals have reduced services such as elective surgery and preventive medicine services. Federal policy has encouraged these reductions. One of the four major statutory changes in the 1981 Medicaid law was the repeal of the 1% penalty on Federal matching funds for states not meeting the performance requirements of EPSDT. Thus, at the present time, although EPSDT services are mandated by law, implementation is largely left to the discretion of the states. In spite of these problems, a beginning has been made, and in some states coordinated interagency plans, improved outreach programs, and more effective case tracking procedures have begun to reorient children's health care to a system of accountable continuing care with a prevention focus. The interagency linkages between EPSDT and Head Start programs are exemplary models of what is possible. Nevertheless, progress has been slow and for many children in poverty families, health care continues to be retroactive rather than proactive.

In summary, the intent of Congress was articulated clearly in the legislation mandating EPSDT, yet to date this intent has not become a reality. Too many children at risk for development do not receive appropriate or effective services, despite the fact that EPSDT provides a comprehensive framework for prevention and treatment of risk conditions. The important and necessary components of an effective delivery system are there: outreach, screening, treatment, and follow-up. Yet the program has been embroiled in continuing political and professional controversy, which has sorely hampered its implementation. The reader is referred to Volume 48, 1978, of the *American Journal of Orthopsychiatry* for a detailed report of the professional debate surrounding the developmental assessment component of this program. The future for preventive health programs is not bright given the current political and economic emphasis on containing costs and conserving public monies. Historically, prevention has had low priority and these services are often the first to be reduced when fiscal cuts are made. This is especially troubling in a time when economic conditions have increased the numbers of children and families without adequate health care services.

In this section, we have focused on delivery of services to low-income populations via EPSDT. It should be emphasized, however, that problems in securing adequate preventive and therapeutic services are not limited to families in lower SES groups. Middle- and upper-income families also face problems, as the barriers to comprehensive services for risk or handicapped children are organizational as well as financial. The Coalition of Labor Union Women and the American Academy of Pediatrics (Austin & Miller, 1982) suggest that current health insurance plans actually discriminate against children. That is, health insurance is mostly reactive—it becomes effective when there is an illness or accident, and it often excludes coverage of regular pediatric services so important in early detection and/or prevention of developmental problems.

In addition, comprehensive care for children at risk or with problems involves institutions other than traditional medical services: schools, public health, community organizations. Ireys (1981) notes that competing interests, contradictory values, and difficulties in communication among diverse caregivers hamper the implementation of comprehensive services for chronically disabled children. Findings from Project REACH (Bernheimer & Keogh, 1982; Young, 1980) provide compelling examples of the effects of a fragmented service system on well-educated, Anglo, middle-class parents of young developmentally delayed children. For many of these parents, the search for comprehensive care was financially and emotionally draining. Too often, professional services were short term, limited to a specific problem, and reactive rather than preventive, despite awareness of the long-term needs of developmentally delayed children.

Conclusions and Recommendations

The editors of this volume asked us to address the question: Prevention and Service—How exact does our information need to be before we should offer preventive services to at-risk children? In our view, the answer is unequivocal. The evidence is already exact enough to warrant implementation of comprehensive programs of prevention. Powerful data demonstrate that prevention works. In this chapter, we have merely skimmed the surface of an increasingly voluminous empirical literature that attests to the profound and long-term consequences of preventive services. Whether it is immunization against polio, genetic counseling for parents with a high probability of Down's syndrome children, special treatment of low-birthweight newborns, early education programs for children from poverty homes, social services for families with developmentally delayed children, or psychological counseling for potential child abuse parents, it is clear that early and appropriate interventions and services reduce the incidence and negative consequences of risk and handicapping conditions. The link between prevention and risk condition is supported on many levels and from different professional or disciplinary perspectives. It also makes good sense economically. Most importantly, it explicitly acknowledges the value of human resources. Why then have preventive programs been slow to be implemented? We suggest a number of interrelated influences.

First, the definitions of health and risk are ambiguous. Does health refer only to physical conditions, thus restricting the definition and limiting the nature of the services? Does risk refer to a broad set of conditions, including emotional and psychological development, necessitating involvement of a range of professional expertise and treatment programs? Screening and identification for risk children differ dramatically as a function of inclusionary and exclusionary definitional criteria; clearly, different professional perspectives dictate screening for different conditions. The ambiguity of the definitions of what constitute health and risk is one of the contributors to the problem of providing adequate prevention.

Second, despite real progress, the state of the scientific art is still limited. Major advances have been made in some specific risk-related areas, as for example, polio immunization or screening for PKU. Yet, there is continuing uncertainty, sometimes controversy, about recognition and treatment of a number of health conditions, especially those relating to emotional and/or social or educational development. Fears of inaccurate identification of children as at risk, of the negative consequences of labeling, and of possible distortion or disruption of family interactions have made professionals properly wary of implementing full-scale screening programs for children who might be considered at risk because of their economic and social conditions (Hobbs, 1975). The problem of identification is compounded by limitations of validity and reliability of many screening instruments aimed at detecting early learning and/or social–emotional problems. Yet, on balance, the effectiveness of screening has been demonstrated; if anything, screening programs tend to underidentify rather than overidentify.

Third, preventive services must be considered within the social and political climate of the country as a whole. Since the mid-1960s, the United States has been involved in a series of social conflicts focused on civil rights, economic conditions, and changes in minority and women's status. Where health concerns have been considered, they have often been tied to these other social and political issues. Health needs for the most part, have not received independent consideration. That they are embedded in other, often volatile, social issues adds to their complexity. As noted by Albee (1982), prevention may also pose an apparent threat to well-established professional interests.

Fourth, service programs tend to develop when there are strong advocates to argue for them. In the case of children, especially at-risk children, there have not been well-organized and powerful advocacy groups. Where such groups exist they are sometimes fragmented, and may even be at odds with each other. Lack of a cohesive and powerful voice of advocacy has surely hindered the development of programs ensuring comprehensive health services for children.

Overall, then, ambiguity of definition, professional and technical limitations, confounding of social, political, and economic considerations, and limited advocacy have led to selective and often fragmented preventive services for infants, children, and youth. The goal of optimum development for all children is supported with considerable rhetoric, as evidenced by Brandt's (1982) statement that "the ultimate goal of federal health policy today is the development and adoption by every citizen of a practical prevention ethic" (p. 1042). Yet, even a cursory examination of demographic statistics suggests that substantial numbers of children and youth continue to be at risk for physical, social, and educational growth. We have summarized evidence documenting links between risk conditions and services. We suggest that the state of the scientific art is advanced enough to argue vigorously for the effectiveness of early treatment and prevention programs. In contrast to some instances where policy precedes knowledge, in the case of preventive care for children at risk, we have good evidence on which to formulate policy. The problem in implementation appears to be one of commitment, of willingness to expend resources. As noted by Wilcoxen and Keogh (1982) in their review of EPSDT, implementation is a "political rather than a scientific problem" (p. 8).

Select Panel Recommendations

In 1981, the Select Panel for the Promotion of Child Health submitted a comprehensive report to the Congress on the health status of the nation's children. The Panel was composed of 17 members, including the Surgeon General of the United States, who represented a range of health-related disciplines. The Panel identified five overriding concerns that summarize the issues discussed in this chapter. First, although many forms of disease prevention and health promotion are demonstrably effective, they are still neither widely available nor adequately used. Second, there are large disparities in health status and the use of health services, according to family income, ethnic background, parental education, and geographic location. Third, health care today is not solely concerned with medical problems; there are psychological, environmental, social, and behavioral components that must be addressed, and the health care system is poorly organized to cope with these components. Fourth, the current health-care system does not sufficiently recognize or support the role of the family as the primary source of health care for children. Finally, federal and state maternal and child programs are not working together effectively; there are gaps in services, fragmentation and duplication of services, and conflicts among various levels of government and among programs.

The Select Panel report formulated goals in three major areas: impoved availability and accessibility of personal health services, reduction of environmental risks and promotion of nutrition and health behaviors, and a more comprehensive scientific and professional knowledge base. Six specific goals were identified for the area of personal health services. As these goals have direct implications for preventive services, we quote directly from the Select Panel summary:

(1) To ensure universal access to three sets of minimum basic services: prenatal, delivery, and postnatal care; comprehensive care for children through age 5; and family planning services.
(2) To bring about the more effective operation of governmental activities aimed at improving maternal and child health.
(3) To improve the organization of health services to reach those population groups with special needs or at special risk.
(4) To ensure that a family's economic status shall not be a bar to the receipt of needed health services or determine the nature and source of such services, and that the use of such services shall never reduce a family to penury.
(5) To ensure that every child from birth to age 18 and every pregnant woman has access to a source of continuing primary care.
(6) To ensure that every family, child, and pregnant woman has access to all services identified as "needed," not merely those basic minimal services which are part of our first goal. (1981, Vol. 1, p. 20).

The Select Panel report provides a backdrop against which to formulate a comprehensive program for services to at-risk children. A number of important components to be included in such a plan are identified: The family is viewed as central in the health and development of children; high risk populations and vulnerable periods are specified; the importance of comprehensive and coordinated services is underscored; the necessary and unique contributions of many professional perspectives are recognized; and the potent impact of economic, social, and administrative or organizational influences on health and development is taken into account.

It is somewhat ironic to note that the EPSDT program, as well as many other mandated health related programs, contains all of these components. The framework is there. In contrast to many social–scientific issues, we know a good deal about children's health and problems, and have evidence to show that appropriate and timely intervention and treatment can be effective. We are led to conclude that prevention programs will be implemented when we have successfully addressed the social–political, not just the scientific problems.

References

Albee, G. W. (1982). Preventing psychopathology and promoting human potential. *American Psychologist*, 37(9), 1043–1050.

Anderson, K., & Garner, A. (1973). Mothers of retarded children: Satisfaction with visits to professional people. *Mental Retardation, 11*, 36–39.

Austin, G., & Miller, J. (1982). *Bargaining for your child's health*. New York: Coalition of Labor Union Women and American Academy of Pediatrics.

Bell, R., & Harper, L. (1977). *Child effects on adults*. Hillsdale, NJ: Erlbaum.

Bernheimer, L. P., & Keogh, B. K. (1982). *Project REACH summary report. Preschool longitudinal study*. Los Angeles: University of California, Graduate School of Education.

Bernheimer, L. P., Young, M., & Winton, P. (1983). Stress over time: Parents with young handicapped children. *Journal of Developmental and Behavioral Pediatrics, 463*, 177–181.

Berwick, D. M., & Komaroff, A. L. (1981). Cost effectiveness of lead screening. New England Journal of Medicine, 306, 1392–1998.

Birch, H. G., & Gussow, J. A. (1970). *Disadvantaged children: Health, nutrition and school failure*. New York: Grune & Stratton.

Bobath, B., & Finnie, N. (1970). Problems of communication between parents and staff in the treatment and management of children with cerebral palsy. *Developmental Medicine and Child Neurology, 12*, 629–635.

Brandt, E. N., Jr. (1982). Prevention policy and practice in the 1980s. *American Psychologist, 37*, 1038–1042.

Bricker, D., & Sheehan, R. (1981). Effectiveness of an early childhood intervention program as indexed by measures of child change. *Journal of the Division for Early Childhood, 4*, 11–27.

Brock, M. (1976). The problem family. *Child: Care, Health and Development, 2*, 139–143.

Broman, S. (1979). Perinatal anoxia and cognitive development in early childhood. In T. M. Field (Ed.), *Infants born at risk*. New York: Spectrum.

Bromwich, R. (1981). *Working with parents and infants: An interactional approach*. Baltimore: University Park Press.

Bronfenbrenner, U. (1977). Toward an experimental ecology of human development. *American Psychologist, 32*, 513–531.

Brunswick, A. F., & Josephson, D. (1972). Adolescent health in Harlem. *American Journal of Public Health*, (Suppl., Pt. 2), 1–62.

Caputo, D., Goldstein, K., & Taub, H. (1979). The development of prematurely born children through middle childhood. In T. Field (Ed.), *Infants born at risk*. New York: Spectrum.

Caputo, D., Goldstein, K., & Taub, H. (1981) Neonatal compromise and later psychological development: A ten-year longitudinal study. In S. Friedman & M. Sigman (Eds.), *Preterm birth and psychological development*. New York: Academic Press.

Children's Defense Fund. (1977). *EPSDT. Does it spell health care for poor children?* Washington, DC: Washington Research Project.

Clunies-Ross, G. (1979). Accelerating the development of Down's Syndrome in infants and young children. *Journal of Special Education, 13*, 169–177.

Colorado Department of Education. (1983). *Effectiveness of early special education for handicapped children*. Denver, CO.

Connaughton, M. (1978). Management of child health care. In J. Neisworth & R. Smith (Eds.), *Retardation: Issues, assessment and intervention*. New York: McGraw-Hill.

Cutler, B. C. (1981). *Unraveling the special education maze: An action guide for parents*. Champaign, IL: Research Press.

Ehrlich, C., Shapiro, E., Kimball, B., & Huttner, M. (1973). Communication skills in five-year-old children with high-risk neonatal histories. *Journal of Speech and Learning Research, 16*, 522–529.

Featherstone, H. (1980). *A difference in the family*. New York: Basic Books.

Field, T. (1979). Interaction patterns of pre-term and term infants. In T. Field (Ed.), *Infants born at risk*. New York: Spectrum.

Field, T. (1983). High risk infants "have less fun" during early interactions. *Topics in Early Childhood Special Education, 361,* 77–87.

Field, T., Hallock N., Ting, G., Dempsey, J., Dabiri, C., & Shuman, H. (1978). A first year follow-up of high-risk infants: Formulating a cumulative risk index. *Child Development, 49,* 119–131.

Fitzhardinge, P. (1976). Follow-up studies on the low birthweight infant. In L. Gluck (Ed.), *Symposium on organization for perinatal care*. Philadelphia: W. B. Saunders.

Fox, D. (1982). The impact of compensatory education programs on social and emotional development. In J. Klayman & S. Moore (Eds.), *Reviews of research for practioners and parents* (No. 2). Minneapolis, MN: Center for Early Education and Development.

Fraiberg, S. (1975). Intervention in infancy: A program for blind infants. In B. Z. Friedlander, G. M. Sterritt, & G. E. Kirk (Eds.), *Exceptional infant* (Vol. 3). New York: Brunner/Mazel.

Garland, C., Stone, N., Swanson, J., & Woodruff, G. (Eds.). (1981). *Early intervention for children with special needs and their families* (WESTAR Series Paper #11). Monmouth, OR: Western States Technical Assistance Resource.

Garwood, S. G. (1982a). Early childhood intervention: Is it time to change outcome variables? *Topics in Early Childhood Special Education, 1*(4), ix–xi.

Garwood, S. G. (1982b). (Mis)use of developmental scales in program evaluation. *Topics in Early Childhood Special Education, 1*(4), 61–70.

Gordis, L. (1973). Effectiveness of comprehensive-care programs in preventing rheumatic fever. *The new England Journal of Medicine, 289,* 331–335.

Halfon, S. T., & Davies, A. M. (1980). Epidemiology and prevention of rheumatic heart disease. In J. B. Borman & M. S. Gotsman (Eds.), *Rheumatic valvular disease in children*. New York: Springer-Verlag.

Hanson, M. (1981). Down's Syndrome children: Characteristics and intervention research. In M. Lewis & L. Rosenblum (Eds.), *The uncommon child*. New York: Plenum.

Hayden, A., & Dmitriev, V. (1975). The multidisciplinary preschool program for Down's syndrome children at the University of Washington Model Preschool Center. In B. Z. Friedlander, G. M. Sterritt, & G. E. Kirk (Eds.), *Exceptional infant* (Vol. 3). New York: Brunner/Mazel.

Hayden, A., & Haring, N. (1976). Early intervention for high risk infants and young children: Programs for Down's syndrome children. In T. J. Tjossem (Ed.), *Intervention strategies for high risk infants and young children*. Baltimore: University Park Press.

Hayden, A., & Haring, N. (1977). The acceleration and maintenance of developmental gains in Down's syndrome school-age children. In P. Mittler (Ed.), *Research to practice in mental retardation* (Vol. 1). Baltimore: University Park Press.

Hobbs, N. (Ed.). (1975). *Issues in the classification of children* (Vol. 1). San Francisco: Jossey-Bass.

Hodges, W. L., & Buzzelli, C. (1984). School change and evaluation: Follow Through revisited. In B. K. Keogh (Ed.), *Advances in Special Education: Vol. 4. Docunuary Program Impact*. Greenville, CN: JAI Press.

Hodges, W. L., Sheehan, R., & Carter, H. (1979). Changes for children in schooling: The role of Follow Through sponsors. *Phi Delta Kappa, 60,* 666–669.

Horton, K. B. (1976). Early intervention for hearing-impaired infants and young children. In T. J. Tjossem (Ed.). *Intervention strategies for high risk infants and young children*. Baltimore: University Park Press.

Hunt, J. V. (1981). Predicting intellectual disorders in childhood for preterm infants with birthweights below 1501 gm. In S. Friedman & M. Sigman (Eds.), *Preterm birth and psychological development*. New York: Academic Press.

Hunt, J. V., Tooley, W. H., & Harvin, D. (1982). Learning disabilities in children with birthweights ≤ 1500 grams. In T. K. Oliver & T. H. Kirschbaum (Eds.), *Seminars in perinatology*. New York: Grune & Stratton.

Ireys, H. (1981). Health care for chronically disabled children and their families. In Select Panel for the Promotion of Child Health (Eds.) *Better health for our children: A national health strategy* (Vol. 4, DHHS Publication No. PHS 79-55071). Washington, DC: U.S. Government Printing Office.

Karnes, M., Schwedel, A., Lewis, B., Ratts, D., & Esry, D. (1981). Impact on early programming for the handicapped: Follow-up study with the elementary school. *Journal of the Division for Early Childhood, 4,* 62–79.

Kass, E., Sigman, M., Bromwich, R., & Parmelee, A. (1976). Educational intervention with high risk infants. In T. J. Tjossem (Ed.), *Intervention strategies for high risk infants and young children*. Baltimore: University Park Press.

Keirn, W. (1971). Shopping parents: Patient problem or professional problem? *Mental Retardation, 9*(4), 6–7.

Keogh, B. K., & Kopp, C. B. (1978). From assessment to intervention: An elusive bridge. In F. Minifie & L. Lloyd (Eds.), *Communicative and cognitive abilities—Early behavioral assessment*. Baltimore: University Park Press.

Kessner, D. M., Singer, J., Kalk, C. E., & Schlesinger, E. R. (1973). *Infant death: An analysis by maternal risk and health care* (Vol. 1). Washington, DC: National Academy of Sciences.

Kopp, C. B. (1979). Mildly to moderately handicapped infants: What should influence your approach to measurement? In T. Black (Ed.), *Perspectives on measurement: A collection of readings for educators of young handicapped children* (pp. 32–38. Chapel Hill, NC: Technical Assistance Development System.

Kopp, C. B. (1983). Risk factors in development. In M. Haith & J. Campos (Eds.), *Infancy and the biology of development* (Vol. 2). In P. Mussen (Ed.), *Manual of child psychology*. New York: Wiley.

Kopp, C. B., & Parmelee, A. H. (1979). Prenatal and perinatal influences on behavior. In J. Osofsky (Ed.), *Handbook of infant development*. New York: Wiley.

Lazar, I., & Darlington, R. (1982). Lasting effects of early education: A report from the consortium for longitudinal studies. *Monographs of the Society for Research in Child Development, 47,* (2–3).

Lesser, G. S., Fifer, G., & Clark, D. H. (1963). Mental abilities of children from different social class and cultural groups. *Monographs of the Society for Research in Child Development, 28*(6).

Lilienfeld, A. M., & Parkhurst, E. (1951). A study of the association of factors of pregnancy and parturition with the development of cerebral palsy: A preliminary report. *American Journal of Hygiene, 53,* 262–282.

Littman, B. (1979). The relationship of medical events to infant development. In T. Field (Ed.), *Infants born at risk*. New York: Spectrum.

National Center for Health Statistics, U.S. Department of Health. (1974). *Prevalence of chronic circulatory conditions, United States, 1972* (U.S. Department of Health, Education and Welfare Publication No. [HRA] 75-1521). Washington, DC: U.S. Government Printing Office.

Nichols, P. L. & Chen, T-C. (1981). *Minimal Brain Dysfunction: A Prospective Study*. Hillsdale, NJ: Erlbaum.

Parmelee, A. H., Kopp, C. B., & Sigman, M. (1976). Selection of developmental assessment techniques for infants at risk. *Merrill-Palmer Quarterly, 22,* 177–199.

Placek, P. J. (1977). Maternal and infant health factors associated with low birth weight: Findings from the 1972 National Natality Survey. In D. M. Reed & F. J. Stanley (Eds.), *Epidemiology of prematurity*. Baltimore, MD: Urban and Schwarnzberg.

Ramey, C. T. (1982). Commentary. In I. Lazar & R. Darlington (Eds.). Lasting effects of early education: A report from the consortium for longitudinal studies. *Monographs of the Society for Research in Child Development, 47*(2–3).

Ramey, C. T., & Finklestein, N. W. (1981). Psychosocial mental retardation: A biological and social coalescence. In M. Begab (Ed.), *Psychosocial influences and retarded performance: Strategies for improving social competence* (Vol. 1). Baltimore: University Park Press.

Ramey, C. T., Trohanis, P. L., & Hostler, S. L. (1982). An introduction. In C. T. Ramey & P. L. Trohanis (Eds.), *Finding and educating high-risk and handicapped infants*. Baltimore: University Park Press.

Ramey, C. T., Zeskind, P. S., & Hunter, R. S. (1981). Biomedical and psychosocial interventions for preterm infants. In S. L. Friedman & M. Sigman (Eds.), *Pre-term and post-term birth: Relevance to optimal psychological development*. New York: Academic Press.

Rescorla, L. A., & Zigler, E. (1981). The Yale Child Welfare Research Program: Implications for social policy. *Educational Evaluation and Policy Analysis, 3*, 5–14.

Roos, P. (1977). Parents of mentally retarded people. *International Journal of Mental Health, 6*, 96–119.

Roskies, E. (1972). *Abnormality and normality: The mothering of thalidomide children*. Ithaca: Cornell University Press.

Rynders, J., & Horrobin, J. (1975). Project EDGE: The University of Minnesota's Communication Stimulation Program for Down's Syndrome infants. In B. Z. Friedlander, G. M. Sterritt, & G. E. Kirk (Eds.), *Exceptional infant* (Vol. 3). New York: Brunner/Mazel.

Sameroff, A. (1975). Transactional models in early social relations. *Human Development, 18*, 65–79.

Sameroff, A. J., & Chandler, M. J. (1975). Reproductive risk and the continuum of caretaking casualty. In F. D. Horowitz, M. Hetherington, S. Scarr-Salapatek, & G. Siegel (Eds.), *Review of child development research* (Vol. 4). Chicago: University of Chicago Press.

Select Panel for the Promotion of Child Health. (1981). *Better health for our children: A national strategy* (DHHS Publication No. PHS 79-55071: 4 vols.). Washington, DC: U. S. Government Printing Office.

Sheehan, R., & Keogh, B. K. (1982). Design and analysis in the evaluation of early childhood special education programs. *Topics in Early Childhood Special Education, 1*(4), 81–88.

Siegel, L. S. (1982). Reproductive, perinatal, and environmental factors as predictors of the cognitive and language development of preterm and full-term infants. *Child Development, 53*, 963–973.

Sigman, M., & Parmelee, A. H. (1979). Longitudinal evaluation of the preterm infant. In T. Field (Ed.), *Infants born at risk*. Jamaica, NY: Spectrum.

Simmons-Martin, A. (1981). Efficacy report: Early education project. *Journal of the Division for Early Childhood, 4*, 5–10.

Smith, B. J. (1984). Expanding the federal role in serving young special-needs children. *Topics in Early Childhood Special Education, 4*(1), 33–42.

Solnit, A. (1976). Obstacles to providing psychological services to disabled children and their families. In D. Bergsma & A. Pulver (Eds.), *Developmental disabilities: Psychologic and social implications*. New York: Alan R. Liss.

Stebbins, L. B., St. Pierre, R. G., Proper, E. L., Anderson, R. B., & Cerva, T. R. (1977). *Education as experimentation: A planned-variation model. An evaluation of follow-through*. Cambridge, MA: Abt Associates.

Tarran, E. (1981). Parents' views of medical and social work services for families with young cerebral-palsied children. *Developmental Medicine and Child Neurology, 23*, 173-182.

Thomas, A., & Chess, S. (1977). *Temperament and development.* New York: Bruner/Mazel.

Tjossem, T. J. (1976). *Intervention strategies for high risk infants and young children.* Baltimore: University Park Press.

Turnbull, A., & Turnbull, J. R. (1985). *Parents speak out.* Columbus, OH: Charles E. Merrill.

Wehr, E. (1982, July 17). Hospitals, insurers, patients feeling pinch of Federal cuts in Medicare, Medicaid funds. *Congressional Quarterly, 40*, 1707–1711.

Weikert, D. P., Bard, J. T., & McNeil, J. T. (1978). *The Ypsilanti Perry Preschool Project: Preschool years and longitudinal results.* Ypsilanti, MI: High/Scope Educational Research Foundation.

Werner, E., Bierman, J., & French, F. (1971). *The children of Kauai: A longitudinal study from the prenatal period to age ten.* Honolulu: University of Hawaii Press.

Werner, E. E. & Smith, R. S. (1982). *Vulnerable but invincible.* New York: McGraw-Hill.

Westinghouse Learning Corporation and Ohio University. (1969). *The impact of Head Start experiences in children's cognitive and affective development.* Springfield, VA: U.S. Department of Commerce Clearinghouse.

Wilcoxen, A. G., & Keogh, B. K. (1982). Preventive health care for children: The networker. *The Newsletter of the Bush Programs in Child Development and Social Policy, 3*, 6, 8.

Young, M. S. (1980). *Factors influencing utilization of resources and support systems by parents of handicapped children.* Unpublished doctoral dissertation, University of California, Los Angeles.

Zigler, E., & Trickett, P. K. (1978). IQ, social competence, and evaluation of early childhood intervention programs. *American Psychologist, 33*, 789–798.

Author Index

Numbers in italics refer to the pages on which the complete references are cited.

Subject Index